D1601394

Stalin,
the Russians,
and
Their War

Stalin, the Russians, and Their War

MARIUS BROEKMEYER

Translated by Rosalind Buck

THE UNIVERSITY OF WISCONSIN PRESS

The University of Wisconsin Press
1930 Monroe Street
Madison, Wisconsin 53711

www.wisc.edu/wisconsinpress/

3 Henrietta Street
London WC2E 8LU, England

Originally published as *Stalin, de Russen en hun oorlog: 1941–1945*
by Mets & Schilt uitgevers, Amsterdam, the Netherlands
Published by arrangement with Mets & Schilt uitgevers, Amsterdam
Copyright © 1999 Marius Broekmeyer, Amstelveen, the Netherlands
English translation copyright © 2004 Rosalind Buck

5   4   3   2   1

Printed in the United States of America

Library of Congress Cataloging-in-Publication Data
Broekmeyer, M. J., 1927–
[Stalin, de Russen en hun oorlog. English]
Stalin, the Russians, and their war : 1941–1945 / Marius Broekmeyer ;
translated by Rosalind Buck.
p. cm.
Includes bibliographical references and index.
ISBN 0-299-19590-2 (alk. paper)
ISBN 0-299-19594-5 (pbk. : alk. paper)
1. World War, 1939–1945—Soviet Union. I. Title.
D764.B75513   2004
940.53′47—dc22   2003020574

Publication of this book was made possible in part by financial support from
the Foundation for the Production and Translation of Dutch Literature.

Contents

Introduction

This book bears a deliberately ambiguous title, which therefore needs some explanation. By *Stalin* I mean the man and his regime, by *the Russians* all the inhabitants of the former Soviet Union, and by *Their War* both the war against the invaders and the war of the regime against its own people (and vice versa).

The book may look, at first glance, like a history of the Russians during the Second World War, but it is not: the military strategic side of the issue is hardly mentioned, the wars against Finland and Japan are dealt with only briefly, the air force and navy are also outside the scope of this work, and I myself am not a historian by profession.

The sources consulted were all published in Russian between 1985 and June 1999. This period was consciously chosen as it only became possible in 1985 to publish books, opinions, and views on the war, which were subjected decreasingly—and finally not at all—to censorship.

Anything that does not appear prominently in my sources is not in this book. I discovered very little about the situation in the occupied areas and the advance through the Balkans and Hungary. I have also omitted anything not published in Russian.

Readers can assume that my sources display a certain degree of partiality. After all, what was once forbidden to write was now suddenly being published, and these were often the negative aspects that had remained unspoken or underexposed in the past. It is therefore impossible to give a balanced view of what the ordinary Russian soldier and civilian went through.

This book contains descriptions of shocking events, which may evoke outraged reactions from readers. You will often read about unlikely and, for us, unimaginable situations. I would therefore, again, ask you to bear in mind that I am unable to provide a complete picture of any of the subjects dealt with here.

I give snatches; I describe episodes; I make—as it were—snapshots in time; I reflect personal recollections, thoughts, experiences, and views of specific individuals. Experienced at time A in place B, written down at time C, and published at time D.

At times the observations of these individuals are simply their own views; at other times they are representative of numerous cases and have a more general significance, which is a major fundamental difficulty. Who is to decide whether something is of an incidental nature or whether it has a more general significance? And on what basis can that be determined?

This might make it all a little disjointed and jumpy, with rapid transitions and changes. That is partly my style of writing, which I feel, in this case, suits the unexpected, strange, and confusing events that are so much a part of war.

The work is divided into four parts.

1. The prelude to the war, from August 1939 to the beginning of the war on 22 June 1941, is discussed in part 1. Questions such as the following are addressed: How did Russia prepare herself for a war? Was the German attack really so unexpected? How did it come to be that Russia let herself be taken unawares? Was Stalin also contemplating starting a war at his own convenience?

2. The events after the German invasion, the Russian retreat, the defense of Moscow and Leningrad, the counterattack at Stalingrad, and the Russian offensives up to and including the capture of Berlin are discussed part 2. In other words, the events have been organized in a more or less chronological fashion.

3. Part 3 contains a more systematic treatment or illustration of individual subjects: women in the war, the Jews in the war, prisoners of war, the Gulag, partisans, people driven from their homes, collaboration, methods of warfare, the generals, the victims, the wounded and missing, and—chiefly—life in general, the characteristics and views of the Russian soldiers. Finally, I deal with opinions concerning the postwar period and discuss issues such as the veterans, Field Marshall Zhukov's fall into disgrace, the war generation, and the postwar famine.

4. By a lucky coincidence S. B. Borisov, lecturer at the Pedagogic Institute in Shadrinsk and enthusiastic promoter of the local culture

there, provided me with several works that were recently written at that institute about the fortunes of the provincial town on the other side of the Urals during and after the war. To my best knowledge the history of such a small town—far more representative for Russia than cities such as Moscow and Leningrad (Saint Petersburg)—has never before been described, at least not for the Western reader.

In this book I attempt to throw light on the human aspect—that is, the aspect of the people—during the war in the East. This book can therefore be seen as a supplement to and perhaps a correction of the image formed of this period in past years.

The tsarist general Mikhail Dragomirov once said that the difference between a historical treatment and a literary interpretation of the same events is like the difference between a topographical map and a landscape. That comparison appeals greatly to me.

In principle, I have used only articles and books written by people who themselves experienced the events of the war. Articles in historic magazines are, naturally, written from a different aspect. What I consider to be my own work is the selection of information and the compilation of the book.

The sources consist of articles, essays, and memoirs published in the magazines *Avrora, Druzhba narodov, Yunost, Kentavr, Molodaya gvardia, Moskva, Nash sovremennik, Neva, Novy mir, Oktyabr, Sever, Sibir, Sibirskie ogni, Ural, Volga, Voprosy literatury, Znamia,* and *Zvezda.* Additional sources are articles in the weekly magazines *Literaturnaya Rossiya* (until 1995), *Literaturnaya gazeta, and Ogonyok.* Furthermore, I consulted articles and reviews from the historical magazines *Voprosy istoryi, Istorya SSSR (Otechestvennaya istorya), Novaya i noveyshaya istorya,* and *Voyenno-istoricheski zhurnal.* These have been supplemented with articles from the daily newspapers. I have endeavored, naturally, to draw material from as many books dealing with my subject as possible.

With respect to the numbers in the margins of the text, the first figure refers to the alphabetically ordered reference list printed at the back of the book of people and books consulted, the second to the work referred to under that number, and the third to the page(s) quoted.

For this book—as with *Het verdriet van Rusland* (Russia's sorrow)—I have made use of the large collection of magazines and books in the University of Amsterdam's Eastern European Institute. Here Mieke Harlaar and Bart Schellekens were extremely helpful. Franz Görner from the Eastern European department of the Staatsbibliothek zu Berlin Preussischer Kulturbesitz—a library I cannot praise highly enough—once more allowed me to benefit from the sizable Russica collection. In Paris I consulted, with great success, the Slavic department of the library in the Grand Palais.

The final editor, Sjoerd de Jong, prevented me from making many mistakes and also considerably improved the text, for which I am extremely grateful.

I thank my dear wife, Ansje, from the bottom of my heart for her patience with a restless husband.

Marius Broekmeyer
Amstelveen, 1 September 1999

History and Documentation

The censor, until the 1990s, strictly controlled the historiography of the Great Patriotic War.

Roughly speaking, initially, the tenor was that all victories were thanks to Stalin, the great inspirer, and, naturally, to the Communist Party. Khrushchev was subsequently pushed to the fore, focusing on his presence in Stalingrad and at Kursk, where he was a member of the political military leadership. After Khrushchev, it appeared that the war was decided on the bridgehead at Novorossisk on the Kuban, as Brezhnev had been the military political chief there.

Errors, defeats, and sheer stupidity were swept under the carpet as much as possible, and taboo subjects were not touched on. Anyone to do so, like the historian Aleksandr Nekrich, was given the push. Writing about the American assistance in the framework of the Lend-Lease Act and "those hundreds of thousands of Spitfires, Aerocobras, Sherman and Valentine tanks and the famous Studebakers" was not a popular move. 309.4.46

Those in the literary and historical worlds were advised that, if they wanted to write about the war, they should begin with Stalingrad or thereabouts. Authors illustrating the way events actually progressed were reviled as "cry babies" who were suffering from "mental self-torture," with a tendency toward "naked naturalism." The war had to be forgotten as quickly as possible; the reconstruction demanded optimistic, cheerful people. And thereafter the slogans were: "epizatsya" (elevating to the epic), "geroizatsya" (the honoring of heroes), and "tipizatsya" (grouping under one large common [optimistic] denominator). 209.4.114

Vladimir Krupin once wrote about a veteran who remarked, after watching a war film: "Look at that, Vitya, the way those people conducted war.

How wonderful. We were always crawling around on our bellies in the mud, doing nothing but digging." Krupin continued: "It was as if he had been in a different war, not the real one; that was full of music and 241.1.39 dancing."

Authors who themselves fought at Stalingrad, like Viktor Nekrasov, had great problems with censorship. Nonetheless their books were published, though in a "modified" form. The manuscript of Vasili Grossman's monumental epic, *Life and Fate*, which I consider the best book ever published about the war in Russia, was seized. All the same, there were sometimes lighter, heavier, or "abridged" books published, sketching a more or less true-to-life picture of the war.

Yelena Rzhevskaya's stories about the war were not published, the reason given that, "the stories are gloomy. You are writing about daily life in the war. Do you really have to describe that? Everybody is tired of the 383.10.214 war." Her work saw the light of day only in 1961.

Memoirs of military leaders were published only by the military press—which was therefore already a barrier—and were constantly supervised by "consultants" and "literary editors." First on the cutting edge of historiography and literature was the great battlefield theme, in which armies and generals were at the fore. Then, when the pressure eased a bit, we had lieutenant prose, which was already closer to the reality and subsequently was referred to rather condescendingly as "trench prose." Since 1985, or thereabouts, it has been possible to describe what happened honestly and truthfully, and to focus attention more clearly on the fate of people, the people in the war.

What happened to the memoirs of Zhukov is perhaps characteristic. The highest echelons of the party constantly made comments on versions and individual chapters. Leonid Brezhnev was determined to appear in the book, even though he had never met Zhukov during the war. They came up with this: "Zhukov wanted to consult Brezhnev. Unfortunately Brezhnev was not present, as he was in [an area] where heavy fighting was tak-397.1.16 ing place."

In Zhukov's work we also come across dozens of people who were not 68.1.13 in the original manuscript. They, too, wished to be mentioned. The tenth edition, from 1990, states correctly where these "additions" have been made.

Zhukov's memoirs were opposed, altered, and delayed by the highest military circles, including the minister of defense, Andrei Grechko, and the chief of the political military leadership, Aleksei Yepishev. The latter commented, "Who needs your truth if it stands in our way?"

According to the military historian N. G. Pavlenko, the twelve-part *History of the Second World War, 1939–1945,* published between 1973 and 1982, "is a step backward." "There has never been and is still not any truthful chronicle of the Great Patriotic War as a whole."   332.2   332.2.5–6

    I quote a number of author's opinions of the historiography of the war in general, in alphabetical order.

    Grigori Baklanov: "The soldiers remained a faceless mass, the background against which the great created their history."   28.1.4

    Yuri Gorkov: "So far, the whole truth about that war has far from come to light."   147.1.12

    Daniil Granin: "Cleansed of limescale and rust, the [new] history of the Great Patriotic War will not seem as brilliant and wonderful as it has been made out to be [up until now]. But it will show more respect for the soldier."   152.2

    A. N. Mertsalov: "After more than half a century, we still lack a more or less truthful chronicle [of the war]. That is insulting to the people."   282.3.228

    A. Mikhailov: "The history of the war is shrouded from our eyes in myths."

    Yelena Senyavskaya: "Memoirs of ordinary soldiers and lower-ranking officers are hardly mentioned in historians' works."   394.1.50

    Innokenti Cheremnikh: "There is little literature concerning the life of the front soldiers."   80.1.81

    Georgi Zhukov: "Take the 'History of the Great Patriotic War' [1960–65]. It is unreadable. It has to be rewritten."   383.2.173

The historian A. N. Mertsalov feels that the historiography goes from one extreme to another. At first all successes were attributed to Stalin, and now Stalin is suddenly out of the picture. "Primitive anticommunism" has taken the place of the earlier "pseudo Marxism," is his opinion. He urges historians to devote attention to the conflicts between the people and the leader, between the army and the "great strategist," between progress and repression, between force and initiative, between Communists and non-Communists, between practical and absurd issues, and between the party and the Communists and "the various groups within the party, depending on their attitude to Stalin and his crimes."   282.2.389   282.2.151

    Where contemporary Russian authors are, almost without exception,

History and Documentation

extremely critical of what they have been fobbed off with until now, one can ask oneself in all conscience what still holds true of the many Western studies of the war in Russia. After all, those studies are founded to a large extent on what was published before 1985 and on material the Soviet authorities allowed to be researched.

A second comment concerns the paradoxical situation in which the very country that has tried so hard to hide the facts of the war is capable, in principle, of revealing more of the views of the military than any other country. Were the archives of the political department of the army to be opened up, with all those thousands of meticulous reports on what the people actually thought, did, and felt, then, according to Mikhail Butov, it would "unearth truly unexpected discoveries, which will provide us all with a painful change of opinion in respect of the events during those years. Take the history of Vlasov's army, for example, which is becoming
65.1.185 clearer."

There is still one untapped source. During a roundtable meeting of historians and literary figures, in 1988, Kondratyev stated that Colonel Ushchapovsky had given him a manuscript concerning the fate of the Twenty-ninth Army, which was encircled in the summer of 1941 at Grodno. It describes the misery, the losses and deprivation, which "were aggravated by the endless executions that the commandant of the army—a protégé of Beria, as we know—had carried out by firing squads, . . . the officers drank themselves silly, everyone knew about it. . . . Every writer was given sheaves of such manuscripts. But what could we advise the authors to do, knowing that their publication [the manuscripts] was impossible? [Tell them to] keep it, to pass it on through the family to be retained for posterity? . . . Evidently no one is interested in that material and no one needs the truth about the war, which could turn out to be quite different from the war described in the memoirs of army leaders and in the official history. There is less and less time left; the veterans are disappearing and
with them the truth about the war."

PART 1

The Prelude

1

Between Pact and War

An extensive amount of literature has been available, particularly since the 1990s, concerning the period between 1939 and 22 June 1941. What were the intentions of the Soviet Union? What did Germany want? And what went on between the two dictators economically, politically, and with regard to military strategy? Was the Soviet Union prepared for a war, in principle and in practice?

Why was everyone so surprised when Germany attacked, and why did all the warnings of an imminent attack fall on deaf ears? Was the Soviet Union itself planning to attack Germany?

Certainly Germany wanted war, was after Russian raw materials and Russian land, and was intent on destroying Bolshevism. Hitler's *Mein Kampf* makes that perfectly clear, and it was proven in practice by the preparations for a campaign against Russia, the first signs of which were apparent in the summer of 1940, on 31 July 1940, to be precise, with the date for the offensive set for "1 May 1941. Duration of the operation: five months. Objective: destruction of Russia's vital forces."

And certainly Soviet Russia made no secret of the fact that its objective was to expand the territory of "socialism," at all costs.

Stalin wrote in 1927: "We will be the last to enter a war to tip the scales" and "plunge Europe into a war, remain neutral ourselves, and then, when the enemies have worn each other out, cast the full might of the Red Army into the fray."

418.1.158;
418.2.14;
418.4.202

In 1928 he foresaw "a constant struggle against social democracy in all areas." The tasks he set were "to destroy fascism, overthrow capitalism, install Soviet control, and free the colonies from slavery." And "a great deal will depend on whether we succeed in delaying the inevitable war with

418.3.288 the capitalist world until the time when the capitalists are fighting one another."

These, of course, are only words and prove little, but they do provide us with some insight into the Soviet leader's frame of mind.

Here follow a few impressions of the prewar mood with regard to a possible war.

Vladimir Nikolayev wrote that in his schooldays he was thoroughly prepared for an imminent war. At school he learned how to handle rifles and machine guns. It was impressed on him, in what he referred to as 315.1.43 his "militarized school life," to "think about the war" and "be prepared." According to one of his peers, V. Farsobin: "Everyone was convinced we 463.222 would be fighting a war on the other side of the border."

In 1938 Konstantin Simonov wrote in a poem: "In Königsberg [East Prussia] in the morning / we were both wounded / a month in the hos- 400.2.42 pital recuperating / and then back into battle." A. Zubov posed some rhetorical question: "Who indulged in idle talk of new republics in the Union and who learned to wield a Voroshilov rifle? A few? A few dozen? Thousands? Hundreds of thousands? Who sang, before the war, 'The Red Army is the mightiest from the Taiga to England'? Who agreed with the poet Eduard Bagritski 'to reach as far as the Ganges so our Fatherland will 500.1.72 stretch from India to England'?"

The lyrics of a song popular before the war, entitled "Tomorrow When We Are at War and the Enemy Attacks," read as follows: "We don't want war, but we are defending ourselves, we are forced to strengthen our defenses. With little bloodshed and one mighty blow we will destroy the enemy in his own land." A 1939 film of the same name showed "how fast-driving tanks and cavalry overrun enemy territory, squadrons of planes 230.1.155 carry out bombing raids, and the enemy raises his hands in fear."

The government also ensured that Nikolay Shpanov's book, *The First Blow* (1939), realized a circulation of five hundred thousand copies in six editions. In this book "fascist Germany was entirely defeated within a day 400.4.44 or two," according to Simonov. In 1995 Yuri Gorkov said, "Many of my peers in military academies around the country remember studying this fantastic novel almost as a manual for the strategic planning of military 147.1.28 campaigns." Mottoes such as "We will never concede an inch of ground," "We counter a blow with a double or triple strike," and "We wage war 155.5.8 with little bloodshed" were the empty words supported by the government that, in the end, gave people the wrong impression.

Lazar Zakharovich Mekhlis, head of the political section of the Red Army, said at the Eighteenth Congress of the Communist Party in March 1939, "If the second imperialistic war turns against the first socialist state in the world, then we will shift the military operations to the territory of the adversary, fulfill our international obligations, and extend the number of Soviet republics."   240.1.196

The party leader for Leningrad, Andrei Zhdanov, openly and cynically declared that the objective was, using "the conflicts among the imperialists . . . to extend the socialist territory of the Soviet Union. . . . That will also be the result of our policy, and it will be clear to you all how the affair will turn out (laughter)."   310.27.81

Vsevolod Vishnevsky, chief of the Defense Committee of the Union of Soviet Writers and, in that capacity, present at all important military political meetings, noted in his diaries from 1939 that expansion of the Soviet Union and the Sovietization of foreign territories was impending. He talked of the access to the Mediterranean Sea, of campaigns in the Carpathian Mountains and in the Balkans, "on the sly, here with persuasion, there with force" and at the right moment.   476.1.105

On 1 September 1939 he confided in his diary, "Now we are taking the initiative, we will not retreat but attack. The policy toward Berlin is clear: what they want is our neutrality and then they will finish the USSR off; what we want is for them to get themselves embroiled in a war and then finish them off." In the publications of his diaries before 1985 all references to a "first blow" were wisely scrapped.   476.1.104

The German-Russian Non-Aggression Pact

In the spring and summer of 1939, regardless of whose fault it may have been, joint French-British attempts to guarantee the safety of Poland by means of an agreement with the Soviet Union foundered.

Earlier Soviet historiography claims that the Soviet Union had little choice but to go along with Germany. In doing so, they could win time, as Russia was not yet ready for a war. This is a rather unconvincing argument, as there was no hint of any German attack on the Soviet Union at that time. According to the Soviet historians, however, this is why the Soviet Union signed the non-aggression pact with Germany on 24 August 1939. The terms of this agreement, referred to as the Molotov-Ribbentrop Pact, after the respective ministers of foreign affairs, were kept strictly secret. During the Nuremberg trials (1945–46) it was forbidden to talk about anything concerning the pact, the invasion of Poland, Polish-Russian relations, or the occupation of the Baltic countries.

The current debate primarily concerns the motives for concluding the pact. Was it to guarantee Russia's safety, or was it a plan to set the capitalist countries against one another? One Russian historian, who is analyzing the current approach to the pact, feels that the two motives are not necessarily mutually exclusive. He also believes that much still remains unknown about the pact, and he wonders what has happened to the correspondence between Hitler and Stalin, and where the documents are concerning a rumored meeting between the two dictators in October 1939.

301.1.160

A New Document

A new document concerning the prewar history was published by *Novy mir* in the December issue of 1994. The editor, T. S. Bushuyeva, stated: "The quoted text by Stalin is based on a French copy, which was probably made by someone from the Comintern who was present at the Politburo. Naturally this text should be compared to the original." *Novy mir* also considered that this was impossible for the time being, as this text, which is strictly secret, is stored in an archive somewhere. Until 16 January 1993 officials denied that a meeting of the Politburo had even taken place on 19 August 1939. It was not until that former date that Stalin's biographer, Gen. Dmitri Volkogonov, wrote that he had read the minutes of that meeting. I give the text from *Novy mir* in translation:

> From captured, secret USSR Osoby [Special] Archives, we have succeeded in establishing that Stalin called together the Politburo and the leaders of the Comintern at short notice on 19 August 1939, in other words, four days before the signing of the German-Russian Non-Aggression Pact [the Molotov-Ribbentrop Pact]. During that meeting he gave an address which had never been published [in *Novy mir*]. Fifty years later Suvorov was to write, "The day Stalin actually started the Second World War was 19 August 1939." What had Stalin talked about?
>
> "The issue of war or peace is entering a critical phase for us. If we conclude a treaty with France and Great Britain concerning mutual assistance, then Germany will forfeit Poland and seek a modus vivendi with the Western states. A war would be averted, but subsequent events could take on a dangerous character for the USSR. If we accept Germany's offer to conclude a non-aggression pact between our two countries, then naturally the

Germans will invade Poland, and French and British intervention will be inevitable. Western Europe will experience serious unrest and disturbance. Under these circumstances we will have a good chance of remaining out of the conflict, and we can hope for a favorable [time to] enter the war.

"The experiences of the past twenty years has shown that, in peacetime, it is impossible to have a sufficiently strong communist movement in Europe to enable a Bolshevist party to seize power. A bolshevist dictatorship is only possible as the result of a great war. We will make a choice, and that choice is clear: We must accept the German proposal and politely send back the delegation from England and France. Our first advantage will be the destruction of Poland up to nearby Warsaw, including the Ukrainian Galicia.

"Germany will give us a free hand in the Baltic countries and will not object to the return of Bessarabia to the USSR. Germany is prepared to allow us to exercise our influence in Romania, Bulgaria, and Hungary. The question of Yugoslavia remains open. At the same time we must foresee the consequences that could arise from either a German defeat or a German victory.

"In the event of a defeat, we will immediately set out to Sovietize Germany and to install a communist government there. We must not forget that a Sovietized Germany will be in great danger if that Sovietization is the result of Germany's defeat in a war that is quickly over. For then England and France will still be powerful enough to take Berlin and to destroy Soviet Germany, and we will not be able to come to the aid of our Bolshevist comrades. It is therefore our task [to ensure] that Germany wages war for as long as possible, so that England and France, drained and exhausted, will be incapable of defeating Sovietized Germany. Adhering to the position of neutrality and biding our time, the USSR will offer to help the current Germany, by providing her with raw materials and food. Nevertheless, it goes without saying that our help must not be allowed to extend beyond certain boundaries and must not undermine our economy or weaken the strength of our own army.

"At the same time, we must practice an active communist propaganda policy, especially in the Anglo-French block and initially in France. We must be prepared for the fact that, in times of war, the party in that warring country will be forced to cease legal activities and go underground. We know that this work will demand many sacrifices, but our French comrades will not waver. Their task will consist, initially, of the dissolution and demoralization of the army and the police. If that preliminary

work is carried out correctly, the security of Soviet Germany will be guar-
anteed, which will aid in the Sovietization of France.

"To realize these plans, it is necessary for the war to last as long as possible, and all the forces we have in Western Europe and the Balkans must
be focused on that objective.

"Let us now consider the second hypothesis, in other words, a German
victory, which some people feel poses a serious threat to us.

"There is a grain of truth in that assumption, although it would be
wrong to think that danger is as near and as great as some imagine. If Germany manages to gain that victory, then it will emerge from the war too
weak to enter into armed conflict against the USSR for at least ten years.

"Germany's primary task will then be to oversee a defeated England
and France in order to prevent their recovery. On the other hand, a victorious Germany will be in control of enormous territories and, in the
course of the next few decades, will be engaged in 'exploiting' these territories and establishing a German order in those countries. Germany will
evidently have other matters at hand than to turn against us. And there is
something else that will strengthen our security. In a conquered France,
the French Communist Party will still be very strong. A communist revolution will take place immediately, and we will be able to take advantage
of those circumstances to come to the aid of France and make France our
ally. Later all those who have been placed under the 'protection' of a victorious Germany will also become our allies. We will have ample scope
for the development of the world revolution. Comrades! It is in the
interest of the USSR—the workers' Fatherland—for a war to break out
between the Reich and the Anglo-French bloc. We have to do everything
we can to ensure that the war lasts as long as possible, in order to exhaust
the two parties. For that very reason, we must agree to conclude the pact
that Germany is proposing and make sure that war, once it has been
declared, lasts as long as possible. It will be necessary to increase the propaganda work in the warring countries so that we are ready by the time the
war ends."

According to German historian Bonwetsch, this text is a forgery, although
the content, he admits, "could very well reflect Stalin's views." I agree:
there may well be different versions of this document, as various Soviet
leaders have since repeated the theme so often.

On 7 September 1939, in a discussion with leaders of the Comintern,
Stalin evidently restated his address of 19 August: "The war is between two

51.1.22

groups of capitalist countries over the redistribution of the world, over world domination. We are not against the idea of them battling fiercely and weakening each other. It would not be a bad thing if, through the fault of Germany, the position of the richest capitalist countries, especially England, were to falter. Without realizing it or wishing to, Hitler himself is undermining the capitalist system. . . . We can maneuver, setting one side against the other, so that they attack each other all the more fiercely. The non-aggression pact helps Germany to a certain degree. The next step is to give the other side a helping hand." 116.1.18

This was expressed even more clearly by the minister of foreign affairs Vyacheslav Molotov in a meeting he held on the night of 2–3 July 1940 with his colleague from Lithuania. In a candid moment Molotov said that not only Lithuania but also the other Baltic States and Finland would belong to the Soviet system "which will dominate everywhere in the future, throughout Europe, first in one area—such as the Baltic countries—and then in other areas. . . . Now we are supporting Germany, but just enough to prevent her from accepting peace proposals . . . and the starving masses will rise against their leaders. . . . At that moment we will come to their aid with fresh forces, properly prepared, and, in the area of Western Europe, somewhere by the Rhine, I imagine, the decisive battle will take place . . . which will decide the fate of Europe forever." After what had to have been a rather alarming conversion for him, the Lithuanian minister immediately noted down what was said.

The annotator of the article from which I have drawn these statements, namely, the second secretary to the Historical Diplomatic Department of the Russian Ministry of Foreign Affairs, then states his view that the Molotov-Ribbentrop Pact was intended to incite Germany to start a war with the West and, indeed, to do so by invading Poland. 99.1.39–40

After the pact of August 1939 antifascist propaganda was toned down in Russia, if not scrapped. Anti-German literature was withdrawn from sale and removed from public libraries. The committee that checked materials for political correctness banned 4,200 items out of a total of 13,200 antifascist propaganda representations, articles, books, and magazines that were considered undesirable. Life became difficult for German antifascist writers in Moscow. The word *fascist* was replaced by "member of the NSDAP (the Nazi Party)." A number of topical films, such as *Action in the Hinterland* and *If We Are at War Tomorrow*, were removed from circulation. Exchanges of books and magazines were set up between German and Russian libraries, and the Soviet Union was invited to the Leipziger 312.2

Messe. Soviet journalists traveled in Germany and—later, in 1940—even
312.1 in occupied France.

The "New Territories"

A week after the pact, Germany attacked Poland on 1 September, after
which, on 3 September, France and England declared war against Germany.
Two weeks after the German offensive, the Soviet Union invaded East
Poland without any declaration of war, with the argument that Moscow
wanted to protect the White Russians and Ukrainians living there. Moscow
wished—and was able—to keep up the pretence of being an opponent
instead of an aggressor and German ally. A supplementary agreement
between Moscow and Berlin, on 23 September 1939, established the border, along the Bug and San rivers, between the two totalitarian powers.

On 31 October 1939 Molotov, speaking for the Supreme Soviet, referred
282.2.217 to former Poland as "a monstrous child of Versailles." His opinion was
that, "Germany is in the position of a state striving for as rapid an end to
the war as possible and for peace, whereas England and France, who only
yesterday were condemning aggression, are now in favor of continuing the
304.1.37 war and are against making peace."

On their leaders' orders, the roughly three hundred thousand Polish
soldiers in East Poland offered no resistance, except at Lvov, where German and Russian soldiers together hunted down Polish soldiers trying to
escape to Romania under the command of the future general Wladislaw
258.1.263–64 Anders. As many as 3,500 men were lost on the Polish side and 737 on the
Russian side.

Approximately 240,000 Poles were made prisoners of war. The soldiers
and lowest ranks were allowed to go home, apart from twenty-five thousand men, who were set to work in constructing a railway line between
Novgorod and Lvov and in the Ukrainian mines. The officers and more
senior civil servants from the newly occupied regions were deported
and housed in three camps: in Kozelsk (4,700), Starobelsk (4,000), and
412.1.14 Ostashkovo (6,500).

On 5 March 1940 the Politburo decided by Protocol No. 144 that these
officers and another six thousand to seven thousand Poles in other pris-
391.19 ons should face a firing squad. At the bottom of the execution order for
21,857 men were the signatures of Stalin, Voroshilov (People's Commissar
for Defense), Mikoyan (Minister for Foreign Trade and a party leader),
and Molotov.

In the autumn of 1943 the Germans sought out "strong lads" in a prisoner-of-war camp near Smolensk for exhumations. Mikhail Lotarev, prisoner of war, Jew, and member of the GPU (the secret political police), signed up and dug up bodies at Katyn. In his words: "Starving and almost lifeless, I puked my guts up; a mask couldn't stop us from being sick." A gypsy gave him schnapps and something to eat. "And so fate brought together slaughtered innocent Poles, a gypsy, and a Jew." In 1943, in the woods near Katyn, 4,143 bodies were found. Until 1990 it was not know where the others who had been shot were buried. Only 3 percent of the Polish officers taken prisoner by the Russians survived; some were wanted by Germany and by several other foreign governments, and a few joined the Ministry of Internal Affairs, the NKVD, which included internal espionage. 269.1.147 271.1

Moscow admitted responsibility for these murders on 13 April 1990, and not until after the document of 5 March 1940 was published did it come to light that Poles were also murdered in other camps in addition to the three mentioned above.

In the meantime, ordinary civilians and the families of deported officers were arrested and exiled to the north and beyond the Urals. Each family was allowed to take 500 kilos worth of belongings: bed linen, clothes, shoes, kitchen utensils, cutlery, and tools. They were given two hours to pack. In various waves of deportations, 388,000 people were expelled. During the long train journeys in cattle trucks, thousands perished from the cold, from starvation, and from exhaustion. 330.1 185.1

It was not until the German attack on the Soviet Union that these Poles were given permission to join up with General Anders's Polish army via Persia. Poles had already attempted to make their way south under their own steam, stealing and pillaging. 330.1.43

In the "new territories" the Soviet government constructed roads, railway lines, and airfields at breakneck speed. These activities were stepped up even further once Georgi Zhukov succeeded Kirill Meretskov as chief of general staff on 1 February 1941. A defense line (the Molotov line) was also constructed along the new border.

With the argument that, in the event of war, the Finnish border was too close to Leningrad, at the end of 1939 Moscow demanded that Finland surrender the Karelian Isthmus, as well as several islands, and make other concessions as well. In March 1940 Stalin remarked on this war with Finland that, "it would be extremely stupid and politically short-sighted not to seize the appropriate moment and attempt as quickly as possible, while the war in the West is still raging, to broach the issue of the security of Leningrad and solve the problem. Putting the issue off for a month or two could mean putting it off for twenty years." The Finnish government refused, following which Russia attacked on 30 November 1939. Despite heavy Russian losses of people and equipment, they did not manage to break through the Mannerheim line as quickly as they had hoped. Only after 105 days, on 12 March 1940, was Finland finally forced to submit and relinquish the territories that had been demanded.

Of the five thousand Russian prisoners of war who returned from Finland, 350 were immediately shot, "and more than four thousand were sentenced to five to eight years in camps." The former aggression on the part of the Soviets was justified by the authorities as "the liberation"; in the case of Finland, the aggression was referred to as "protecting the Northwest border." For the present account, what the Leningrad party leader, Andrei Zhdanov, said on 20 November 1940 is important: "We have become stronger and can take a more active stand. The wars against Poland and Finland were not wars of defense. We have already trodden the path of offensive policy."

German-Russian Economic Relations

Accompanying the German-Russian Non-Aggression Pact was a trade and credit agreement signed on 19 August 1939, which was later added to and extended with agreements of 11 February 1940 and 10 January 1941.

The ensuing supplies were so substantial—for both the Russian defense industry and Germany—that they practically broke the economic embargo imposed by the Allies. Dozens of Russian experts visited German munitions factories, docks, and military installations. "They included the most highly qualified specialists in the areas of aeronautics, artillery, marine ship building. . . . They discovered some extremely useful things," wrote the historian Villyis Sipols. Visitors included the aircraft builder Aleksandr Yakovlev and the future rocket specialist Sergei Korolyov. The leader of those experts, People's Commissar Ivan Tevosyan, said of the Russian purchases, "It is our job to acquire the latest, most advanced examples of arms and instruments. . . . We are not going to buy old types of weapons."

"In the spring of 1941 Hitler ordered us to show the military delegation from the Soviet Union our tank factories and training centers," said the senior German officer Heinz Guderian. "Hitler particularly stressed that we should show everything, that nothing should be concealed. Once the Soviet officers had seen everything, they refused to believe that the T-IV tank was our heaviest tank. They kept insisting that we were keeping our latest tanks from them." At the beginning of the war 778 Soviet engineers and other specialists were working in Germany, purchasing and inspecting supplies.

Germany supplied primarily modern metalworking lathes, optical equipment, and weapons. They provided the Russians with the (unfinished) cruiser, "Lützow," other equipment for marine shipbuilding, ships artillery, hydroacoustic and hydrogeographical equipment, field artillery, anti-aircraft artillery, and a few different modern war planes: Heinkel 100, Junkers 88, Dornier 215, Bücker 133, Focke-Wulf, Junkers 207, and Messerschmitt 109 and 110. Altogether there were thirty units, including bombs, weapons, and spare parts.

Sipols concluded: "All this contributed considerably to reinforcing the defense potential of the USSR and to helping the Soviet Union achieve victory over the fascist Reich in the war. . . . Throughout the four years of the war the USSR used German factory equipment and lathes."

Although Germany was initially skeptical regarding the value of the agreements, the Russian supplies exceeded German expectations, as did "Stalin's willingness to grant national socialist Germany unilateral economic support in its war against virtually the rest of the world." Russian supplies, therefore, were generally also of great importance to Germany, as they themselves admitted, in their preparations for war. There was even talk of a "decisive significance of the Russian supplies from a military point of view . . . indispensable for our military industry and the economy as a whole."

Germany was supplied with approximately 2.2 million tons of grain and 1 million tons of oil, along with cotton, platinum, iridium, asbestos, manganese ore, and other goods. In the first six months of 1941 the mutual supplies increased to such a degree that "on the night of 22 June 1941, contrary to all sense of reason, Soviet trains and ships loaded with grain, oil, and other goods blithely made their way toward Germany."

According to Heinrich Schwendemann, a German economic historian, the Germans' self-confidence was so great that the generous military supplies to Moscow were not considered of any importance for the outcome of the attack on the Soviet Union already planned since July 1940.

The German ocean steamer, *Bremen,* and thirty other German ships found refuge from the English navy in Kola Bay in the autumn of 1939.

Top-secret negotiations were also conducted regarding the stationing of
three German bases on the Kola Peninsula.

200.1.117

The Food Situation in Russia

At the same time that grain was being exported to Germany, in Russia
itself, as a result of the Finnish war, current war preparations, and the
massive repression of previous years, there were shortages of bread and
flour. During this period, of the eight million hectares in the private possession of "farmers"—or, rather, land workers—two million hectares were
requisitioned. Was this measure intended to force them to spend more
time working on the collective fields or to punish them? In any case, in
December 1939, in many places bread disappeared from the shops; indeed,
from that month on, village shops were not even allowed to sell bread
or flour.

Recently published letters to the newspapers, for example, talk of "hunger once again." "All the letters paint a truly tragic picture: a half-starved
existence, desperation among the people, threats of failed production, and
the like. They are filled with implicit accusations laid at the door of the
leaders of the USSR."

In the autumn of 1939 "reserved shopping" was established for the
army, and later for the NKVD, workers in the energy industry, miners, and
railway personnel. This meant that only specific categories of people could
purchase goods in certain shops; the rest of the population had to find
what they could in the few other shops that remained. In the province
of Molotov (Perm), 65 percent of the population had to manage with
whatever food was in shops that were supplied with a mere 2 to 3 percent
of the total available foodstuffs; the rest was sold by means of "reserved
shopping."

Farmers consequently went to town in the hope of buying something
there, so that long queues formed in front of the shops. Infantry and
mounted troops were sent in to solve the "queuing problem." Queues were
broken up, and people were fined or loaded into trucks and then dumped
outside the city.

"Standing in front of the shops was forbidden, so you moved around
into the side streets or into the park, where people stood shivering until
morning, and, at daybreak, everyone took the person before him by the
elbow and we crept like a gray snake through the town to the shop." Whole
families sometimes queued for many consecutive days and were therefore

325.1.24
325.2.4

unable to work. Documents even bear witness to "fatal accidents as a result of hunger." 325.1.25–27

The writer Mikhail Prishvin noted in his diary on 30 December 1939, "There is nothing in the shops—not even any sugar—and tens of thousands of people are queuing day and night. Everyone wants to buy something for the festivities, and, although there is nothing, people hope nonetheless that they will be able to get something." 359.1.144

No wonder the people themselves, unofficially, introduced a kind of coupon system, with local variations, to which the government turned a blind eye. "Ration books in the period from 1939 to 1941 are a historical fact," says the historian Yelena Osokina. The ration book system was only officially introduced in large cities such as Moscow and Leningrad in July 1941. 325.1.17

A Neutral Russia

In April 1940 Germany occupied Denmark and Norway, and on 10 May the Blitzkrieg began against the Netherlands, Belgium, Luxembourg, and France.

Although Moscow had reckoned on a long-term war that would exhaust both parties, on 22 June 1940 France had already surrendered. According to a communiqué dated 23 June 1940, Moscow announced, through the TASS press agency, that the Soviet Union wished to remain neutral and would therefore not be intimidated by Churchill, who warned her, on the day the German troops occupied Guernsey, of German domination in Europe. Stalin's argument was that Churchill, finding himself in a tight spot, would do anything to set the Soviet Union and Germany against each other. Furthermore, the prime minister, who had come to power on 10 May 1940, had never previously shown any concern for the fate of the Soviet Union.

On the other hand, nothing at that time indicated that Germany was afraid of the Soviet Union. Berlin was of the opinion that neither England nor the Soviet Union was capable of posing any military threat and that Germany should therefore take advantage of this favorable situation. Thus it was decided, on 31 July 1940, to formulate secret plans for an attack on Russia (the "Fritz Plan").

While Germany was attacking and conquering Western Europe, on 14 June 1940—the day Paris fell—Russian troops occupied Lithuania. The

occupation of Latvia and Estonia followed several days later. In July 1940
these three states—now Russian military bases—were enlisted as new
USSR republics. In 1941 the Soviet occupiers deported 15,851 people from
these countries to Siberia.

351.1.155

In June 1940 the Soviet army also attacked Romania over the Dnestr,
and occupied and annexed Bessarabia and northern Bukovina. On 23 June
1940 Molotov had already declared that the "solution" to "the Bessarabian
question can permit no further delay." Here, too, as in the Baltic States
and the "new territories," there were immediate deportations of "undesirable elements." On the grounds of a confidential protocol from the
German-Russian Non-Aggression Pact, German inhabitants were allowed
to leave both Romanian territories. They constituted a well-heeled, affluent
group of the population, which had been established there since 1812. In
this way a total of 133,138 people fled the district either with their belongings or with compensation for them. "The nature of the evacuation and
the attitude of the state organizations bear witness to the fact that this was
one of the measures for removing hostile elements, which, in the opinion
of the Soviet leadership, posed a great social and political threat for the
country on the eve of war. . . . From the Soviet Union's perspective, and
in fact from Germany's standpoint as well, the evacuation of the Germans
from Bessarabia amounted to a deportation. Both sides were preparing
for war, and therefore both the USSR and Germany alike viewed any German who wished to remain on Soviet territory as an enemy."

197.1; 331.1

331.2.103

In the mouth of the Danube, and specifically the part "relinquished"
by Romania, a Russian Danube flotilla lay at anchor: seventy vessels with
artillery, three hundred kilometers from the oil fields of Ploiesti, which
were strategically important to Germany. The place where the flotilla was
based, incidentally, was difficult to defend. In fact, it seemed more intended for action upstream.

After the German conquest in the West, on 4 August 1940, *Pravda* wrote,
"How fantastic, how wonderful it is when the entire world shakes at its
foundations, when the mighty and the great fall." On 18 August the same
newspaper reported, "Every war of this kind brings us nearer to the happy
time when there will be no more slaughter among the people. . . . And
when Stalin, the Field Marshall of the Revolution, gives the signal, then
hundreds of thousands of pilots, aviators, and parachutists [will] sweep
down on the enemy with all the might of their weapons, the weapons of
socialist justice. The Soviet air force will bring happiness to mankind."

Yet a third article in *Pravda* intended to reflect or boost the attitude of
the people: "Perhaps there will be others to join the sixteen coats of arms
[of the Soviet republics]. . . . And who knows where we will celebrate New
Year's Day in five or ten years?"

On 27 September 1940 Germany, Italy, and Japan concluded the Three-
Power Pact, intended to organize and divide the world according to their
ideas. At the end of November 1940 Hungary, Romania, Slovakia, and
Bulgaria entered the pact. This increased the German influence on the
Balkans, and, under German pressure, Romania was forced to cede Tran-
sylvania, with its large Hungarian population, to Hungary, without consulting Russia. A German military mission appeared in Romania. All this
caused Russia some concern. Mutual irritation grew.

To dispel that irritation—or to lull Moscow into a false sense of security—Molotov was invited to pay a visit to Berlin, between 10 and 14
November 1940. Germany was eager to discover Russia's intentions. Sipols
cites a document by Hitler dated 12 November, in which he states, "Political negotiations are being entered into in order to gain clarity regarding
Russia's position in the near future. Depending on how those negotiations
progress, we must continue preparations for the East for which verbal instructions have been given."   402.1.149

Molotov's instructions from Stalin included: "1) Objective of the trip
a) to find out the real intentions of Germany and all the parties to the
pact concerning the execution of the plan to form a 'new Europe' and a
'Great Asian Territory': the borders of 'new Europe' and the East Asian territory. . . . The USSR's place in those plans and in the future; 2) to ensure
that a) Finland, b) the Danube, and c) Bulgaria are included in the sphere
of influence of the USSR. Furthermore, to discuss Turkey and Iran."   94

A strange game unfolded. Germany invited Moscow to enter the Three-
Power Pact; Russia agreed in principle but did not wish to be considered
as a partner or as the fourth country. The exact progression of affairs in
this issue is debatable.

The German minister of foreign affairs, Joachim von Ribbentrop,
launched repeatedly into long-winded dissertations regarding the division
of the world once England was defeated. Molotov, who was forced to
take refuge in an air-raid shelter because of an English bombing attack
on Berlin, remarked dryly that England evidently was not yet defeated,
and then he returned to concrete questions, to which, however, he received
no answers. Molotov demanded the deployment of Russian troops in

Bulgaria and in bases on the Bosporus, Dardanelles, and Danube. Russia offered transit traffic to Japan via the Trans-Siberian Railway. Russia demanded the withdrawal of German troops from Finland. Germany, however, rejected all the Russian demands.

After the talks in Berlin, Molotov commented that, "in general, all the members of the delegation were convinced that the inevitability of a German attack had increased unbelievably and that in the near future, in particular, our forces should draw suitable conclusions." Stalin further declared, after having heard Molotov's report, "Hitler is preparing a similar fate for us [to that of Poland and Austria] with this pact, but by signing this non-aggression pact with Germany, we have already gained more than a year in which to prepare the decisive, fatal strike against Hitlerdom. Naturally, we cannot see the pact as the basis for guaranteeing our current security. The guarantee for lasting peace is to strengthen our armed forces."

On 25 November Molotov informed the German ambassador in Moscow that Russia was prepared to become a party to a Four-Power Pact under the following conditions: that German troops be withdrawn from Finland, that a pact be concluded with Bulgaria because of the straits, that the "area to the south of Batumi and Baku in the general direction of the Persian Gulf be recognized as the center of the USSR's aspirations," and, finally, that Japan refrain from demanding concessions in Northern Sakhalin. The Russian demands were so thoroughly unacceptable that Berlin did not even respond; nonetheless, the Germans did pass them on to their allies in the Balkans, to point out Russia's aggressive intentions.

A few short weeks later—on 18 December 1940—*Weisung Nr. 21, Unternehmen Barbarossa* was signed, the definitive formation of the plan for the war against the Soviet Union.

Military Preparations

Between 21 and 30 December 1940, 270 military leaders and politicians conferred in Moscow regarding the military situation. The experiences of the war against Finland a year earlier had demonstrated the relative weakness of the Soviet army. Both the military leaders and the politicians lamented "the poor skills of the overwhelming majority of the commando structure of the Red Army."

A partial explanation for this situation was that, as a result of the purging, which had hit the army hard, inexperienced officers had been

promoted rapidly to senior ranks. The words of General Ivan Tyulenev
were unsettling: "We have no up-to-date, founded theory of defense."   46.1.15

In January 1941 two strategic exercises were held: one from 2 to 6
January, for the northwestern battle scene, and the other from 8 to 11 January, for the southwestern battle scene where the "attack operation" was
simulated.   46.2

The exercises were based on the assumption of a minor advance by the
enemy, which would be stopped and repelled on their own territory. This
was the usual Soviet interpretation of the beginning of a war. Not until
the timely counterattack did the exercises begin.

The future field marshal of the tank troops, Mikhail Kazakov, who took
part in the maneuvers, referred to the "Reds" as the "aggressor." "But   195.1.57–58
nothing was mentioned in the task of how the 'Easterners' succeeded so
quickly and consequently repelled the attack. . . . The exercises did not
even attempt to deal with the actions of the 'Easterners,' in other words,
the Red Army, in the event of an offensive by a real enemy." It was assumed   46.3.8
that "the 'Westerners,' together with their Allies, would attack the 'Easterners' without being fully prepared, on 15 July 1941." "Kazakov therefore
appears to have been right in seeing the 'Easterners' as the aggressor in the
exercises—in which case the following question arises: if offensive action
was formulated for the 'Easterners,' was that then related to the operative
plans of the general staff in the event of a war in the West? The answer to
that question is, in our opinion, yes, it was related." "What it boils down
to is that the author of the 'clarified plan' [in other words, the general
staff's plan for what to do in the event of an attack] and those who formulated the task for the operational strategic exercises were working on
the assumption of an unconditionally favorable defense against enemy
attack in the initial period of the war, after which the Red Army's attack
was to unfold. The cornerstone was not defense but attack, although,
again, only after the successful repulsion of the aggressors."   46.3.11

Commander-in-Chief Leonid Sandalov explained, perhaps superflu-
ously: "The commando and staff exercises throughout the entire winter
period and in the spring of 1941 were only executed on the theme of
attack." And, finally, in a speech during the autumn of 1938, directly from   339.39–41
the horse's mouth, Stalin himself declared: "All that fuss about defense;
it's nothing but a cover."   169

2

War Approaches

On 18 December 1940 Hitler gave the definitive order to prepare Operation Barbarossa, the attack on the Soviet Union. Although utmost secrecy was the aim, Russian counter-espionage already knew the main points of 180.1.16 the plan less than two weeks later.

This is the appropriate moment to write something about the military events in the areas of Poland occupied by the Soviet Union. Despite the great lack of barracks, other accommodations, and roads, an army of some considerable size had been stationed in these "new territories." Stalin forbade the military force to encamp behind the old border in and around the Stalin Line. He ordered that, "not an inch of ground must be conceded to the enemy." This meant that the troops had to advance to the 199.1.9 new border. Worse still, despite objections from the General Staff, the former Stalin Line along the old borders, considered to be extremely 155.5.6 strong, was dismantled; some parts were conserved, others blown up, 126.1.239 while no new defense line had yet been prepared along the new border. As a result, afterward, it proved that, at a strategic moment, the forces were deprived of weapons and left unable to defend either the old or the 70.1 new border.

At the beginning of February 1941 an increasing number of Russian troops was directed to the new border as a start, because "a full concentration of Soviet armies along the German border was planned for 300.2.11 10 July 1941."

Between 25 March and 5 April four hundred thousand men were called up and "infantry, mechanized and tank divisions, and airborne troops 312.6.164 were transferred from the Far East to the West."

20

Then "in April 1941 Stalin undertook a demonstrative campaign by concentrating units of the Red Army in Bessarabia, on the border with Romania, which had joined the Three-Power Pact."   312.4.58

And Zhukov tells us, "The character of the military operations itself
determined the necessity of a considerable expansion of the airborne
troops. April 1941 was the beginning of the formation of five airborne
brigades. . . . With the intention of frightening Germany, in May 1941
major exercises were held with the Red Army's airborne troops." Later   475.1.96
those airborne troops—not needed in a defensive war—turned up again
as the first guard divisions.

In the meantime, war was approaching rapidly: in a Blitzkrieg in March–
April Germany attacked Yugoslavia and Greece, and, with the exception
of Crete, occupied both countries.

Stalin's Speech of 5 May 1941

Stalin's speech of 5 May is long and unpublished and was addressed to the
graduates of military academies. Even now we know only of a summary.   418.6

The official summary, written on 28 June 1948 and intended to be included in Stalin's collected works, part 14, reads: "The actual experience
for reforming our army we have gained from the Russian-Finnish war
and the current war in the West. I have said that we possess a modern
army, equipped with the latest weapons. We have tanks of the first order,
which will break through the front." According to Stalin, at that time
the Red Army had three hundred divisions, more heavily armored tanks
were available, the artillery was better and the planes faster. There was no
reason, therefore, to feel inferior to anyone. "Is the German army really
invincible?" he asked his audience. "No, there is no invincible army in the
world, and, from a military point of view, there is nothing special about
the German army with regard to its tanks, artillery, or air force."

After his speech Stalin proposed several toasts. The third was as follows: "We were temporarily applying a defensive policy, as long as we had
not rearmed our army and had not equipped our army with modern resources. Now that we have reformed our army, however, and saturated it
with material for modern warfare, we have become powerful, and it is
now that we must change from a position of defense to one of attack. In
organizing the defense of our country, we are obliged to act aggressively.
When changing over from a position of defense to a military policy of
offensive action, we need to bolster our agitation and propaganda, and our

press, with an aggressive spirit. The Red Army is a modern army, and a modern army is an offensive army."

According to one of the officers present, Enver Muratov, Stalin declared that "the German army was not invincible" and that a war against Germany "will inevitably accelerate into a victorious people's liberation war." He also said that is was necessary to analyze the experience of the Soviet-Finnish war. The lessons of that war were hard. "We have to admit that the Red Army has been shown to be unprepared to fight a modern war. We are carefully studying these lessons and extra measures are being taken to eliminate the serious shortages in military armament and in the military training of the troops." And he warned his audience: "I am asking you not to talk about this." Muratov writes that, "after several speeches, General Grigori Sivkov stood up and proposed the following toast: 'Comrades! Let us drink a toast to peace, to Stalin's peace policy, to the creator of this policy, to our great leader and teacher, Josif Vissarionovich Stalin!'"

In response, Stalin held up his hand in a gesture of protest. The guests were confused. Stalin said something to [General Semyon] Timoshenko, who said: "Comrade Stalin would like to speak." Applause. Stalin waved them back to their seats. Once it had become quiet in the hall, he began his address. He was absolutely enraged and stuttered a little, a strong Georgian accent creeping into his speech: "This general has understood nothing. He has understood nothing. We Communists are not pacifists; we have always been against unjustified wars, against imperialistic wars for dividing up the world, against slavery and exploitation of the workers. We have always been for just wars for freedom and independence, for revolutionary wars to free the people from the colonial yolk, for the most just war to defend the socialist Fatherland. Germany wishes to destroy our socialist state, which the workers won under the leadership of Lenin's Communist Party. Germany wishes to destroy our great Fatherland, Lenin's Fatherland, the results of October, wipe out millions of Soviet people and enslave those who are left. Only a war with fascist Germany and a victory in that war can save our Fatherland. Raise your glasses and drink to the war, to aggression in that war, and to our victory in that war." Stalin emptied his glass, and everyone else did the same. Silence descended on the room.

On returning to his military academy in Stalingrad, where he was a lecturer, Muratov was asked if a war was in the offing. "In reply, I started to quote Stalin's speech almost literally. A major from SMERSH [the organization of the Soviet Counterespionage Service, short for Death to Spies]

294.1

294.1.285

demanded to know on what grounds I was spreading rumors regarding the possibility of a war with Germany. I answered calmly that I was simply carrying out Comrade Stalin's orders to the letter, as he had expressed them at the reception in the Kremlin on 5 May."

At the beginning of the war, Gustav Hilger, who had previously been attached to the German Embassy in Moscow as a diplomat, interrogated several captured Russian officers, who independently described what they remembered of the meeting on 5 May 1941: "We have to abandon defensive solutions, as they are obsolete. . . . The Red Army has to get used to the idea that the time for the aggressive expansion of the socialist front has dawned. Anyone who does not understand the necessity of an offensive approach is a narrow-minded idiot. Praise of the German army must also come to an end." 294.1.287 42.1.246

The historian Oleg Vishlyov, who works more on suggestion than on evidence, felt that the testimonies of these Russian officers and the reputation of their interrogators were unreliable. 475.3.95

The writer Vsevolod Vishnevski, already known to have too loose a tongue, was also present on 5 May. He noted the following in his diary on 13 May: "A speech of enormous significance. We are embarking on a true ideological attack. . . . I am not consulting my notes [on that speech], but I do remember clearly the prediction that it is we who are beginning the fight against Germany; we will conduct a grandiose battle against fascism, against an extremely dangerous military neighbor, on behalf of the revolutionary philosophy of Europe and, naturally, Asia. . . . A crusade to the west lies before us. The future holds possibilities of which we have long dreamed." After a conversation with Voroshilov, Vishnevski, who was well 90.1.91 informed, had already noted in his diary on 14 April: "Our hour, the time for open battle, for holy war, approaches rapidly." 312.3.65

Other Propaganda

During May 1941, evidently as a consequence of the meeting of 5 May, several important conferences were held with newspaper and magazine editors, political leaders and propaganda chiefs from the Red Army, writers, and filmmakers. Participating actively in these meetings, indeed setting the tone, were Andrei Zhdanov, Georgi Malenkov, Aleksandr Shcherbakov (secretary of the party's Central Committee), Georgi Aleksandrov (the party's head of agitation and propaganda), and A. I. Zaporozhets (head of propaganda for the Red Army).

The eight directives adopted at these meetings included "The Task of the Red Army's Political Propaganda in the Near Future," "The Current Role of Propaganda," and "The Current International Situation and the Foreign Policy of the USSR." Here follows several passages from those documents:

"Focus all forms of propaganda, agitation, and education on the single goal of the political, moral, and military preparation of military personnel for conducting a just, offensive, and totally destructive war."

312.3.62

"Every war the Soviet Union conducts will be a just war." Evidently it no longer mattered who the aggressor was.

"The increased political, economic, and military might of the Soviet Union enables us to apply an offensive foreign policy and resolutely liquidate hotbeds of unrest near our borders by expanding our territory."

312.5.159

"We are not ruling out the possibility that the USSR will be forced to take the initiative to proceed with offensive military action by virtue of the situation that has developed. . . . In the current particularly tense international situation, the USSR must be prepared for all kinds of unexpected eventualities and keep the powder dry for any imperialist state, regardless of the existence of pacts and agreements with that state."

281.2.79–80

"An attack on the Soviet Union by the imperialists is possible any day at any moment and we must be prepared to anticipate this attack by means of offensive action. . . . The experience of military action has shown that a defensive strategy against dominant, motorized units has had no success whatsoever and has ended in defeat. Consequently we must apply that same offensive strategy against Germany, supported by powerful equipment. . . . Such a conflict is no longer so far away." Here Aleksandrov added a handwritten note: "You should absolutely avoid employing such phrasing. That would mean showing the enemy our cards."

281.2.82

The historian Mikhail Meltyukhov concluded, "In our opinion, with information on direct preparations by the Red Army for an attack, such considerations in documents determining the official line of the party's Central Committee prove indisputably the intentions of the Soviet leadership to carry out an attack on Germany in the summer of 1941." He continues: "The primary objective of the USSR was the expansion of the 'front of socialism' over as large an area as possible. In Moscow's view, the following circumstances were favorable for executing that task: the German occupation of the majority of the continent, a long, drawn-out war with no prospects, growing dissatisfaction among the populations of the occupied countries, fragmentation of the Wehrmacht over several fronts, a brooding Japanese-American conflict—all this gave the Soviet leadership the unique chance to destroy Germany with a sudden blow and 'to liberate' Europe from 'rotting capitalism.' In my opinion, all the activities of the Soviet leadership between 1939 and 1941 were aimed at that objective."   281.2.83

This opinion, which Meltyukhov and others held, is strongly contested. Critics argue that those documents had not yet been approved by the top leadership nor had they been passed on to the troops. In my opinion, however, they do indicate the precise aim of the propaganda, and there seems little room for doubt that ideological preparation was under way. After all, it is impossible that the statements and phrasing quoted above did not have Stalin's approval, when his watchdogs were present at the very time the statements were being formulated and perhaps even suggested the wording themselves. One of those watchdogs, Shcherbakov, also stated, on 20 May 1941, "The land of socialism is obligated to take advantage of the favorable developments in the international situation and to take the initiative for offensive action against the capitalist encirclement in order to expand the socialist front."   281.2.80

The historian Vladimir Nevezhin, whose book on all these propaganda documents was published in 1997 and extensively documented, concludes that an accurate analysis of such documents "permits one to suppose, first, that they were founded on Stalin's instructions, given in his speeches to graduates of military academies on 5 May 1941; and, second, that they were formulated in mutual cohesion and contain the same views and positions. The guiding principle of all this material boils down to the necessity for an all-around, ideological preparation of the Red Army personnel and of the entire people for an offensive war. In some of these projects, the idea was directly postulated to take the initiative into their own hands and deal a fatal blow to the capitalist encirclement so as to bring about its definitive destruction and to achieve victory for socialism."   312.6.234–35

The writer Vsevolod Vishnevski, naturally, did not determine the policy. He does, however, indicate what the most aggressive members of the leadership were thinking. A typical example is his diary entry of 21 May 1941: "If the warring parties continue to spill blood, we could become the super arbitrator in Europe and Asia. Hitler is aware that we are aiming to give him a licking, preferably somewhere in 1942, once Germany has exhausted itself."   312.3.66

The "Considerations"

The first version of the Soviet strategy for 1941 was formulated on 14
October 1940. A revised version appeared on 11 March 1941, to which were
added the "Considerations concerning the Plan for the Strategic Development of the Soviet Union's Armed Forces in the Event of a War with
Germany and Its Allies," dated 15 May 1941. Although the view was maintained, even by General Volkogonov, that no Russian plan of attack existed,
413   after the publication of the "Considerations," this standpoint became entirely untenable, and one can only dispute the significance of that document. I quote:

> As Germany is currently keeping its army mobilized, with a developed
> hinterland, it is capable of *getting us first*, once they set the wheels in
> motion, and dealing [us] a sudden blow. To prevent this eventuality, I
> believe we must not let the German commando take the initiative under
> any circumstances but must *be one step ahead of* the enemy and attack the
> German army at the point when they are at the development stage and
> still unable to form a front with any interaction with military units. . . .
> The first strategic objective of the Red Army's action is to ensure the
> destruction of the main body of the German army, which is positioned to
> the south of the Brest-Demblin Line and to arrive by the thirtieth day of
> the operation at the Ostrolenka front, at the river Narev, at Lovic, Lodz,
> Kreuzburg, Oppeln, and Olomouc.
>   The following strategic objective is to destroy large forces from the
> center and the northern wing of the German front with an attack from
> the area of Katowice in a northerly or northeasterly direction and gain
> control of the area of former Poland and East Prussia. The next task is to
> destroy the German army to the east of the Vistula and in the direction
> of Krakow, come out at the Narev and Vistula rivers, and gain control
> of the area of Katowice, achieving this by a) launching the main attack
> with the forces from the south-west front in the direction of Krakow and
> Katowice and so cutting Germany off from its southern allies, b) launch-
> ing a supporting attack with the left wing of the west front in the direc-
> tion of Sedlec and Demblin, with the objective of uniting the Warsaw
> divisions and gaining control of Warsaw and also supporting the south
> front by destroying the enemy's Lublin division, and c) conducting active
> defense against Finland, East Prussia, Hungary, and Romania and being
> prepared to strike at Romania, circumstances permitting. In this way, the

Red Army will begin offensive action from the Cizev-Lyutovisko front
with a force of 152 divisions as against the Germans' 100. An active defense
will be conducted at the other parts of the state border.

After several passages on numbers of divisions and which would be
deployed where, the document continues:

> In order to guarantee the execution of the plan set out above, it is essen-
> tial to take the following measures in time, without which it is impossible
> to strike unexpectedly at the enemy, either from the air or overland:
> 1. A secret mobilization of troops under the guise of military exercises
>   with the reserve;
> 2. Under the guise of leaving for the encampments realize a secret con-
>   centration closer to the western border, first concentrating all the
>   armies of the Supreme Command;
> 3. Secretly bring together the air force from the distant districts at newly
>   built airfields and make a start on the development of the air force
>   hinterland;
> 4. Gradually develop a hospital base and the hinterland under the guise
>   of maneuvers and hinterland exercises."

Finally, the "Considerations" state:

> 'ix I request:
> 1. Confirmation of the proposed plan for strategic development of the
>   USSR's armed forces and the plan for the proposed military action
>   in the event of a war with Germany;
> 2. Permission for prompt, gradual execution of a secret mobilization
>   and secret concentration of, first, all reserve armies of the Supreme
>   Command and the air force
> 3. That the People's Commissar of Railways be requested to carry out
>   a complete and timely laying of railway lines in accordance with the
>   plan of 1941 and, in particular, in the direction of Lvov.

The document is marked "top secret," "highly important," "strictly personal," and "only copy." It is handwritten, dated May 1941, and was probably formulated between 7 and 15 May 1941. Halfway through May, in the
Kremlin, the future marshal Aleksandr Vasilevski, then vice chairman of

the Chief of General Staff, handed it personally to Zhukov, who reported on the document to Stalin, as well as Timoshenko, the People's Commissar for Defense, according to Danilov.

90.3.37

P. N. Bobylev, historian and reserve-colonel writes: "The 'Considerations' are valuable and convincing proof of the response of the Red Army's general staff to Germany's action at that time. . . . The general staff considered a preventive strike a way of thwarting what a great deal of information pointed to as an inevitable German attack on the Soviet Union."

46.3.14

There is nothing in the "Considerations" about a mobilization after a German attack. What is absolutely new is the "preventive strike," which did not fit in with views on the beginning of a war until that moment.

Critics make use of the fact that Stalin did not sign this document to undermine its importance. The lack of his signature, however, means nothing; the most important orders were given verbally. In any event, the document was discussed on 24 May 1941 during a top-secret meeting between Stalin and the highest civil and military leaders, when the latest plans were discussed in detail. "It can no longer be doubted that the strategic planning of the war in the USSR was being realized to the full extent," writes Yuri Gorkov, according to whom, "absolutely no tasks of an offensive nature were assigned to the troops of the western military districts." Nor was there any known document "concerning the Soviet Union's preparation for an attack on Germany."

90.1.85

147.1.35–36

147.2.115

147.2.109

Molodyakov, however, voiced the question, "Is absolutely nothing actually acknowledged in the documents, then, about the Russian plan of attack?" Both Gorkov and Molodyakov may very well be right that nothing was said about the plan of attack in those documents. Indeed, it is most unlikely that the Russians could have settled such a matter in a couple of weeks, when the German plans of attack required at least six months of preparation.

289.1.184–85

According to Zhukov, the idea of a preventive strike evolved "between Timoshenko and himself in connection with Stalin's speech of 5 May 1941, in which he spoke of the possibility of acting offensively."

312.4.61

Zhukov later wrote that he had given Stalin a memorandum concerning a preventive attack, although a message was then passed on to him through Stalin's secretary, Aleksandr Poskryobyshev: "Tell Zhukov not to write me

any memorandums for which I need to call in the public prosecutor." 147.2.111; 17.2.41
Zhukov told military historian V. A. Anfilov Stalin's reply to the memorandum: "Have you gone mad?" These seem unlikely remarks to me, as
the idea of the preventive attack was clearly present in the "Considerations," and one must assume that the "Considerations" were discussed
thoroughly on 24 May with a large number of military and political leaders. Molotov later told the writer Ivan Stadnyuk that in May 1941, partly
because of the arrival of Rudolf Hess in Scotland, which caused Moscow
great concern, a preventive attack on Germany had indeed been considered but that the decision had been made at the time "to wait a while." 142.1.9
Erik van Ree writes in his manuscript of a Stalin biography of Stalin and
the Zhukov plan: "He may well have rejected it, or accepted it and post-
poned its execution. But that he was preparing for a stroke against the
Germans in the long run is almost certain."

A start was also made on the execution of the plans for the "Considerations." A total of 802,000 men were mobilized under the guise of
maneuvers. On 10 July 1941 the Twenty-second, Sixteenth, Nineteenth,
Twenty-fifth, Twentieth, Twenty-fourth, and Twenty-eighth Armies, "the
second strategic echelon," were supposed to be transferred to the west. 337.1.47
Supplies and hospitals were transferred to the border. 7,113 aircraft were
stationed near the border, where airstrips were constructed.

In May and June 1941 an increasing number of troops were concentrated
on the western borders: 77 divisions were already there, and now 114 more
of the "first strategic echelon" joined them. Troops from the Transbaikal 73.1.68
area, Siberia, the Urals, and the Caucasus were directed westward and
arrived at the Dnepr and Western Dvina. 199.1.16

Most remarkable is that the troops did not entrench themselves, bar-
riers were removed rather than installed, and bridges were not mined. Nor
did the troops prepare themselves for winter; they were often quartered
in provisional encampments and other less suitable accommodation. Was
the intention, perhaps, not to let the troops spend the winter there?

The strongest army, the Ninth, was positioned opposite Romania with
seventeen divisions and two mountain divisions (the Twelfth and Eighteenth Armies) in the Carpathian Mountains.

None of the sixty-three Russian armored divisions had any personnel
for blowing up bridges, but they did have soldiers who were trained to
build pontoons across rivers. 278.1.350

On the day of the German attack 47,000 railway wagons loaded with
war supplies were still on their way, and 1,320 trains, loaded with trucks,
were standing ready at the border. As a result, the Soviet army lost roughly
85 percent of all supplies of the People's Commissar for Munitions during the first weeks of the war.

A hundred million maps were lost at the border. The Germans saw
piles of burning maps at Tiraspol and Shaulyai. Top military topographer
Kudryavtsev maintained that roughly two hundred wagons full of maps
were lost in the first few days of the war. Many Russian topographers
perished at the border. Why were the topographers and the maps even
there?

The Soviet troops hardly had any maps of their own territory. Colonel
N. Lyubimov declared, in a statement taken by German officers, that his
regiment possessed only one or two maps on a scale of 1:200,000, which
were of absolutely no use to the artillery. Stalin's son, Yakov Dzhugashvili,
taken prisoner by the Germans, is reputed to have told German interrogators, "The maps worked against the Red Army, as, contrary to expectations, the war was taking place to the east of the state border."

According to Marshal Konstantin Rokossovski, "The orders to the
troops to direct the artillery to the maneuver sites in the border zone and
other ridiculous orders under those circumstances did not exactly inspire
confidence. Judging by the concentration of our air force at airfields in
advance positions and the positioning of supplies . . . in the border area,
this looked like preparation for a step forward." Rokossovski also wrote,
in a passage formerly deleted from his memoirs, that "the staff of the
Military District of Kiev was transferred from Kiev to Tarnopol. We were
not told why."

A major from the Historical Institute of the Ministry of Defense wrote:
"In general, the deployment of the Western Military District troops seemed
more as if it were for an attack than for defense."

According to the historian Danilov, the positioning of supplies just
behind the border was not an "error" but was "dictated by the necessity to
facilitate the planned attack."

The main Russian forces, with 4,200 tanks, were in the Military District of Kiev, as opposed to only 383 tanks in the Northern sector and 109
in the Baltic sector. Meanwhile the GRU, the Russian military intelligence
service, had continually reported that the Germans' main attack would
take place not in the south but to the north of the Pripyat marshes.

Warnings from the Intelligence Service

Despite the purging that had utterly devastated its ranks, the GRU was entirely up to date with the German's real intentions. Moscow knew as early as the summer of 1940 that Germany planned to attack. On 28 December 1940, ten days after the signing of the preparations for the Barbarossa Plan, Moscow was already aware of what was going on, including the planned directions of attack. The later German troop transfers to the east did not go unnoticed, and yet the politicians did not respond efficiently. 180.1.10

This was primarily a result of Stalin's extreme paranoia. Behind the GRU reports he suspected the hand of the British Secret Service, which had, indeed, done everything possible to set Germany and Russia against each other. Furthermore, Stalin was convinced that there would be no German attack until Great Britain was forced into submission. Stalin was also convinced that Germany would not repeat the mistake of waging war on two fronts. In addition to this, I should point out, it is not even certain that the GRU reports actually ever reached Stalin. The point is that everyone was afraid of providing Stalin with news, statements, or reports that contradicted his fixed views and convictions. This was made evident by a report dated 20 March 1941 by the head of the GRU, Fyodor Golikov. In the report he states the exact positioning of the Germans but concludes that the attack will only be carried out after the defeat of England and that "we must treat rumors and documents that talk of the inevitability of a war against the USSR in the spring of this year as disinformation originating from the English or even the German intelligence." 334.1.56

On 1 April 1941 Richard Sorge, the GRU spy in Japan, reported that there would be "an attack in mid-June 1941."

On 11 May 1941 there was a report from Bucharest: "The military operations against the USSR will begin in mid-June. The strike will be unexpected." 334.1.55

On 13 May Sorge specified an attack on 22 June 1941 with 150 divisions. 90.2.18

Sorge refused, however, to return from Tokyo, for fear of repression, and therefore his reports were not believed. Sorge's wife died in a Siberian prison camp in 1942. 102.1.180
425.1.132

On 21 May the spy Leopold Trepper reported that the attack would begin on 22 June. General Tupikov, military attaché, reported the same from Berlin. Lavrenti Beria, the People's Commissar for Foreign Affairs, expressed himself as follows concerning these reports, "I repeat my urgent advice to recall and punish our ambassador in Berlin, Dekanozov, who, as before, is bombarding me with [reports concerning] a so-called attack by Hitler on the USSR." In Stalin's view: "This information is English provocation. Find out who the author of this provocation is and punish him."

On 30 May Sorge reported, "The German attack will take place in the second half of June. The mightiest blow will be struck by the left flank of the German army." On 17 June 1941 People's Commissar for State Security Merkulov stated: "The source working in the staff of the German air force has reported, 'All Germany's military measures for an armed offensive against the USSR have been taken, and the attack can be expected at any moment.'" Stalin wrote on this document in his own hand: "To Comrade Merkulov. Perhaps you should send your 'source' in the staff of the German air force back to his fucking mother. This is not a source but disinformation. I. St." The same day Merkulov ordered, "Check this again carefully and send another report."

On 21 June Beria said to Stalin, "Lieutenant-General Golikov, the chief of the GRU, where up until recently Berzin's gang was operating, has been complaining about Dekanozov and his Major Novobranets, who is lying about the fact that Hitler has assembled 170 divisions against us on our western border . . . but my people and I, Josif Vissarionovich, are staunchly maintaining your view: Hitler will not attack us in 1941." And, "A lot of functionaries have recently fallen prey to shameless provocation and the sowing of unrest. We have to reduce [those] secret agents . . . to the dust of concentration camps, as aids to international provocateurs wishing to bring us into conflict with Germany."

Incidentally Dekanozov had received this information personally from the German ambassador in Moscow, F. W. von der Schulenburg. Stalin remarked, "That disinformation is now taking on sizable proportions at the level of ambassadors."

Moscow had, however, been extremely worried about Rudolf Hess's flight to—or arrival in—Scotland, in the vicinity of the Duke of Hamilton's estate on 10 May 1941. It was assumed that Hitler, who, quite unusually, had held a four-hour meeting with Hess shortly beforehand, had wanted to come to an agreement with Great Britain to eventually launch a joint attack on the USSR. Moscow reasoned that such a flight by Hess would have been impossible without the knowledge of both the Germans and the British.

"Churchill's government said nothing for several days about the arrival of Hitler's deputy in England. Berlin, too, remained completely silent." Somewhere around 20 May 1941, G. Rozanov wrote: "Moscow received a message from London saying that the British cabinet had discussed proposals made by Hess and recommended continuing the negotiations with him at a higher level, bringing in Lord Chancellor Simon, an advocate of an agreement with Germany." "As Stalin was informed, negotiations took place in the strictest privacy on 10 June in a villa near Aldershot between Simon, the British diplomat, Kirkpatrik, and Hess." 168.112

376.1.148

The historian V. S. Lavrov wrote that, on 5 May, Hess discussed a letter with Hitler from the Duke of Hamilton dated 28 April. The "negotiations" concerning Hess's proposals were continued between Kirkpatrick and the German ambassador in Dublin. 255.1.22–23

The bungling diplomacy of Sir Stafford Cripps, the British ambassador in Moscow, who, by suggesting the possibility of a British-German rapprochement, hoped to incite the Soviet Union into adopting an offensive policy toward Germany, was counterproductive. As the English archives regarding this point still remain closed until 2017, little can be said of any value on the matter. When it was opened, the Foreign Office archive for 1941 contained no documents concerning this affair. 458.1.41

During discussions over the course of the war with his English partners, Stalin returned continually to the same subject: what message had Hess actually taken to them? He never received a reply. What is highly suspicious is that when Hess wished to talk about what he knew of this affair under oath during the Nuremberg trials against German war criminals, the president of the court, Sir Geoffrey Lawrence, forbade him to talk about it. 168.112–13

German Deception

Berlin did everything possible to keep the plans of attack secret.

The concentration of troops in the east was supposed to act as a "distraction," or to allow the troops to rest before their invasion of England. Alternatively the troops were intended to advance via the Balkans to Iraq and Iran. It was also suggested that Germany was planning to make demands of the Soviet Union in this context, requesting a passage through the Caucasus, for example, which could make Moscow believe that those troops were positioned there as a way to persuade them to grant concessions. 475.1.71–74

Minister for Public Information and Propaganda Joseph Goebbels devised an ingenious deception. He wrote an article in the *Völkischer Beobachter*, entitled "The Example of Crete," in which the recent invasion of that island was seen as a general rehearsal for the invasion of England. He then had the issue of the party paper in question seized before distribution (13 June 1941), which achieved the desired effect: Goebbels has let the cat out of the bag; an attack on England is indeed imminent. This would, naturally, support Stalin in his idée fixe that they need not fear a German attack before England had been defeated. Rumors were also spread that Stalin was to visit Berlin.

180.1.13

The Military Balance of Power

The Soviet Union had prepared thoroughly for war. Military expenditure rose from 25.6 percent of the state budget to 32.6 percent and then to 43.4 percent between 1939 and 1941. In that same time span the war industry produced 17,000 aircraft, 7,600 tanks, 80,000 pieces of artillery and mortars, and 200,000 machine guns and automatic weapons. They might not all have been the most modern arms, but at the moment of the attack the Soviet Union had 3,719 aircraft of the latest type and 2,083 of the most modern tanks.

In the space of a year or two 125 new divisions had been formed. The number of military personnel increased from almost 2 million in 1939 to nearly 6 million men. Of these, 2.9 million were posted at the western borders.

394.1.76

The historian Mikhail Meltyukhov, whom I have quoted above several times, provides us with the following comparison of the state of affairs (G. I. Gerasimov gives slightly different figures):

281.2.82
128.1.8

	1 January 1939	22 June 1941
personnel	1,943,000	5,710,000
divisions	136	303
artillery and mortars	55,800	115,900
tanks	18,400	22,300
aircraft	17,500	22,400

In contrast, the Germans had 4.6 million men in 155 divisions, 43,407 pieces of artillery and grenade launchers, 3,998 tanks, and 3,904 aircraft.

281.1.17

The most modern Soviet tanks were far superior to the German tanks,

and they generally outnumbered them by a ratio of 4 to 1. From January 155.5.11–12
1939 to June 1941 Soviet industry produced eighteen thousand fighter
planes and more than seven thousand tanks. 282.2.219

The German planes were better than the Russians.

It should be noted that the new divisions certainly had a lack of equipment and experienced commanders. Communications, radio equipment,
tractors, vehicles, fuel, and repair facilities were in short supply. The eight
hundred thousand reserves who had been called up—virtually untrained
men—were meant to make up the numbers of the Ninety-ninth Infantry
Division on the western borders. 124.1.114

As the Amsterdam historian Dr. R. Veltmeijer noted: "In 1941 forty-
eight motorized divisions, twenty-two armored divisions, and sixteen cavalry divisions were positioned in the salient at Lvov and Bialystok alone.
The mass concentration of troops in a bulge at the front can generate
advantages in the event of an attack. On the other hand, for a defensive
force, such a configuration is extremely risky." 470.1.257

The Russian army was actually in a state of complete confusion and a
phase of reorganization, and its leaders were worried, afraid of taking any
responsibility. The men saw that the officers were insecure and lost respect
for them. A large proportion of the commanders had been hastily promoted, since the persecution by the Old Guard in the 1930s had left huge
gaps in the ranks, which had to be filled with relatively inexperienced personnel. Lesser requirements, shorter training, and rapid promotion: the
consequences could be easily predicted. It seems likely, certainly, that if
the higher-ranking officers had not been so decimated the war might have
taken a different turn. The struggle might not even have come to war—
at least that is what Konstantin Simonov feels. After the war Marshal Vasi- 400.4.44–46
levski wrote: "Were it not for the year 1937, there might well have been no
war at all in 1941. . . . A major role was played by the assessment of the
level of destruction of military officers that had taken place in the USSR." 256.2.186

Gerasimov opines that a successful beginning to the war could have
been achieved by, as Zhukov had suggested, anticipating the Germans
(which had been forbidden by Stalin) or mobilization. After all, the Soviet
Union was "absolutely and relatively quantitatively superior where all
types of armaments were concerned." The initial defeats were a result
of the fact that the army was not yet completely organized; they needed
at least another thirty days. And Stalin only gave the order on 21 June,
although "a partial secret mobilization and deployment of the troops had
already been carried out as early as May." 128.1.10

The Final Phase

On 14 June 1941 TASS published a communiqué that is difficult to explain as anything other than a desperate act. The press agency wrote that rumors such as a reputed desire by Germany to attack the Soviet Union,

> have been clumsily fabricated by the propaganda of forces hostile to the USSR and Germany who have an interest in further expanding and stirring up the war. . . . Even before the return to London of the English ambassador in the USSR, Sir Stafford Cripps, rumors began to circulate in the English press, as well as in the international press, of an imminent war between the USSR and Germany. . . . The USSR is said to be preparing herself quickly for a war with Germany and concentrating her troops at the borders. . . . Rumors that the USSR is getting ready for a war with Germany are lies and provocation. . . . According to USSR information, Germany is adhering to the conditions of the German-Russian Non-Aggression Pact just as strictly as the USSR, and therefore, in the opinion of Soviet circles, the rumor concerning Germany's intention to break the pact and undertake an attack on the USSR is entirely unfounded, and it must be assumed that the recent transfer of German troops newly available after the operations in the Balkans to the eastern and northeastern areas of Germany bears no relation to any other motive concerning Soviet-German relations.

Was Moscow playing the innocent here? Did Moscow wish to adopt the attitude of the victim of aggression from the start? In any event, this TASS report caused a great deal of confusion among Russian civilians and military personnel alike.

There was no reaction to the TASS report from Germany, which fueled Moscow's fears of a German-British tête-à-tête. Every effort was made to keep Germany in a good mood and hold off an attack. No response was made to German aircraft flying overhead. A German parachute unit taken prisoner at Grodno on 21 June was, however, interrogated and the incident 278.1.354 reported to the authorities, but the operation was seen as a bluff.

Between 18 and 20 June Moscow asked Berlin to receive Molotov. Berlin, however, stalled for time; in the words of the Secretary of State for Foreign Affairs, Ernst von Weizsäcker, they did not want "to give Stalin the oppor-475.1.79 tunity to upset the applecart at the last moment with a friendly gesture."

Molotov made a final attempt when, on 21 June, he summoned the

German ambassador "and asked him to explain the reasons why the German leadership was dissatisfied with the government of the USSR and the rumors of an approaching war." "The Soviet government," said Molotov, "cannot see any reason for such German dissatisfaction and would be grateful if someone would let them know what has caused the current state of Soviet-German relations and why there has been no response from the German government to the TASS statement of 14 June 1941."

This was all very embarrassing. Was Moscow planning to comply with any demands the Germans might make, to play for time and delay a war as long as possible? In the meantime, the Germans were dropping spies and saboteurs behind Soviet lines, often dressed as soldiers of the Red Army. Border incidents became more frequent. 283.1.29; 251.2.170

Last Orders

Despite urging by the military the troops were not allowed to advance, and Beria's men made certain that this remained the case. Military commanders wanting to prepare for an attack were accused of "panicking." Mekhlis and other political leaders insisted that supplies were placed as close to the border as possible, as an attack could rapidly be warded off anyway. 124.1.134

When, on 13 June, Timoshenko suggested to Stalin that the troops be brought into a state of readiness, Stalin advised him to read the TASS report of the following day. In May and June 1941, as Simonov established shortly afterward, military commanders "were given what amounted to demonstrative leave en masse." In fact, by doing so, the war could surprise the army in its barracks and encampments. Marshal Zhukov, as recently as 14 June 1941, had requested that Stalin bring the troops into a state of readiness, but his request was to no avail. Later the marshal said that he should have insisted more strongly on other occasions. "But what did it mean at that time to oppose Stalin in judging the general political situation? We all remembered only too well what had happened in preceding years, and, to put it simply, saying out loud that Stalin had the wrong end of the stick, that he was mistaken, meant that before you even left the building you were taking coffee with Beria." 466.1.156 282.2.233

400.8.73

During the evening and into the night of 21–22 June 1941 the Russian generals and leaders met with Stalin; when the order was to be given to bring the troops into a state of emergency, Stalin remarked, "It is (still) too early

508.1.233 to give such an order. Perhaps the problem can yet be solved peacefully. We must give a brief order indicating that an attack may begin after provocation by German units. The troops in the border districts must not respond to provocation to avoid creating any conflict situations."

When it became obvious that the war had begun, by Order No. 3 of 22 June 1941, signed by Timoshenko, Zhukov, and Georgi Malenkov, the Fifth and Sixth Armies were commanded to attack in the direction of Lublin 312.5.165–66 and take the city by 24 June. In any event, Königsberg was bombed, and the Ploiesti oilfields were attacked from the air. The Danube Flotilla even occupied the Romanian town of Kilija for a few days, and the Red Army also attacked at Tilsit and Suvalki.

Farsobin, a historian who served in the war, wrote of the war's beginning: "The army did its utmost, but the order to attack was not countermanded." He then recalls a conversation between A. A. Korobkov, commanding officer of the Fourth Army, and his commissar, F. I. Shlykov, held on 22 June: "We have to ask the district to confirm our decision to start our defense." This was the answer he received: "Do you want them 112.2.123 to call us cowards and deprive us of our command of the army?"

The Red Army was attacking when it was clearly not prepared for defense or attack. Here the price was paid for Stalin's misjudgment of the Red Army's capabilities, which Russian commanders such as Zhukov and 112.4.167 Rokossovski later repeatedly pointed out.

The Polemics

On the Soviet side, for decades writers described the start of the war as a "treacherous, double-crossing attack, for which no one was prepared in any way and which came like a bolt from the blue." Had they then not been warned? Were they so trusting? Indeed, that is the impression that was created.

Viktor Suvorov, a GRU officer who defected to England in 1978, wrote the following in his book *Ledokol* (The icebreaker) (which he later reiterated in *Den M* [M Day] and *Poslednyaya respublika* [The last republic]): "To conceal the unparalleled preparation for a 'liberation' that did not take place, the regime made us all out to be fools. The regime tried to hide its crime with the myth of our general, boundless, unfathomable stupid-429.1 ity. We have all been painted as idiots, starting with Stalin and Zhukov."

Suvorov now passionately and demagogically defends the view that the Soviet Union had planned an offensive war against Germany for July 1941 and that the German attack of June 1941 upset those plans. In other words, the Soviet Union had indeed prepared for war, but for an offensive rather than a defensive war. Moreover, Suvorov tries to show that Stalin had already been helping the German National-Socialists to get into power by, for example, forbidding the German Communist Party to unite with the German Social Democrats against National Socialism. Once in power, the Nazi regime was then to be encouraged to wage war against Western Europe, to pave the way, as an "icebreaker for the revolution," for the subsequent liberation and Sovietization of Europe by the Red Army.

Suvorov's books have helped to initiate a closer study of the history between 1939 and 1941, and, possibly only since 1985, a more accurate and honest one.

Suvorov's idea of a planned Soviet attack has been criticized from many sides and often justifiably, as he exaggerates, is inaccurate in his quotes, and suggests more than he can prove. He appears, nonetheless, to be correct regarding the issue of a Russian attack at some time in the future, as not only the targeted propaganda but also the strategic views and their partial implementation give every reason to support such an interpretation. That the Soviet troops were not trained in defense is also well known: the intention was, in fact, to attack. And in that regard Suvorov says nothing new, because everyone knew Russia's military doctrine was active, aggressive defense.

Suvorov is often accused of describing the German aggression as a preventive war and therefore excusing Hitler's war in the East. The response to this is clear: of course it was not a "preventive war," as it had long been established that Germany wanted to attack the Soviet Union and even the exact time this would take place. The facts are indisputable: Germany was the aggressor, Russia defended herself, and not one iota of what actually happened has changed.

Suvorov's books are widely read in present-day Russia and enjoy "scandalous popularity" among a broad readership. In the scientific and military world, furthermore, they have prompted an almost unprecedented flood of reactions. Recently Oleg Vishlyov eloquently defended the view that Russia was purely defending herself.

475.2

The reasons for the popularity of Suvorov's books are, first of all, that they throw light on a blind spot in the shady history of the last years and months before the war; and, second, because the author depicts Stalin as a criminal rather than as a victim of aggression. This harmonizes well with the current view that everything Stalin did and everything that occurred during his regime was wrong and criminal. And thus Stalin carries World War II with him into his downfall.

This situation places Russian critics of Suvorov in the unpleasant position of having to adopt the role of Stalin's defenders, at least in this aspect. And anyone reading more into Suvorov's views is leveled with the equally unpleasant accusation of adhering to the version of the "preventive war" and, in doing so, wishing to exonerate Hitler—absurd insinuations.

In 1998 the Moscow historian V. P. Petrov, in an article in *Novy mir,* advanced a third version of the start of the war. This rejects not only the official Russian version but also Suvorov's account and poses the question of whether the clearly awkward preparations were part of the "general chaos or were conscious acts by those in authority in an effort to conceal a complete lack of preparation for fascist aggression behind reports on paper." "Yes, and all that preparation took place in such a way that, under the guise of reinforcing the defense, measures were implemented that eventually caused the maximum disorganization of the troops in all military border districts, just at the time when Germany attacked."

Petrov, too, points out the evidently stupid orders. He suggests that, actually, everything possible was done to suffer a defeat. In a remarkable postscript to Petrov's article, one Yuri Kublanski writes that those incomprehensible deeds and orders were both inspired and executed by "secret opponents of the Leader, who were probably hoping for a collapse of the Stalin regime in the event of a military conflict with Germany." All these were vague accusations and were contradicted by L. Lazarev: There is not a trace of proof of the existence of treachery or any anti-Soviet attitude on the part of high-ranking officers in June–August 1941. The littérateur and publicist Lazarev refers to Petrov's article as an example of "the replacement of the old, stupid, official lies with amazing and shocking fabrications" that has occurred in recent years.

Finally

In compiling this chapter I was continually torn between two views: Was the Soviet Union indeed planning an attack? Was she preparing for it, and, if so, when was it to occur? If the latter is true, what incredible stupidity, in view of the proven weakness of the armed forces and the progression of the war, not to mention the huge discrepancy between the militant propaganda and the obviously insufficient military preparations for war. It seems that a final assessment is not yet possible, if only because the archives, including the archive of the president of Russia and the captured Wehrmacht archive stored in Podolsk, are still not entirely accessible. It would appear that the evidence points strongly to a planned offensive action at some point on the part of Russia.

According to Nikolay Kuznetsov, Admiral and People's Commissar for the Navy, and member of the Central Committee, Stalin's error was "a misjudgment in the timing of the conflict. I. V. Stalin realized the preparation for war—a widespread and many-faceted war—based on a schedule he chose himself. Hitler threw his plans out of gear." 251.1.321

Semyon P. Ivanov, head of the Academy of the General Staff from 1968 to 1973, wrote, "The German fascist supreme command managed literally to anticipate our troops in the last two weeks before the war." S. Skryabin, 300.212 currently reserve colonel wrote: "The sudden, treacherous attack by fascist Germany on the Soviet Union foiled the military plans in the early period of the war." 403.1.34

Suvorov quotes, unfortunately without accrediting the source, what General Pyotr Grigorenko is supposed to have written, "We were prepared entirely for an offensive war. And it is not our fault that we did not carry out that aggression." The writer Vyacheslav Kondratyev gives his opinion, 429.2.173 "If Stalin was not ready for a war in 1941, then he was doubtlessly planning to start a war against Germany himself in 1942 or 1943. By that time, we would have been able to rearm our forces. I therefore feel that there are grounds for seeing the character of the war that had been started as preventive." 209.27.79

The historian Gabriel Gorodetsky, who emigrated to Israel, set out to disprove the arguments of Suvorov and his supporters, in his book *Grand Delusion: Stalin and the Invasion of Russia*. Based on thorough research 148.1 into the diplomatic history of the year prior to the attack, he concludes that Stalin consistently attempted to avoid war and implemented a peace policy. Unfortunately Gorodetsky ignores any reasoning or circumstances that argue against his view.

Distinguishing three phases in the Russian plans might help to clarify matters:

1. The "classic" phase: the Russians let the enemy come and then strike back (offensive defense).

2 From April to May 1941 the Russians plan their own attack at the last moment, as there is no point in defense, as the French experiences bear witness; they then change from one plan to another, rearm, and reorganize the army.

3. In June panic strikes, and, even at the cost of a humiliating loss of face, the Russians attempt to pacify Germany. They evidently try to avoid the German attack at all costs, at least until autumn, when they believe that the climate and soil conditions would make an attack impossible before the spring of 1942.

In any event, we currently have no more to go on regarding a Soviet attack on Germany (and Europe) than clues and strong suspicions, and these are based only on indirect or unconvincing evidence or both. It goes against all logic to attempt to prove subsequently that an individual (or a state) had been considering a particular action when, in fact, that action was never carried out.

PART 2

The War

3

The Beginning of the War

While the Soviet troops on the border watched German bomber squadrons flying overhead and heard explosions ringing out from 4:00 in the morning, between 3:00 and 4:00 they received Order No. 1: "1. A sudden attack by the Germans is possible in the course of 22 to 23 June 1941. The attack may start with incidents of provocation. 2. It is the task of our troops not to respond to any provocation [as] this could have great implications. . . . At the same time, troops must remain in a state of emergency, prepared to face a possible sudden strike by the Germans and their allies."   124.1.137

Shortly afterward Order No. 2 was given: "Throw yourselves on the enemy forces with all your strength and resources, and destroy them in those areas where they have breached the Soviet border. Until [further] special order, the land forces may not cross the border."   124.1.140

At 3:15 on the morning of 22 June Admiral Nikolay Kuznetsov telephoned to say that Sebastopol had been attacked. He could not get through to Stalin. Malenkov answered the phone and said, "Do you understand what you are saying?"   251.2.176

General Zhukov woke Stalin at 3:25. Stalin's response: "That is provocation . . . do not open fire." When the German ambassador declared   147.1.79–80
the beginning of the war to Molotov at 5:30, the People's Commissar for Foreign Affairs complained that "absolutely no concentration of Red Army troops had been carried out on the border with Germany." Furthermore, he felt that "it must be possible to discuss this issue, as the German government had not made any complaint to the Soviet government up until the last moment."   256.2.185

It was only in the afternoon of 22 June that Molotov announced on the radio that war had broken out with Germany. One of the first to respond

to the attack was the metropolitan bishop, Sergei. 22 June was, coinciden-
tally, the holiday "in remembrance of all the saints who have shone in
the land of Russia." In his sermon, and later in his letter, he stated: "Our
Orthodox Church has always shared the joys and sorrows of the people.
And she will not abandon the people today. . . . The Church gives its holy
blessing to the coming battle." Sergi talked of the fight against the Swedish
king, Karel XII, and about the war with Napoleon, and also spoke of historical heroic figures such as Alexander Nevski, Dmitri Donskoi, Alyosha
Popovich, and Ilya Muromets. Only later did the official Soviet propaganda pick up this patriotic theme of harking back to Russian history, but,
even then, "behind this facade stood, nevertheless, the terrible image of
'the leader of all time and all peoples.'"

Reports concerning Stalin's behavior in the first two weeks of the war are
contradictory. One inaccurate version, on which Nikita Khrushchev and
Anastas Mikoyan later expanded, implies that he was totally confused and
refused to speak to the people (which Molotov did for him on 22 June),
that he retreated to his dacha in Kuntsevo, and that he did not want to see
anyone. The second version refutes this and points out that, according to
Stalin's visitors' book, 117 people spoke to him in the period between 21
and 28 June. Zhukov says that Stalin was only thrown for the first two
hours of the war.

It is generally accepted, however, that after 28 June, when he was told
that Minsk had fallen and the way to Moscow lay practically open, he
became depressed, which only ended when the Politburo came to look for
him in his dacha on 1 July. He then acted strangely, asking: "What are you
doing here?" and was, they say, scared of being arrested.

Not until 3 July did Stalin address the country over the radio. "Comrades! Citizens! Brothers and sisters! Soldiers of the land and sea! I am
turning to you, my friends." He spoke with a heavy Georgian accent and
was audibly nervous. Listeners could hear him drinking water, his teeth
knocking against the glass. He was not speaking the truth: "The enemy's
best divisions and the best part of their air force have already been
destroyed. . . . The main force of the Red Army, armed with thousands of
tanks and aircraft, is entering the battle." And he gave the order to destroy
everything that could be useful to the enemy, deploying a scorched earth
policy, in other words.

In the meantime, the Luftwaffe had already destroyed twelve hundred
aircraft, practically wiping out the Russian air force in the west. The

commander of the air force at the western front, Kopets, committed suicide the same day.   400.2.59

The munitions supplies and "70 percent of the mobilization food supplies were lost," so that, in the winter of 1941–42, the state grain reserves
needed to be drawn on. One month after the German invasion, there was   497.1.23
an "unexpected" lack of rifles: those supplies, too, had fallen into enemy
hands.   284.1.103

Hour by hour "the Germans advanced as if carrying out maneuvers,
while our troops retreated in disarray, that is, they fled to the east."   33.1.47–48

That they were taken by surprise is beyond doubt: many of the troops
were in the barracks or encampments, transports of men and equipment
were still on the way, ammunition had to be unloaded prematurely, many
officers were on leave, those who had been mobilized could not find or
reach their unit nor their supplies and stores of fuel, and munitions and
food fell into enemy hands.   94.1.172

Not everyone was surprised. The fortress and garrisons of Brest had
anticipated an attack and were prepared for it. For several weeks, isolated   387.2.23
at the border, the Soviet troops stubbornly resisted. The German troops,
too, came up many a time against fierce resistance, even when the situation for the defending party was hopeless. Admiral Kuznetsov had taken
it upon himself to bring the fleet into a state of emergency, and his losses
were therefore minimal.   224.1

Mobilization

On 27 June a new mobilization was announced. In the space of two
months, five million men were called up and more than three hundred
new divisions formed. Not surprisingly the training of officers was very   495.1.162
brief and therefore elementary. "We were only shown a Tokarev rifle," the
operation of the Maksim machine gun was only explained, and "we all
looked at it." In the division of future author Mikhail Kostrov there was   257.1.71
only one gun to every five men, and Kostrov was not given one. He therefore refused to fight and was sentenced to the firing squad. The first salvo
missed, as did the second, after which the commander of the firing squad
whispered to Kostrov, "Do me a favor, friend, and fall down." Kostrov
complied and so both were satisfied.   225.1.66

Konstantin Simonov made his way to the front by train from Moscow
on 22 June. The train was filled with officers returning from leave. "Judging by our carriage, it looked as if half the Western Military District had

been on leave. I couldn't understand how it could have happened." A group of officers elsewhere was told, "You will have to get to your division by yourselves, hitching or on foot, however you can. . . . Hell, I don't know if you can make those two hundred kilometers in four days or not." On the way, Simonov saw long columns of civilians called up for service on the road, looking for their division. "They did not want to be taken for deserters, and at the same time they were not sure, did not understand, where they were going. . . . They were on their way to their mobilization destination." In Roslavl Simonov saw how recruits were given weapons training, all still in civilian clothes and unarmed.

361.1.65

400.2.19
400.2.155

The departure of recruits in the villages was traditional. "They had to gather everything together quickly: mug, spoon, towel, and underwear. The people stormed the shops and took all the bottles of Moscow Special [vodka]. Everyone was drinking, those who were being taken away and those who were staying. And they were all in tears, as though they were saying good-bye forever. . . . Father turned around, took a deep bow and spoke with a quavering voice. 'Farewell village, perhaps I will never see you again, farewell fields, farewell everyone.' Then he came to us, kissed us one by one, and said to Mother, 'Go home and take care of the children.'"

290.2.80–81

In the village of Drankovo "everywhere you looked, our beloved Russia was crying its heart out. At this late hour there were no officious commissars around, the people made no effort to restrain themselves, but mourned freely and without shame. The women wailed and lamented, howling inconsolably as if for the dead, knowing in their heart of hearts that this was the final farewell."

232.1.13–14

The Military Retreat

Most units—or what was left of them—retreated in a state of disorder. Communications had either broken down or were entirely lacking. Troops were searching for their officers, officers for their troops. Roads were hopelessly blocked with endless comings and goings of people. Rumors abounded—about German parachutists and saboteurs in Russian uniform, about encircling—and many soldiers had just been mobilized and were therefore still inexperienced. Some officers committed suicide on the way. Yevgeny Dolmatovski had been encircled in August at Uman, was spattered by the brains of a battalion commissar, but he managed to escape: "We retreated alongside beautiful cornfields full of cornflowers

400.3.59

and poppies, leaving behind villages that could have been painted by Kuindzhi and towns depicted by Chagall." After returning to his own division, Dolmatovski underwent a thorough interrogation, which included many insulting insinuations. He was not executed only because he knew where the Sixth Army had buried the regimental flags. The panic was indescribable.

98.1.10, 33

On seeing the chaotic, fleeing, demoralized soldiers by a bridge, some in uniform, others in civilian clothing, some with weapons, some without, some wearing insignias, others having torn them off, General Rokossovski remarked out loud: "Tomorrow all our papers will be reporting on the heroic withdrawal of the Red Army." A lieutenant from SMERSH overheard him, and said, "You just got out of prison. Do you want to go back?"

269.1.144

In Western Ukraine, Ukrainian nationalists shot at retreating Soviet troops "as if we were retreating over enemy territory." There were white flags, blue and yellow Ukrainian flags, and flags with swastikas. Some of the people welcomed the German troops with flowers and the traditional bread and salt.

67.1.12; 188.4.110; 30.1.232

In December 1941, at a barbershop in the area of Tula, Simonov saw a sign that read, "For gentlemen German officers"; other signs were written in German and Russian. Elsewhere people looted shops after bombing raids. The Volokolamski Monastery in the little town of Monastyr was plundered and destroyed by Russian soldiers.

400.2.558

214.1.180–81

The author Emmanuil Kazakevich remarked that, in retreating, the soldiers "openly expressed their feelings . . . they remembered with contempt the continual boasting and the unparalleled jubilant mood that Stalin had cultivated over the course of many years."

256.3.228

Vladimir Karpov wrote, "Many soldiers, first and foremost those from enemy-occupied areas, fled home," not only Ukrainians but also Russians. According to Viktor Astafyev, initially there were soldiers who wanted to "fight against their own mates at the front, rather than the fascist enemy," but this accusation needs further investigation. According to Solzhenitsyn, in the summer of 1941 the country was hoping for liberation by the Germans: "You can't think of anything more convincing than this voting with the feet." In a letter to Ales Adamovich dated 21 March 1980, Kondratyev said that the war could also be seen as a "continuation of the civil war. . . . In my opinion, Stalin was also afraid of that at the beginning of the war. Let's face it, how many people were not dissatisfied or affected?"

191.1.131; 426.1.16

95.1.156

20.2.204–5

209.12.173

General Rokossovski wrote, "There were many instances of cowardice, panic, desertion, and willful mutilation in order to get out of fighting." And Zhukov adds: "There were unstable troops who not only retreated but fled and started to panic. . . . At the beginning of the war we fought badly, not only in the higher ranks but also among the ordinary men." I. Chernov noted, "The officers varied, the divisions varied, their resolve varied . . . in the unwillingness to recognize that a tendency could be discerned toward believing that 'only the leaders were at fault.'"

Lieutenant V. Osten described the causes of the first defeats as "not only the incompetent command of the troops and the lack of equipment, weapons, ammunition, and communications equipment but also demonstrative executions of 'cowards and scare-mongers' and desertion and panic prompted by fear of tanks and plenty of other things."

In August 1941 it was hot as hell and dust clung to everything, "dust, white and red dust, thrown up by sheep's feet, pigs' trotters, horses, cows' hooves, carts full of refugees, army trucks, officers' buses, tanks, artillery, and tractors; the dust hung like a cloud drifting above Ukraine" was how Vasili Grossman described the scene. October came with cold rains, impassable roads, and wet woods, "People are silent; no one is smiling or joking. Angry at everything, jaws set. Watch your step," adds Chernov. "Small units wander around, retreating with or without orders, having shot their last cartridge. Try and sort out who comes from where and why here. All trudge forward in silence in the interminable rain, day and night, hungry and wet."

Encircling

The rapidly advancing German tank columns had already encircled millions of Soviet soldiers in the first months. Some units managed to break out; others attempted individually or in small groups to rejoin their own troops by getting through the front line, which was not continuous, at night, avoiding the roads, seeking and finding shelter with villagers, sometimes even helped by the newly appointed heads of the villages. Initially, after the passage of the troops, there were no Germans in the villages, no newly appointed mayors or police. "The villagers lived in a state of expectation," and wherever a new local government had been appointed, it turned a blind eye to the Soviet soldiers wandering around, having escaped from encirclement.

400.5.52
238.1.9
326.2.475
157.1.159
84.2.142, 156
506.1.171

Encircled soldiers and hastily mobilized home reserves trickled back through the lines by the thousands, sometimes having seen neither hide nor hair of the Germans. Others deserted and returned home, but then had to form groups to resist the partisans by force, since the partisans saw them as traitors. Still others found shelter with lonely women or hired themselves out as farmhands. "Many of them married in church, to wives of mobilized soldiers or to girls or simply set up house together. With regard to these '*primaki*' [newlyweds] no one asked any questions." 400.2.85 243.1.96 407.4.157

Yelena Rzhevskaya described how the farmer Darya removed a wounded soldier from a prisoner-of-war camp, cared for him, and took him into her own house. The new head of the village (*starosta*) approved. "One more worker," he commented. Initially—was this only in Ukraine?—people were allowed to fetch sick family members from assembly points for prisoners of war. After escaping, wounded, from such a camp, Yevgeny Dolmatovski found shelter with a woman on a farm. "The wound in my hand was full of maggots. I was unable to withdraw my hand when the old woman started to kiss it, as it were: she sucked up the crawling white larvae, spat them out, and started sucking again." Lieutenant Vsevolod Osten trekked through the South Ukrainian Taurian Steppe, searching for the Russian lines. He almost always found shelter and food in the houses of farmers, since word had spread of the inhuman treatment in the prisoner-of-war camps. The only place not safe for the soldiers was the Crimea: military police were everywhere, "and, in the hills, mounted Tatar units were wreaking havoc." Tens of thousands of retreating and escaping Soviet soldiers were milling around the Ukrainian steppes in the summer and autumn of 1941. 383.5.207–24 383.3.3–11 98.1.25 326.2.204

The journalist Boris Runin, an encircled Muscovite home reserve, described how shabby his comrades looked in their civilian clothing and how their reception, when they retreated unharmed, was anything but friendly. The civilian population who had helped with food and shelter in occupied areas closed their doors to them in Soviet territory. Agents from SMERSH arrested them and their fellow soldiers, subjected them to intense interrogation, and told them that suicide would have been more fitting.

Being encircled aroused suspicion, but, all the same, it was not as bad as being taken prisoner. "We will soon see what you are, deserters or, worse still, spies." They were shut up in camps, where Runin first heard that "a step to the left, a step to the right is seen as an attempt to escape." Ultimately the army had no idea as to what to do with all those "return-ers." They were also quite understandably afraid of German infiltration. 381.2

They were a burden; after all, the home reserves were totally inexperienced, and most of them were either too old or too young. Nevertheless, in 1941 the majority was called up to the army, and, even worse, in 1942 escaped and returning soldiers were assigned to "penal battalions and storm groups."

98.1.43

Military Operations

The Soviet troops continually attempted to carry out counterattacks in accordance with the strategic doctrine. On 9 September 1941, for example, after twenty-six days of heavy fighting, a German salient at Yelnya was retaken. Most attacks, however, were fruitless and were accompanied by enormous losses. "Dilettantism, incompetence, and cruelty" was how Mertsalov summed up the Russian leadership. He gave the example of the 350th Infantry Division, which was fighting at Selizharovo in December 1941: "The guns wouldn't fire (the grease used in manufacturing had not yet been removed) and the Germans kept them under heavy machine-gun fire. Screaming, cursing, swearing . . . the division commander was stupid and stubborn, sending in one battalion after another . . . so much for the battle cry, 'For the Fatherland, for Stalin.' Try asking the men coming out of the trenches . . . what they were yelling," wrote T. Pilipenko, who fought in the war.

282.2.260

A. N. Mertsalov quotes a document dated 12 October 1941 signed by Zhukov, vice premier Nikolay Bulganin, and the western front chief of staff, Vasili Sokolovski: "To the Supreme Commander of the Forty-ninth Army. Counterattack to restore the former situation. Otherwise, the commanders of the units, and you, too, will be shot for unauthorized withdrawal from the town of Kaluga." In October 1941 Zhukov told Rokossovski, "I will have you shot if you retreat one more step. Is that understood?" Rokossovski replied that he did not wish to hear such a tone and such language. A couple of days later Zhukov apologized, after Stalin had hauled him over the coals. Evidently someone had informed Stalin of the incident.

282.2.316–17

275.1.72

"All our exhausted troops were capable of," wrote Simonov, quoting Rokossovski, "was to drive off the enemy here and there, using up their strength without any decisive results. They inched forward. . . . The regiments and divisions had too few men. Machine guns, mortars, artillery, munitions, there was too little of everything, there were only a few tanks left. . . . The paradox was that it was the strongest who were defending and the weakest who were attacking, up to their waists in snow." 400.2.103

After a furious row with Stalin, on 6 October, Zhukov was dismissed as chief of the General Staff and was appointed Supreme Commander at the western front to replace Ivan Konev, who had fallen out of favor with Stalin. Stalin wanted to have Konev court-marshaled, since it was Konev's fault that six armies had been surrounded near Bryansk and Vyazma, leaving the way to Moscow open for the Germans. Zhukov, however, managed to arrange for Konev to be his deputy. This did nothing to change the fact that Zhukov and Konev couldn't stand each other, up to and including the recapturing of Berlin, three and a half years later. 191.1.124–25

A disaster had also taken place at Kiev. Four armies had been encircled because Stalin refused to allow their retreat behind the Dnepr in time. Consequently the Germans took 665,000 soldiers prisoner. Kiev itself fell on 19 September 1941. A few days later the notorious massacre of the Jewish population took place in the Babi Yar ravine. In occupied Kiev, almost immediately, young men, wearing yellow and blue armbands, were seen armed with carbines. These Ukrainian nationalists initially considered themselves German allies. Their euphoria was quickly over, however; Hitler had no use for them, and many were shot. Tongues started wagging 221.1.177 among the population of Kiev: about the arrests, the terror, the hunger, the mass murders, people being driven out, starving to death under Soviet rule; "sometimes the accounts were told in the spirit of Hitler, more often they were simple and unaffected. But however they were told, they told the truth," said Naum Korzhavin. And Belyayev recalled, "Two months 221.1.176 after the arrival of the Germans, 'Galacians' appeared in Poltava, a battalion of 'Mazeppa boys,' as everyone referred to them. They spoke a kind of Ukrainian-Polish language, were terribly arrogant, and even lashed out at old women when they heard the 'Muscovite' tongue, while many of the inhabitants of Poltava knew no language other than Russian." 33.1.50

In the autumn and winter of 1941 the attitude of the people changed considerably. The initial confusion was more or less over. The people, who had at first been extremely impressed by the Germans' strength and their fearlessness as they attacked with rolled-up sleeves, woke up to reality. In the beginning, "in many villages that had experienced the full misery of the kolkhozes, people welcomed the guests with bread and salt," but as they learned more of the guests' wrongdoings, the mood changed. 267.1.105

When the tide turned in December—not yet for good—and villages were recaptured for Moscow, the attitude changed finally from amazement and a certain admiration to hate and the desire for revenge: "The troops moved through villages that had been razed to the ground by the Germans. . . . In the villages stood gallows from which people hung by the Germans had been removed sometimes only hours before."

Konstantin Simonov reported how captured Germans who had been guilty of applying the scorched earth policy in their retreat were shot without mercy. And, in general, he wrote, "our soldiers were reluctant to take prisoners of war, and it is hard to blame them for that."

400.2.530, 535–36

Not Prisoners of War but Traitors

The high numbers of prisoners prompted Stalin, on 16 August 1941, to implement the inhuman, unjust Order No. 270. "The State Commission for Defense must admit that some officers and soldiers are not conducting themselves in a steadfast manner; they are exhibiting panic and scandalous cowardice, casting down their weapons, forgetting their duty to the Fatherland, blatantly breaking their oath, turning into a flock of sheep fleeing in panic from the insolent enemy." This order treated prisoners quite simply as traitors. The order, unpublished until 1988, was that every member of military personnel was to shoot any other not willing to fight to the death "and push forward bold, courageous men from among the younger officers or soldiers in their stead." This order was evidently aimed at the commanders of the Twenty-eighth and Twelfth Armies who had surrendered when encircled. Anyone deserting or tearing off his insignia could be shot and his family members arrested. These men's families lost their pensions. When Stalin's son, Yakov Dzhugashvili, was taken as a prisoner of war, Beria arrested Yakov's wife, Yulia Isaakovna Meltser.

357

497.2.10

58.1.10–11

Of course, some soldiers had surrendered immediately and others had deserted, but most prisoners were taken as a result of the errors of the Russian military leaders. After all, whose fault was it that 3.6 million men were taken prisoner? Surely it could only be the fault of the man who had congratulated Hitler on his triumph in the West and had failed to prepare the people properly for war.

282.2.327

296.1.236

Evidently a fury of executions followed, because, on 4 October 1941, an order was issued "concerning repressions taking the place of instructive tasks"; the order mentioned specific commanders who had been guilty of "unlawful repression and the most gross misuse of power" with regard to their subordinates.

Repression of the Military

Just before the German invasion, a large number of high-ranking officers were taken out of the camps and prisons, including General Aleksandr Gorbatov, the future marshal Konstantin Rokossovski, and the generals Lizhakov, Petrovski, and Vasili Yushkevich. Lizhakov was killed on 25 July 1942, after which Stalin forbade the army newspaper, *Red Star*, to publish his obituary.

400.2.80

As we know, the army had been robbed of many competent commanders as a result of the purges of 1937 and 1938. It has been reputed that of the 48,773 military commanders arrested during that period, roughly 12,000 returned. Young, often inexperienced, less well-trained officers filled the places of those who did not return. Gorbatov is of the opinion that, if those officers had not been killed, the Germans would not have gotten as far as the Volga or even the Dnepr. On 23 June, along with several other commanding officers, General Kirill Meretskov, commanding officer of the Leningrad front and former Spanish civil war veteran, was arrested. He was forced to confess to being the leader of a group of "military conspirators." He was badly beaten by five NKVD thugs, now identified by name: "Rodos broke his ribs. The unfortunate man rolled around on the ground, trying to ease the unbearable pain by screaming." Beria, during his own trial in 1953, admitted that Meretskov's "treatment . . . had been sheer butchery." They humiliated him, urinated on his head, and then, a short while later, he was released and was received by Stalin with the words, "Good-day, Comrade Meretskov, and how are you feeling?" The statements of those who were tortured make grizzly reading: "How Vannikov screamed, clutching at his heart, how Meretskov was beaten to a pulp, how Smushkevich rolled, groaning across the floor, how Shtern lost consciousness because of the pain." Their wives were shot with them; the wife of the Jewish general Stern was imprisoned in a camp until 1956 and labeled as "the wife of an unmasked German who had carried out spying assignments for the Abwehr [the German Military Intelligence and Counterintelligence Organization]." Those not murdered in the Lubyanka Prison were transported during the evacuation of Moscow to Kuybyshev or Samara, to be shot there.

147.1.16; 281.3.116

141.1.24

21.1.75

464.1

332.2.8

155.1.195

75.1.12

In the meantime, the front was crying out for experienced commanders. Of the aforementioned, Meretskov and the People's Commissar for Armaments, Boris Vannikov, were released. Meretskov was appointed as the commander of the Fourth Army at the Volkhov front. Alongside him

was a political commissar who was there, or so Meretskov thought, to spy
on him. It turned out, however, that the commissar had also recently been
released. "Nevertheless, we have to go on," said Commissar Dobrovolski,
"you can see what the situation is." "Yes, I can see," replied Meretskov,
259.1.116   "that's the only reason I want to go on living."

Naturally, scapegoats had to be found for the catastrophic defeats. The
commanding officer at the western front, General Pavlov (replaced by
Timoshenko) and many of his officers were singled out. Lazar Mekhlis,
Stalin's permanent representative at the various fronts, sought out even
more "guilty parties" and proposed arresting and punishing them. Stalin
telegraphed back, "agreed," and welcomed this measure as one of the cer-
17.1   tain methods for cleaning things up at the front. Zhukov also signed the
document that meant the execution, on 23 July 1941, of Pavlov and his
282.3.227   officers. Days earlier, Pavlov's parents, wife, and five-year-old son had been
147.1.104   exiled to Siberia.
        According to David Samoylov, a soldier on the front and a poet, such
a beginning to the war was "the moment of Stalin's deepest humiliation,
386.1.43   and he never forgave the people for that humiliation."
        The fate of those taken prisoner by the NKVD was grim. As soon as
the Germans approached, the prisoners were killed on the spot in the
prison courtyards. There were reports of such massacres, where many
hundreds of prisoners died, from Lvov, Drogobych, Orel, and Stanislav
(today, Ivano-Frankovsk). In Stanislav "they sent a tank in and mowed
down the prisoners with machine guns as they were driven into the
188.4.143   courtyard."

Scorched Earth

The retreating troops and the population were given the order to destroy
anything that could be of use to the enemy, including homes, factories—
or those that had not already been transferred to the hinterland—crops
in the fields, buildings, barns, and supplies. This ensued from Order 0428,
dated 17 November 1941, which states: "destroy and burn all inhabited
places in the hinterland of the German troops up to a distance of forty to
sixty kilometers in depth from the front and in an area of twenty to thirty
147.1.143   kilometers to the left and right of the roads." This order came in the exceptionally harsh winter of 1941–42, when thousands of innocent people
could be affected.

This did not sit well with the people. They looted shops—why not, if everything is to be destroyed anyway?—and fought against those starting the fires. "They rushed at us, trying to spit at us and punch us. 'Herods! You are destroying the entire population.'" A lieutenant in the little vil- 214.1.176 lage of Syanino refused to set any fires and was shot. But the following morning a group of German scouts attacked and killed all those who had started the fires. 232.1.19

Things became uncivilized. "The red cavalry . . . smashed the windows with rifle butts, shouting, 'You've got five minutes. Get that stuff out here! We're going to burn it!' They threw bottles through the windows and, when there were no more, straw was fetched and piled up around the buildings." The Moscow party organization had the task, among other 232.1.19 things, of organizing "partisan units and sabotage and destruction groups" to work behind enemy lines. In the beginning of December 1941 a Musco- 60.1.78 vite Komsomol girl, who had set fire to barns at the request of her masters in Moscow, was abused and subsequently hanged by Germans. This was Zoya Kosmodemyanskaya, feted afterward as a heroine. Furious villagers had turned her over to the occupiers. 306.1.215

Refugees

Floods of refugees tried to escape to the east. In Kiev, Naum Korzhavin saw members of the NKVD first getting themselves and their family members to safety, and then immediately afterward helping party and government officials. "I saw a truck laden with household effects, as if they were going to their dacha. What kind of defense is that if the people who are supposed to form the core are quietly sneaking their families out? Expecting heroism of others and making a run for it themselves . . . sowing panic which they themselves were supposed to be combating. That was Stalinism." Korzhavin himself fled with his family up the Dnepr by ship. Ukrainian village girls on the banks refused to sell them anything to eat. "They were glad we were fleeing. Probably, to a considerable degree, that was because of anti-Jewish feeling, but, more important, the hated government and those who they believed were connected with the government were leaving." 221.1.189, 192

On 22 June a train full of refugees departed from Vilnius heading, via Minsk and Smolensk, to Moscow. The train escaped being bombed because the driver, it was later discovered, had placed a flag with a swastika on the engine and the carriages. This was the work of the sabotage groups brought in just before the attack. 351.1.156

At a bridge over the Sozha (at Krichev) "people were trudging eastward in an unending stream with bundles, traveling on carts with children, old people, and all kinds of cargo. Among the refugees, alone and in small groups, walked wounded soldiers. Here, too, people were driving livestock from the collective farms over the bridge, the cattle plunging, bellowing, into the water, the herders yelling their heads off at the crazed beasts."

39.1.64–65

On his way from Moscow to the front, on the Minsk highroad, Simonov saw a motley crew of people: men with beards and headgear from the previous century, carts and broken bicycles, flowerpots and washboards. And a lot of Jewish women, "from the west of White Russia judging by their clothes, dressed in foreign jackets with high shoulders, reduced to dusty rags." Viktor Safronov remarked of the refugees that they were "primarily Jews. But not our Jews. Ours are kind, friendly people, but these, wherever they came from, from the west, keep themselves to themselves, are fearful, anxious. Dark eyes like saucers." Marchenko, as a young boy, already on the road with his mother for six weeks, was forced to beg for food on the way: "I knocked on the first window. 'In the name of Christ, please give to the refugees.' 'God will provide,' the people replied, sadly. I knocked on a second window. 'We've had nothing to eat ourselves since yesterday.'"

400.2.18–19, 84

385.1.115

276.1.53

Valeri Alekseyev sensed hostile feelings toward refugees. He heard a woman say, "the Germans hang people like our family or put them in special camps, but they do nothing to the others." The trains that were still running ferried the wounded to the east and the military transports to the west. Trains carrying refugees could be uncoupled at any time and sometimes had to wait days before continuing on their way.

12.1.37

"Like all stations in wartime," remarked Aleksandr Zhuk, "all the benches, the whole area, was enveloped in a smothering, choking stench, full of people sleeping beside or on their bags and bundles with their children. They jumped up nervously at any sign of a steam locomotive, jostled one another at the exit, saw it was not their train, and went back to where they had been lying."

506.1.155

Evacuation of Factories

Factories essential to the war industry were systematically dismantled and moved to the east, mostly to the Urals and Siberia, in a matter of weeks or months. The factories, along with their personnel, sometimes accompanied by their families, were taken to the east, where they were immediately reestablished. Thanks to this evacuation, the Soviet Union was

already able to produce more for the war in 1942 than ever before. This
operation involved 1.6 million railway wagons and 18 million people, and
2,593 industrial firms were evacuated. The T-34 tank, for example, initially   228.1.43–44
produced in Kharkov, was now being manufactured in Nizhni Tagil in
the Urals.

But the living and working conditions those millions of people endured—can you imagine? Furthermore, eight hundred thousand horses
and 2.5 million cows were driven to the east. Simonov was stuck for hours
at Smolensk, the herds of cows blocking the way. Vasili Kozhanov described   400.2.154–55
the scene: "Cattle-driving brigades were hastily formed. The collective
farms were obliged to take the herds to designated places, using their
own personnel and at their own cost. One of those places was in Rzhev,
for example, 'where you could hear the continual lowing and bellowing
of the cows from way off' . . . a real cattle concentration camp. They were
bellowing for lack of water and fodder; the veterinary surgeons, who
had been summoned from throughout the entire region, had the task of
selecting the animals. The weaker cattle were sent to the slaughterhouse,
the healthy ones . . . were driven under their own steam another five hundred versts to the provinces of Vladimir and Ivanovo." Between July and   232.1.43, 45
September 1941 a regimental vet drove a herd of cows from Chernigov to
Saratov, a distance of some two thousand kilometers.   189.1.9

4

The Mood in Moscow

Before the war Moscow had 4.2 million inhabitants; over the course of the summer and autumn of 1941 that number, by November, had dwindled to 2.4 million; and by January 1942 the population of Moscow numbered 2 million.

Immediately after the invasion Aleksandr Fadeyev chaired a meeting of the Writers' Union in Moscow. "The half-empty hall was a sorry sight; in general people were dejected . . . the meeting was not exactly a success: two years of strict banning of antifascist material in the press had left its mark." The NKVD, as always, closely studied the mood of the people. Recently published NKVD reports speak of rumors, hoarding, panic, and belief in German supremacy against which there was nothing to be done. "Although patriotic feelings flourished among the majority of the population of the capital, at the same time many citizens had an openly anti-Soviet attitude . . . a hatred of Communists, including the families of Communists, and anti-Semitism." One individual, who was eight years old at the time, remembers what some people said: "Why should we be scared? The Germans are civilized people."

The NKVD reports distinguished three sorts of people: patriots, rumormongers, and defeatists. While one was indifferent, another prepared himself for new masters. Some hoped that the Germans would sweep away the Stalin regime, opting for the "lesser of two evils." "Some members of the intelligentsia looked forward to the arrival of the Germans, but not specifically because it was the Germans. They were simply dreaming of the Leninist-Stalinist system being polished off at the hands of Germany." And, to achieve that, "one could put up with being under German rule for a while."

Evacuation of Artists

Writers, musicians, and other artists were evacuated promptly. Aleksei Tolstoy, Vsevolod Ivanov, Fadeyev, and Katayev, for instance, went to Tashkent. Others, including Fyodor Gladkov, Leonid Leonov, Boris Pasternak, Konstantin Fedin, Vera Inber, Ilya Selvinski, and Mikhail Isakovski went to Chistopol, a small town on the Kama. The train journey to Tashkent and Chistopol took a long time (from several days to weeks), as trains carrying the wounded and military transports had priority. When a train intended for the Writers' Union was canceled: "Panic. The waiting room packed with suitcases. Soldiers ripping off their insignia before your eyes." 254.1.77 Kornei Chukovski, a well-known children's author, was traveling in a luxury train and saw, in Kuybyshev, a train standing next to his. Behind a window he could make out "the doleful face of Mikhail Kalinin. I greeted him, and he pulled down the blind. Evidently the government had arrived on that train, which is why planes were crossing back and forth over the train on the way, and there was anti-aircraft artillery mounted on the last few wagons." Kalinin was, at least in name, the head of state of the USSR. 88.1.173

Everywhere, of course, people were forced into extremely cramped accommodations, "often two or three families in one room." People were 91.1.123 starved of reliable information, insecure about belongings left behind. There was no lack of the usual writers' quarrels. In Tashkent, which was dubbed "Soviet Athens" because of the number of writers there, "a Slavicization of writers" was to be implemented; in other words, Jewish writers were to be expelled. This occurred after Shcherbakov, secretary of the Central Committee, had remarked to Fadeyev, pointing to *Literatura i iskusstvo* (Literature and art), "What kind of surnames are those? Where are the great Russian people?" The obedient Fadeyev, already a rather heavy drinker by then, subsequently fired all Jews from the magazine. 172.1.112–13

Tashkent was also full of wounded soldiers from the front; in the winter the people were plagued by a typhus epidemic transmitted by lice. In the course of 1942 and 1943 most of the evacuated Muscovites returned; those who had remained in the capital saw them as cowardly refugees.

The Moscow Home Reserves

In the absence of regular armies, battalions and divisions of home reserves were hastily set up in Moscow. Hundreds of thousands of men, sixteen divisions, volunteered freely, including the musicians Emil Gilels and

David Oistrakh. Runin feels the home reserves were also used to get rid
of unwelcome writers! Dressed in civilian clothes and their own footwear,
they went off to the front, led by virtually untrained members of the party
or the Komsomol. Sometimes the reserves were given a couple of days'
instruction. People with a "past," such as those whose family members
had been arrested, were put into the "labor army," such as Yuri Smirnov,
whose father, a hero of the civil war, had been shot, and whose mother
was in a camp.

"We must never forget those young men and women who flew to the
flame of war for love of their Fatherland, and with fierce willingness to
give their lives for that cause. . . . But neither should we forget," writes
Kondratyev, "how carelessly and cruelly our leaders abused that youthful
enthusiasm, without a trace of compassion for those young lives, using
them to fill every breach and rent caused by our woeful lack of preparation for war and the incapacity of many of our military leaders to wage a
modern war. Without preparation by artillery, with nothing more than
type 1891/30 rifles and a 'hurrah,' they cast brigades and divisions into
the fray to recapture occupied Russian villages, after which, owing to the
panic among the leaders and the lack of communication, millions of soldiers and officers were taken prisoner by the enemy during the first few
months of the war."

The losses among the reserves were enormous: "A few survived. It
sometimes happened that men were thrown into battle unarmed. 'You can
find yourself weapons in the fight.'"

The reserves, also known as extermination battalions, were set up by
order of 24 July 1941, with the aim of fighting enemy parachutists and
saboteurs.

At Vyazma the Second Home Reserves Division lost ten thousand of
its twelve thousand members. "On both sides of the road to Minsk, by
the town of Vyazma, lie tens of thousands of defenders of the Fatherland, buried by the local inhabitants under threat from fascist weapons,
in trenches, bomb craters, without a mass grave. In the spring the Vyazma
River washes their remains away, swamp mud dissolves the remains of
papers, while all over the country there are hundreds of thousands of
people who have received the bitter message that their father, grandfather,
or brother is 'missing,'" wrote Filatova, president of the Veterans' Committee of the Second Home Reserves Division in 1989. As many as 240
cadets fared no better, all being wiped out—except two to four men—
before Moscow. Later Aleksandr Bek based his *Volokolamsk Highway* on

the subject. It was a crime, writes Mertsalov, sending untrained and virtually unarmed civilians into battle as home reserves.   282.2.338

Erecting a Defense

When it became clear that the military situation was deteriorating, young
people, students, and others eligible for service were called up to build
antitank ditches and other defenses. Men reported in civilian clothing,
with a few toiletries. Where was their journey taking them? "On a special mission," was the reply. "We walked to the accompaniment of an
orchestra, in disorganized rows, but singing cheerfully through the center
of Moscow, in the direction of the Byelorusski Station," wrote Vladimir
Nikolayev. "First thing in the morning the field kitchen gave us something
to eat; we were lined up and divided into sections. We were all given a
spade and shown how to use it. Most diggers went toward Smolensk,
to the Dnepr and Desna. Alongside the Dnepr I saw girls from the top
class of school fleeing in high heels from the bombs and machine gun fire
from the air."   315.1.52–53

The Muscovite home reserves also dug defenses: "A badly instructed,
poorly dressed troop, consisting of boys and intelligentsia." Schoolchil-   386.1.45
dren were dropped behind the German lines as saboteurs. Hardly any of
them survived.   114.1.44–45

When the enemy neared the Dnepr, the young people were ordered
to return to Moscow on foot in groups of three to four men, each taking
responsibility for one girl. Sleeping in the woods or the fields, avoiding
the main roads by day, many did not make it and were captured by the
enemy. In October 1941 three hundred women were deployed to dig a
hundred kilometers west of Moscow. Let down by everybody, in complete
confusion, divided by mutual quarrels, cursing Stalin's draconian methods of punishment for turning up late for work, some women said, "We'll
give him war one of these days!" Little to eat, attacked by Messerschmitts,
many dead. Those who survived returned on foot, empty-handed, to
Moscow.   215.3.3, 5

Evacuation to Kuybyshev

The armies intended to defend Moscow were poorly equipped. Grigori
Baklanov wrote about the lack of weapons. There were discussions as
to whether rifles should be given to divisions going to the front or to one

28.3

of Beria's divisions that guarded the camps. In the Sixteenth Army stationed before Moscow, 1,080 men did not even have any footwear or warm

191.1.113

clothes.

By October the situation west of the capital was critical. There were continual breaches in the front. "The troops brought in from the hinterland to close the breach," said Grigorenko, "were given the order 'to shoot the traitors who have opened the front for the enemy.' People who had selflessly offered resistance day and night and finally managed to break

155.5.20

out to their own troops were therefore greeted with fusillades." In other words, soldiers who, although encircled, had managed to break out were

381.2.101

considered traitors.

On 7 October Georgi Zhukov was summoned posthaste from Leningrad to Moscow. He made his report in Stalin's office, where both Stalin and Beria were present, expressing his opinion that there was literally no front, as such, west of Moscow and that the troops were entirely without leadership, and only a few encircled units continued to fight at their own risk. According to Zhukov, Stalin turned to his police chief and said, "Try to use your channels to test the waters for concluding a new Treaty of Brest with Germany, a separate treaty. We can relinquish the Baltic countries, White Russia, part of Ukraine . . . whatever terms possible." Beria explored the possibilities through the Bulgarian envoy, but he was disappointed, as

332.2.7

Hitler believed that Moscow would fall into his hands anyway.

On 19 October Zhukov took over responsibility for the defense of Moscow, a state of siege was announced, and panic mongers were shot

191.3.135

on the spot. On Stalin's orders, the government, general staff, and foreign ambassadors were evacuated on 16 October to Kuybyshev on the Volga, the patriarch himself went to Ulyanovsk on the Volga, and even Lenin was removed from his mausoleum and brought to safety.

The center of Kuybyshev was cleared to make room for the evacuated official bodies and for important persons, such as the former minister of foreign affairs, Maksim Litvinov, who, with his wife and young son, Pavel,

266.1.158

the future dissident, was given a three-room apartment. For the privileged the train journey to Kuybyshev took five days; others went by boat via Gorki.

Vasili Grossman, in his novel, *Life and Fate*, described the situation in Kuybyshev: "It was a capital city, temporarily evacuated from Moscow, with the diplomatic corps, the Bolshoi Ballet, famous writers, Muscovite cabaret artists, and foreign journalists. All these thousands of Muscovites moved into communal flats, hotel suites, and rooms, and went about their usual business—heads of departments, directorates, and ministries supervised their subordinates and ran the economy; extraordinary ambassadors and plenipotentiaries rode in luxurious cars to receptions given by the leaders of the Soviet Union's foreign policy. Ulanova, Lemonov, and Mikhailov entertained the public with ballet and opera. Henry Shapiro, the representative of United Press, posed loaded questions at press conferences to Salomon Abramovich Lozovski, the head of the Soviet Information Center. Authors wrote articles for national and foreign newspapers and radio stations; journalists wrote on military themes based on material they had collected in hospitals."   157.2.59

In Kuybyshev David Samoilov was struck by "a sense of the eternal loneliness of Russia, which I heard reflected later in the second movement of Shostakovich's Tenth Symphony."   386.1.48

State of Siege and Panic

All through the summer and autumn floods of refugees streamed in from the west to Moscow. On hearing their stories, people started to believe the Russian propaganda regarding German atrocities—at first it had been thought that the Germans only had it in for Communists and Jews. "The Hitlerites themselves were far quicker to let our people feel that Russia was under a deadly threat."   209.8.202

Moscow was repeatedly bombed in October; a total of two thousand German aircraft took part. During a meeting concerning the defense of the capital, Beria said, "Moscow is not the Soviet Union. It is a waste of time defending Moscow. It is dangerous to remain in Moscow; they will pick us off like partridges."   60.1.75

On 15 October the decision was made to evacuate the capital. The party packed its bags, and everyone attempted to flee. Workers were not told, or at least they were not told properly, that factories were partially set with explosives and that certain sections needed to be evacuated. "Workers in a dairy factory stopped their director from escaping with his milk products. They took the food and the car and thrust him headfirst into a vat of cream."   60.1.73

On 20 October martial law was proclaimed in Moscow in wording dictated by Stalin himself, which deliberately evoked reminiscences of the words used during the Napoleon invasion.

The air was heavy with the smell of burning: people were burning documents and leaders' books; official bodies burned their archives. The street was littered with chunks of plaster from smashed busts of Lenin and Stalin. The writer Aleksei Novikov-Priboi said that any resistance was hopeless. "Out of the Woodwork" is the title of an article from that time, dealing with anti-Soviet stories, anti-Semitism, and people who would even draw up lists of "undesirables."

267.1.104

188.4.150–51;
282.2.251

Boris Runin, having escaped from being encircled as a home reserve, returned to his Moscow home. His neighbor had raided his library to feed the stove and removed the plate with Runin's (Jewish) name from the door.

381.2.97

From July 1941 on, the manager of the Writers' Union club, Aleksei Alekseyevich, was in charge of the club's bar. All kinds of dubious-looking types were to be seen in his establishment, tanking themselves up with liqueurs and Spanish wine (the Spanish government's payment in kind for Russian military aid during the civil war). He did not stint on the measures, his philosophy being: otherwise the enemy will soon have it all.

"The Germans were close at hand and shady forces emerged, expecting at any moment an end to the struggle for the capital that would be favorable to them. And while outsiders conducted themselves as a rowdy rabble," wrote Runin, "among us writers there prevailed an atmosphere of defeat." After a couple of days, however, this "fiddling while Rome burned" of mid-October 1941 was over for the Moscow underworld, and, from then on, Aleksei Alekseyevich treated soldiers returning from the front and writers to his drink free of charge.

381.2.97

381.2.84

Colonel N. Lyubimov stated: "Up until 16 October 1941 I kept reassuring myself that after the war we will get back at Stalin and his cronies. Not only for our slaughtered fathers, mothers, sisters and brothers, friends and acquaintances, not only for the destruction of the Russian culture, but also for the friendship with Hitler, for the marvelous preparation for the war, and the fulfillment of the promise: we will not concede an inch of the Fatherland to the enemy. We will put off the day of reckoning until 'after the war,' as now is not the time; until the day of victory we have a common enemy."

267.1.98

Flight from Moscow

On 20 July thirty-six hundred members of the NKVD and state security personnel were already evacuated. Their families would follow later.

132.1.20

In the course of October 1941 the flight from Moscow took on increasing proportions: directors ran off, sometimes with, sometimes without, the cash. Sometimes their workers were given a few weeks' salary or a "Stalinpud" (sixteen kilos) of flour, sometimes not. As I noted earlier, "in the October days archives burned. Black ash swirled through the air like snow on a negative, covering the streets and pavements. The ash seemed sticky to me, it was a ghastly feeling when it wafted into your face, blown up by the wind," recalled Aleksandr Lavrin. By mid-October hundreds of thousands had left the city, fleeing eastward. Shops were closed or looted, or everything was simply doled out. 340.1.184–85

254.1.76

188.5.49

On 16 October Andrei Nazarov noticed strangely decked-out figures among the refugees, "hung with garlands of sausages; 'They're looting the slaughterhouses!' came the cry of respectful amazement from amid the crowd." 305.1.16

The privileged fled by train or official cars, while most Muscovites left on foot, pushing carts. As soon as war broke out, 1,077 people were arrested in Moscow as spies or Trotskyists. In the first few days of panic the NKVD massacred two hundred to three hundred members of the military who had been imprisoned since 1937 in the cellars of Lubyanka. Other prisoners were taken to Kuybyshev and shot there. Inmates of other prisons were also killed. "Day and night they transported them to the Butovo region and shot them there, hastily shoved them under the ground and brought on the next lot, then the next and the next." 397.1.15

262.1.71

Panic spread from the top downward. "According to incomplete information, 779 leading functionaries from 438 factories, official bodies, and organizations fled, taking 100 vehicles, 1.4 million rubles in cash, and 1 million rubles in goods." This led later to the expulsion of some four hundred members from the party. The "man in the street" remained calm, and thought: what will be will be. David Samoilov heard his neighbor saying, "Come on, Hitler, come on pal!" Kids on the street jeering mockingly, "The Soviet Information Agency reports that our troops have left all the cities." 60.1.75

60.1.77

267.1.103

386.1.46

267.1.101

"Here and there people stop cars, drag out the occupants, beat them up, and throw their things into the street. You hear cries such as 'Beat the Jews.' People are starting to remember the insults, the oppression, the injustice, the bureaucratic humiliation by officials, the boasting and smugness of the party people, the draconian *ukazes* (decrees), the systematic deceit of the masses, the nonsense spread by the newspapers and the sweet-talkers. . . . It is terrible to hear. People are expressing the pain in their hearts." 145.1.20–21

In Moscow, in mid-October, Yevgeny Vorobyov saw "an enormous herd of pigs and piglets on their way to the slaughterhouse. . . . Pigs dropping from exhaustion were stuck on the spot and thrown onto the carts following the herd. Weary women in headscarves from the collective farms trudged along, stick in hand, worn out, their cheeks stained with tears."

Sergei Golitsyn, the descendant of a very old noble family, also came across these pigs as he passed through Moscow. He described the fleeing masses: "There was every make of truck, stowed full with people, not so much with governmental property but more with personal luggage. There were private cars, also stuffed with belongings and people. I saw bakers' delivery vans, a yellow beer truck, a red fire engine, hose trucks, Number 2 Moscow-Kuntsevo buses. . . . Pedestrians were struggling along next to the road, with suitcases and bundles, leading and carrying children of all ages. Important people with felt hats, fat children in overcoats, boys from the technical school with packs on their backs, a loaf of bread under their arm, all walking along chatting merrily. A respectable family, father with a paunch, a lady with a substantial rear, two boys and two girls, were strolling slowly along as if they were out for a Sunday walk. A slim lady in a fur coat was dragging an enormous suitcase, limping on both feet, in high heels."

"It was simply a miracle the Germans did not move into Moscow right then: they didn't know, they couldn't have imagined they could have marched into Moscow unhindered. For about two days Moscow was an open city," wrote Yuri Levitanski. "During those three days the abandoned city could have been captured by the enemy," says economist and ex-prisoner of the Vorkuta camps, Vladimir Zubchaninov. "But the Germans did not take advantage of the situation. Only when Siberian military units arrived did the panic calm down."

The 7 November Parade

Despite the extremely perilous situation, on 7 November, the anniversary of the October Revolution, the traditional parade was held in Moscow's Red Square. On Stalin's orders, there was also a parade in Kuybyshev, where the diplomatic corps was currently present. "The parade was an unexpected, shockingly joyful event for the whole country. . . . It was a parade, traditional but extraordinary. Not only a military parade but also a political parade—a challenge, a defiant thumbing of the nose at the

enemy: you may be bragging about the capture of Moscow, but we are
holding our normal, festive parade."   191.3.135–36

It had been snowing heavily the previous evening and during the night.
The fire brigade had put up the usual decorations on the facades around
the square. Apart from that, everything was white: the pavement, the
houses, the sandbags. Photographer Dmitri Baltermants wrote, "To say
that it snowed says nothing of the snowstorm that literally raged on the
square. If you looked hard, you could just barely see the Spasski Tower,
the Vasili Blazhenny Cathedral, and GUM (the huge department store
on Red Square) through the thick curtain of enormous flakes of clinging
snow." A participant recalled, "We were standing in a square formation   29.1.10–12
under the snow of a gloomy, dingy Moscow day. Everyone was feeling
gloomy, too. The Germans were in the area of the city. Everyone had the
same thought: can we stand our ground? Can we keep it up? The people
were panicking. Everybody who was able was heading eastward as quickly
as possible. The highway to Vladimir was full of cars and trucks." Con-   33.1.49
trary to what was announced, the troops did not go directly from the
parade to the front.   454.1.62

The parade passed by: the home reserves, still in civilian clothes, the
infantry with a rifle or sometimes a carbine over the shoulder, 160 tanks,
motorized infantry, and artillery. Because of the otherwise conveniently
bad weather, the air force, standing ready with three hundred planes, was
forced to stay on the ground.

Stalin addressed the troops: "The war you are waging is a war of liberation, a just war. May the encouraging example of our great forefathers—
Aleksandr Nevski, Dmitri Donskoy, Kuzma Minin, Dmitri Pozharski,
Aleksandr Suvorov, and Mikhail Kutuzov—inspire you in this war. May
the victorious banner of the great Lenin light your way." That he made far
too little of the Russian casualties and grossly exaggerated the German
losses was good for morale but it was not the truth.   188.6

At the same time the traditional meeting of the Moscow council was
held in the Mayakovsky metro station. Stalin, as chairman, and hundreds
of guests on chairs fetched from here, there, and everywhere. "A metro
train arrives. Everyone looks its way. Usually trains come from the other
direction. The members of the government have obviously arrived and
take their seats behind the table covered with the red cloth. Stalin in military jacket with flat collar, without insignia or badges. He looks older but
has a tranquil expression, a concentrated gaze"—so recalled the editor in
chief of the *Red Star* in 1984.   323.1.246

Saved

The Germans continued to attack, although exhausted by the intense cold and practically at the end of their strength.

On 27 November 1941, sixteen kilometers from Moscow, Krasnaya Polyana was occupied, if only for one day. Two days later, in an attempt to kidnap Stalin, German parachutists landed on the Vorobyovy Gory and at the Neskuchny Sad, only four kilometers from the Kremlin. Both airborne landings were quickly suppressed.

Marshal Rokossovski no longer had any extra men or tanks. "It was God who ordered Hitler to stop his troops at Tula, when the anti-aircraft artillery had been removed and when the Soviet Supreme Command had managed to send Siberian divisions to a panic-ridden Moscow, which you could have taken with your bare hands in October." The future marshal Andrei Yeryomenko wrote in his memoirs: "At the beginning of the attack, some divisions, the 360th, had not a single day's food rations left. We had to find a solution to the situation by taking the scanty supplies from one section and giving them to another that had nothing. Bread was taken from the 358th Infantry Division and passed on to the 360th, so the men at least had something to eat the evening before the first day of the attack."

General Andrei Vlasov, one of Stalin's favorite generals, recklessly attacked in December, in a heavy snowstorm, trusting to luck and without any information about the enemy. Vlasov had already distinguished himself in the battle of Kiev (in 1942, however, his career took a dramatic turn when the Germans captured him). During and after Vlasov's attack, the fresh Siberian divisions, which had arrived on 3 December 1941, warmly dressed and equipped with new weapons, were able to do their job.

The attack, incidentally, cannot really be called a Russian offensive, Zhukov told Simonov in 1950, as the Germans were already retreating on their own accord. Later Simonov wrote: "It has now long been acknowledged that, at the beginning of our counterattack at Moscow, the German troops had already been given the order to retreat. But at that time, in 1950, it was not appropriate to talk about it. . . . It was only acceptable to say that we launched a counterattack on the Germans while they were still advancing toward Moscow."

Nonetheless, the ground gained and the spoils won at Moscow were a welcome piece of good luck after months of virtually nothing but defeats. The great danger for Moscow was over for the time being.

5

Leningrad

The German troops rapidly advanced into the Baltic countries and Northwest Russia. Initially there were no problems: trains with food destined for Leningrad were diverted as they were not needed by the Neva city, according to party leader Zhdanov; stocks were, after all, sufficient. _{83.1.14; 405.1.115; 497.1.22}

In the first two or three weeks of the siege, workers employed in Leningrad went home in the evening to occupied territory. They were extremely positive about the polite, helpful Germans . . . until Communists and other opponents began to be shot. _{450.1.150}

During the first few weeks of the war children were evacuated from Leningrad, without their parents, to the south, in the direction of Novgorod—the precise direction of the war, a sign of the confusion prevalent at the time. Nor was there any thought of evacuating noncombatants. The _{182.1.182} military was, however, already supplying the future members of the resistance with false papers, and "in the city it stank of smoke, dying gray butterflies of burning pages from the works of Stalin, Lenin, and Marx fluttered on the breeze." Thousands of civilians from the area surrounding _{194.1.54} Leningrad sought refuge from the approaching enemy in the big city, sometimes with their livestock, which had to be slaughtered because of a lack of cattle fodder. These people had not been given a *propiska* (residence permit) and were therefore not issued ration cards. Later most of them were among the first to die during the blockade. _{378.1.186}

As long as it remained possible, that is, as long as the city was not yet encircled, civilians and the sick were evacuated by rail, first to Vologda and further inland, to the Urals, the Caucasus, and Siberia. The trains full of evacuees crawled along the line; lacking sufficient locomotives and fuel for the boilers, they covered no more than one hundred kilometers a day. It took more than a day for farmers, drummed up from the surrounding

8.1.113 area, to dig one train out of the snow. Some of the trains remained idle
8.1.115 for as long as five or six days.

Deceased passengers were unloaded on the way. On the 131 trains that
ran via Vologda, 1,619 people died and were taken off the train during the
8.1.117 journey; another 490 died in Vologda.

In August 1941 those who remained viewed the people who were leaving as cowards and traitors. The evacuees were by no means welcomed
everywhere with open arms: after all, they aggravated the housing shortage, brought on food shortages, and prices soared.

"How long the years of evacuation lasted! . . . We lived on messages,
rumors, letters, and news from Leningrad and from the fronts. We planted,
sowed, built reed constructions, felled trees, signed up for state loans, collected items for the front, and much, much more. . . . We didn't suffer
from the excess cares and work; it was the greed, the powerlessness, the
narrow-minded egotism, and the indifference that finished us off. Those,"
wrote Nina Ivanova-Romanova, "were disguised as difficulties related to
the war; that's how they kept us quiet. And that's what made life so mis-
173.1.97–98 erable and oppressive."

The real evacuation only began when it was far too late, which explains
the enormous losses during the siege. In January and February 1942 some
two hundred thousand people starved to death in Leningrad. It was not
until 22 January 1942 that the decision was made to evacuate half a mil-
8.1.106 lion civilians via the frozen Lake Ladoga. Most of them arrived in a piti-
ful state, psychologically confused, suffering, among other things, from
diarrhea and other intestinal problems. Between 26 January and 15 April
8.1.118 1942, 554,186 people from Leningrad were evacuated through Vologda. In
Vologda itself the bodies were taken to the military cemetery, where mass
8.1.109–10 graves were excavated with dynamite because of the frost.

"What distressed me most," recalls a commissar from the No. 1 Evacuation Hospital in Vologda, "was a big cart in the courtyard, with two
decks . . . filled to bursting with frozen corpses that you had no way to get
rid of . . . we lacked the courage and the strength to hack them apart with
an ax. What's more, there were no graves ready; anyway . . . it was decided
8.1.114 to leave them until spring, until it thawed."

Evacuation of the Intelligentsia

In August and September 1941 academics, composers, writers, poets, and
89.2 winners of the Stalin Prize were evacuated from Leningrad by civil aircraft.

Not all, just those the regime considered important enough. Mikhail Zoshchenko and Shostakovich flew out in September. In March 1942 Shostakovich's sister and nephew were evacuated to Kuybyshev. 411.1.176

Leningrad's university lecturers went to Saratov, which, from Lake Ladoga, was another twenty days by train. The poetess Anna Akhmatova was taken first to Moscow by plane—"in the belly of a flying fish," as she experienced it—and then on to Tashkent by train. Her companion, Lidiia Chukovskaya, noted on 5 November 1941, "A train full of Germans from the Volga area. They have nowhere to go. Cattle trucks, the doors open. You can see children, women, washing on a line. They say they have been traveling for more than a month already and no town will take them in." In her train, in a carriage full of soldiers, Chukovskaya heard someone say, "You should leave those Yids to Hitler, let him bury them all alive." Hearing this, Anna Akhmatova remarked, "Such people should be killed." 87.1.143

To qualify for evacuation, you had to have special permission and fill in all kinds of papers. The author L. Panteleyev, who had been instructed to leave Leningrad within a few hours, as a "socially alien element," was determined to stay. He asked his colleague, Vera Ketlinskaya, to help him. This was her reaction: "If the security organizations find Panteleyev guilty, then he is indeed guilty, and I am not going to put myself out for him." Panteleyev went into hiding "and lived for several months without ration cards." 329.1.169–71

The Home Reserve

In the summer of 1941 home reserve battalions were set up in Leningrad to ward off the approaching German troops. There was nothing close to sufficient weapons available for this motley crew of young and old, intelligentsia, farmers, students, and civilians, all mostly untrained. The LANO (Leningrad People's Home Reserve Army) had a total of some two hundred thousand volunteers.

Unlike regular soldiers, as a home reserve you had a few privileges: you kept the salary from your job, and, as a Communist, you could not be deployed for illegal, dangerous work behind German lines. Farm children managed better than city kids: they could bear hardship better, did not get blisters on their hands and feet so easily, and could walk longer distances. By August the food supplies for the home reserves were already critically low; although there was still enough food, the transport was not functioning properly. There were hardly any field kitchens for these unfortunates. Vasili Belov wrote about young girls and women recruited 89.1.215

3.1.3

89.1.216

from the villages to dig antitank ditches, only to be robbed and mistreated by their "supervisors."

The home reserves were the first to be sent in against the enemy, and they suffered unimaginable losses. After one month, of the ten thousand men in the First Guard Division, only seven hundred were left. Whole regiments were wiped out, down to the last man. In the home reserves the dead were hardly ever registered; the family therefore received no death announcement. Anyone inquiring was told they were "missing," which meant that widows of home reserves could not remarry and received a far smaller pension than the widows of those officially listed as dead; orphans were not orphans.

Skeletons and equipment belonging to dead home reserves can still be found in the area around Leningrad.

One volunteer home reserve said to his commanding officer in the train, "We'll be at the front soon. When do we get our weapons?" "One more question like that and I'll have you in front of a firing squad," was the reply. "When we start fighting, we'll get weapons." SMERSH also carried out "demonstration punishments" in the home reserves.

The writer Daniil Granin described his experiences in the Leningrad home reserve. Thanks to them, he says, Leningrad was not taken by storm; the Germans were even afraid of the raggle-taggle bunch of doggedly battling civilians. He also wrote of the initial fear and panic that can arise merely at the mention of the word *siege*. Of his own fears, he wrote: "The planes screamed; bombs fell with an even more heartrending scream. Their screaming bored into your brain, your chest, and your belly, churning up your innards. The screaming wiped out all my feelings; it was impossible to think about anything anymore. The boom of the explosion was a relief. . . . Heaven abandoned me; neither qualifications nor knowledge could help me. I was entirely alone with this death that came at me from all directions. Clamped tight together, my lips whispered: 'Lord, have mercy on me. Save me, don't let me die; I pray you let it fall further up, not on me. Lord, have mercy.' Suddenly the sense of those three words known since time immemorial became clear: 'Lord, have mercy.'"

Over a Frozen Lake Ladoga

The extremely harsh winter of 1941–42 was a solution for many Leningrad inhabitants; indeed, the cold claimed more victims than hunger. Lake Ladoga froze. On 20 November the frozen lake reached a thickness of

36.2

282.2.338
436.1.97

89.1.219

472.1.77
89.1.218

152.3.141–42

eighteen centimeters, and "a sleigh brought some flour to Leningrad." Two days later the road over the ice, dubbed the "Road of Life," officially the VAD-102 or Military Highway No. 102, was opened. Trucks disappeared into the ice cold water through thin patches and holes made by bombs. The future renowned author Fyodor Abramov, evacuated over the ice with heavy wounds, saw trucks full of children in front of him and behind him disappear under the ice.

Thanks to the ice route, it was gradually possible to increase and improve the rations very slightly in Leningrad. Military equipment and fresh Siberian troops could also be brought in and evacuees taken out.

In a very short period of time, between 26 May and 16 June 1942, an oil pipeline, thirty kilometers long, was laid across the bottom of the lake, enabling some four hundred tons of oil products to reach the city per day. 447.1.145 The Life Road became impassable on 24 April 1942, after an additional 86,041 tons of goods had been transported across it in March. At the exit to Lake Ladoga, when traveling from Saint Petersburg, there is now a memorial plaque: "Those who come after us! Be aware that, in the barren years, true to people, duty, and Fatherland, that we laid the Road of Life from here over the ice of Lake Ladoga so that life should not die." 467.1.124

Hunger

One thing after another disappeared from the besieged and continually bombed city: first food became scarce, then the public transport stopped, after which the power failed, the telephones no longer worked, the fuel ran out, and finally no more water came out of the taps.

The winter of 1941 was terribly cold. "January 1942. 30 degrees Celsius below freezing. Piles of snow in the street. Little paths between them, someone on his way to work, another fetching a bucket of water, a third pulling a sledge carrying dead relatives wrapped in sheets. Not everyone has the strength to take them to a cemetery." Many people left the "swaddled" (*pelenashki*) on the street. Each district had a PST, a collection post for bodies. People slept in their clothes because of the intense cold. To 176.1.250 get fuel for the winter, in the summer of 1942 civilians were ordered to demolish wooden houses in the area surrounding Leningrad. They had to keep the streets free of snow in the winter and dispose of household waste. Much of this work was left undone; the people were so weak. Water was finally fetched from the Neva with a sledge, sometimes a walk of a couple kilometers. When the cats had all been eaten as well, there was an explosion in the rat population, which feasted on the corpses lying in the streets. Even in the factory halls, "they tapped their terrible way endlessly with their clawed feet across the concrete floor." Another inhabitant reported: "I saw a swarming, living army of rats before me. They crossed the road as one solid mass." In the end, cats were brought in from the Urals to keep the food stores free of rats.

153.1.262

176.1.257

176.1.266

The siege of Leningrad became official when, on 8 September, Schlusselburg fell, and the circle around the city—with the exception of Lake Ladoga—was closed. The only contact with the outside world was by air. As early as September the Badayev food stores were bombed and burned out. This gave rise to food shortages. "The storehouses were an enormous sea of fire. Stocks of margarine melted away, rivulets of liquified sugar formed on the dirty ground, flour burned and smoldered. Mixed with the choking stench of fire and smoke you could smell the aroma of cinnamon, cloves, and other spices." In December 1941 a cup of that sugar-soaked earth fetched one hundred rubles.

47.1.203

368.1.18

At the beginning of September a previously unknown product appeared: *duranda*, a sort of cattle cake.

Rationing was introduced. In the autumn of 1941 rations were continually reduced. In October "people rushed to the land outside the city and dug up potatoes on their own initiative, pulled carrots out of the ground, and cut cabbages. A whole series of 'bag carriers' moved to the city. The trams were packed."

166.1.10

On 7 November, to celebrate the anniversary of the October Revolution, people were given a little extra: children received 200 grams of cream and 100 grams of potato meal; adults were given five salted tomatoes.

415.1.158

Not until the end of December, thanks to the transport over the ice of Lake Ladoga, was slightly more provided: 350 grams of "bread" per worker and 200 grams for others, an improvement on the previous 300 and 150 grams, respectively.

"On the 190th day [of the siege] there was more bread for the first time. General elation in the streets. People were hugging and kissing total strangers. Their lips, turned to stone by the cold, refuse to comply. Nevertheless, more bread: workers 100 grams extra, others 70 grams."

415.1.166

Companies, official bodies, and hospitals were forced to serve increasingly low-calorie meals, usually a sort of thin soup. Later, intellectuals—who obviously did not receive any workers' ration—were affiliated with particular institutions where they could get a meal.

153.1.204

People queued for hours in front of the food stores: "It was pitch black in the shops, terribly stuffy, a babble of voices, threatening, pleading," wrote Lidiia Ginzburg. "The sales staff behind the counter fought the crowds. Hundreds of people queued for bread from 4:00 or 5:00 in the morning, in the dark, in the freezing cold." "The salesman comes into contact with the customer. Neither says a word, the wrestling focused on every gram over- or underweight." People sometimes queued all day for nothing, for by then no food supplies were left.

131.1.95

131.1.98
166.1.14

Ginzburg noted with amazement that men pushed into the queue. Perhaps, she surmised, they did this because they felt queuing was women's work. "The queue," writes Ginzburg, "is a forced unification of people who are irritable toward one another, while they are concentrating on a common interest and goal. Hence the mixture of rivalry, enmity, and the sense of a collective, direct willingness to close ranks against the common enemy: the transgressor . . . the lines of hungry people in the winter were horribly quiet. Gradually, as the bread ration increased, with the warmth of spring and the upcoming green, the behavior of the queues changed. People started to talk."

131.1.95

131.1.96

Valuables, furniture, books, the starving population offered everything in exchange for food. A Becker grand piano was worth 1.5 kilos of bread; a man's new suit, 1.5 to 3 kilos of flour. "With a quavering voice and a wan smile, they asked for a loaf of bread in exchange for a ring, earrings, bracelets," wrote Oleg Shestinski.

443.1.123

People, exhausted by hunger, collapsed in the street—sometimes for good. Women and girls ceased menstruating. "With the siege and the hunger, every flirt in the city stopped flirting." People didn't recognize their own bodies anymore: "There were continually new angles and caved-in hollows, patchy and raw. The skin was a spotty sack, too big for its contents," remarked Lidiia Ginzburg.

43.1.112

131.1.86–87

Dogs, cats, pigeons disappeared from the urban landscape: eaten. Old shoes, leather belts, old wallpaper were cooked up.

190.1.161

Finally, even human flesh was eaten. If you went out with small children, you had to be careful they were not stolen. Cannibalism is mentioned repeatedly. Auntie Nastya "killed her own daughter, hid her under the bed, and cut pieces off, bit by bit." Special services were set up to combat cannibalism. Anyone caught faced an irrevocable death sentence. Only in 1992 were Aleksandr (Ales) Adamovich and Daniil Granin allowed a till then unaccepted chapter on cannibalism in their *Siege Book*.

219.1.126
96.1.190; 43.1.111
153.1.240

5.2.5–6

Some eked out their meager food allowances over the day, others ate

131.1.105–6   everything in one go, and each scorned the other's method. Most people
were easily irritated, "started to curse over the slightest thing; people were
96.1.181; 43.1.113   continually swearing in the tram, no one spoke normally or politely." All
sense of respectability had disappeared.

On 30 January 1942 Zhilinski noted in his diary on the subject of American (!) flour, some of which had evidently reached Leningrad: "the bread
is so wonderful, tasty, marvelously baked, with such delicious crusts, that
505.1.13   you could cry, you are allowed to eat so little, a total of 250 grams a day."
On 22 February 1942 the bread ration was increased again to the level of
453.1.107   rations in Moscow, but the increase was already too late for many.
In May 1942 "matches, salt, mushrooms, garlic, 200 grams of cranber-
153.1.275   ries, and even some candy" were added to the ration cards.
In the autumn of 1942 the vegetables people had planted and sown
everywhere in former municipal parks were harvested. After the summer
of 1942, "there was still the same hunger and cold, but it was not quite as
bad. The winters were not as harsh, and more was brought in via our Lake
Ladoga. What's more, America brought us first this, then that . . . there
58.1.197   were no more corpses in the streets." Refectories were also opened where
219.1.128   hot food was served.
When, in 1943, the Soviet Union's harvest fell short of expectations,
453.1.107   rations were reduced everywhere except in Leningrad.
Vitali Bianki described the stages of starvation: "diarrhea—swollen
legs—catastrophic weight loss—pain in the spine—flaky nails—blurring
of the consciousness—pasty complexion—ruddy cheeks—foaming at the
mouth—splits in the skin—then you die resignedly, almost without pain,
43.1.109   usually in your sleep."
The personnel of the famous institute where all kinds of seeds were
stored refused to touch them: "they protected the edible collection while
149.1.193   they themselves were starving to death."
Olga Berggolts described women in a Leningrad bathhouse during the
siege: "Dark bodies with raw skin . . . no longer looked like women. Their
breasts were shrunken, their bellies caved in, purple and blue blotches
from the scurvy on calfless legs, the thickest part at the ankle. Some had
scandalously distended stomachs. There was an extraordinary politeness
in the bathhouse, no one swore, everyone kept their distance, shared the
soap . . . that was the politeness of the hungry."
One old woman especially caught Berggolts's attention: "She was completely bald, with a round, protruding belly her spidery legs were hardly

able to support, she looked just like a spider. Yes, that was how war looked. Not a soldier, not a helmeted gorilla, not a tank, but this feeble, barely living old person." Then suddenly a healthy young woman came in:

Firm, round, pert breasts with cheeky pink nipples . . . a milky skin. . . . Oh, how ghastly she is with her normal, blooming health and eternally feminine flesh. . . . Yes, how dare she come like that into this terrible building where the monstrous humiliation and horrors of the war were displayed, how dare she, the bitch, how dare she insult all that with her lovely, healthy body?
—She must have been sleeping with the manager of a restaurant!
—She has been robbing us and our children!
—Hey, beautiful, stay away from here, otherwise we'll eat you up!
Everybody avoided her, recoiled from her. . . . She gave a scream, started to cry, threw down her washbasin and fled.

40.2.116–17

Children

In August 1941 children were already being evacuated with their crèches and schools in the direction of the approaching enemy. In panic, the parents snatched their children away at the last moment. Still, a total of 467,000 children remained trapped in the besieged city.

A second evacuation took place in October 1941. These were primarily orphans and street children, who sometimes did not even know their own name or their parents' names. First, they were given new clothes, underwear, and felt boots. One orphanage was evacuated via Buy, where the train remained stationary for two weeks. "Many children went searching through the rubbish for anything that might be edible. The smallest children, particularly the girls, suffered the worst. It was cold in the carriages; there were icicles hanging in the corners, and almost all of us had shoes on [as opposed to felt boots] and flannel clothing. The quietest and smallest children suffered from frozen hands and feet." They finally arrived in Irbit, in Siberia, via Sverdlovsk, on 21 December 1941.

153.1.230

19.1.167

A third evacuation took place in June and July of 1942, by train to Lake Ladoga and then further by boat. At the beginning of 1943, many of the wounded were evacuated to the province of Kalinin (now Tver).

Much later, L. Razumovski wrote an impressive account, with the help of twenty-eight survivors from the orphanage. Another account told of the effects of the blockade on the subsequent development of adults.

368.1

443.1

The children were initially taken care of in Leningrad. During the day they were kept as long as possible at school, where they also received a hot meal. Children's homes, crèches, hospitals, and relief centers did what they could. Many of the children suffered from skin ailments. "You could only be amazed at the patience of the little ones when the doctor or nurse came around every morning to remove the blankets from a child, as carefully as possible, blankets saturated with pus and blood. You didn't hear them cry; there was no screaming, not a whimper."

While the pupils of the nautical college ate their lunch, some twenty young boys would be standing silently, unmoving, outside the fence, clutching their pans, mugs, jugs, and jam jars, gazing hopefully at the source of the smell of cabbage soup and barley. Sometimes they were allowed in, and then those little lads would chatter like frozen sparrows, glancing thankfully with sunken eyes at boys just like themselves, only a little older. Some children would take a couple of mouthfuls, lay down the spoon after having carefully licked it clean, and ask, "May I take some for my mama, my little sister, my little brother?"

The principal of a boarding school took the orphan girl Lena into her home. "When they lay down together in the same bed and Natalia Ivanovna, the principal, closed her eyes, Lena woke her, crying, 'Don't go to sleep; otherwise you won't wake up either, just like my mother.'"

Despite all efforts, however, virtually all infants died during the blockade, from insufficient food and, in particular, the intense cold.

In the period between 1942 and 1943 the situation improved. "For breakfast, in addition to porridge and a slice of bread with half an egg or cheese, the children had hot chocolate or tea with milk. . . . The army at the Leningrad front often gave up their gifts from Georgia and Central Asia for the children. Then they had fresh fruit as dessert." But whether this applied to all children in Leningrad is another story.

The Victims

Many people lost their lives in the shelling and bombing, but the hunger, the cold, and the deprivation took a far higher toll. For a long time it was reported that there had been 623,253 fatalities, which is far too low a number as not all the dead were registered, for example, the tens of thousands of refugees from the area who were the first to die. The men, and mostly those who were unmarried, died more quickly than the women as they did not take proper care of themselves and were less capable of adapting.

378.1.87

16.1.215

246.1.20

153.1.205

153.1.217

Many of the dead were buried at the edge of a cemetery, most of them in mass graves dug as antitank ditches, which were only closed once full. The dead were seldom laid in coffins; most of them were wrapped in sheets or a blanket. They were delivered to collection points at hospitals, where you could see the frozen piles of corpses stacked like wood. In the Botanical Gardens, fallen soldiers lay in one area, dead children in another, and the remaining dead in yet another. Burial teams took the bodies away later in trucks.

37.1.18–19

"Once, a driver brought a full trailer and when someone from the cemetery asked, 'How many?' he answered, 'Four hundred.' 'Are you crazy? We'll never get four hundred in.' 'Look who I brought.'" In the trailer lay the tiny corpses of children from the infants' home.

153.1.255

In 1995 a report from 1942 by the Directorate of Public Works in Leningrad was published: "According to incomplete information from the cemeteries, 1,930,625 dead were buried in the city between 1 July 1941 and 12 July 1942."

256.1.188

No one will ever know, therefore, just how many victims there were. More than two million seems highly likely. If you were to read out the names of the victims over the radio, day and night without pause, it would take 208 days.

453.1.108

Culture in the Besieged City

The radio, more than anything else, instilled courage. Especially loved were the poems. Olga Berggolts reported: "I don't think people will ever listen to poetry the way the hungry, distended, barely alive Leningraders did that winter." "There was a tremendous thirst for information," wrote Lidiia Ginzburg. People spoke to one another on the street; they recounted their life stories to total strangers, an expression of "the desire to give themselves and their lives some meaning."

40.1.9
131.1.84
153.1.250

The language changed. Men no longer talked of "the Germans," "the enemy," or "the fascists" but, instead, used the word *he:* "he is quiet during the day." People did not say someone had "starved to death" but that he "didn't get up."

153.1.251

In besieged Leningrad "a feeling of freedom prevailed. Yes, cut off from the rest of the country they were free to work without being bossed around by the leaders, without the instructive and punishing hand they had been used to."

182.1.189

At the end of October 1941 a concert hall was reopened. "The violinist

Barinova gave a solo concert in the Great Hall. The hall was unheated, people sat there in their coats. It was dark; only an unnatural light illuminated the figure of the artist. You could see her breathing on her fingers from time to time to warm them up a little."

Before he was evacuated Dmitri Shostakovich had been working on his Seventh Symphony, the *Leningrad*. On 27 December he completed the score in the evacuation destination of Kuybyshev, where, on 5 March 1942, the première took place. Musicians were brought back from the front to Leningrad for rehearsals and given a little extra food. The symphony was performed in Moscow on 29 March 1942 and also in the packed Philharmonic in Leningrad on 9 August. That day was referred to as "a day of victory during the war."

It was said of that concert: "The first violinist is dying; the percussionist died on his way to work; and the French horn is on his deathbed." Conducting the symphony was Karl Ilyich Eliasberg. As Berggolts recounts: "He was in tails and the coat hung on him as if he were a coat-hanger, he had become so thin over the winter. . . . From the very first bars, we recognized ourselves [in the symphony] and our journey, the entire already legendary epic of Leningrad . . . and we, who had not yet mourned our nearest and dearest who had passed away that winter, were able and willing to let our joy, our silently burning tears, flow freely, and we were not ashamed."

Daniil Granin, who wrote the *Siege Book* together with Ales Adamovich, a book based on conversations with survivors after the war, feels that "morale was one of the major characteristics of the heroic battle for Leningrad, not patriotism, but rather the perseverance of the intellect, the protest against the humiliation of hunger, against the dehumanization. Those who saved others were saved themselves. Art and culture helped."

During those conversations with survivors Granin and Adamovich heard such terrible tales of suffering and baseness that they have always refused to write about them: "There are some things a writer should not repeat; there is a limit to human suffering."

A Little Relief

After the spring of 1942 people became more cheerful; the worst was over, or so they thought and hoped. Snow and rubbish were cleared away in March 1942 with the aid of 244,000 men, the bodies finally buried. "Cars loaded with 'white shrouds' removed their grizzly burden." A million

219.1.124–25
401.1.177
40.1.9–11
152.3.318

people were buried in the Pishkaryov cemetery. Olga Berggolts wrote a poem for this graveyard, ending with the words, "Nobody is forgotten, nothing is forgotten."

For months the courtyards had been used as a kind of rubbish dump, which started to stink terribly once the thaw set in. After the big cleanup, life started to become a little more normal. On 15 April, 116 trams began running again. The worst of the hunger was over. Well, at least you got more food in Leningrad than in the Urals or Siberia!

176.1.264

Profiteers

Of course, some people did take advantage of the situation to get their hands on valuables for the price of a loaf of bread. Those in strategic positions were open to temptation: kitchen personnel, those in charge of supplies. If they were caught, the death sentence usually followed.

A baker, because of her work, had no lack of "friends and acquaintances." She moved to more luxurious accommodations and bought a grand piano for a kilo and a half of bread. A nurse, who had been caught pinching food intended for children in the hospital, said, "Why are you looking at me like that? The children here won't die, they have something to eat, but my own children will surely die if I don't take something home for them. So go ahead and report what you've seen here."

368.1.41

153.1.202

Men who were able to obtain food organized eating parties for women and girls, who expressed their thanks with their bodies. A political functionary from the army invited young girls to his house: they were given a lavish meal and drink in exchange for physical remuneration.

176.1.257–59

It is said that the local party leader, Andrei Zhdanov, and Mayor Pyotr Popkov, as well as those functionaries working for the city and the party, lacked for nothing. Food is reputed to have been sent to them, especially from Moscow. Zhdanov was rumored to have a private cow, which was heavily guarded, at least better guarded than the army staff's cow, which had been stolen and eaten by the soldiers.

174.1.4

176.1.260

Just as inequitable, on 18 November 1941 Lev Uspenski spied "a luxurious abundance" of food at the naval staff base. Authors Tatyana Tolstaya and Fyodor Abramov also reported: "those running the city were provided with food the existence of which Leningraders had simply forgotten."

462.1.191

497.1.22–23

There were "special shops" for party functionaries, where "the shelves groaned under the weight of exquisite foodstuffs." While people in Leningrad were starving to death, "self-satisfied, fat bosses and rosy, well-fed

401.1.180

97.1.186 ladies had 'settled themselves close to the food.'" No historian wrote about that, complained Anna Dolinina, nor about the corruption. According to Dolinina, any kind of medical certificate could be purchased at
97.1.186 polyclinics, "including exemption from military service."

After the war Granin and Adamovich, as mentioned above, held intense interviews, for their aforementioned book, with people who had experienced the siege. To the horror of these authors, they heard tales of city leaders hosting parties during the hunger of 1941 and 1942. On every single day of March 1942 a recently appointed personnel official from the Leningrad party committee saw, in the canteen, "meat, mutton, chicken, goose, turkey, sausage (all kinds), fish, caviar, cheese, pies, chocolate, coffee, tea, 300 grams of white bread and sometimes brown bread a day, 30 grams of butter, and 50 grams of drink at lunch and dinner. . . . Yes, such a holiday during the front and the long siege of the city is only possible with
231.1.251 Bolsheviks, only with a Soviet government."

Fighting at Leningrad

On 10 September 1941, on Stalin's orders, Georgi Zhukov was suddenly taken to Leningrad in a heavily escorted Douglas plane. Without ceremony, he took over the command there from Klim Voroshilov. Zhukov acted ruthlessly, cruelly, but the front stabilized. Punishments were merciless: the commandant and the commissar of the Aurora—the legendary ship from the October Revolution, which at that time, incidentally, only shot blanks—were put in front of a firing squad because they had sought
347.1.25 cover during an air raid. The crew of a tank was executed because they had escaped to their own lines without their tank, which had been shot
24.1.205 to pieces.

There was extraordinarily heavy fighting on a Russian bridgehead over
161.1.64 the Neva. One division after another was wiped out. "There were places there where you could not see the ground for bodies. And outnumbering the dead were the wounded, asking for help, but already a fresh layer of
473.1.57 corpses lay on top of them." The Nevskii Pyatachok bridgehead was lost
206.7 anyway. A total of seventy-five thousand Russians died there.

As the months went by, shelling and bombing in the city became a normal occurrence; "people tried not to take any notice of it and no one
153.1.245 bothered to seek shelter any longer." Later, it turned out that launching sites for V-2s had been built at Pskov to shell the city, a year before
453.1.109 the bombing of London. It was not until 25 January 1944 that the Soviet

armies at Oranienbaum and Leningrad made contact: the siege was now
finally broken, at the cost of "more than two hundred thousand victims."   153.1.245
"The time for defense was over. The German war was over, and now the
Russian war began," remarked Lev Rubinstein poignantly.   80.1.44

The Second Assault Army

Despite heavy counterattacks, for more than two years it had been impossible to break the siege of Leningrad and unite the Volkhov front with the
Leningrad front.

After Zhukov's successes at Moscow it is said that Stalin wished to lay
claim to a great operation himself, at Leningrad. On 29 December 1941 he
wrote a letter to General Kirill Meretskov in which he urged him "to let
the attack turn into a general attack on the enemy." "Ten lines that cost
the lives of ten thousand," wrote Immanuil Levin, referring to the letter
recently unearthed from the archives.   259.1.117

Meretskov, unwilling to find himself back in the cellars of Lyubanka
Prison, spurred the troops ever onward. The attacks were poorly prepared.
There was a lack of munitions and support, and many soldiers who came
from Central Asia were not used to the woods, the swamps, and the bitter cold of 30 to 40 degrees below freezing. They ate grass, frogs, hedge-
hogs, ants, bark, leaves, and horses. One commanding officer, whose men
were starving to death, was shot because he had had a horse slaughtered.   459.1.8–9
Vitamin deficiencies spread scurvy and night blindness.

Luckily cranberries and mushrooms could be found in the marshes.
Boris Runin, who was working for the paper of this Second Assault Army,
noted that sacks of mushrooms gathered there were taken to the propaganda sector of the Red Army in Moscow as a "special assignment," after
which his editor was promoted to the rank of colonel and awarded a
medal, although no fighting had taken place in that time.   381.2.120–21

Further north there was fighting over the possession of Tikhvin. David
Samoilov wrote, "When the defenses were covered with snow and we were
issued felt boots, everything looked more like a village and our lives
continued at an even pace, like in an old-fashioned fort on the borders
of the country. When it was still dark, before daybreak, the field kitchen
arrived. You could hear the rails of the sledge crunching in the snow and
Vashka, the cook, swearing. The sergeant brought dried bread, rolling
tobacco, and sugar. He measured out the vodka with the shell of an antitank grenade."   386.1.64

At one point Meretskov left the scene, and the command was transferred to the aforementioned Andrei Vlasov, one of Stalin's favorite generals. In August and September 1941 Vlasov, as supreme commander of the Thirty-seventh Army, had defended Kiev, and, as commander of the Twentieth Army, he had driven back the Germans before Moscow at Volokolamsk. Now he had to make sure that the almost entirely encircled army broke through to Leningrad. The Lyubanskaya operation to break the siege was poorly prepared. The result was that the assault army had to dig itself in first and was then driven back into the simply impassable, expansive marshes next to the Volkhov River and Lake Ilmen. Of battalions that numbered 318 men, no more than 12 remained.

One of the last telegrams from this army, dated 21 June 1942, read: "The troops have had 50 grams of bread a day for the last three weeks. For the last three days there has been no food at all. The men are completely exhausted . . . there is no ammunition."

Finally, they were forced to retreat under continual enemy fire through a three-hundred- to four-hundred-meter-wide corridor at Myasnoi Bor. Most of them died there.

To this day the unburied skeletons of soldiers from the Second Assault Army still lie in the marshes at Myasnoi Bor. Young volunteers, in their spare time, are currently burying them and discovering their names. Officially ten thousand men died there; others say the number was closer to twenty thousand to twenty-five thousand or even as many as one hundred thousand.

In January–February 1944 Myasnoi Bor was liberated. "The snow was red with patches of blood." The other side also suffered great losses. The 1st, 126th, 254th, and 291st Infantry Divisions, a police division, two Estonian SS battalions, and the "Nederland" and "Vlaanderen" legions were, according to Levin, "virtually wiped out."

On 27 June 1942 General Vlasov was taken prisoner, or allowed himself to be taken prisoner, by the Germans. Later, he set up the Russian Liberation Army (ROA), which fought on the German side. When this became known, his first wife, a military doctor, was arrested as the wife of a traitor and spent five years in prison, after which she was banished for an unspecified time.

For decades, the existence of the second assault army was hushed up, as it was considered to be an army of traitors. . . . The writer, Sergei Krutilin, who fought in it himself, was forbidden to write about this army.

The NKVD

"Even during the very first weeks of the war" the NKVD started to arrest people. "For three long weeks a great wave of arrests swept through the city." I. I. Zhilinski, born in 1890, was sentenced to ten years in a prison camp for keeping a diary; he died in Leningrad before the ten years expired.

161.1.56

505.2.5–6

In October 1941 the authorities concocted a case concerning the "coun-terrevolutionary activity by corresponding academy member Ignatovski and his group." Vladimir Ignatovski was tortured, and, dying with him, were "127 highly respected scholars from Leningrad." The majority of those arrested worked in the defense industry.

138.1.17

248.1.74–75

Every night there were arrests, and therefore many slept in their clothes, their boots within reach. An NKVD report, dated 5 November 1941, states: "There are even dedicated traitors among the party leaders." The writer Veniamin Kaverin was pressured to spy and inform on his fellow authors. To his relief, he was evacuated on 10 November 1941.

185.1.120–21

181.1.13

194.1.59–60

Leningrad Falls from Grace

On 4 December 1943 a decision was made to place on exhibit "The Heroic Defense of Leningrad." On 30 April 1944 the exhibition, concerning the defense and life of Leningrad during the siege, was set up in a museum and occupied twenty-six halls. The director of the museum was L. L. Rakov. The museum, continually expanded by gifts from Leningraders, was renamed the "Museum of the Defenders of Leningrad." On display, among other exhibits, was a pyramid, more than eight meters high, of German helmets full of bullet holes and the recipe of the famous siege bread: 50 percent rye flour, 10 percent cattle cake, 2.5 percent soya meal, 5 percent chaff, 10 percent malt, 15 percent cellulose, and 5 percent wall-paper paste. Many Soviet and captured weapons were also exhibited.

72.1.291

After the war, fear and terror reigned once again in Leningrad. In 1946 and 1948 former leaders of the resistance and the defense were arrested, tortured, and shot. Actually, wrote Granin and Adamovich, the siege con-tinued after the war: "The city, which had fallen from grace, was encircled by insinuations, initiative was stifled, [and] it was not permitted to restore either dignity or honor."

5.2.19

Sixty passages were deleted from their book. Scrapped, among other things, was the fact that during the war men and women washed together in the bathhouse: "Try to explain that, by then, they had lost all sexual characteristics."

5.2.8

In August 1949 the museum—which had been visited by Zhukov, Eisenhower, and Mrs. Clementine Churchill—closed its doors: the exhibits were distributed in various locations and the weapons melted down or given to the army. Photographs and paintings of famous defenders of the city were burned, personnel were dismissed, and, at the end of 1952, the museum finally closed its doors.

135.1.147

Rakov was arrested, tortured, and accused of having collected the weapons in the museum in order to surrender Leningrad to the Fins after an uprising. On 21 February 1950, during the so-called Leningrad Affair, Malenkov stated: the personnel "were accused of having made a myth out of the special siege fate of Leningrad . . . that the city was considered to be outside the general battle . . . that the role of enemies of the people such as Popkov, Kuznetsov, and Kapustin were artificially differentiated, while Stalin's role, on the other hand, was diminished" (see further, page 237).

6

The Tide Turns

The Kalinin Front

After the retreat from Moscow in December 1941 and the months that followed, the enemy was only able to hold its ground in and around the provincial town of Rzhev, which remained in enemy hands for seventeen months, from October 1941 to 3 March 1943.

Rzhev was referred to as the gate to Moscow and also the access gate to Berlin, as it formed a strategic railway junction between Novgorod, Vyazma, and Moscow. The Germans dubbed Rzhev the "operational base for a decisive renewed attack on Moscow . . . a dagger aimed at Moscow." 383.5.386

There is every reason to speak of the "battle of Rzhev." It was fought on the territory of the provinces of Kalinin (modern-day Tver), Moscow, and Smolensk, bitter fighting that is said to have cost more than 1.6 million Soviet lives. Continual Russian attacks were intended to distract 129.1.174 German troops from the southern front in Ukraine. Nevertheless, it was precisely there that the Germans broke through in 1942, enabling them to thrust ahead to the Volga at Stalingrad.

The fighting on this Kalinin front was unusually protracted, exhausting, bloody, and mostly in vain. Persistently the soldiers had to attack, and when a little village or hill was lost, they had to attack until it was recaptured or face a court-martial or death sentence.

The Russians fought there initially with obsolete rifles, generally without any support from artillery or tanks. The trenches filled with water in the spring and autumn. "The rain had already been pouring for a week, monotonously, as if no spring or warmth was coming. God created heaven and earth, but the devil the roads of Kalinin, cursed the drivers." 383.5.174

Whining dogs dragged sacks of bread through the mud. The army interpreter, Yelena Rzhevskaya—her nom de plume taken from the town of Rzhev—never saw more ghastly fighting than here, and she went all the way to the Reichskanzlei in Berlin.

383.9.60

"There was hunger, violence on the part of the occupiers, cruelty and treachery. German front soldiers were transformed into devils. Only the Fins were worse," wrote Rzhevskaya. "At the liberation of Rzhev, all the commanding officers of the infantry companies and platoons were killed. . . . Over the entire field lay mutilated, stiff soldiers spread out or in groups,

383.1.57, 21

under or on top of the snow."

The occupiers committed acts of unheard of cruelty in and around Rzhev. They took warm clothing from people on the street, drove them out of their houses. At one point a large number of inhabitants were transported to Germany by train. The place was plagued by hunger and typhus. Because of the constant bombing, at the time of liberation in 1943, there were only 362 of the former 60,000 inhabitants left and 300 of the 5,500 prewar houses. In the area of Rzhev, 96 hamlets and villages disappeared from the face of the earth.

Vyacheslav Kondratyev devoted all his work to the fighting on the Kalinin front, at the villages of Usovo, Chornovo, Panovo, and Ovsyannikovo, where he himself had fought from the winter of 1942. In an epilogue I wrote to his last account, *To Redeem in Blood*, I explore this subject in

209.26

detail. Here, at the Kalinin front, brigade after brigade was sent into the fray, the dead serving as "cover" for the next lot. "There were mounds of

209.4.122

dead in front of every village."

The worst sight he witnessed was, in his words, "the bodies of our own soldiers, stripped down to their underwear, which blended into the snow. All that could be seen clearly was the head, the wrists, and the feet." This is why the Russians hoped that, if they should die, it would be close to German lines, in other words, far away from their own people, who were

209.5

after their uniform and boots.

"Only later did we find out that there were two other infantry brigades in addition to ours; we hadn't noticed them. They had arrived before us and lost almost their entire strength in a few days. We saw them, the dead, lying on the field the first morning of the battle and hid ourselves

209.4.122

behind their bodies as we leaped forward." Kondratyev had further comments: "We attacked all the same, more than once, knowing we couldn't

get through; we went without complaint, carrying out the order." "I don't 209.15.75–76
know how many we lost, but I remember the mountains of bodies in front
of every little village at Rzhev. I can still remember how we attacked without artillery preparation, with no more than firearms and a 'hurrah,' how
we were constantly thrown into ill-fated, unprepared, useless attacks again
and again until the brigade had been wiped out, until there were no more
than fifteen or so soldiers left in the company." 209.6

Kondratyev wrote to a former comrade in arms, "And something else,
Misha. You walked those 160 kilometers from the front to the evacuation
hospital, a road alongside devastated, half-burned Russian villages. You
were walking in the winter, so naturally you found shelter and a place to
stay for the night in those little houses where Russian women took you in
and fed you with what little they had—there wasn't much then—perhaps
they shared their last potato with you. How many wounded came through
every village? Thousands! And every night there were strangers sleeping
there, filthy from the front, sometimes covered in lice, in these women's
houses, but they let us into their *izbas*." 209.1

The life expectancy of a company commandant at the Kalinin front was
approximately two weeks. One general on inspection had his horse stolen
and eaten by the hungry soldiers. "Bodies, frozen fast to the ground, 216.2.51
shielded us from fire. . . . The wounded bled into the frost, the dead grew
stiff, the living cursed everything and hoped for an end to it all, alive or
dead. As long as that end came quickly," wrote Maksim Korobeynikov in 216.2.160
his impressive memoirs on the Kalinin front. 216.2

In March 1942 Korobeynikov and his comrades were starving; no bread
had been supplied for eighteen days. In March–April 1942 a general was 216.2.219
dismissed because of the precarious food supplies at this front. "A great 323.4.8, 83
deal of food and equipment was misappropriated . . . theft and crime were
rife at the expense of the blood of soldiers: that dark side still demands
investigation." 348.1.123

Kondratyev and Korobeynikov's descriptions are more than confirmed in
Vladimir Klipel's *Soldaty Otechestva* (Soldiers of the Fatherland). Klipel, 202.1, 2
who served in the Seventeenth Infantry Division, also describes the "demonstration attacks": you must never retreat, you have to keep on attacking, no matter how weak your division. "Willful freezing is considered to
be self-mutilation" and is therefore heavily punished. "Already for more 202.1.22

than a week we have been battling without mines or grenades, and you simply have to trust to the self-sacrifice of the soldiers walking into the machine guns."

202.2.95

And, in Klipel's words: "The same thing for almost two months and you never get used to it. Humiliating and exasperating, but we cannot answer the Germans. Our artillery has been silent for some time now . . . and the Germans let the grenades rain down, they do not spare them, as if there is no spring and no thaw, as if a road leads straight from Berlin to this accursed Ovsyannikovo, an asphalt road that provides them, unhindered, with everything they need."

209.18.105, 125

348.1.122

"I draw a veil over the night blindness, the diarrhea, the boils, the diseases caused by the cold, the damp, and the swamp water." The Germans had the upper hand during the day; at night the Russians had the advantage. "And so we freeze, lying for days in the snow, without sleep or rest of any kind, without any hope that the casualties have not been in vain. . . . Once more we have to round up all the living and send them back into the machine-gun fire. After all, the village has not yet been taken, and nobody has countermanded the order to do so."

202.2.95

Klipel also writes, "The frost has fettered the rivers, snowstorms have covered them with a white blanket. The woods are swathed in snow, the trees bowing under their burden. The weight of the snow has bent slender trees over the road, forming wonderful arches. A heavy, oppressive sky hangs above the earth. Sometimes the sun breaks through for an hour or so, and then the wintry woods are lit up with crystal; the virgin white of the open fields is blinding. But that rarely happens, nature is often in a somber mood; soft snow falls continually in great flakes out of the dark depths of the heavens."

202.1.8

Ukraine

The great German breakthrough and major gaining of ground were accomplished in the south, in Ukraine. Stalin had gathered the main forces at Moscow, "more than half our army, almost 80 percent of the tanks, and 62 percent of the aircraft. But in the Caucasus, where the main force of the Hitlerites was being confronted, there was a mere 5.2 percent of our divisions and only 2.9 percent of the tanks," wrote Vladimir Shubkin.

448.1

Against the advice of the military, Stalin gave the order to attack. Kharkov was, indeed, captured, but then the Russians walked into the German trap. Once again the battle ended in a devastating encirclement.

German, Hungarian, and Romanian units then quickly advanced in the direction of the Volga and the Northern Caucasus, where they received support from various Cossack settlements.

233.1.156

In 1963 Zhukov wrote that a great deal is left out of the official historiography of the war. For example, "the most important issues are not mentioned: he [Khrushchev] was a member of the Military Council for the southwestern front. You can reproach me on the initial period of the war. But 1942 is not the initial period of the war. Starting with Barvenkovo and Kharkov, he rolled back as far as the Volga, and no one writes about that. They took to their heels with Timoshenko, taking one group of Germans to the Volga, another to the Caucasus. And the southwestern and southern fronts were subordinate to them. It was a considerable force."

383.11.18–19

In the summer of 1942 the enemy reached the river Don. It was crossed by force at the end of July. A frantic flight followed. An unimaginable number of troops, wagons, and cannons jostled for position at the crossings, shelled by virtually unimpeded Junkers and Messerschmitts. At these

74.1.137

crossings the future renowned writer Vladimir Tendryakov saw "burning vehicles . . . bodies falling into the water, wounded soldiers on stretchers, forgotten by everyone. They called out for no one; they maintained a doomed silence. Wounded people might have been quiet, but the wounded horses screamed with terrifying, hysterical, almost female voices." Writer

456.2.58–59;
456.1.151

Nikolay Gribachov states, "On the bridge was a stream of retreating people, cargo, vehicles, trucks, and tractors. Gaunt soldiers and officers, unshaven, in filthy or torn uniforms, black with soot and dust, their nerves stretched to the limit, hastened to the other side, no-one daring to stop and wash or drink from the Don." One overzealous official went off to

154.1.54

check the wagons, wanting to cross the river at Belgorod. He caused a blockage of three thousand vehicles, easy prey for German planes.

100.2.11–12

Between the Don and the Volga, the Luftwaffe was still so mighty that planes even hunted down individual, wandering soldiers.

11.2.30

In the spring and summer of 1942 the warring parties tore through and over Ukraine and the more easterly steppes. In the occupied area, one eyewitness reported in 1994, as quoted by Zinich, "People hardly slept in the last few days of spring. During the day they worked in the kolkhoz; in the evenings and at night they were busy on their own land. The horses, already worn out in the daytime, had to be pulled along and, anyway, there were too few. Everyone tried to get by as best he could. One would harness up his cow, and those who were stronger formed a group, three to four women harnessed to the plow and pulling, pulling. . . . But mostly they trusted in the spade. . . . The men worked like devils; behind the house, in the hayfields, the whole night long you could hear the sound of digging and the groaning of women harnessed to the plow."

497.1.65

"By August 1942, in an entirely depopulated strip of land, twenty or thirty kilometers deep, stretching across the whole of the front, right across Russia, there was a harvest unprecedented in size, a gift from the Lord," says Penkov. "The women from the villages stole off to the front line in the night, under artillery fire, and harvested all the grain by hand, almost stalk by stalk. . . . Mother came back with several sacks of grain she had earned. It helped us get through the difficult winter of 1942."

336.1.14

During the retreat through Ukraine and between the Don and the Volga, commandants advised their men to save themselves as best they could. Officers were seen tearing off their stripes. Soldiers, dressed as farmers, tried to get home by keeping a low profile. "There was only one way out: to melt into the population, wait, act cautiously, and begin a clandestine struggle." What Viktor Nekrasov noted is almost unimaginable. In the spring of 1942 Nekrasov, as an officer in the engineering corps, had only seen mines and other weapons in pictures. When his troop left the barracks in the Northern Caucasian Cossack village of Serafimovich for the front, the soldiers were parading with wooden sticks instead of rifles and the artillery was symbolized by tree trunks loaded on wagons. The women in the village wept over this nonsense. "Who had devised that farce? God only knows." Only a day before the battle of Kharkov were they given rifles, the obsolete model 1891/1931. Officers were given a pistol. They were not allowed to practice. Only one or two officers knew how to strip down a rifle and put it back together again. "So that was how the famous Timoshenko attack on Kharkov began in May 1942. We all know how it ended."

375.1.41

64.1.65

309.4.32–33, 46

309.3

"Not One Step Back!"

On 28 July 1942, as a result of the panicky retreat from Ukraine, notorious Order No. 00227 was implemented. The two zeros meant top secret. The order was read out to all members of the military, from the lowest ranks to the highest, and was only published in 1988. Known as "Not one step back!" the order reflected the unadulterated truth about the absolutely critical situation of that summer of 1942. According to David Ortenberg, then editor in chief of the army newspaper, *Red Star*, Stalin himself had dictated the order.

356

We have far less territory, far fewer men, far less grain, metal, and factories. We have lost more than seventy million people, more than eight
hundred million pud [1 pud = 16 kilos] of grain a year, and more than ten
million tons of steel. We are already no stronger than the Germans, either
in men or stocks of grain. If we retreat any further we are digging our
own graves and letting our Fatherland go to the dogs. It is therefore time
to end the retreat: "Not one step back!" . . . The people of our country,
who love and respect the Red Army, are becoming disappointed in the
Red Army, are losing faith, and many of them curse the Red Army for
sentencing our people to the yoke of the German oppressors and even
retreating into the east. What are we lacking? We are lacking order and
discipline in every company, battalion, regiment, division, tank unit, and
air squadron. We must introduce the strictest order, initiate an iron discipline in our army, if we wish to save the situation and defend our Fatherland. . . . We must immediately end all talk of forever being able to retreat,
of having a great deal of territory, of our country being big and rich, of
having a large population, and of always having grain available. Such talk
is not true and is dangerous; it weakens us and strengthens the enemy,
because if we do not halt the retreat, then we will lose grain, fuel, metal,
raw materials, factories, and railways.

Drastic measures were announced:
—Penal companies and penal battalions were to be set up for soldiers
  who had surrendered, retreated without an express order, or shown
  cowardice.
—Police troops ("blocking detachments") were to be established behind
  their own lines and were to shoot cowards, panic mongers, and
  deserters.
—The family of those punished were to be arrested.

According to Viktor Nekrasov, it was not the Red Army but Stalin who
had lost the people's confidence, as he had not been properly prepared for
a war, and also because leaders such as Voroshilov, Semyon Budyonny, and
Timoshenko had caused one defeat after another through their incompetence. Zhukov later referred to Order No. 00227 as "the most scandalous
order, which unjustly slandered the military and moral qualities of our
soldiers."
  Another question is whether the Red Army was even motivated to fight
at that time. Most soldiers were, as we know, poorly trained, if at all, had

309.4.33

147.1.144

no proper uniform, and were not equipped with the best weapons. Would
they have felt like sacrificing themselves? Krushchev wrote in his memoirs
that, whereas in World War I farmers fought for their own home and
business, in 1941 and 1942 that motive was lacking: "We retreated because
soldiers did not see why they should fight, why they should die."

The Red Army was made up mostly of farmers. "They had been treated
so atrociously by the whole collectivization operation, with taxes, hunger,
being tried for gleaning corn left on the fields after harvesting or a careless word, that—to put it mildly—on the whole, they were not exactly
keen to fight."

The White Russian author Vasil Bykov wrote a story about a political
commissar, who, in order to encourage his soldiers, told them that, after
the war, there would be no more kolkhozes, that life would be different.
The colonel came to a bad end. One officer who fought at Stalingrad
writes: "The country that existed before the war entered into the war.
And everything that prevailed at that time—the capacity for self-sacrifice
and suspicion, cruelty and mental impotence, naive romanticism, an officially demonstrated devotion to the leader and deeply buried doubts, the
crass sluggishness of bureaucrats, scare-mongering and the brave hope
that everything would turn out all right in the end, the heavy burden of
insults, and the feeling that this war was justified—the people took all
of this with them to war."

Penal companies (for soldiers and lower-ranking commandants) and penal
battalions (for officers) were deployed in the most difficult and dangerous places at the front. Those who were wounded had "paid their debt in
blood" and were dismissed; the rest were either dead or had to return to
battle. Anyone with a large unit retreating on orders under the command
of a commandant went unpunished, but anyone managing to break out
of an encirclement or a prisoner-of-war camp in small groups and get
back to their own lines, often after weeks or months, had to account for
themselves to the "Special Section" (Osoby Otdel) of SMERSH.

As the German troops advanced, the NKVD shot its prisoners in Orel. Tank
general Heinz Guderian showed the victims to the local population. Georgi
Vladimov wrote: "Between the rows [of murder victims], crossing back
and forth repeatedly through the living and the dead, a pope was walking up and down in a lilac cassock, a fat, gray-haired, worn-out Russian
pope, seemingly a drunkard and a glutton, but with a heart overflowing

239.1.139

71.2.29

68.2.29

66.9.8

448.1

with love. He mourned them all with real tears, wiping his eyes and nose now and again on his cassock."

Guderian called him over and asked, "Why is your flock looking at me like that? Did someone tell them my tank personnel did this?" And the pope answered, "No one thinks your men did this. But perhaps it might not have happened if your tanks had not been here?" Lev Anninski writes that the pope added, "This is our pain, not yours." 480.1
20.1.220

In Voronezh NKVD henchman Lutkov killed prisoners while German Junkers bombed the city. 504.1

Stalingrad

Stalingrad spanned a distance of twenty miles alongside the Volga, with not only modern factories and blocks of flats but also many wooden houses. When, in the summer of 1942, the enemy approached over the burning hot steppes, all kinds of materials, two million cattle, thirty-five hundred agricultural machines and carts, and people, too, were transported to the other side of the river by means of six different crossings. 196.1.149

"Clouds of dust thrown up by a thousand head of cattle, sheep, horses, tractors, combine harvesters, all evacuated from Poltava, Rostov, Voroshilovgrad, Voronezh, Kalmykia. . . . By the beginning of August approximately two hundred thousand animals and a mass of machines were stockpiled on the right bank and still the flow didn't stop." 196.1.147

Russian troops rushed hastily to Stalingrad. According to Rokossovski, 23 August 1942 was the heaviest day of the war. The German tanks broke through and reached the Volga. L. Shubkin, an officer in the artillery, writes, "At least we are being transported. But the infantry looks terrible. They stumble along the road like sleepwalkers, laden with rifles, kit bags, heavy artillery, mortars, and submachine guns. The marching had already been going on for several days, and the boundaries of human strength have long been passed; black faces with a tortured look, uniform jackets white with salt, bloody feet cut to ribbons that refuse to do further service." Shubkin's unit suffered heavy losses both to artillery and men. "The losses were not made up. There was a continual shortage of munitions, not to mention our daily bread. The soldiers were prepared to keep themselves on their feet at any cost and went into the steppe in the night, where, miraculously, a small field of wheat had been left. They cut it down with their bayonets and knives, and dragged it back to the trenches on their groundsheets. There it was threshed, winnowed, and cooked without salt. It often seemed as if we were the last soldiers of the Fatherland. . . . Officers and soldiers discussed where they could find something to eat over a roll-up. Their mutual relations took on a new dimension. The officers no longer formed a clique as before, but pushed the cannons forward with us, even helped dig the trenches. . . . That's how it always is when danger is near, when you have real work to do, then the relationships between people become simpler, friendlier."

455.1

The importance of Stalingrad was in its control of the Volga River, by which oil and Allied goods supplied via Persia reached the front. After the Russian victory at Stalingrad, in particular, the Germans threw mines into the Volga in an effort to continue to disrupt shipping traffic.

On 23 August 1942 Stalingrad was heavily bombed. The wooden houses went up like matchwood.

"The soil of Stalingrad was thrown up, everything became black. It looked as if a monstrous hurricane had swept into the city and tossed it into the air. . . . The screaming of bombs raining down from above mingled with the thunder of explosions, with the creaking and rumbling of collapsing buildings and the raging of roaring fires."

463.192–93

On 3 September the German troops broke through at another point near the Volga, partly because a Russian commando post had driven Russian tanks out of their hiding places. "Have you ever heard of any military commandant being punished for [the destruction of] that tank regiment and the burned men, or is everything put down to the war?"

80.1.75–76

German planes dropped pamphlets—the paper was extremely good for rolling cigarettes—with the heading "Pass" and the letters B.I.G. ["Bayonet in the Ground," meaning do not resist]. "Russian soldiers! Behind you is the Volga. Soon you will all be *bul-bul* (dead meat). Do not listen to the Jewish political commissar. Do not read Ehrenburg! He is only wasting ink, and you, your blood. Give yourselves up, and then you can save yourselves. Come over to our side. You only need to shout, 'Stalin *kaput!* Bayonet in the Ground.'" In Mikhail Alekseyev's platoon the bayonets suddenly disappeared: the soldiers had interpreted the text literally and buried the bayonets.

11.4.13

The fighting at Stalingrad was, without precedent, the heaviest, the most persistent, and the most bitter on both sides. Soldiers fought over every house, over every story of a house, for each hollow, each pile of stones.

In the beginning of autumn 1942 the Russian side was experiencing a great shortage of men. Men who were young, inexperienced, or elderly were simply taken from the fields and thrown into battle. A brigade of marines arrived on 17 September from Severomorsk (near Murmansk); in a couple of days not one of them was still alive.

On 21 January 1943 Mikhail Alekseyev was looking for a place to spend the night. "I found a hole in the snow and crawled into it. In the dark I could feel a pile of sacks. I laid down my fur coat and lay on top of it. In the morning I awoke and saw that they were not sacks but the bodies of German soldiers, stacked up neatly, German-style."

In the beginning the fighting took place in the stifling heat; later, in autumn and winter, in the bitter cold and the blizzards. "It was suffocating in the trenches. When the wind came from no-man's-land it was impossible to breathe. It was there the unburied corpses lay and everything we threw out of the trenches. We defecated into tin cans and threw them in that direction." Driven back to a narrow strip of land alongside the Volga, the Russians—General Vasili Chuikov's Sixty-second Army— still managed to hold their ground with an almost incomprehensible perseverance. "The battle for Stalingrad lasted 145 days and nights. The dead remained, in mass graves, in the rubble of the city. Who counted them, who noted down their names or how any Red Army soldier died and where he is buried? No one concerned himself with such issues. It is no longer possible to find any mass graves since the postwar development. Maybe they lie under that new block of flats or under that factory complex?"

One woman recounted: "When it was all over in Stalingrad, we were ordered to evacuate the most seriously wounded by ship and longboat to Kazan and Gorki. It was already spring by then, April! But we found so many wounded, they were lying on the earth, in trenches, in subterranean shelters, cellars, there were so many, I can't tell you how many. It was dreadful! As we dragged the wounded away from the battlefield, we kept thinking that was it, that even in Stalingrad there were no more, but when the fighting ended there turned out to be so many it was unbelievable."

The great encirclement movement of the Soviet army started on 19 November 1942. "Echoes of the artillery fire in the misty morning of 19 November, the rumble of the T-34 tanks advancing toward the breach, scattering the Romanians, who offered little resistance, over the snowy steppe. . . . The Romanians threw down their weapons, driven forth by a merciful blizzard, disappearing in all directions, looking for someone who

11.2.57

13.2.89

11.1

109.1.142

290.1.174

13.2.89

might want to take them prisoner. But nobody was interested in them or
how many of their frozen bodies subsequently lay until the spring in the
ravines and woods of that little bend in the river Don."

In December the Russians marched "day and night, taking only brief
pauses, along the roads and paths of the snow-covered fields, alongside
woods and deserted, burning villages. . . . The troops walked some fifty
kilometers a day, in the direction of the Don, which they were able to cross
over on the ice."

Fresh troops "were dressed in new army jackets, most of them with felt
boots, many of them with automatic weapons instead of rifles. The soldiers marched along with a spring in their step, smiling cheerfully. How
many of them got as far as Berlin?"

Justifiably, perhaps, thousands of articles and books have been written
about Stalingrad, by far the best-known battle of World War II, the beginning of the end of the German army. What else is there to say?

The first novel about Stalingrad was written by Viktor Nekrasov, who
himself had fought as an officer in the engineers' battalion. The book was
initially entitled *Stalingrad* but that title was not allowed, as the censor did
not want the descriptions to apply to the whole of Stalingrad. Instead, *In
the Trenches of Stalingrad* was settled on. Later a film based on Nekrasov's
document—that was, after all, what his book was—was entitled *Soldiers*
(1957). The generals leveled heavy criticism at Nekrasov's description of
the retreat from the Don to the Volga, as if the Russian soldiers were
"a ragged troop of bandits, definitely not a heroic Soviet army." "No," was
Nekrasov's retort, "you didn't see that shabby troop, for you had long
since fled east with your jeeps." Nekrasov himself had retreated from
Rostov-on-Don by foot, with his largely inexperienced engineers' battalion. Only in Stalingrad did they get to see dynamite, and each soldier fired
one shot. In Stalingrad he saw "stones, pieces of concrete, tables, a cupboard turned over . . . we come to the Tractor Factory. Where are the
Germans? There, behind the rolling mill, there's a ravine there, Mechet it's
called, they are shooting with mortars. Our organized units are not here
yet; the workers are holding [the Germans] off."

Nekrasov was the first author to write about the moral responsibility
of the commandant in sending soldiers to their deaths.

Nekrasov, who was forced to leave the Soviet Union in 1974, said that
the most valuable commodity in Stalingrad was not clothes, a hat, a pistol, or an automatic weapon but, rather, because everything was frozen,

427.1.199

441.1.98, 95

137.3.15

309.4.30

309.3

309.4.34

the little pickax, spade, and ax. "We stole those, we went out in search of them. The best was the German one, which was only issued for important assignments—and you had to sign for it." Worst of all was "the intermin- 309.4.48
able hunger . . . we scratched bread crumbs mixed with tobacco out of our bags to still our hunger." 74.1.139

Nekrasov—a great friend of Vyacheslav Kondratyev—tells how he managed to get two engineers to join the artillery, where a special dagger was to be manufactured for Yemelyan Yaroslavsky, the visiting people's commissar. "I hadn't heard such cursing and swearing as I heard that night in a long time." 309.4.37

Although officially fiction, the most impressive, thought-provoking book about Stalingrad, the war in Russia, and the war between the two dictators in general is *Life and Fate,* written by war correspondent Vasili Grossman. Initially publication of the book in the Soviet Union was impossible. The ideology chief, Mikhail Suslov, said, "Perhaps in two hundred years' time," and then had the manuscript seized. Thus it was not published until 1988. It is the *War and Peace* of the war in Russia. The setting switches from Stalingrad to the Kremlin, from scientific laboratories to Auschwitz.

The main theme of this impressive epic is the fighting in Stalingrad, and the central point is "Building 6.1," where a small group of Russians is holding its own under entirely impossible conditions in a building shot to ruins, where soldiers fight for every stone. Under the command of Captain Grekov, they speak freely about politics; they are no longer afraid of anything. Commissar Krymov, who has been sent after them, reports that anarchy is rife among their ranks, "a Parisian commune." He complains that reports on the fighting are not submitted every day at 19:00 hours. How free and strong they felt, there amid the rubble, independent and fighting for freedom, and after the war, too. "And they try to imagine a future they would be willing to fight for. . . . I want freedom. That's what I'm fighting for. We all want freedom. 'Forget it. What do you want that for? You only have to see to the Germans, nothing more.'"

"Building 6.1" was "like a fishbone in the throat," not only for the Germans, who were attacking in vain, but also for the political leaders, who first and foremost demanded strict obedience and subjection from the defenders of Russia.

"The proximity of death, the possibility of being killed at any moment, makes men free," writes Igor Zolotusski. "Freedom loosens tongues,

freedom unites them, officers and soldiers, young and old, former intelligentsia, former foremen. No one is superior to anyone else. Here, the
dream of self-management and of individual freedom is realized. But
there are also 'informers' in this free society. Here, a spy from the commando has been sent to check on them or, to put it simply, an informer
who reports on the conduct and conversations of the defenders of the
building. Discussions on freedom, spirit, friendship, the argument for the
total subjection of mankind in the light of the total violence in the twentieth century develop in Grossman among the bullets, within the walls
of Building 6.1 and on the threshold of the gas chamber, in the homes of
learned men in Kazan, and in the cells of Lubyanka. Grossman's novel
hovers like a great bird above the country and above the war."

498.1

Indeed, at Stalingrad, everyone was rewarded according to his per-
formance and attitude. Here, there was no distinction made between "sons
of enemies of the people" and others. At the front, those young men could
become officers; after the war they were once again "stepchildren of the
time," as Grossman called them.

188.2.136–38

Throughout and after the battle of Stalingrad, writes Grossman,
people regarded the Germans differently. Stalingrad "aided a new self-
consciousness of the army and the people." The historian Senyavskaya
wrote later, "The whole period up until the victory of Stalingrad . . . is
characterized by the fact that there was a real threat of defeat. . . . Everyone was aware of that possibility."

157.5.309

394.1.78

When the Sixth German Army, under General Field Marshal Friedrich
Paulus, had surrendered in Stalingrad on 31 January 1943, "they trooped
past our officers' quarters in endless rows with their knapsacks stuffed
with God knows what and, with a sad smile on their frozen faces, slipped
us their watches and fountain pens so we wouldn't take their albums with
photographs of dear Gretchen and kindly old people, Mum and Dad. . . .
We were kind, we just breathed alcohol fumes in their faces and laughed,
'Okay, Fritz, we won't touch you, but think about your Frau, you won't be
seeing her for a while . . .' So began February 1943."

309.4.39

And that is what happened to all 330,000 prisoners, says Nekrasov. No
revenge, no insults, humiliation, or cruelty. Golitsyn, however, saw how a
German prisoner, unable to follow, was shot down.

137.3.16

After the capitulation, groups of Germans wandered along the Volga,
hoping someone would capture them and take them further away. Later,

151.1.113

Russian schoolchildren were given German underwear and parts of uniforms, taken from prisoners of war who had frozen to death during transport to the camps.   139.1

"Romanians were dressed in green leather jackets with high woolen
hats. . . . People laughed about the Romanians, but they looked at them
without anger, with a sympathetic indifference. . . . They behaved even
less nastily toward Italians." Quite other feelings were evoked by Hun-   157.5.57
garians and Fins and, in particular, the Germans. The German prisoners
looked terrible. "They had their heads and shoulders wrapped in pieces
of blanket, on their feet they wore cloth bound around their boots with a
string. . . . The ears, nose, cheeks of many of them were covered in black
blotches of frost gangrene. The quiet clink of mess tins hanging from their
belts reminded you of the sound of handcuffed criminals."   157.5.57–58

Before and after Stalingrad, part of the front ran through the Kalmyk
steppe in the direction of the Northern Caucasus. "The Kalmyk steppe is
open space up to the horizon, covered in the winter with rock-hard frozen
sand. Not a tree or bush for as far as the eye can see. Settlements are
extremely rare. Cruel, penetrating winds blast all winter long, starting
in October or November. We had to transport water from Astrakhan,
because both the Hitlerites and those Kalmyks who had collaborated with
them had poisoned all the rare springs. . . . Sometimes we came across the
carcass of a horse, stinking terribly . . . chunks of the meat were roasted
on a fire and we wolfed it down—hunger is the best sauce," wrote Isaak
Tsidilkovski in 1996.   74.1.140

"The infantry," adds Yuri Shishenkov, "walked on for two hundred to
three hundred kilometers, their faces blackened by frost and wind, their
hands red. The supply units remained behind the infantry, which had
gone on ahead. The people walked, chewing on hard dried bread as they
went along. It was certainly not every day that there was a pan of soup." 445.1.217

Between the Volga and the Dnepr

The Russians quickly advanced further westward, in the direction of
Rostov-on-Don. With the liberation of this city, in the summer of 1943, it
was clear that the superiority of the Russian air force over the Luftwaffe,
which had begun at Stalingrad, had increased substantially.   74.1.141

Kharkov was taken, too, for the second time. The film director Dovzhenko noted in his diary on 28 August 1943, "Repeat of the arrests of last

winter in Kharkov. Around twenty-five hundred people were then banished from the city after we had captured it. A scandal. That scandal is repeating itself. No wonder so many people fled with the Germans."

In the spring of 1943 hungry, poorly dressed, untrained, and inexperienced soldiers continually attacked the little village of Grebennikov, near Rostov, where the enemy was thoroughly entrenched. They kept on attacking, without the aid of tanks or artillery. These "soldiers" were "mostly from the recently liberated areas" and had never held a rifle. Three times a day, for almost a month, they attacked—to no avail. When their duty officer, Selivanov, complained about the unit having to continually attack, the response was, "Do you think your rabble can be compared to a select NKVD division? Do you know where you are? This is the south: the Vendée, the Don, the Kuban, the Northern Caucasus [and they] have always been a bastion of the Whites. Now, too, it is an enemy nest, each one is a bigger traitor than the other. No uniforms? Why give that crap uniforms? Are they starving in the trenches? So what . . . they're all tarred with the same brush. They should all be sentenced without exception. Get them in front of a court martial! Well, do you understand now why you are doing 'nothing' but attacking?"

Here we come up against what, in my experience, is a rarely described phenomenon: in great haste the advancing Russian armies "mobilized" all men who had lived under occupation and, viewing them as inferior, threw them straight into battle as cannon fodder. Sometimes these unfortunates were even forced to attack without weapons. "They told us, 'Get on with it, you can find weapons there and get one when someone dies,' and we went empty-handed."

These hastily mobilized troops were known as "seized soldiers"; in this case they were inhabitants of the Donets Basin. They went into battle without uniforms, dressed in their black everyday clothes, under the "protection of the blocking detachments behind them." The members of the Special Section called them "black jackets." These virtually untrained soldiers were even spotted at Kursk.

The phrase "has been under enemy occupation" became a humiliating qualification, as if the people in question were enemies. They were suspicious characters with whom you could do as you wished; their stigma could only be erased with blood. Was this a way of taking revenge, or was it premeditated murder? Or did the army have a shortage of men at that

---

100.1

64.1.64, 63

64.1.65

64.1.64; 232.1.35

37.1.21

349.1.162

426.1.16

100.1

426.1.16

time? Or was it a combination of all those elements? On 11 October 1943 the military council for the southern front gave orders for all new reinforcements to be investigated and "all politically dubious persons to be removed from the divisions" and, "after investigation," to "send them on to NKVD camps, place them in penal battalions, or let them go back to their units."

282.2.323

The Forcing of the Dnepr

In September 1943 the Russian armies stood before the Dnepr, which is difficult to cross from the east; the western banks are high and the eastern banks low.

Viktor Astafyev wrote several chilling pages on the crossing of the "Great River" at Velikie Krinitsy. As the day of the crossing approached, the agitation and propaganda moved into high gear and, with that, a great number of people suddenly had to go away on official business or had important tasks to fulfill elsewhere; others claimed they were nonswimmers or were sick. Many others had to organize conferences and meetings. In other words, they were "up to their neck in affairs that would tolerate no delay and which kept them far from the river and the approaching battle."

23.8.68

There were generally no pontoons or bridges. The soldiers had to "cross the river by self-devised means." There are photographs of the crossing: "hay or straw stuffed into a sack and then trust to luck, God help them. Others managed to build a raft."

2.1.206; 479

80.1.78

Thousands drowned before reaching the other side, and those who did make it arrived in another hell: continually under fire, herded together on a small bridgehead without sufficient food or munitions. Those caught up by the current and swept back to their own bank were chased back into the river by the blocking detachments that had hidden themselves in the reeds. Anyone in the river who had already been hit by these detachments was left to drift downriver. "Just let them see what we do with that scum, those cowards who confuse the left bank with the right."

23.8.102

23.9.61

The blocking detachments actually had the most modern weapons—which they used to chase their own people to their death—and they "will defend their cushy jobs more fiercely than the Germans do their trenches."

23.9.97; 60–61

According to Astafyev, some twenty thousand were killed, wounded, or drowned in this crossing. Russian officers also considered it a poorly prepared enterprise.

23.9.54

23.10.60

Although only one telephone line was working over the Dnepr, the head of the political section, Lazar Isaakovich, found it necessary to deliver a speech on that line, but they dragged him away. "I'll get you for this," he said furiously. Shortly afterward he stepped on a mine and died. He was buried with a great deal of pomp and circumstance, while on the other bank the dead were unceremoniously being tossed into mass graves with hooks.

23.10.75–76

23.10.133

"Insects, crows, and rats celebrated their sinister feast on the bank," said Astafyev. "Crows picked out the eyes of the drowned, gorging on human flesh, casually helping themselves to drifting corpses. On the bank, engineers walked back and forth, pushing the bodies into the water, hoping that civilians living along the banks would fish them out and bury them." "Next to and under some of the corpses rats had already taken the opportunity to bear their young and hide the tiny naked baby rats under rotting soldiers' clothes. Startled, the rats fiercely defended their nests and, screeching, attacked the men, who then bashed at them with spades and stones, stamped on them with their boots."

23.10.116

23.10.131

Did events progress in this way only at the crossing Astafyev witnessed? No. At a crossing over the Dnepr, eighteen kilometers south of Dnepropetrovsk, the following occurred: "What happened that night, it's hard to remember after forty years. There were roughly five hundred of us, one battalion, one machine gun, and one company of engineers. About twenty men got across the river swimming."

247.1.26–27

Liberation of Western Ukraine

The male population of Western Ukraine was "mobilized" mercilessly. The people were picked up and thrown into battle practically untrained. A considerable part of the reinforcements consisted of Western Ukrainians, and these "escorted regiments" were deployed in the most dangerous places. At the end of 1941 there were 3,185,000 Ukrainians in the Soviet army, and "from the beginning of liberation up to the end of the war almost four million Ukrainians were mobilized."

416.1.124

360.1.184

General Pyotr Grigorenko described how villages were surrounded, the villagers driven together, and "volunteers" requested for the Red Army. Anyone refusing had to explain why and that usually meant arrest. "No one went home a free man. All ended up as either 'volunteers' or as arrested enemies of the Soviet powers."

155.4.168

The army in which the Ukrainian Grigorenko served consisted largely of such "volunteers," "mobilized men," and "recuperated wounded." The military hospitals were informed of how many recuperating cases there should be and when they should be sent back to their units. Strict punishment awaited those doctors who failed to fulfill their appointed tasks. Fleeing was virtually impossible: roaming figures were targeted by the people of the "special section," and families of "deserters" were also punished.   155.4.168

"The lack of manpower was so tangible that the mobilization had, in reality, become a manhunt," says Grigorenko. The mortality among this contemptuously named *chornosvitki* (black jackets) was extremely high, noted A. Dovzhenko in his diary on 28 November 1943.   100.1

Yelena Romanova wrote: "There were all kinds among them: border soldiers surprised by the war, who had made it through the difficult years, some in cellars and woods, others as the husbands of local widows; very polite but suspicious 'Westerners,' who communicated little with strangers. People who had committed some misdemeanor and could not remain in their job, but had nevertheless decided not to flee abroad with the foreign soldiers, had become stuck here. People who had resisted being sent to Germany . . . the majority had lost their nearest and dearest over the years or even in the previous few days. . . . The political commissar with his new epaulettes and shiny boots parades up and down in front of the unshaven men in their ragged clothes and worn-out shoes, delivering a speech. He employs words and turns of phrase that the newspapers use, too, words all the other commissars and political chiefs have bandied about, words used in letters to us, words—incantations—with which we answered without thinking in our letters from the front—clichés, as you would say now. But our entire soul lay in those clichés and in those days all our souls were alike."   374.1.6

Near the Ukrainian city of Zhitomir, in 1943, the Soviet troops came across a large store of drink. They got drunk, and subsequently the Germans easily drove them out. It was not until almost the start of 1944 that Zhitomir was recaptured for the second time. "Our truck, a half-tonner, was bouncing over the bumps in the road, [when] something cracked under the wheels. We went up a road covered with sticky mud and in that mud lay bodies, compressed into gray slabs, and we drove over those corpses of our soldiers for ten or twenty kilometers. We all fell silent, and   23.11.5

then a believer among us started to pray in a trembling voice: 'Lord! Forgive the innocent people. And forgive us all, for we know not what we do.'"

Astafyev wrote about himself and about the bloody fighting: "I fell
down behind a little hill, where I was spattered with mud by the bullets
smashing in; I was splattered with flecks of gray matter and blue-black
flesh; it turned out I had sought cover behind a corpse. I wanted to wipe
the stinking spatters from my face and lips, but I dared not even spit in
case I gave myself away." Mud, snow, and cold was typical in the Car-
pathians. And battalions were forced to trudge two hundred kilometers
on foot. "Soldiers sometimes even fell asleep walking, only waking up
when they stumbled over uneven ground or bumped into their comrade
in front of them."

In the western part of Ukraine the Soviet troops also came across massive resistance from the local populace, plagued by one kind of military
or pseudo-military outfit after another. Some Polish units supported their
government in London; others supported the Communists. The Ukrainian Insurgent Army (UPA) was fighting the Germans and Russians; the
Organization of Ukrainian Nationalists (OUN) was fighting the Russian
partisans; and the infamous Galicia SS Division fought with the Germans
against everybody. The men following Stepan Bandera, the leader of the
OUN, were particularly active and dangerous. In Stanislav, wrote V. Kardin,
they occupied "the hospital for several hours, took bandages, medicines,
and instruments, and then disappeared again without harming a hair on
anybody's head."

For two months, Bandera worked on the side of the Germans, after
which he turned his army, then numbering 180,000 men, against both the
Germans and the Russians. The resistance in Western Ukraine lasted until
approximately 1952.

The villages received the Soviet troops in silence. There were hardly any
men there; the men were either dead or had been taken away by the Germans, the villagers said. In fact, many men had hidden in the woods. It
was "quiet" in these areas during the day; at night the enemy was murdered, especially newly installed heads of governmental organizations and
teachers. These eastern Ukrainians—originally from the Russian-speaking
part of Ukraine, beyond the Dnepr—were hated in the western part of
Ukraine.

The Soviet army was virtually powerless against these activities. According to Astafyev, this is what happened to villages suspected of nationalism:

"They surrounded a dozen villages and, at night, drove their inhabitants into trains standing ready, sometimes in such a haste that the villagers could take nothing with them. . . . If there was any shooting, they simply set fire to the villages, and, like cattle, to the accompaniment of desolate howling, children, women, and old people, sometimes men, too, were driven into the road, where they were loaded into trucks and onto carts and taken to a station, mostly to an unremarkable stop." 23.12.49, 40

How voluntary was the activity witnessed by Ivan Stadnyuk in the spring of 1944 in the Twenty-seventh Army? "To the left and right of us, women, teenagers, and old men walked past, up to their knees in mud. It seemed as if long chains of people stretched from horizon to horizon. They carried grenades, mines, and cartridge cases in the direction of the front in sacks, cloths bound onto their backs or simply in their arms." 416.1.131

The Soviet troops had to be constantly on the alert for ambushes. General Nikolay Vatutin was seriously wounded by a Bandera bullet. Only American penicillin could save him, but Stalin, fearing an American trap, denied him this, and Vatutin died. From January 1945 to at least 1947 71.3.16 the Thirty-eighth Army remained in the Carpathian Military District, fighting against the Ukrainian Insurgent Army and those who supported them. "Many UPA fighters had been trained in the Soviet army and were 188.4.131–32 fighting against their former regimental comrades." UPA fighters were not 188.6 considered prisoners of war and were either shot immediately or sent to the camps in Kolyma. 188.4.123

The territory in Western Ukraine was also extremely difficult to access in the spring of 1944. After every ten or fifteen steps in the mud you had remove kilos of black, sticky soil from your boots. And it was constant marching, never a sanitary stop. Men simply unbuttoned their flies and urinated while they walked; women "had to pee straight into their quilted trousers." 416.1.142–43

Konstantin Simonov describes the way the Russians advanced as follows: "Now, what is it that the ordinary infantryman does, one of the millions who walk along these roads, who . . . march forty kilometers a day . . . a submachine gun around his neck, his full kit on his back. He carries everything a soldier needs en route. People can get where no vehicles can, and, in addition to what he already has to carry, he also carries what should actually be driven. He marches under conditions that sometimes approach those of the cavemen; sometimes for days on end he can forget what fire is. The jacket of his uniform has not once been completely dry for a month, and he constantly feels that damp on his shoulders. When marching, sometimes he finds nowhere to rest for hours: all around him it is so muddy he sinks into it up to his knees. Sometimes he doesn't see a hot meal for days, because sometimes it is not only the trucks that are unable to get through but also the horses with the field kitchen. He has no tobacco, as the tobacco has gotten lost somewhere along the way. Every day, so many trials and tribulations mount up in a concentrated form that another will not experience in a lifetime. And, naturally, apart from that and above all, every day he is involved in bitter fighting, exposed to mortal danger."

400.3.375–76

After the war, entire village populations were banished: "They didn't mess around," says Kardin, "guilty or innocent, it was simply a boot in the backside and into the cattle truck." "The war was over, but soldiers now died from bullets fired in an ambush, from snipers, from mines hidden in the road."

188.4.152

188.4.134

Posters warned the Russians to go home if they did not wish to be killed by the UPA. "Brave Red Army soldiers! You have broken Hitler's neck. Now break Stalin's." Russian soldiers were forbidden to marry a Western Ukrainian. Such a marriage meant contact with a foreign country. Western Ukraine continued to resist until long after the war.

176.4.107

188.4.117

At this time Astafyev was serving in Western Ukraine and says that, of the various military and paramilitary organizations, Sidor Kovpak's partisans "had delivered an enormous, devastating blow to the German hinterland; they kept many German troops busy, forcing them to maintain large garrisons next to railway lines and bridges, in cities and at stations. I have seen the Kovel railway line, which was literally littered with railway carriages on both sides, with locomotives and military equipment." But all those partisans needed to eat, sleep, keep warm, have their laundry done, and so forth, "and like a thundercloud, an all-consuming cloud of locusts, the partisan troops—who naturally included all sorts—roamed through Western Ukraine. Our partisans did not, however, pay too much attention to what was 'mine,' 'someone else's,' or 'ours.' It was too much for the patience of the farmers, who had joined up with the already destroyed movement of the *samostyniki* [fighters for the independence of Ukraine] and took up arms. . . . The Kovpak heroes . . . looted, stole, and raped as before, ran the villages as they saw fit, judged and condemned those in Lemberg, which had once again become Lvov, in the area of Rovno, Kovno, Stanislav, and Uzhgorod, in all the western areas. It also caught on over the 'old border,' to the Soviet Ukraine, where a hidden, cruel war was taking place, to which there was, at that time, no end in sight."   23.14.54

Andrei Zubov believes that the enmity of the local population in Western Ukraine and the Baltic countries—caused by their experiences under the Soviet regime—contributed considerably to the collapse of the Soviet Union in 1990 and 1991.   500.1.76

7

The Advance to Berlin

After the German invasion of Russia, on 12 August 1941, Moscow decided not only to release all the Poles who had been taken prisoner or interned—391,575 people—but to form a Polish army on Russian soil. After all, Poland and the Soviet Union were now actually allies in the war against Germany. That army was to have six divisions, a total of ninety-six thousand men. This was General Wladislaw Anders's army, which already had approximately sixty thousand men on 1 March 1942. It soon proved, however, that these Poles were extremely anti-Soviet. Some said openly that, once they were at the front, they would turn against the Red Army. They also refused to acknowledge the annexation of the eastern Polish territories in 1939. Many Poles, Beria reported, traveled south on their own initiative in order to leave the Soviet Union as quickly as possible.

In the summer of 1942 the Polish government in London decided to evacuate its subjects via Persia, both soldiers and civilians. Tashkent was an intermediate stop for many Poles: shabby people with worn-out shoes, some barefoot, accompanied by sick, hungry children. Shortly afterward "soldiers appeared on the streets of Tashkent dressed in a smart uniform of English cut, with 'Poland' embroidered on the right sleeve," says Svetlana Davydyuk. At the end of 1942 the Poles left the country via Persia. A number of members of the military under the command of General Berling remained in the Soviet Union.

In May 1943 the first Polish division had been formed at Ryazan. Then in April 1944 a Polish military training school was set up there, where Polish citizens could join an army that was, indeed, prepared to fight on the Soviet side. At the time this army was established, it had many Russian

419.74

419.65–66

37.1.123

37.1.124

419.59

officers, and many of the personnel knew hardly any Polish. Later, several 233.1.159; 221.2.161
more divisions were formed. 37.1.135

As a result of the break between the Polish government in exile and Moscow—partly because of the massacre of Polish officers at Katyn—a Union of Polish Patriots was set up in Russia, which pushed for the formation of a Polish army with the aid of Soviet instructors.

On 26 March 1944, with the world watching, these Polish patriots pledged an oath to Russia in the little village of Staroletovo. Davydyuk 37.1.128
writes: "I swore allegiance to a country I had never seen and in a language I could not yet speak. Nevertheless, I saw no difference between Russians and Poles; we shared everything." And she was with them from Ryazan to Berlin and the Elbe.

In August 1944 the Red Army entered Poland. "All night long, columns drove with their full headlights on. The light from the headlamps tried to bore through a thick curtain of rain. Sometimes, in a bend in the road, the corner of a house was lit up or ruins in a border village. No light, not a living soul to be seen. Soaked to the skin, with wet overcoats, we drove until dawn. The mists parted grudgingly for us. We drove past Brest without stopping. We crossed the Bug by bridge. The little town of Terespol. Poland." In this way the troops marched over the river Bug into Poland, 386.2.67
sometimes with soldiers who had never seen a machine gun: "My soldiers were children of all nationalities: Ukrainians, Kirghizes, and Russians and there they underwent the baptism of fire." 92.2.234

At the Bug, others, such as Davydov, saw, "a dark sky, throbbing with purple streamers, slashed with tracer bullets. We trudge forward through the sucking mud of a country road, sinking up to our knees in the clinging, doughy soil. On the wet horizon, an enemy plane drones irritatingly, heavy drops of rain beat against your face, the wind smells of fire and stench." 92.1.37

Anatoli Rybakov recalled, "The roads were strewn with vehicles and groups of refugees, Germans and Poles—men in black and white caps milling around. Signposts at the side of the road, saying '500 kilometers to Berlin,' 'Roll on Berlin,' 'Onward, victory is at hand.' And German signposts that had not yet been removed. A crucifix by the road, a little further the pointed roof of a church. There are prisoners, liberated from German camps, Frenchmen with their little flags, in raggedy uniforms, unshaven, emaciated, pushing little carts containing their paltry possessions." 382.1.49

"The death factory at Majdanek, near Lublin, left a terrible impression in Poland," says I. M. Tsidilkovski. "When we entered Majdanek, the air was still permeated with the nauseating smell of burning." Simonov, who wrote the first article on Majdanek, says that the scene "wiped out everything that was in my memory before." He describes the camp, the ovens, the piles of little children's shoes, the administration lying spread over the ground, sees that there, in May 1943, Jakob Borghard, born in Rotterdam on 10 November 1918, was killed. The Russians forced thousands of German soldiers to see the camp and its horrors.

"I can remember," noted Rybakov, "how we liberated German concentration camps in Poland. Cheering triumphantly, the prisoners from other countries set off, free, for their Fatherland. And how the people from SMERSH registered our prisoners of war, emaciated, tortured, gloomy prisoners, interrogated them, drove them into trucks and sent them off to fresh investigations and interrogations; after all, according to Stalin, they were traitors. Finally, our NKVD boys had some real work."

In eastern Poland, the Soviet occupation ensured that the previously quarreling Poles and Ukrainians were now united against the Russians. The men they came across there, the *zapadniki* (Westerners), were given a brief training and then immediately signed up for the army. They were, says Astafyev, "half-farmers, half-Ukrainians, half-Poles, half-Hungarians, half-Bessarabians, half-Slovakians, and goodness knows what else," and most of them took to their heels at the first opportunity.

Poles were furious for being treated as White Russian; others refused to take the Russian oath, saying, "We don't want to betray our country."

In the former western territories, in particular, the resistance against the Russians was marked. This large area was plagued by all kinds of paramilitary units, each demanding their tribute from the people in succession.

From 6 to 8 February 1945 the NKVD executed a major operation against those units in the area around Baranovichi in White Russia. This "Plan for the liquidation of units of the Armia Krajowa [Home Army] in western White Russia" was primarily aimed at Poles supporting their government in London and devoting themselves to a "united, indivisible Poland" with the borders of 1939. Those in the Armia Krajowa said, "We are taking the reins of the resurrected state into our own hands, as no one can replace us in exercising the power in our Fatherland." An NKVD report declared that the NDK, the Polish National Democratic Party, "has appointed mayors and commandants without authorization, implemented

74.1.144

400.3.432
400.3.438–39

382.1.58–59

23.14.5

394.1.108

106.1.23

orders in the name of the expatriate government and the Supreme Command of the Armia Krajowa, and carried out propaganda against the activity of the Krajowa Rada Narodova [the Polish government formed by Moscow] and against the forming of the National Committee for the Liberation of Poland."

106.1.199

Armed resistance was detected in this area as early as August 1944. "It has been established that they [the National Democrats] are exercising influence on unstable soldiers of the Red Army, most of them from Western Ukraine. They are supplying them with civilian clothing to encourage them to desert and are offering them hiding places, in exchange for which they get weapons."

106.1.28

On 3 August 1944 Stalin already ordered units of the Armia Krajowa, "and other organizations including German agents, to be disarmed immediately on discovery, the officers interned, and the lower ranks taken to special reserve battalions and to Berling's Polish army."

106.1.16–17

Up to 15 July 1945 a total of 576 traitors to their country, 852 bandits, 206 counterrevolutionary elements, 139 members of the Armia Krajowa, 127 contact persons, and 1,728 gang collaborators were arrested on White Russian territory—all, of course, on the NKVD's terms.

106.1.25

Thus the Polish people did not exactly welcome the Russians. Kardin, reporting on the city of Stanislav, said that the people did not "understand" the Russian language, that soldiers received poor service in the shops, and so forth,

188.4.145

Tsidilkovski, on his way back to Slutsk in White Russia in August 1945, wrote that "the attitude of the Poles toward us was often openly hostile." In general, therefore, the Russians were not keen about being in Poland, and the Poles were happier about the Germans' retreat than the Russians' arrival. Although the Soviets were not exactly soft on any remaining Germans, I read a great deal of criticism by Russians about the way the Poles treated Germans—mostly women, children, and old people—molesting them, confiscating their possessions, and driving them out. In Torun, Grigori Pomerants saw German women sweeping the street, a particular kind of cloth sewn to their backs, "like the Germans forced the Jews to wear . . . why are we repeating cruelty that we ourselves considered to be something from the dark ages?" Some German refugees asked the Russians for help, which they received, in protecting them from Polish mistreatment. In Bromberg, Yelena Rzhevskaya noted, "The government decided not to feed the Germans. It still gives me the shivers years later."

74.1.146

349.1.155

383.4.13

"What I remember most clearly is the expulsion of the Germans from the areas to the east of the Oder," wrote Golitsyn. "We saw the way Polish soldiers would enter some little German village, go from house to house, giving the people twenty-four hours to gather their things together. Obediently, without a word of protest, without tears or pleas, the law-abiding Germans, women, old men, and children, efficiently got themselves ready, leaving almost all their possessions and livestock behind. Several roads met at the bridge over the Oder. Along those roads walked an endless tide of evicted Germans. There was a bottleneck of people on the bridge. And the Polish soldiers, armed with sticks, hurriedly drove the women on, screaming and swearing at them to quicken their pace, hitting them with sticks. . . . The Poles did not cross the bridge. Our soldiers were on the other side, and, there, liberation awaited the refugees. Some people were already sitting there; exhausted newcomers joined them. They understood that now they could catch their breath—and not only catch their breath but also drink and eat something. You only had to stand in the queue by the nearest field kitchen, and there were no fewer than ten field kitchens, 137.4.74 drawn by horses."

And with regard to the horses: captured German horses could not understand the Russian orders. "Tprrr" meant "whoa," and the animals failed to understand "nu, pashli" (giddy-up). According to Golitsyn, "The Russians didn't even know the magic words, the words you rarely see in 137.1.191 print, that always help to make a horse obey."

Although sexual contact with Polish women was strictly forbidden, of course it occurred—either out of love, because of poverty, or for money— 395.1.105, 109 and that applied to German women in Poland as well. In Poznan a Russian colonel wanted to shoot two men for raping a German. "But the colonel was behind the times. That had already been allowed on the way 383.4.59 to Germany." According to Kardin, confiscating food was seen as a mere trifle in Poland, "but when we get to Germany, then we'll give their Frau 188.4.136 what for. Blessed hate. Blessed revenge. How blessed are they?"

Warsaw

At the approach of Soviet troops in August 1944, an uprising against the Germans broke out in Warsaw. Although the Russians took the suburb of Praga on the eastern bank of the Vistula, they did not come to the aid of the rebels. Several battalions managed to cross the river, but they suffered heavy losses and were forced to retreat. Six Polish battalions, however, were successful in their crossing. Some members of the Russian military $_{179.1.103}$ were counting on coming to the aid of the rebels, but no order was issued to do so. Not until January 1945 was the utterly devastated city of Warsaw liberated. There were six divisions on the Russian side. In the words of Pomerants: "All day long we were ashamed to look each other in the eye. And the blatant lies! How did I manage to swallow those lies? I could never have done it myself. But we, our battalion, our army, swallowed them, and I with them." The Soviet army stood by and watched the SS $_{349.1.149}$ raze Warsaw to the ground. One Russian aviator, Captain Gorodetski, had escaped from a German camp, found himself in Warsaw with the rebels, and escaped from there, too, through the sewers, swimming over the Vistula, and then falling into the hands of SMERSH, "where they knocked me around to such an extent that I was no longer able to deny that I was planning to murder Stalin. . . . I signed a paper saying that I would not reveal anything about what I had seen in Warsaw." When Gorodetski later $_{410.1.233}$ recorded his experiences on paper, no publisher would touch it. $_{410.1.238}$

David Samoilov noted that the Soviet troops "spoke little and were unwilling to answer any questions about the uprising in Warsaw. The army was absolutely uninformed regarding the events taking place there." $_{386.2.71}$

Evidently Stalin wanted to teach the Poles a lesson and "show the rebels that they were shit, a zero, and that they only amounted to something when the Russians put a one in front." $_{349.1.149}$

The official Russian version is that the Polish government in London had intended the uprising to be a provocation, that the Soviet troops were tired and incapable of attacking, and that the Russians had not been informed in time of the plans for an uprising. $_{179.1.103}$

When the Russians entered Warsaw on 17 January 1945 "Warsaw was dead, silent, empty, the ruins covered in snow. Maybe someone saw the remains of his own house in those ruins? I don't know; no one felt like talking." $_{91.1.135}$

D. Zatonski later recalled some of the worst things about the war. One was "doing nothing at the Vistula when, on the other side of the river—within hand's reach!—SS troops were smothering the uprising of Warsaw in blood." A second grizzly event concerned "our tanks boring into crowds of refugees in East Prussia." $_{490.1.12}$

Another, Svetlana Davydyuk, wrote, "My worst memory of the war is the fear and humiliation in the eyes of children. I've seen it in the eyes of both our children and Polish children liberated from the camps; I've seen it in the eyes of German children, too." $_{91.1.143}$

East Prussia

Soviet troops approached the border of East Prussia, and, understandably, this stirred up all kinds of angry, vengeful feelings. Signs were set up on the border, saying, "Well, there it is, bloody Germany." And prompted, if not provoked, by the years of, bitter, slating articles that journalist Ilya Ehrenburg had written almost daily in the army newspaper *Red Star* against the German infiltrators, a fury of revenge and hate raged among the Soviets regarding East Prussia, which lay between Danzig (Gdansk) and Lithuania.

The reports and photographs of the liberated destruction camps in Poland, in particular, fanned the flames of fury to unprecedented heights.

Most places in East Prussia had already been deserted by the terrified population. Messages were chalked on the walls everywhere, saying, "Sieg oder Sibirien!" (Victory or Siberia!) and "Roter Tod geht" (Red death go home). Golitsyn wrote, "East Prussia was empty and all the people's fury because of the millions of murdered and tortured people, the burned cities and villages, a fury that refused to be contained by institutions or political organizations, was wreaked on these solid houses, on furniture made of walnut and oak, on railway carriages full of wood, on little apple trees, on the entire affluence of those who, for some unknown reason, wanted to conquer our country." A poem written at the time reflected that sentiment, "Learn what Russian fury means. / We are not in Paris; we are not Danes. / Turn pale with fear, Germany!"

The Germans resisted fiercely, and the fighting was unusually heavy. The Russian attack was initially planned for 20 January 1945, but at the request of the Western Allies, who felt threatened by the German Ardennes offensive, it was pushed ahead to 13 January 1945.

Before the troops reached the border, having any contact with German women was strictly forbidden, as that interfered with discipline. Catching a venereal disease was treated as willful mutilation.

Towns and villages were plundered and anything edible—of which there was plenty—was confiscated on the spot. "The nicest things were turkeys, piglets, preserved fruits, and jam. And an orgy of eating set in." Glassware, crystal, furniture, everything was smashed to smithereens. Golitsyn's engineers' battalion took wagons full of slaughtered chickens and beef.

Once the troops had crossed the state border, "the men were permitted to send one package home, the officers two. The higher one's rank, the fewer restrictions and the more possibilities of getting rich. 'Confiscated'

pianos were loaded into the trunks of Studebakers, on Lend Lease from
America, 'requisitioned' bidets went by plane," writes Kardin. This con- 188.3.8
fiscation was carried out mainly by the units that arrived after the front
soldiers, who were too busy fighting.

On the road the Russians saw men and women in carts and wagons
with flags, "Czechoslovakian, Polish, Dutch, and French. There were girls
on foot with big breasts and fat cheeks, enormous bundles on their backs
and on their chests." 137.4.57

Königsberg, a strong fort, fell only after weeks of unbelievably heavy
shelling. Any remaining German citizens—a fraction of the former population—were initially deprived of any food. Until the end of 1946 some
four thousand to five thousand Germans died every month. Many Ger- 143.1.172
mans were arrested, interned, and set to work for several years somewhere
in the Soviet Union (discussed below). Liberated Russian prisoners were
sent straight back into battle after a brief training. Golitsyn, on his own 127.9.130
initiative, took wandering Russian ex-prisoners of war into his engineers
unit and, later, took in seventy women and young girls, so the unit ended
up looking like a love company. 137.4.62

According to David Samoilov, the Russians' revenge could have been far
more horrifying had it not been for the Russian character. They were 386.2.93
happy to express themselves by "gaily destroying, burning, and generally
carrying on with a fierce determination, like Stepan Razin and Pugachov—
and that desire was continually fueled by slogans, by poems, and especially
by articles" about German atrocities. Someone had asked a newly liber- 386.3.304
ated farmer's wife in Ukraine what should be done with the Germans and
received this reply, "Be so good as not to touch their children and wives."
The future author Grigori Baklanov, who noted this down, commented
that "this magnanimity was the foundation of our victory." 28.1.10

Back to East Prussia: "The black ribbon of the road led past cars that
had been destroyed or burned out, alongside the bloated bodies of horses,
by wet, bullet ridden cushions spewing matted feathers onto the asphalt,
past abandoned bicycles and perambulators lying in the ditches at the side
of the road, past all the signs of a hasty flight, the remnants of a foreign,
unknown life," writes Grigori Simkin. 399.1.19

Heavy losses were suffered in East Prussia and Pomerania. In one
company, only seventeen men remained. "'No matter, you still have four
female snipers.' The day before the attack, reinforcements were sent. Never

having been under fire, they were terribly young and extremely old people with scared faces in new gray uniform jackets. . . . A gunnery bombardment started; they scattered at every explosion. They weren't soldiers yet. They went into the attack and every jack man of them was killed, as if in one salvo. An absolutely horrific spectacle. We could hardly expect a second lot of reinforcements," wrote the sniper Yevgenya Markova. "The officers wanted the sharpshooters to be able to ride on the wagons, but the drivers protested: the horses were also dead tired. But to tell the truth, those drivers didn't like us. They were convinced we were not up to anything serious, and they couldn't accept that those, in their opinion, self-satisfied, horribly healthy, shameless hussies were not after their exhausted horses. Sometimes a furious commandant ordered the drivers to take us on their wagons, but once they did, the drivers threw such abuse at us that we preferred to get off again."

All eyewitnesses tell of the white down feathers lying all over the street, the remains of the bedding on which the Soviet soldiers had cooled their anger. According to Pomerants: "Down is the sign of a pogrom, a sign of the complete freedom [to do as you wish], which dances, rapes, and burns. Beat the Germans to death. Take revenge. And then get the German women. That's how it is, the soldiers' victory celebration. And then roll out the barrel!"

With what pogrom had the war ended, Pomerants wondered: a relaxing of nerves, the anarchical national spirit, or wartime propaganda?

There are numerous accounts of rape of both old women and very young girls, as well as reports of the murder of civilians and soldiers who had already been captured. "At the end of the war I was amazed at how much lechery a hero who has come all the way from Stalingrad to Berlin can indulge in. And with what indifference everyone regards such lechery." According to Sergeant Anatoli Genatulin: "Petrified with fear, the German women did not resist; they obediently lay down with the Russian Ivan, the Cossack, the Bolshevik . . . as long as he did not kill her. The war distorted the human soul, sometimes deprived the eighteen-year-old boys of their youth and purity, I can certainly tell you about that." And Genatulin tells how one evening, at Wittenberg, he and three other soldiers, of whom only one had ever had sex with a woman, overwhelmed with curiosity and lust, went into a barn where terrified Germans were sleeping. First, he let a mature woman go, crying, "nein, nein," as her child started to cry. Then he grabbed hold of a young woman. He tried to

reassure her by constantly saying, "gut, gut." Then she became the victim
of his "experienced" comrade. "And then I heard something I have never
heard since, in all my life. I heard her parents crying." His three comrades
were killed just days later. What had they known? Love? No. "All they
had known was terrified refugees and the senseless overpowering of a
daughter of the overthrown enemy."   127.14

There was no end to the destruction. Towns and villages that had fallen
virtually unscathed into the hands of the Russians were subsequently
reduced to ashes by the units that came along later.   346.1.104

And then there was the looting. It was at that time, as I mentioned
earlier, that Stalin permitted members of the armed forces to send home
packages of goods—"bought" at the Voyentorg (military shop). This opportunity did not fall onto stony ground. True, a week later the order was
given in East Prussia that anyone caught looting or raping would be shot,
"but by that time the rear guard had moved in and they allowed themselves a few pleasures, despite any orders."   309.4.40

The second and third waves of soldiers, in particular, behaved bar-
barically. Apart from that, the infantry was unable to take a great deal of   127.11
booty with them in addition to watches, jewelry, and other small items.
Artillerists and drivers, not to mention officers, had better opportunities.   400.3.183
Kardin suspected that, by allowing the soldiers to take booty, Stalin was
seeking support from the men and also trying to get his hands on compromising material against higher-ranking officers and generals. Until   188.3.8
1947, army leader Vasili Chuykov had to warn against "banditry, robbery,
and rape of the civilian population."   393.2.94

On 21 January 1945 Rokossovski issued Order No. 006 in East Prussia,
which commanded that the Russian hate should direct itself against soldiers on the battlefield, not against civilians, and anyone guilty of looting
or rape would be shot on the spot.   394.1.80

Molotov maintained later that Stalin burst into a great rage when he
heard of the plundering, murder, and rape. "He called the commandants
together, banged his pipe on the table, and threatened to demote any commandant and have him court-matialed if his troops did not desist from
such scandalous behavior."   252.1.111

The future well-known author Lev Kopelev believed, incidentally, that
only a minority of the Russian military indulged in such excesses as described above. Major Kopelev, as an officer, protested against such exces-   212.1.23
sive conduct. On 5 April 1945, although wounded, he was removed from
the hospital, arrested, and locked up in a camp for three years, to which

another ten years were added in 1947 on the accusation of "bourgeois
humanism propaganda and sympathy with the enemy." He was not released until 1954.

101.1.116–17

From August 1946 on, Russian migrants were settled in East Prussia. The
remaining German population was transferred to the Soviet-occupied
area in Germany.

143.1.173

Ehrenburg

Ilya Ehrenburg visited East Prussia and reported on what he saw at the
Frunze military academy in Moscow on 21 March 1945. He said, for instance, "They drink themselves senseless, and, in their drunken state,
they rape women and set fire to houses." And further: "The culture of our
troops is base, and, as a result, our soldiers walk off with everything they
can get their hands on . . . needless destruction of property, food, livestock." In an editorial he wrote in his paper, *Red Star*, he is reputed to
have said, "Russians returning from forced labor look good. The girls are
well fed and well dressed. For our soldiers, our articles in the press about
the slavery of people deported to Germany are unconvincing." And he
added, moreover, that "the second echelon of the Red Army is reputedly
on the point of breaking up and collapsing; they are plundering, stealing
valuable possessions, and getting drunk, and they do not refrain from
'fraternizing' with German women." Count Einsiedel, a great-grandson of
Bismarck and vice president of the Comité Freies Deutschland (National
Committee for a Free Germany) set up in Russia by German officers who
had been taken prisoner, also returned with shocking tales from a visit to
East Prussia.

371.1.50–51

371.1.51

371.1.50

The sinister Viktor Abakumov—head of the dreaded SMERSH from
December 1942 and executed in 1953 together with Beria—reported Ehrenburg's comments on 29 March 1945 to Stalin, who subsequently made a
typical move. He commissioned Alexandrov, head of the agitation and
propaganda sector of the Central Committee, to write an article in *Pravda*
on 18 April 1945, entitled, "Comrade Ehrenburg Sees It Too Simply."
The article accused the writer of being bloodthirsty and making "provocative calls for revenge on peaceful inhabitants of Germany and spreading
erroneous propaganda of hate against the German people." This was not
correct behavior, as "Hitlers come and go, but the German people will
remain." Two birds with one stone: Ehrenburg's formidable authority had
been challenged—no one would print his articles until 10 May 1945—and

the Germans were given to understand that the excesses would not (any longer) be tolerated. Ehrenburg's motto, "Death to the Germans," would no longer apply, because now a distinction had to be made between Germans and Fascists.

Stalin hoped that this article would calm the German resistance, which was becoming increasingly fierce, but his hopes were in vain. The article did little to help the troops. The men, on hearing the article read to them, made remarks such as "go and read Ehrenburg . . . followed by general sounds of agreement." One soldier wrote to Ehrenburg from Austria, "My friends and I would like to ask you to see it 'too simply,' as before."

386.3.304

119.1.270

Order No. 0143 of 20 April 1945 also says much in this respect: "Ensure that the troops change their attitude toward the Germans concerning both prisoners of war and the civilian population and treat them better. Cruel treatment of Germans makes them fearful and encourages them to resist stubbornly and refuse to surrender. The civilian population, fearing revenge, is organizing into gangs. Such a situation is unfavorable to us. A more humane attitude toward the Germans will make our military operations in their territory easier and undoubtedly will decrease the Germans' resolve to defend themselves."

393.2.93

But even after the *Pravda* article, court-martials continued to convict soldiers and officers suspected of "civil humanism with regard to the conquered people."

386.2.91

Between the Oder and Berlin

"We drive through smart, clean toy villages, all alike as peas in a pod," wrote Anatoli Davydov. "Churches with pointed roofs and from every window hung clean towels and sheets—a sign of surrender. When we take a break, we are eager to stretch our legs. In the empty villages it still smells of the life that has just left it, although there is not a single inhabitant to be seen. They have all gone away, hidden themselves somewhere. Not a living soul in the cozy little houses. Coffeepots still warm on the stove, rows of pots of jam and preserved fruits in sideboards and cellars. A strange picture of health, cleanliness, and comfort in contrast to the empty reality. A soldier sits, glowing with health, on a gun carriage, dipping into stewed fruit, spitting out the pits, and swearing with relish."

92.1.41

"Along the highways, the trees have been pruned. Ruddy, brown spring mud. Houses on fire, crackling dryly, hot tiles tumbling down from the roofs. In the black sludge alongside the road, twisted skeletons of wagons, red cushions slashed open, swollen horse carcasses, white down under the wheels of heavy Studebakers. A pall of smoke and stench lies over the land, bitterly catching in the throat. An odd, dark purple, wet sky."

Vasili Grossman noted, "Enormous crowds on the roads. Prisoners of war of all nationalities: French, Belgian, Dutch, all heavily laden. Only the Americans are unburdened, even bareheaded, all they need is a drink. Some of them greet us, waving bottles. Along other roads flows the civil international of Europe. Women in trousers, all pushing perambulators full of things. An idiotic, cheerful chaos. Which way is east? Which way is west?"

"For the first twenty or thirty kilometers after the Oder we did not come across one peaceful inhabitant," recalled David Samoilov. "All of Germany was determined to escape from the terrible revenge they expected, from which there was no escape possible." According to Rybakov, the following was read aloud in all army units: "We must make it clear to everyone, it has nothing to do with sympathy for the Germans [but] we must not throw away the honorable image of the soldiers of the Red Army, which is not one of fascist rapists and looters." Genatulin was amazed. "What a people! It doesn't even stink in the toilet. The hole is covered with a lid. You can't stand on it with your feet; you have to sit down. There is a bag of paper next to you. Such a neat and tidy nation and look how much blood they have spilled."

According to Vladimir Nikolayev: "Our soldiers and officers who entered Germany and the Eastern European countries were swamped with a flood of new impressions. In a military hospital I lay with a young marine who had entered Germany from the sea. The war had failed to leave the impression on him that the German villages had. He, a farmer's son, could talk endlessly about what he had seen there." And Kardin reported: "Our soldiers, farmers' boys, were amazed when they saw the villages of Czechoslovakia, Poland, Germany, and Hungary at the end of the war. They could never have dreamed of such a level of agriculture. The question arose automatically: shouldn't we get rid of the kolkhozes after the war?" On the other hand, the affluence they came across also evoked feelings of anger, envy, and hate, which led to destruction.

There are many witnesses to the attitude expressed toward the German women. Sometimes—or usually?—it went hand in hand with violence, "the pistol as the language of love." Elsewhere there was talk of "elements of light force." "In Reichenbach," wrote Rybakov, "there were many lonely

92.1.41

157.1.170

386.2.87

382.1.50

127.9.149

315.1.56–57

188.3.33
394.1.198

349.1.158;
230.1.167

women and they were longing for male company as much as we desired women. Young, accessible, friendly, well-groomed, sweet-smelling Germans dressed in a 'foreign' style—in our scanty prewar Soviet time we had never seen women like these. And our officers and soldiers were young, healthy, manly, and attractive in their military uniforms. . . . 'Herr Lieutenant,' 'Herr Hauptmann,' 'Herr Major,' and even simply 'Herr Soldat' . . . Germans are keen on rank and position."

382.1.53–54

Boris Slutski writes that rape and looting were committed by members of the military who were able to move more freely than the fighting troops. The Viennese women, or so he claimed, surrendered themselves extremely easily to the victors.

407.2.54

In other places, brute force was used and women were sometimes taken by four or five men, one after another. "It is a known fact that, as the Soviet troops approached, German women took their own lives in droves, to save themselves from falling into the hands of the conquerors. And those who did fall into their hands have kept their silence for fifty years. It is not something to talk about in Germany."

349.1.157–58

247.1

In 1992 two German women published interviews of women raped at that time, and the picture this produced "contrasted sharply with the idealistic image of the soldier liberator from Treptowpark" in Berlin. Long after the war Helga Sander produced a film about, and with, raped German women. The film was also shown in Minsk. Women present at that showing denied that it had happened, "but when the female soldiers from the front were alone with me [the writer, Svetlana Alekseyevich], they told of things far worse than had been portrayed in the film. They were unwilling—and perhaps unable—to talk to a German about it."

265.1

13.4

Although sexual contact with German women was officially forbidden, not everyone complied. If brute force was used, a court-martial could step in: a German woman could get you five years, a Czech woman ten. A German woman once said to Plimak, interpreter for the Soviet army, "One man, two men, but so many? That's impossible." To which he replied: "Stay hidden for the next two or three days, if you can. Then the commandant will be in town."

349.1.158

346.1.100

Sometimes they spoke of "semi-prostitution," when women gave themselves in return for food. "In the months following the war this contact with women became part of army life, continually increasing until it caused an explosion of venereal disease," writes Viktor Kozlov.

230.1.168

In Poland and Germany discipline began to crumble toward the end of the war, as is shown in recently published reports by the political sector

of the army. In the Nineteenth Army, for example, there were reports of
an increase in venereal disease (14 April 1945), organized drinking sprees,
plundering and rape (also 14 April 1945), the discarding of uniforms and
"wholesale changing into civilian clothes" (12 April 1945), destruction of
household goods, and the like (8 April 1945).

394.1.209–12

At Sonnenburg (present-day Slonsk, near Kostrzyn in West Poland) a
German concentration camp was liberated. Lev Kukuyev wrote, "There
was a mountain, meters high, of bodies in which rigor mortis had not
yet set in. . . . The wounds were still bleeding, above the corpses hung a
warm cloud of steam. I had fought for several years, seen it all, but
now, for the first time, I saw human blood flowing like a stream from
under the mass of bodies into a rubbish pit. . . . The terrible news of the
new camp, one hundred kilometers from Berlin, quickly reached the regiments, the divisions, spreading throughout the entire army." After Babi
Yar, Katyn, Majdanek, and Auschwitz, it was quite understandable that the
Soviet troops were seized by an incredible, pent-up fury.

247.1.40–41

The merciless behavior of the Red Army toward the German civilian
population resulted in the resistance of the German troops becoming even
more dogged. Stalin therefore penned a letter to all officers and Communists, telling them to be more humane with the conquered people. "To
my absolute amazement," says Grigori Pomerants, "neither officers nor
Communists could give a damn about the letter from Stalin himself! It
would take more than Stalin to stop the army."

349.1.150

Berlin

On 16 April 1945 the definitive attack on Berlin was launched, with four
thousand tanks, twenty-three thousand pieces of artillery, and more than
four thousand planes. It started with heavy artillery fire on German positions in Seelow Heights.

"The artillery preparation began with salvos of Katyusha rockets. In
the entire war I had not heard such a barrage of artillery," wrote Sergeant
Farsobin. "There was a continual drone of rocket installations. The flam-
ing tails of reactive grenades, aimed at the enemy defense. It didn't look
as if anything could possibly survive on the other side."

463.229

Golitsyn noted, "The entire earth, black with smoke, was littered for
several kilometers with our tanks. Burned out, destroyed, and twisted. It
was there that the Germans had first used a new, terrible weapon, the

Faustpatrone. A tube propelled an enormous stream of fire of an unbelievable temperature for more than fifty meters and incinerated a tank within
seconds . . . a terrible slaughter took place in Seelow Heights. One tank went
down, another moved up, and then that one went down, too. . . . We suffered innumerable losses to take those heights." One general reported to   137.4.73
Zhukov that the Soviet advance was being held up by the Faustpatrone. The
marshal replied, "You will be telling your grandchildren about the Faustpatrone after the war, but now, you advance and attack, willy-nilly." Zhukov   332.1.17
even wanted to shoot an engineer as an "agent of enemy espionage" because
he had suggested welding metal shields onto the tanks, which would
afford them better protection but would delay the advance by several days.   120.1.153

According to Golitsyn, "exceptionally bitter fighting commenced as we
entered the last ten days of April. With neither soldiers nor noncommis-
sioned officers to spare, our Supreme Command threw new units into the
battle, one after another. Those that were killed were replaced by others.
We—and not the Allies—should occupy as much territory as possible, as
quickly as possible, and take Berlin! That's what Marshals Zhukov and
Konev called on us to do—Stalin had so ordered."   137.4.70–71
    Everything humanly possible was done to take possession of Berlin
before 1 May 1945. "There was more than enough foolishness and stupidity bordering on criminal activity in the final battle—the rivalry between
G. Zhukov and I. Konev in the capture of Berlin was blasphemous."   282.4.228

Ivan Konev's tanks were forty-five kilometers ahead of the Sixty-ninth
Army. Konev was ordered to retreat "and not spoil the show arranged   307.1.93
beforehand."   349.1.159
    Bitter street fighting: "a black firestorm . . . the roaring of fires drowned
out the sound of shots and explosions. Something collapsing in burning
houses; there was a crunching and a groaning, a waterfall of smoke and
sparks. A greasy, choking cloud of smoke lit up with purple fire. . . . And
the street, blanketed in smoke and flames, ringed with scorched trees . . .
from time to time, from out of the fire and the darkness, you could hear
heartrending human cries, hopeless, desperate. Already many years have
passed," wrote V. Mindlin in 1985, but "still now, I sometimes wake in the
night, and I seem to hear those cries, quaking in horror."   286.1.148

"Dusk. We approach the half-destroyed walls of the zoo. Pillars from the
city's railway. Many bodies, lying side by side, on top of one another, on

their backs or face down. Semi-congealed blood on the road, still red. It
has all just happened. A small SS unit was fighting here. Two twisted
machine guns by the pillars and fifteen bodies, including two dead women
in SS uniform."

400.3.762–63

Let us hear what Simonov has to say: "Siegesallee. Dead bodies, tangled
anti-aircraft artillery. So much destroyed anti-aircraft artillery, more here
than anywhere else. Overturned German trucks, wrecked tanks, German
and ours."

400.3.766

"3 May, a dusty, sunny day. Some of our armies that have taken Berlin are moving toward the city in various directions, throwing up incredible amounts of dust. Tanks, mounted artillery, Katyushas, thousands and
thousands of trucks, rolling artillery, heavy and light anti-tank guns, all
bumping along over bricks and rubble, marching infantry in an endless
army train. All either walking or driving into the city from all sides. Dazed
inhabitants stand in the ruined streets, at crossroads, looking, in defeat,
out of windows at it all advancing, rumbling, incredibly legion and
entirely infinite. I myself had the feeling that it was not simply divisions
and army corps advancing into Berlin but all of Russia passing through
in all directions. Columns of prisoners, blocking all the roads, coming the
other way."

400.3.768

Yuri Nikolayev was slightly less triumphant. "When, in 1945, after being
liberated from a camp (I, too, had been treated to their 'hospitality') I
arrived in Berlin and looked at the victors, bristling with medals, I suddenly discovered that there was something wrong with all these conquerors. . . . They had almost all lived under occupation, their parents had
been banished as kulaks, they had been prisoners of war or their parents
had experienced occupation or imprisonment or 'had rested in the encirclement of 1941.'"

314.1.220

Pomerants was ashamed of his people's conduct in Berlin: "Soldiers
drunk, officers drunk. Soldiers from the engineers battalion looking for
hidden drink in the bushes with mine detectors. They drink methyl alcohol and go blind. Their first words in the interrogation of prisoners are,
'*Ring, Uhr, Rad, Wein*' [Rings, watches, bikes, wine]."

349.1.158

Apart from the tanks and cannons, recalled Samoilov, on the road between
Warsaw and Berlin you could see a donkey, "calmly walking along in the
verge at the side of the road. An elderly Uzbek, wearing a hat like traditional headgear, a rifle over his shoulder, was dozing on the back of his
donkey as it made its way alongside the ditch. He was riding at his ease

toward Berlin . . . just such a contrast as the camels on which the Eighth
Army had come from the steppes of Stalingrad. Haughtily, sedately, they
swung their aristocratic heads from side to side. Their riders, with brown
cheekbones and slanted eyes, possessed the cruel indifference of Asia and
the desire for a ruthless invasion. This seemed more horrific to the Germans than the tanks. 'Die Kalmüken,' they called our Cossacks and Uzbeks,
not knowing the fate of the real 'Kalmüken.' What did they think of the
toothless smile and the avaricious breath of Asia, eager to prize open the
legs of Europe's maidens with their knees?"   386.2.86–87

As a war correspondent in Berlin, at the beginning of May, Vasili Grossman saw "a wounded German soldier sitting on a bench, his arm around
a girl, a nurse. They look at no one. For them, the world has ceased to
exist. When I walked past again an hour later, they were still sitting there
like that. They are happy."   157.1.174

Grossman also describes "a cold, rainy day, undoubtedly the day of the
fall of Germany, in smoke, among ruins, in flames, in the midst of hundreds of corpses lining the streets. Bodies, crushed by tanks, squeezed out
like tubes, almost all of them clutching grenades and automatic weapons
in their hands—killed in the fighting. Nearly all the dead wear brown
shirts—these are the activists from the Nazi Party, who were defending the
access to the Reichstag and the new Reichskanzlei."   157.1.171

Russian losses in and around Berlin were terribly heavy. Although officially the figure is said to be three hundred thousand casualties, author
Grigori Baklanov maintains that it is more likely five hundred thousand.   27.1.8
The day before the capitulation, more than one hundred thousand Rus-
sians were killed in street fighting. The actual number of casualties is not   141.1.24; 223.2.32
known. The troops blockading Berlin from the west to prevent the escape
of German troops breaking out lost thousands more in fighting, but the
Russian "artillerists, too, hacked at the furious, crazed Fascists with axes
and spades."   23.1

The military historian N. G. Pavlenko feels that the Berlin operation
was "one of the least successful attack operations" of the war. "Zhukov
himself admitted as much in discussions with me," he stated in 1991.   332.4.90

Much has been written about who was the first to plant the red flag on
the Reichstag. We know that many sections were given organized lengths
of red fabric. Officially the flag was planted by Yegorov, a Russian, and Kan-   260.1.117
taria, a Georgian, as Stalin had ordered. The man who actually planted the

flag is Alyosha Kovalyov, a Ukrainian, who kept silent about it for fifty years. Only then did he say, "They summoned me to the NKVD and said, 'Keep your mouth shut about it being you. It has to be as Stalin said.

489.11   And if you reveal the fact that you are on the photograph, you will be in trouble.'"

Even before the Reichstag was taken, incidentally, members of the mil-

311.1.134   itary had already been congratulated. Viktor Nekrasov wrote that there were as many as twenty groups wandering around with flags. And this he

309.4.52   heard, he says, from Yegorov and Kantaria themselves.

For the first few hours after the conquest, things were quiet. In the words of Ilya Krichevski, who also tells of the staging of the flag photograph, "It was, indeed, quiet. The victors, tired from the long battle, slept in the Reichstag. When we arrived at the Reichstag with the correspondent from our newspaper, in the early morning of 2 May, there was not a living soul to be seen. Later the pilgrimage to the Reichstag by other sections began, crowds of visitors writing their names on the walls and pillars. The famous scenes of the storming of the Reichstag were not shot until 3 May. The film directors and photo-correspondents, who had arrived too late, attempted to re-create what they had missed after the event. And why was that? Because another army had been designated for the taking of the Reichstag, and the correspondents, filmmakers, and artists were all gathered there, waiting for the historic events to take place. At the same time, our modest Third Army of storm troopers, which had been allotted a secondary role, suddenly came to the Reichstag and came to an abrupt halt, not knowing what to do. The Supreme Command had no choice but

236.1   to give them the order to start the storming." Here, too, Russian losses were heavy. "And they were all too tangible, because you had to squeeze his throat with your hands and then shoot him or stick a knife in him;

236.2   you were spattered with their blood."

David Samoilov wrote, "At the end of the battle of Berlin, perhaps our army did not realize it, but they felt the possibility of an ongoing campaign against Europe. A war with our current allies did not seem unlikely to my regimental comrades or to me. The military success, the feeling of victory and invincibility, the yet unquenched thirst for attack, all this

386.2.89   supported a sense of the possibility and feasibility of conquering Europe."

PART 3

Part

People and Systems

8

The People

Women in the War

The women living in the hinterland bore an extremely heavy burden during and after the war. They generally replaced the men at work, had to bring up the children and take care of older family members, suffered from shortages of virtually everything, and were plagued by hunger, cold and exhaustion.

How did they manage? "Through patience, the highest degree of self-sacrifice. Year in, year out, day in, day out, every night for the entire war and even longer."

331.1.146

I deal with these women in the hinterland in more detail in part 4; here I deal with women who were in the army or traveling with the army.

Hundreds of thousands of girls and women participated in the war in one way or another. Initially they joined up voluntarily; shortly afterward—still voluntarily—550,000 more were recruited by means of the Komsomol (Communist Youth Organization).

They reported to the mobilization centers, accompanied by their weeping mothers—"they were not weeping, they were howling." Their hair was cut short, and they were given a uniform, often much too big. The training was harsh, for both medical and military jobs.

13.2.63

They were taken away in freight trains. In the so-called reserve regiments, or training regiments, newly arrived sharpshooters were hungry and were truly put through the mill.

When the women finally arrived at the front, wrote Yelena Markova, "we were given a luxurious meal, a pan of soup made from dried vegetables and pork, and army bread. How delicious that soup was after our

frugal meals in the reserve regiment. The soup was so thick and so fill-
ing that you could stand the spoon up in the pan. Of course you ate every
last bit. I needn't say anything about the bread. Ration bread is quite different: thick, aromatic, not so dark and so dry you have to bite pieces off.
If you are hungry, you can keep a piece in your mouth for a really long
time, even that is enjoyable."

There were a total of eight hundred thousand women deployed and
trained for the most diverse functions and tasks: operating anti-aircraft
artillery, making telephone connections, taking care of military mail, and
picking up the wounded, which was extremely dangerous work that involved carrying the wounded off the battlefield on your back during fighting, delivering them to the first-aid post, and then going back into the
field. Women also worked as nurses at first-aid posts, field hospitals, or
evacuation hospitals in the hinterland; they worked as doctors, lawyers at
field court-martials, engineers, aviators, sharpshooters, political functionaries, sailors, drivers, traffic controllers, washerwomen, cooks, bakers, sabotage agents—which risked being called a German spy on returning from
your assignment, being asked "What took you so long?" They also worked
as railway officials and ordinary soldiers. Among the most dangerous non-
combatant categories were the female medical orderlies (*feldshers*) and the
sanitarka, the women who fetched the wounded from the battlefield.

Three air force regiments consisted of women; there were several
women's infantry regiments and separate schools for female sharpshooters.

In 1942 women were mobilized for the army, not for air defense but
for dangerous jobs in the engineers' battalion, such as laying connection
cables, laying mines, and building defenses.

Svetlana Alekseyevich collected statements from hundreds of women about
their experiences at the front. Her book is entitled, quite justifiably, *War
Has No Woman's Face* (1985). Below I quote mostly from her work.

"I was capable of anything then: sleeping next to a corpse, I shot, I've
seen blood, I remember very well that blood smells very strange in the
snow. . . . When I say it now, I feel terrible. But then I felt nothing. I was
capable of anything then."

A woman, whose family had been massacred, tortured and killed
German prisoners with pleasure. "I can't blame her for any of it," writes
Alekseyevich, "because my family was not burned."

A 45-mm antitank gun was operated by seven women in the battle of
Kursk. Five of the women were killed.

277.1.18

229.1.85–90

153.1.212;
115.1.132

13.5.207

13.5.207

13.5.203, 211

There was even a woman in a firing squad. Only one woman was shot
for desertion, because she had gone to look for her lover in another unit.   383.10.205–6

One nurse "saw so many amputated arms and legs that I could hardly
believe there were any whole men any longer. It seemed as if they had all
been wounded or killed."   13.2.70

A cook had this to say: "Sometimes there was no one left after the fighting. You cooked a pan of soup, and there was no one to give it to."   13.2.70

"Dirty, unkempt, we looked like pathetic little orphans. And we endured the eternal feeling of danger and the absolute impossibility of evad-
ing improper proposals from men under those circumstances." A baker   348.1.118
said: "As eighteen-year-old girls we lugged seventy-kilo sacks of flour
between two of us." "Many girls got chapped skin from the washing, from   13.2.76
the heavy loads, from the stress or eczema from the soap. Nevertheless,
a day or two's rest and then you had to start washing again." Men can   13.2.77
relieve themselves while marching; women had to let the urine run into
their padded trousers. Many women told Svetlana Alekseyevich that "it
was not as bad in battle as it was after the fighting, a woman alone day
and night among hundreds of men. And I mean our own men, those we
had rescued from the battle, dragged out of the fire."   13.4

And delousing with all those men around?   13.2.80

Captain Rabinovich instructed the "young patriots he had recruited on
how to worm military secrets out of a German officer in bed. . . . Inexperienced as they were, the women simply fell into the hands of the
police before they had a chance to carry out their assignment."   280.1.158

"A couple of years after the war I still couldn't get rid of the smell of
blood that had followed me for so long. When someone gave me a red
blouse . . . I couldn't wear it, because it was red. . . . I couldn't go into a
butcher's shop—my husband went for me."   13.2.89

"Someone is dying before your very eyes. You know it, and you can
see that there's nothing you can do to help him. You kiss him, stroke
him, say kind words, and then say good-bye to him. Those faces are still
engraved on my memory. I have forgotten no one; I can see them all [she
cries]."   13.2.89

The same woman on the celebration of Victory Day (9 May): "I wait
for that day and it scares me. I collect washing for a couple of months
and I iron all day long. I have to have something to do . . . and when we
meet one another, there are never enough handkerchiefs."   13.2.91

The soldiers came into contact mostly with nurses, who comforted
them, cheered them up, and gave them courage. The nurses brought a

touch of home into their harsh existence. It was hard, nerve-wracking work, and they were often very young girls. "At the time, those girls personified the image of the Fatherland for us, of home, of everything we went to defend in heavy, bloody fighting. . . . Sometimes the girls gave us their love. . . . There are no words for what that meant to us. You carried a kiss on your lips and then dying was no longer so bad," said Vyacheslav Kondratyev.

209.1

A member of the communications unit, Praskovia Petrovna Boitsovaya, wrote, "We seventeen-, eighteen-year-old girls accepted no privileges because of our youth or our sex. Personally I was permanently in a communications unit, among soldiers of all ages, with no mother or friend around. You had to watch every step you made, every word you spoke. I can count the number of times I was able to wash in a bathhouse on one of the fingers of one hand (in an earthen shelter, during a short pause in the fighting). Even in the summer, by a river, how can you bathe with men around?" She continued, "I can't remember even spending one night in a building in-between the fighting. You couldn't even stand up in the signals corps' earth shelter: water streamed in from the sides, mud sucked at your feet, a narrow strip of uniform fabric soaked in oil smoked day and night."

23.2

With eight hundred thousand women in the armed forces and male soldiers, in principle, never having leave—except in the event of serious injury—and with no brothels like they had in the German army, that's asking for problems. And problems arose. Not without reason did mothers warn their daughters, afraid they would get into trouble.

General Antipenko is reputed to have told the Czech historian B. Snajder that, in the summer of 1944, with the permission of the Supreme Command, two "rest homes" were set up for officers. The experiment was rapidly terminated, as those officers took the personnel—"There were plenty of suitors"—back to their units, "and new personnel were not recruited."

446.1.109

Well known are the reports, too numerous to mention, of female conscripts living with their commandant and, when he was killed, moving in with his successor. The commandant and the chief of the political department had first "choice."

247.1.79

"Everyone is scared to death of us *osobisty* [members of the "special section" charged with spying on their own soldiers]. . . . 'If you accept,' said a girl to her friend, 'then you can wave good-bye to army soup and eat chocolate, canned meat, and fruit.'"

293.1.64

Vasili Grossman quoted a rhyme:

One autumn night
The commandant called her
'Til the morning light
He called her his "daughter"
Now one night to another
She lies with his brothers.

156.4.42

Sometimes women acted as maids or housekeepers for the officers. Some generals, like Grigorenko, were accompanied by their own wife later in the war.

155.4.172

At some point many girls went to the hinterland on "sick leave" to give birth. Getting pregnant, of course, was one way to avoid the front. Some mothers even encouraged their daughters to do so. Officially pregnancy was seen as "willful mutilation" and was punished in exactly the same way that people were punished who mutilated themselves to avoid service. Women also deliberately sought a protector in order to evade the approaches of other men, as Kondratyev writes in his novella, *Sashka*.

209.21

A war woman like that was referred to as a PPZJ (a march-and-crusade woman).

Ordinary soldiers had to make do with brief encounters. Many soldiers acquired a pen pal (*zaochnitsa*) who cheered them up, sent them packages, and sometimes claimed a "monetary attestation": if you were in service, you could have part of your salary paid to someone else for six or twelve months.

250.1.114

Bykov writes that the soldiers were generally too tired and exhausted for sex, and often too young as well, because, according to him, the infantry consisted largely of seventeen and eighteen year olds. Snajder also quotes Viktor Nekrasov: "Officers lived with nurses and communications personnel; there was nothing left for the ordinary soldier but masturbation."

446.1.108–9

446.1.109

Raya was standing watch, when she was overpowered by a tank mechanic. She was given three days' arrest, and he got nothing, to which he said, "There is no rule saying it is forbidden to fuck sentries." One evening Sergeant B. visited Raiska, who never refused. He said, "I love you." She replied, "Stop that. Do you think I don't know you draw lots to see who can come to me? Look, it's all right with me, I mean, I feel sorry for all you poor saps."

229.1.185

363.1.93–94

Konstantin Simonov was later heavily criticized for one of his poems about these brief encounters:

For those who must back to the fighting
And have only but glimpsed love's charms
Death is perhaps much less frightening
When he remembers one night in her arms

22.1.175

The telephonist Miturich was seen as "odd." She made no distinction between the men: "When someone came to call for her, then she went with him, she didn't refuse, she expressed no preference or dissatisfaction; they were all alike to her." Lieutenant Lyova Rubinstein was alone with her for half an hour. His commandant had arranged this meeting for him without the latter's knowledge, as motivation. Later Miturich said, "He could not say, 'Take your pants off,' and I could not do it without being asked."

380.1.25

Elsewhere, two cooks slept with all the officers in turn. "The two women were mildly contemptuous of them."

407.3.51

Another woman said, "Love? What kind of love is it when your arms are steeped in blood to the elbows? Other people's and your own. I've had enough of that kind of love. If he wants to sleep with me, well . . . but love?"

380.1.40

And still elsewhere, three scouts employed "corrective measures" to "persuade" a SMERSH major who was pestering a girl to change his ways. He was beaten up and, shortly afterward, transferred.

353.1

Men returning from the war were heroes. The women and girls received no such honors.

After the war civilians—and particularly wives—regarded women who had served in the war with suspicion. What did our husbands do with them? And what did they do with our husbands? Jealousy, made worse by the terrible excess of women after the war.

The other side of this coin can be seen, for example, in a village where only one man remained. Maria Belaya, an eyewitness, wrote, "He got married every week. Celebrated the wedding, lived with her for a week, and then went on to another woman. The women did not argue over him; everything progressed quite calmly. It was only his first wife who spat on the ground in fury and chased him into the bathroom after every wedding." One village woman complained of men after the war: "They

31.1

couldn't care less now—they can do as they like. There are so few men
left after the war." 204.1.45

The authorities gave demobilized women little support in choosing a
profession or finding accommodations.

After the war one nurse, who had donated blood thirty-two times, lived
in a "windowless room, 4.5 square meters . . . I could only start cooking
after two other families had finished. . . . That went on until 1962." 388.1.156

When Ksenia Osadchaya came home after the war, she was so changed
that her mother did not recognize her. 13.2.65

If you came back from the war and tried to find a husband, "even your
own sisters were jealous, not to mention the neighbors in the communal
house." 13.1.16

T. Umyagina, married to a soldier in the war, returned home. Her par-
ents-in-law turned to their son and said: "'Who have you gone and married? A girl from the front! You have two young sisters. Who will want to
marry them now?' . . . They destroyed all my photographs from the front." 13.2.90

Girls who had not been at the front defended themselves. "What do
you expect? Go to the front, become someone's possession, and come
back with a big belly." 209.20.14–15

Girls with a child—and no husband—certainly had a hard time because
of a lack of sympathy, the housing shortage, and lack of attention.

The medal for military service often awarded to women was certainly
not very highly respected and was mockingly referred to as the medal for
sexual services. 408.1

Viktor Astafyev, who was generally cynical about the war, wrote with
understanding and sympathy:"I swear that half, if not more, of our girls
bear their over-ripe innocence like a lead weight. After all, they are not
made of stone; they want love, but that despised flesh enslaves them. They
suffer patiently, but they wantonly spout dirty limericks. Some satisfy
themselves with masturbation, others occupy themselves with a lesbian
relationship. . . . You don't know anything, and you don't need to know.
And don't let our people know everything about the war. Better for the
mind; purer for the body." 23.18.21

Astafyev feels that a memorial should be erected to the hospital sisters,
"not only because they cleansed you of dirt, pus, and lice but also because
they helped you to become men." 23.18.20

Films and books about the war falsely portray the women who were
in the war. They are pictured in a respectable dress and a soldier's hat,
neat and clean. This was nothing like the reality of filth and mud. "Not

until the end of the war were we given dresses as smart clothes. Then we were given flannel underwear as well, instead of men's stuff. We were as 13.2.68   happy as can be; we unbuttoned our blouses to show off."

Jews in the War

German behavior toward the Jews in the occupied areas defies all description. Special Einsatzgruppen operated behind the front troops, executing Jews wherever they found them.

Ghettos were set up in Odessa, Minsk, and Vilnius (Wilno) (with the cooperation of elements of the local population), to name but a few places. After robbery, hunger and mistreatment, the end was always death, a miserable death.

Vasili Grossman described the massacre of Jews and of his family in 159.6   Berdichev. I stopped reading after a few pages.

An accurately maintained, virtually day by day report of the herding together and ultimate destruction of the Jewish population in Wilno was recently discovered there, hidden under a roof. It was first published in Dutch, *De Joden van Wilno* (The Jews of Wilno), and subsequently translated into Lithuanian; several copies were given to every secondary school in the country. This moving account, also translated into German, Russian, and Italian, is, like Grossman's tale, almost too terrible to read.

In 1984 people who had dug up Jewish bodies and robbed them of gold teeth and the like were tried in court. This case gave other people the idea, 486.1.6   so more treasure hunters appeared: "They're digging again, the bastards."

In Kharkov, behind the tractor factory, twenty-eight thousand Jews 407.2.48   were murdered. In the area of Odessa German colonists murdered their 406.1.164   Jewish neighbors.

On 24 September 1941 powerful remote-controlled explosions destroyed 940 large buildings in the center of Kiev, leaving the German occupiers with heavy losses. As a result, although the Germans, incidentally, needed no pretext to wipe out the Jewish population, on 29 and 30 September 1941, just outside Kiev, in a gorge known as Babi Yar, thirty-three thousand of Kiev's Jewish inhabitants were cold-bloodedly murdered.

The possessions of the murdered Jews were confiscated and offered to 407.4.155–56   civilians in Kiev or elsewhere in exchange for food. One woman from a block of flats where Aleksandr Zhuk's aunt had once lived said to friends of hers: "'Here, take this, absolutely new Jewish things. Hardly been worn. . . . The Jews knew what to make underwear from . . . this is Lenochka's, a really smart girl she was, such a funny happy girl on our block. There were a lot of good Jews. Don't worry, it's all clean linen. I knew them all well. Now there are none of them left, they've all been destroyed.' And it was impossible to tell whether she was expressing sympathy for the murdered people or indifference." 506.1.173

In August 1943 the German occupiers had the corpses at Babi Yar exhumed and burned. How many people, and not only Jews, were murdered in Babi Yar? Was it seventy thousand? Was it even more? What is certain is that when Kiev was liberated on 7 November 1943 only a few Jewish inhabitants were found there. 416.1.113–15

71.3.16

In 1990 Arkadi Elyashevich wrote: "A deep gorge where one hundred thousand were destroyed in three days' time, they filled it with earth. . . . Every year on 29 September—after the war, of course—people came to the gorge. They walked over a piece of barren ground, crying, casting flowers left and right; they knelt, kissed the earth, and took a handful of dirt away with them. And even on the twenty-fifth anniversary, no one took the trouble to meet them, to comfort or support them. A new asphalt road has been built over the gorge; blocks of high-rise flats have appeared all around. There is long since nothing left of the past." At times the militia has even stopped people from going to Babi Yar. In addition to the slaughter in Babi Yar, in Ukraine there were "more than 630 places where Jews were executed en masse." 107.1.199

49

227.1.21

Some Ukrainians helped Jews to escape or to go into hiding. This is documented in letters to *Ogonyok* (illustrated Soviet weekly) from M. G. Mindlina, B. Volfson, and D. Szonyi, director of the Jewish Foundation for Christian Rescuers (New York), which describe "tens of thousands of Soviet citizens who risked their lives to help Jews." Unfortunately, of course, there are also numerous accounts by survivors concerning Ukrainians who swore at them, threatened to turn them in, refused any help, and took their belongings from them. Others pretended not to know their Jewish neighbors in the street; former Communists also supported the persecution of the Jews. 287.1.4

482.1; 431.1

406.1.159

Vasili Grossman devoted paragraph 18 of his magnum opus to a Jewish ghetto, where the Jews were first robbed of everything and then killed. 157.2.38–44

In 1942 Naum Korzhavin overheard someone say, "When the Germans come, we'll show you a thing or two!" Gerschelman recalled that when he 221.3.129

returned to occupied Kiev a woman who was his neighbor said, "'Hey, Jew, come for your rubbish? It's at the Gestapo's,' and she shouted to a boy in the courtyard to go to the Germans and get them to come and fetch

407.4.155   the Jew." And others cried, "Get the Jew!" The son of an aunt, with whom Gerschelman, fleeing, sought refuge in Kharkov, said, "Get out of here,

407.4.156   Jew. I'll give you thirty minutes and then I'm going to the police." He finally found shelter with farmers, where he hid as a "newlywed" (*primak*). "There were a lot of such *primaki* in Ukraine: encircled Russians, those fortunate enough to have escaped from camps, sometimes high-ranking officers, very occasionally Jews. A close-knit group, they were part of the everyday life of the Ukrainian village. The Ukrainian police were afraid of

407.4.157   coming into contact with them."

In July 1941 one woman overheard someone say in a train, "Why should we Russians suffer because of the Jews; after all, the Germans are going

372.1   to destroy you, aren't they?" The wife of the writer Perets Markish, evacuated to Uzbekistan, wanted to buy bread for her children, who were, incidentally, being bullied by other children in a sanatorium. "We don't

172.1.99–100   sell to Jews. The war is your fault!"

Evacuated Jews were not called up for military service until 1943 and

349.1.151   were therefore given the cold shoulder. "Jews were fleeing for safety, leav-

221.1.153   ing us to fight for them." Evacuees were generally received with mixed feelings.

It was impossible to stamp out the false supposition, "I suppose your

221.1.159   Daddy has got a million stashed away in his case?" Nevertheless Korzhavin, too, denies that he came across any "real anti-Semitism." Yelena Bonner feels differently; she writes of the war: "I survived it and became Jewish . . . in the outburst of military anti-Semitism . . . with the crude officers' anecdotes and stories that the Jews were conducting the war in

50.1   Tashkent."

According to Tsidilkovski, some people claimed that Jews were attempting to avoid service at the front and that the Jewish victims of the Ger-

74.1.142   mans had let themselves be led like lambs to the slaughter. "That is a malicious lie," he writes, in view of the Jewish resistance groups and the uprisings in the ghettos. But, as a soldier, he claimed not to have come across any anti-Semitism. Contradictory messages, in other words.

In the army, and certainly in the army in the field, there was (supposedly) little or no anti-Semitism:

—Are you Russian, Lieutenant?
—No, I'm a Jew.
—You don't look or act like one.   380.1.42

Lieutenant Rubinstein refused a quartermaster's training he was offered
in the hinterland. "They would all say: that Jew has found himself a cushy
job, run away from the front, but we Orthodox have to take revenge on
the Germans for you and die here." According to Yuri Levitanski, the   380.1.42
anti-Semitism only began to raise its head in 1943, as a result of German
propaganda in Ukraine, and it was strongly reinforced when the Red Army
entered Europe. It is not clear to him why.   262.172–73

There were relatively few Jews in the infantry, which led to "passive
anti-Semitism," according to Boris Slutski. He continues: "Toward the end
of the war Jews already constituted a considerable section of the artillery,
the engineers, and other technical units, as well as in espionage and, to a
lesser degree, in the tank sections . . . but few Jews were in the infantry.
This was because of their high level of education and the fact that, from
1943 on, the infantry contained mostly farmers from areas liberated from
the Germans—areas where the Jews had been completely wiped out."   407.4.153

Approximately half a million Jewish citizens participated in the war.
Slutski writes that Jewish soldiers often tried "to compensate, with their
own self-sacrifice, for the absence at the front line of their cowardly com-
patriots," evidently believing that Jews had been too scarce at the front.   407.4.153

The virtually global anti-Semitism was founded partly on intolerance
and enmity toward emancipated groups, toward "newcomers," particularly
when they were generally better educated. In the words of the historian
Mikhail Koval:"Many Jews, particularly the younger generation, had every
reason to exhibit feelings of gratitude and even dependence toward the
Soviet government. After all, the Soviets had freed them from isolation,
given them equal rights with non-Jews, and opened the doors wide for
every Jew's ideal—education. The Jews were aware of what they owed the
Soviet state and strove to repay that debt honestly by working, not only
in the economic and cultural spheres but also by serving in the army
and the organs of state security."   227.1.17

During the war, a virulent nationalism emerged, stimulated from above,
that placed the Russians and all that was Russian at the fore. The "national
minorities," who were often unaccustomed to modern technology and
the harsh climate, were, as a rule, compared to the Russians. The Russian

soldier at the front saw that it was the Slavic peoples of the Soviet Union, in particular, who fought and were used to military work. According to Slutski, the war caused an outburst of chauvinism: Russians against Poles, Estonians, Lithuanians, Moldavians, and Kalmyks; and commandants and political officials encouraged the chauvinism. He adds: But at the lowest level there was no animosity, only friendly teasing, and "the foreign campaign contributed to a unification of the nations." Here again, contradictory messages.

In 1940 Yelena Rzhevskaya, the military interpreter quoted earlier, heard that Jewish female translators were not being sent abroad and that they had even been fired from the Peoples Commissar for Foreign Affairs. "I thought: Soviet fraternization with the Germans has already gone that far."

At the beginning of the war Stalin had already conceived of the idea of an anti-Jewish campaign.

In the summer of 1942 Aleksandr Shcherbakov, chief of propaganda for the Red Army, drew up lists of "non-Russians in art and culture" and "non-Russian people" in music criticism. On 17 August 1942 an associated resolution was adopted.

In the spring of 1943, at a meeting in Moscow, it was decided that too many Jews were working for the magazine *Literatura i iskusstvo* (Literature and art). The result was an article entitled "Concerning the Russian National Pride" (10 April), in which such phrases appear as "people who have lost their own soil" and "slavish toadying to things foreign." Thus, just after the victory at Stalingrad, the persecution of "cosmopolitans" began.

There was a secret instruction, for example, that Jews could not be given promotion in the media. Further, in 1943, Jewish names were removed from the editorial team of a medical journal. As one member of the Academy of Medical Sciences said about that period after the war, "There is a resolution to reduce the number of Jews in editorial positions. You see, Hitler drops leaflets pointing out that there are Jews all over the Soviet Union and that the culture of the Russian people is therefore diminished."

Tsidilkovski, who had been raised and educated as a Jew, spoke Yiddish and had met with great difficulty in trying to register his language as "Yiddish" when he joined the Communist Party in 1943. According to him, a report by Georgi Malenkov, Politburo candidate member, "at a Plenary

Session of the Central Committee at the beginning of 1944 . . . stressed
the necessity for a special, cautious attitude regarding the Jewish nationality in the USSR."

After the war Jews repeatedly faced resistance and opposition by the
authorities, whether in their efforts to find a suitable job or to enroll in a
university. Tsidilkovski was shown the door at all higher-educational institutions, and he finally became a bicycle repairman. Yelena Rzhevskaya,   74.1.147–48
who graduated in 1948 from the Literature Institute, also experienced
great difficulties. Kardin was asked in 1945 whether "he was aware that a
secret resolution had been passed by the Central Committee in 1944 that
prohibited people of a series of undesirable nationalities from obtaining
membership in the party." Jewish authors who were arrested were said   188.4.141
either not to have fought in the war or to have deserted.   56.1

That Jewish issues were being hushed up became apparent with the
reporting on Babi Yar. Initial reports indicated that the victims were Jewish, but later, from 1943 on, that was no longer mentioned. Reports on the
Jewish ghettos also disappeared. Only Ilya Ehrenburg continued to write
about the ghettos. The original text written by the committee responsible
for registering war crimes and war damage regarding Babi Yar were
altered. The words "of the Jewish population," in the sentence "The Hitler
bandits carried out a mass destruction of the Jewish population," were
changed; the massacre was now apparently carried out against "thousands
of peaceful Soviet citizens." This revision was agreed on only after a great   42.2.192
deal of deliberation and compromise, in which, incidentally, Aleksandrov,
Molotov, and Khrushchev all participated. Reports on the liberation of
Auschwitz were similarly altered. Here the victims were "Slavic peoples";
the word *Jew* or *Jewish* was mentioned in one sentence regarding "a Jew-
ess from Greece."   42.2.199

Only in 1978 were the Russians able to read in just one sentence in
Rybakov's novel, *The Heavy Sand*, that six million Jews were murdered in
the war.   264.1.185

Prisoners of War

In the first few months of the war millions of Soviet soldiers were taken
prisoner. The exact number is disputed; estimations vary from 3.8 million
to 5.7 million. Equally unclear is the number of fatalities among them.
German figures record 2.8 million deceased prisoners of war.   282.2.357–58

The prisoners were first herded together into fields cordoned off with barbed wire and then into barns, schools, stadiums, and churches, under little surveillance. Deprived of food and drink, their treatment was clearly inhumane. They arrived at their destination, along with the sick and wounded, only after long, exhausting marches. Those who could not keep up were shot.

These were no isolated incidents; the policy was clearly aimed at killing as many Soviet soldiers as possible. On 8 July 1941 Hitler ordered the killing of Jews and Communists, and on 17 July 1941 the Gestapo ordered that all prisoners of war who might be dangerous be killed.

As soon as the prisoners had been placed in a camp, Jews, Communists, and political commissars were singled out and shot. Aleksandr Zhuk, a Jew, was initially to be shot, but, because of heavy protest, he managed to avoid that fate. He ultimately fled to Kiev. There he heard people address one another as "Mr." and "Dear Sir," instead of "Citizen" or "Comrade."

That the Soviet government had not signed any international agreements concerning the treatment of prisoners of war and no modus vivendi was found for them during the war did not, of course, give the Germans carte blanche to treat Soviet prisoners inhumanely. It did enable the Soviet government, however, not to recognize prisoners of war, to brand them as traitors and defectors, and not to lift a finger to help them.

"Unfortunately a large number of Soviet soldiers and officers who had been taken prisoner ended up collaborating with the enemy." The total number who did so in 1944, including Vlasov's Russian Liberation Army, was 1.2 to 1.6 million men.

Initially women were allowed to fetch their husbands and family members from the primitive camps, and new village chiefs could reclaim their villagers. This applied to Ukrainians but not to Russians. Up to the end of January 1943, as many as 280,108 prisoners of war were released in this way, including 270,095 Ukrainians, in an apparent effort to placate the Ukrainians.

Anyone wishing to work in "labor battalions" or volunteering (!) to go to Germany as an Ostarbeiter (worker from the East) was also released.

Some of the Ukrainians were given papers to prove that they had been released from a German prisoner-of-war camp. They had to fill in their own names. In the camp where Zhuk was being held, those who had taken a nationalistic stance were given bread. If a prisoner had no mess tin, he was given soup in his hat. Zhuk writes that higher-ranking officers were looked after and "were even given food."

At the end of 1941, when the Blitzkrieg had failed, the Russian prisoners of war appear to have been treated better. After all, there was now insufficient manpower. From May 1942 on, political commissars were not killed immediately but were deported to the Mauthausen camp.   282.2.360

Numerous camps were established, and each name evokes a more terrible image than the last, that of hunger, cold, neglect, sickness, dampness, trigger-happy guards, barbed wire, and men with machine guns in watchtowers.

Infamous were the camps in Rzhev, the Millerovo Pit, Zhitomir, Smolensk, Salaspils (where people held out for no more than two or three weeks under the watch of inhuman Ukrainian guards), Uman, the village of Volosovo (where six thousand men were killed), Riga, Kaunas ("no sooner were the gates of the camp open than the SS charged at the thick crowd of prisoners, shouting inhuman cries and killing them"), Vyazma, Klin, Shaulyai (nine camps here alone), Sumy, and the village of Rozhdestvenno. It was in this latter camp where the Tatar author Musa Dzhalil was a prisoner; "he was forcibly recruited into the Tatar legion, where he formed an illegal patriotic group, was unmasked, and then executed." Equally numerous are the reports that Russian prisoners of war were found murdered in large numbers during the later Russian advance westward. On 23 November 1942, at Stalingrad, Soviet troops found "a pit filled to the brim with the bodies of their comrades."   308.1 9.8.1 27.1.172 183.1.254 27.1.173 37.1.7 11.2.63

It has been shown that in later years, in some places, things progressed more humanely. A. Lysenko writes that the Germans who were then in Ukraine allowed the local population to give prisoners food parcels, which were collected by the church, by teachers, and by village heads. Reputedly these parcels amounted to thousands of tons of food. In *Ogonyok* Aleksandr Afanasyev wrote that older German guards exchanged food with prisoners, that there was some degree of medical care, and that in "Belgorod there was an entire hall full of our soldiers with bullet wounds, recuperating on double rations—one from the commandant and one from the mayor—who cried 'hurrah' as our fighter planes shot down a German plane in flames above the city."   270.1.48; 6.1.38 6.1.38

A Jewish GPU agent, Lotaryev, a member of SMERSH, ended up in the concentration camp in Lamsdorf (present-day Tambinowice, near Opole in South Poland). He managed to stay alive by acting as the compere for a Russian orchestra for prisoners of war from other countries and in other barracks, in exchange for food. The orchestra was led by another Jew,

Ginzburg, who passed himself off as a Russian German. One poem he performed went like this:

> Behind the towers of the Kremlin stands a building
> Red stars shine from it
> Let all aggressors remember
> Where it stands, where that building stands.

269.1.146

The camp at Rzhev was hell on earth—twenty thousand men all crammed together into one square kilometer, the sick next to the wounded and the dead, all mixed up. They left the camp during the day to build German fortifications. Hundreds were buried every morning, even as early as 1941. Yelena Rzhevskaya writes, "It was a sinister situation. The prisoners all knew they would die of hunger, suffer unimaginably, and yet they did not go to Vlasov or join the politsay (the police force recruited from the local population). . . . Death by torture and humiliation approached rapidly. Above all, bloody diarrhea and typhus took Russia's sons."

232.1.26

383.1.20

The guards would throw frozen potatoes onto the ground "and then, laughing and shooting automatic weapons, they watched living skeletons fall on the potatoes and eat them raw. More victims."

383.1.20

Kondratyev, the chronicler of Rzhev, based his book *Borka's Road* on this camp; it is an account of an observer who has been taken prisoner. On the way to the camp Borka sees how villagers throw food to the soldiers as they trudge past, even though it is strictly forbidden. "Boys," one of the prisoners, an older man, says, "if we are still alive when the war is over, then we should get down on our knees for every farmer's wife and thank her. After all, what would we have done without them?" Kondratyev describes the selection process in the camp: first Jews, then Communists; a third group consisting of officers, and a fourth Ukrainians. "The Ukrainians form volunteer units. They are given German rations and German uniforms—they found scum like that."

209.17.496

209.17.493

"Everybody walked in columns to the camp: common criminals, the sons of kulaks—yes, there are people who are dissatisfied with the Soviet government . . . there are not many of them, but it is because of them, the bastards, that all the mistrust arises."

209.17.496

And Kondratyev describes Rzhev itself: "A high barbed-wire fence, a watchtower with searchlights every fifty meters. Inside, rows of long barracks." In the barracks, the criminals ruled the roost, as "they have things

209.17.498

organized here. For them, a camp is a camp, whether it is a Soviet or a
German camp." In the camp "it appeared to Borka that some among them
were not unduly sorry to be imprisoned; from barely noticeable signs,
more by instinct than reason, he concluded that you should not discuss
anything with these guys." 209.17.487

Anyone wanting to escape on the way to the camp was aware that, for
the first escapee ten men would be shot; for the next, twenty; and then ten
more for each escapee after that. Mutually suspicious, no man trusted
another, and everyone understood that his own comrades would stop at
nothing to prevent an escape, even violence if necessary. 209.17.495

Borka finally escapes from the camp but is later recaptured. He con-
fides to his new fellow inmates that he wants to escape again. One man
points out what is waiting for him back home; whatever you think it may
be, it certainly won't:

—Ah, how marvelous to see you unscathed, old man! Do you think
that's how it goes? They'll get you straightaway.
—Have the Germans taught you such rubbish?
—The Germans, yes, but we've got brains ourselves. You've broken
your oath by getting yourself captured. 209.17.531

Yuri Nikolayev adds: "The primary concern of our prisoners of war,
at least in 1944, was not how to survive captivity but how they would be
received back home." 314.1.220

Konstantin Vorobyov was taken prisoner in 1941 as one of the "Kremlin
cadets," an experience he later recounted in *Killed at Moscow*. He was
shifted from one camp to another, survived it all, and, having escaped and
gone into hiding in Shaulyai in 1943, he wrote the story "It's Us, Lord,"
based on the experience. This horrific account of the suffering of Russian
prisoners of war in the Rzhev camp, in the officers' camp of Salaspils, and
in the Shaulyai prison remained unpublished until 1986.

Vorobyov describes the hunger, the thirst—there was never any snow
in the camp, everything was immediately licked up—the lice, in the hundreds, that crawled over everyone, the typhus, the mass destruction, the
stench of corpses and excrement, the frozen toes that fell off when someone took his boots off. The beer bottles you had to queue up for, so
you could use them to crush the lice in your clothes against the hard 485.2.34
ground. And the continual execution of prisoners: because they picked up

209.17.500

a cigarette butt, because they wavered while standing in line, because they groaned, and also for nothing, simply out of what Vorobyov called "a sporting interest."

He managed to escape twice. He also served as an officer from 1944 to 1945 but was dismissed in 1946 as "someone who had been in a prisoner-of-war camp."

Major Gavrilov, a regiment commandant from Brest, was unconscious when the Germans took him prisoner. In 1945 he was liberated and sentenced to ten years in a camp. In 1987 he was declared a "Hero of the Soviet Union." "And there are thousands like him who died before they were freed of the scandalous stigma." Some were captured because they had not been given weapons in time.

Soviet citizens who had fought in Yugoslavia on Tito's side also had everything taken from them and were sworn to silence over that period.

Later Vorobyov wrote that "former prisoners attempted to conceal, with a dull sense of shame, the horrors they had had to endure, and therefore few know what those people were forced to go through. Books on imprisonment were far from the truth; they were not worth reading." "All those years I was under special surveillance by the state security forces . . . lived under the constant threat of arrest at any moment," one author wrote.

In addition to prisoners of war, other Soviet citizens were also sent to Germany, such as the Ostarbeiter, chiefly Ukrainian girls, recruited and deported by force. The Feldgendarmerie was at the station while they were being deported. "The Germans did not interfere with anything, they simply observed," noted Vsevolod Osten. "The preparation for the departure of yet another party of young Ukrainians to Germany was organized by the local politsay. . . . They were mostly girls between the ages of sixteen and twenty, almost no boys. Judging by their appearance, the girls were not ordinary farm girls. More like village intelligentsia, you might say. The Germans first skimmed off the 'cream,' freeing the Ukrainians from those capable of spreading 'Bolshevik contagion.'"

The mortality among the prisoners of war was, as we have seen, excessively high. Postwar German sources quote a total mortality of 57 percent; most died before and during transport before February 1942. Mortality among British prisoners of war amounted to 3.6 percent.

As we know, Russian prisoners of war received no help from either their own government or the Red Cross. One could save oneself from certain

485.2.20

79.1.282

191.3.100
457.1.226

184.1

485.4.620

389.1.15

221.2.259

282.2.358

death by entering the service of Vlasov's army or reporting as a nonmili-
tary *Hilfswillige* (HIWI). There were around a million of these.   243.1.86–87

Stalin's son Jakov was taken prisoner on 18 July 1941 as a major at
Vyazma. He refused all German offers, was taken to Sachsenhausen,
became depressed, and threw himself into live barbed wire after an argument. Stalin refused to exchange him for a high-ranking German officer.   203.1.79

Family members of soldiers who were taken prisoner were subjected
to repression; in other words, they were arrested. Such arrests were made
of 12,128 family members in 1941, 12,429 in 1942, 8,817 in 1943, 5,698 in
1944, and 8,817 in 1945.   497.1.33–34

In the 1990s Chancellor Helmut Kohl handed over fifty-three volumes
of the names of prisoners of war who had died in German camps. Of the   98.1.74
808,146 Soviet prisoners in cemeteries in Poland, no more than 611 had
been identified at the beginning of 1989.   497.2.57

Later, prisoners of war worked in German agriculture; civilian prisoners
or those who had been forcibly recruited worked in factories, in domestic service, or agriculture. German farmers and industrialists came to what
amounted to a modern slave market to see which workers they liked the
looks of. Women from the east were strictly forbidden to have a child: if   290.2.81
they became pregnant, they were forced to have an abortion.   210.1.83–84

For many years there was no mention of the Ostarbeiter in the Soviet
Union, until, in 1976, Vitali Shomin was able to publish *Badge of the
"OST,"* a documentary novel about the labor camp where he ended up as
a fifteen-year-old boy. Hunger, cold, hard work, and beatings were quite
normal for the Ostarbeiter. It has been claimed that 4,978,000 Soviet citizens were deported to Germany as cheap labor, but here, too, the figures   4.1.171
are disputed: the number has also been said to be 2.1 million civilians.   370.1.168
This number included, incidentally, Soviet citizens who had left with the
Germans, afraid of vengeance by the Soviet government.   210.1.87

Treatment by the Fatherland

Not all Soviet citizens in Germany—prisoners of war or deportees—
looked forward with such longing to liberation. The rumors that the Soviet
authorities would view them as traitors and turncoats had filtered through
to Germany as well, and the Germans expressly confronted the Soviet citizens with such rumors in detail. On their return, prisoners of war were
asked, "Why didn't you commit suicide?" or "Why didn't the Germans kill

you?" Invariably this question was asked by those who had found cushy desk jobs for the duration of the war.

Probably typical is what happened to Yeleazar Meletinski. Encircled and captured in the Donets Basin, he managed to escape from a prisoner-of-war camp. On his return he was accused of "anti-Soviet agitation," because he had said there was not an unbroken front line and you could escape alive from encirclement. "That remark was treated, first, as misinformation and, second, as praise of the Germans: how could it be that they had not killed all prisoners in one go?

"But it's the truth, I said. What should I have said, then?' 'You should have said that the Germans hang everybody, cut them into pieces, murder and nothing else.' But I did talk about the German atrocities. 'Too little, because it seemed as if there were atrocities, but you still managed to escape from the encirclement.' But I really did escape, didn't I? 'That is not important. What is important is what you said.'" Meletinski writes further that, on seeing what the "special section" did, his comrades preferred to live under occupation. According to Meletinski, in June 1942 in the Donets Basin it was not difficult to escape capture. The confusion was so great at that time that when soldiers came across one another wandering around Ukraine, they did not ask which unit they were from but which army they had been in.

After the war the prisoners of war who had been liberated or taken prisoner by the Western Allies, in particular, were under suspicion as spies for the West—and those numbered 2,048,974. They were not allowed to settle in Moscow, Leningrad, or Kiev, even after verification. Incidentally, on 17 June 1944 the Western Allies were surprised to find that 10 percent of the prisoners of war in the West at that time were Soviet citizens.

In any event, "[in 1945] columns of tens of thousands of people, women and even children, headed east from the zone border. They went by foot, some with their meager possessions on carts and with bicycles. Transfer camps, endless interrogation by a state security officer, threats and humiliation awaited them," says the historian Mikhail Semiryaga.

"Prisoners from fascist concentration camps were driven to Siberian camps. The atmosphere of the postwar years was sinister—an atmosphere of treason, of fear. And we, the victors," wrote Grigori Baklanov, "felt conquered in our own country by the system we had defended in 1,418 bloody days. Scum, who had been in the hinterland or had managed to save themselves in the military hinterland, started to rise to the surface and were prepared to act unscrupulously, to snatch and grab."

Margin notes: 280.1.177, 280.1.164, 393.1.27, 28.1

Deported girls, in particular, had a hard time after liberation. They were asked: "So, you've been working for the Germans, have you?" Rybakov tells how the girls made desperate attempts not to be repatriated: they quickly entered domestic service with the Germans, worked in bathhouses and laundries or as a cook, or married a lower-ranking officer. "Do you have the moral right to refuse the soldier liberator anything if you are under suspicion?" 382.1.57

430.1.230

According to Astafyev, "On the way home the military police stood like a wall, guys even more vicious than the Gestapo thugs. They undressed the girls—for disinfection and humiliating examination—turned out their pockets and took anything of value, crushing cheap jewelry and baubles underfoot. Doctors and nurses, already hostile before they started, swore at them, kicked them, insulted them, and, after examination, took those with a venereal disease away. It was rumored that they were shot." Many committed suicide from fear and humiliation. 23.18.36

The military police were taking revenge on the girls because they felt they had been amusing Germans "while the Soviet soldiers, in their shelters and trenches, wasted their sperm in masturbation." 23.18.36

Anyone who had been in Germany ended up in a filtration camp, where people coming from the West were searched, their identity verified, and their conduct under occupation established. Some were then sent on to Soviet concentration camps, and every one of them had great difficulty getting proper work or accommodations. The same question had to be answered on all the forms: "Have you been in a prisoner-of-war camp?" All their lives they were discriminated against, treated with suspicion, slandered, and intimidated. They received no benefits, no invalidity pension (welfare for disabled servicemen). It was virtually impossible for them to get a higher education. Even years later people still had a black mark on their "biography" because they had been in another country.

In 1954 Marshal Zhukov attempted to scrap the question concerning having been a prisoner of war and to relegate the associated discrimination to the past. He failed. Only in 1990 were prisoners of war rehabilitated as honest soldiers during a ceremonial in Moscow in remembrance of the forty-fifth anniversary of the Soviet victory. 508.4

One bizarre story concerns Major Mikhail Novobranets, head of the information department of the Red Army intelligence service. He spent time in many German camps, escaped in northern Norway, where he founded a partisan group, liberated other prisoners of war and part of northern Norway, and stood at the head of what amounted to a small army. On their way home he and all his people were arrested, locked up in prisoners' vans, guarded by dogs, and taken to camps. He spent ten years in Siberian camps. Years after the war his Norwegian resistance comrades were in Moscow and wanted to see their hero. "Then a miracle happened. Within two days he was brought to Moscow by special plane, returned to the army, and given the rank of colonel. A meeting with his Norwegian friends was then arranged."

The commandant of the heroic defense of Brest was only released from a camp in 1956. Russians who had fought in the Maquis and been decorated by Charles de Gaulle returned to Moscow. They had been told that Stalin would receive them. They were put up in the hotel Moskva and picked up the next day by an officer who was to take them to the Kremlin. There they were lined up and the resolution by "special consilium" was read aloud to them: instead of the death penalty, they were sentenced to twenty-five years in a camp. "The masters of ceremony of the Lubyanka tore off the men's Légion d'honneurs and snapped handcuffs on the wrists of the heroes."

After his last escape Borka, from Kondratyev's novel, ended up in a filtration camp near Gryazovets. At night he could hear isolated shots, and then the following morning there were a few more missing. The verification camp near Ryazan was infamous; soldiers had to stay there for three months, and officers six. There was high barbed wire, guards armed with machine guns in watchtowers. An ice-cold attitude was shown toward the soldiers to be verified, which already boded ill.

In the northern Russian concentration camp of Ustvymlag, Lev Razgon came across "people from camps in the west of Germany. The Americans had liberated them, fed and clothed them, and then handed them over to our own people." They were received with great celebration at stations during the return trip—"until they got deeper into our country. Then the cattle trucks were closed, the guards came onboard, and the former prisoners were shunted off, posthaste, to the camp."

Others finally ended up in camps at Kolyma, Vanino, and Sovietskaya Gavan on the Pacific Coast. "At the end of the war the liberated prisoners were brought together in special battalions and forcibly sent to far-flung corners of the country as permanent labor in forestry and coal-mining companies," writes Semiryaga.

Kondratyev did, however, feel that verification camps were necessary for soldiers returning from encirclement. After all, what do you do with soldiers who come back without weapons or papers? Military service record books in the Soviet Union do not include a photograph of the holder.   209.12.272

Although figures by no means say everything, nevertheless I shall quote a few here. On 1 March 1946, 4,199,488 Soviet citizens were repatriated. Of those, 2,427,906 were allowed to go home, 801,152 were recruited into the army, 608,095 were placed in labor battalions, and 272,867 formed a "special contingent" of the NKVD, while 84,468 were still being investigated. Later another hundred thousand or so were repatriated.   493.1.36

However strongly repatriation was enforced, 451,561 people nevertheless remained in the West. Of these, 7.03 percent were Russians, 32.1 percent Ukrainians, 3.18 percent White Russians, 24.19 percent Latvians, 14.04 percent Lithuanians, 13.05 percent Estonians, and 7.42 percent represented other nationalities.   493.1.39

The repression of prisoners of war and those who had been outside the Soviet Union was embarked on once again in 1948 and 1949, when "persons who may constitute a danger because of their anti-Soviet contacts and hostile activities" were banished to Siberia, even if they had already served their sentence. The standard punishment was twenty-five years in a camp.   424.104

According to Kondratyev, as well as others, the reason for this repression was that Stalin wished to silence everyone who had seen something of the West, and not because they had supposedly been "traitors."   209.13.29

In 1956, as mentioned earlier, the attitude toward former prisoners of war underwent some degree of change. Only in 1988 did this subject begin to elicit heavy discussions. Yet in 1996, however, recommendations were still being made regarding the complete rehabilitation of prisoners of war.   424.110–12

The Gulag

At the outbreak of war there were 2.3 million prisoners in the camps of the Chief Directorate of Labor Camps (Gulag). The regime immediately became stricter: less food, longer working days, and no radio, newspapers, or correspondence. There were, however, executions by firing squad, particularly in the event of defeats at the front.   52.1

As many as 750,000 prisoners were evacuated at the beginning of the war. "Many of them traveled the thousand-kilometer route on foot."   175.1.19

361.2.134–35
"In the three years of the war 2.9 million people disappeared from camps and colonies, and 1.8 million arrived. . . . 975,000 men went into service."

361.1
394.1.129–30
303.3.78
Political prisoners, in particular, asked the camp commandant if they could be sent to the front; the request was usually refused. Criminal prisoners were eligible, however. In one way or another, 420,000 Gulag prisoners entered the army in 1941. Many died during the encirclement at Vyazma and Bryansk. At the defense of Murmansk in 1941 the Arctic Division consisted entirely of released prisoners. One commandant at the Volkhov front said that 59 of his 78 soldiers were criminals and had taken to their heels.

320.1.10
320.1.6
364.3.57
Andrei Obrosov noted in a Siberian camp in June and July 1941: "I saw many people who could not conceal their joy when reports came in on our first fiascoes at the front and the enormous losses . . . but most of them . . . did not expect anything good [and] foresaw a hardening of the regime, repression, and reductions in the rations." Obrosov himself escaped from a Siberian camp with two comrades in 1941, walked four hundred kilometers through the taiga, obtained false papers, joined up and fought at the front, was arrested in 1945, and was rehabilitated in 1955. In 1942 a certain Kostya fled from a camp where he was serving a sentence for stealing a chicken. He volunteered for the army, was not allowed to become a party member, but was allowed to fight. On 9 May 1945, two hours after the war, he was again arrested in order to complete the remainder of his sentence.

499.1.87
298.1.143
220.175
The worst time for the Gulag prisoners, so they say, was the autumn of 1941. In Vorkuta recently released prisoners were again picked up and others were shot, whereas another group was released as "socially allied" and allowed to join the army. None of the political prisoners was waiting for Hitler, but some criminals were: "When Hitler comes we'll hang you after all." It is known that there were political prisoners who, when war broke out, called on their fellows to work even harder, to carry out so-called Stakhanov labor, named after a mine worker who is supposed to have dug dubiously large quantities of coal in 1935. "We buried the majority of the forced laborers, alias Stakhanov laborers, in the first winter of the war; the heroes of forced labor were buried without coffin or clothes, naked corpses that the guards ran through with a bayonet at the gate to make sure no one left the camp alive." In the city of Gorki prisoners called for workdays to be lengthened to more than twelve hours, for the "defense fund." As thanks, they were accused of a conspiracy. "We want no gifts from enemies of the people," was the response.

"The war was under way and there were millions of healthy men in the camps, former specialists from all walks of the country's military and economic life. Furthermore, it took considerable manpower to guard them. This was a heavy burden on the country." 263.1.310

Because the country needed coal from Vorkuta, rations were increased there at the end of 1942, and the prisoners were given American white bread and canned meat, butter, American clothes, and fashionable shoes with thick soles. Later the Volga Germans arrived here, too. Not officially 499.1.105–6 prisoners, but closely guarded nonetheless. One sadistic camp comman- 499.1.106 dant, Korotkov, tossed a coin to decide who might "be allowed" to go to the front to pay his debt "with his filthy blood." Vladimir But describes 64.1.37 the camp guards as "specially selected, preferably with an education of no more than three or four primary school classes, preferably from isolated villages and with a poor knowledge of Russian." Even better were guards with physical or mental disabilities, as "they are malicious and vengeful, just what we need." 64.1.38

A total of 448,000 Gulag prisoners worked laying railway lines, 310,000 were deployed in the construction industry, 320,000 in lumberjacking, 171,000 in mines, and 268,000 in building roads and airfields. All things considered, the Gulag made an extremely important contribution to the war effort. There was never any lack of camp guards. 361.2.136; 27.1

In the winter of 1941–42 "more than half the prisoners of Vyatlag" died. 37.3.171 In 1942, in some camps in the area of Komi, the entire camp population died within 150 days. 497.2.100

In the period between July 1941 and June 1942, 862,760 people were sentenced to various punishments in the Gulag. Up to 1 July 1944 the Gulag 243.1.97 received 1.8 million new prisoners, and 621,637 prisoners died in that time. 282.2.322; 175.1.23

Who ended up in the Gulag? People who had praised the efficiency of German weapons, for example, earned five to ten years. "In 1942 parties of children aged fourteen and fifteen arrived, all sentenced to five years for breaking the law concerning willful absence from work in the war industry." These were the *ukazniki* or *trudoviki*. 497.2.50

From 1943 on, citizens from formerly occupied areas that had been liberated arrived in the Gulag. Thus, after the first capture of Kharkov, it was not the real traitors who were arrested—they had retreated with the Germans—but cobblers, cooks, and "German whores" and, as we saw, former prisoners of war and Ostarbeiters, people who had been liberated from German concentration camps. Author Varlam Shalamov describes 364.1.76–77

how hardened front soldiers were locked up in Kolyma: spies, pilots, officers, and soldiers. Only when they reached Kolyma did they see that
Vlasov's people had been right, that prisoners of war could count on a
Siberian camp as traitors. Shalamov's *Major Pugachov's Last Battle,* from
his "Kolyma Tales," is fantastical. As former front soldiers, Pugachov and
those in his group could handle weapons well. They overpowered the camp
guards and found their way to short-lived freedom. After a few weeks the
whole group was found and killed in fierce fighting.

There were several uprisings in the Gulag camps during the war. One
was in January 1942 in Ust Uzha at Vorkuta, for example, under the leadership of a certain Retyunin. All were shot, even the prisoners who had
not participated.

German Prisoners of War in Russia

Approximately 3.2 million German soldiers were taken prisoner by the
Russians. Russian figures talk of 2,389,560 men. Of course, most of the
prisoners were taken at the end of the war. Of the ninety-one thousand
Germans taken prisoner at Stalingrad, only six thousand survived.

According to German information, approximately 1.1 million of the 3.2
million prisoners died. At the end of 1941, 9,417 German soldiers had been
made prisoners of war. By 1 March 1944 that number was 252,028, of whom
105,285 were still alive.

The most difficult period was between 1945 and 1949—owing to poor
food and poor health care—but the Russian population was also living in
poverty and hunger at that time. All prisoners of war were put to work:
clearing up rubble, building houses, rebuilding factories, and constructing electrical power stations. Virtually all postwar construction, in other
words, all construction up to 1950, was carried out using German labor.
They were given accommodations not only in camps but also in garages,
monasteries, and barns. There were repeated escape attempts.

The cemeteries of deceased prisoners have virtually all disappeared.
The soldiers' graves with the birch crosses left there by the Germans in
Russia, in particular, have been plowed over.

Antifascists and converts to communism received better treatment.
The system of informers and "reeducation" was widespread in the camps
and included indoctrination, readings, antifascist clubs, and all kinds of
courses, but "the prisoners of war, particularly the officers, had difficulty
accepting antifascist ideas."

437.1

499.1.100–103

206.5.187

110.1.133

110.1.133

206.4.14

110.1.137

110.1.136

Irina Bezborodova wrote: "Prisoners of war were encouraged to produce works of art for propaganda purposes. Hundreds of plays appeared, novels, stories, operettas, watercolors, and drawings, all produced by prisoners of war in Soviet camps." Before the Germans were repatriated, the Ministry of Internal Affairs (MVD) first demanded "political reports on their life in captivity, in view of 'the great significance for the refutation of slanderous and provocative remarks outside the country.'" Repatriation depended on attitude. Those who were unprepared to change their attitudes could expect to be tried. This applied even to Walter von Seydlitz, the chairman of the voluntarily formed Union of German Officers, which, after Stalingrad, the Soviet government set up among cooperative prisoners of war. He was sentenced to twenty-five years, and his wife and four daughters were persecuted, first by the Nazis and later by the German Democratic Republic (DDR) authorities. Von Seydlitz was released in 1955.

Just before repatriation people were better fed, had more opportunities to rest, and could take part in excursions. At the end of 1947 proceedings were instituted against 143 members of the military, including 23 generals. Some of them committed suicide. "Between 1947 and 1950 more than thirty thousand German prisoners of war and internees were tried."

There were trials in Kharkov, Smolensk, Bryansk, Leningrad, Nikolayev, Minsk, Kiev, Riga, and Velikie Luki. But as early as 1943, in Kharkov, a case was already brought against German war criminals, in this instance, the operators of a Vergasungswagen, a mobile gassing unit, the forerunner of the gas chamber.

General G. Weidling, the last commandant of Berlin—who retained the position for only a matter of days—was given a twenty-five-year sentence because he refused "to confirm Stalin's version of Hitler's flight from Berlin." He died a broken and confused man, and was buried in Vladimir.

The last prisoners of war returned only in 1955, after Chancellor Konrad Adenauer paid a visit to Moscow. In 1948 there were 100,025 German prisoners of war missing. The figures have often, incidentally, been manipulated. Viktor Konasov, the Russian historian who specialized in prisoner-of-war issues, writes, "The repatriation of around two hundred thousand men is not confirmed by any document; the mortality among the prisoners was, judging by all the circumstances, considerably higher than those two hundred thousand."

41.1.171

206.1.56

41.1.171

41.1.170

400.3.356

112.3.148

206.5.188–89

Were There Excesses?

"According to the calculations of German historians—which we consider too high, anyway—90 to 95 percent of the German soldiers and officers in 1941–42 were killed upon surrender or died shortly afterward," says Konasov. Exact figures are difficult to provide, since many died on the way to the command centers or assembly points.

Kondratyev and Viktor Nekrasov both claim to be unaware of any incident of mistreatment of prisoners of war. Nekrasov writes that, in Stalingrad, all documentation was taken from the prisoners, but they were allowed to keep photograph albums, which was seen as "one of the greatest forms of sympathy." Friendly, teasing remarks were also made about their photographs. "Take what you want, but let me keep this," was written all over the Germans' faces, and, in gratitude, they gave their "watches, pens, toiletries: *bitte, bitte, Herr Oberleutnant.*"

Prisoners were killed, however, if they refused to give up information, generally when no one had the time or energy to take them to the hinterland. In that case, this is how it went: "We [Germans and Russians] had agreed, as it were: we do not take each other prisoner." The commandant of the Fifty-first Army at Stalingrad killed all his prisoners of war. "Well, what was I supposed to do with them?" he said.

During marches, too, many died; those unable to keep up were shot. "That was quite normal then, all armies acted that way," says the German, Gerulja. Of the eight thousand German prisoners of war in a camp near Prokopyevsk, 6,189 died between 13 March and 1 May 1943: 1,526 died on their way to the camp, and the rest died from hunger.

There are countless descriptions of prisoners being killed. This happened chiefly after the soldiers had seen the German destruction camps.

A train in which Boris Slutsky was traveling stopped at the station of Mikhurinsk on 20 February 1943. Next to him was a train full of prisoners, "Italians, Romanians, and Yugoslavian Jews from a labor battalion. . . . In the open wagons lay dozens of yellow corpses, victims of hunger."

Farsobin recounted in 1946 that, in the little village of Ulybyshevo in 1942–43, several Russian officers had to spend a couple of nights unloading a train full of frozen prisoners of war and burying them.

In the steppes by the Don, Prince Sergei Golitsyn—he was careful to conceal his old noble background—found an Austrian soldier who had been left behind, Friedrich Stettiner, a car mechanic from Vienna. This was an extremely handy coincidence, as Golitsyn's engineers' trucks had

206.1.61

112.3.147

309.4.42

61.1.38–39

71.4.10

130.1.41

206.3.209

127.9.276

407.4.152

407.3.46

112.5.172

broken down and Stettiner got them going again. The Viennese stayed with
Golitsyn and his unit throughout the entire war. He was a true Fascist,
despised the Slavic race, and scoffed at the impoverished Russian farms.
On the way, in Russian villages, he repaired buckets, samovars, gramo-
phones, clocks and watches, and sewing machines. The farming community looked on him with curiosity. He married a Russian girl, and only
after the war was he taken to a prisoner-of-war camp.   137.3.16

On 14 March 1943 Golitsyn—who never managed to rise any higher
than commandant of a military construction department—crossed with
his engineers through an area that had never been in German hands. "To
my amazement, there lay half-stripped and entirely naked German corpses.
I assumed they were prisoners of war who had been shot, but nothing was
written about it then."   137.3.21

Not until 1996 was the theme of the German prisoners of war and their
fate touched on in the Soviet Union and then in a book by Viktor Konasov.   206.2

Viktor Sofronov once saw captured Germans working in a village. Russian
women brought them food, bread, biscuits, and potatoes. "Strange. Why?
Was it because they had slaughtered and burned them in Ukraine and
White Russia? Was it human compassion for all living things? It was compassion. Russian compassion." When one of the Germans dropped from
a roof, dead, those women wept—"sniffling and sobbing, thinking of their
own men who had not come home from the front."   409.1.116–17

Another person reported in 1946 that "people regarded prisoners without hate." Children exchanged pieces of bread with them for little toys.   341.1.222

It is also known that many German ex-prisoners of war did not foster
any feelings of revenge for the Russians. That was true as well for the emi-   152.1
nent literature historian Wolfgang Kasack, who was taken as a seventeen
year old from Berlin to Kuybyshev. Russian farming women gave him and
his fellow prisoners something to drink during the short stops, and the
Russian guards turned a blind eye.   192.1.178

Let me close these terrible pages on the fate of German and Russian
prisoners of war with an account written by Vladimir Vinogradov entitled
"Kein faschist." Toward the end of the war, a fire breaks out in a hospital in Lvov. The wounded quickly need to be rescued. German prisoners
of war, working there as orderlies, are called on to save the Russians. The
Germans, still in uniform, wearing their stripes and insignia, eagle and
swastika and all the trimmings, cry out the famous "*Raus, schnell, schnell.*"

The wounded protest, but there is nothing else to do, and now the help-
less Russians have to surrender to the Germans in order not to be burned
alive. The Germans cry, "kein faschist," and the Russians are "obliged to
put his arms around his neck, the sworn hated enemy . . . a bizarre, impossible, unnatural fraternization."

474.1.27–28

Partisans

Shortly before the war, training centers, bases, and command centers for
saboteurs and partisans were dismantled and disbanded. After all, a partisan war could not be reconciled with the strategic views of a rapid
advance of their own side into enemy territory. According to Starinov, one
of the famous partisan commanders, more partisan leaders died during
the 1930s than during the war. When it came down to it, therefore, there
was a lack of knowledge, addresses, and professionalism—and that was
partly the cause of many arrests and defeats at the beginning of the war.
Once the war started, opinions changed once again. A party resolution
dated 18 July 1941 contained the following order, "Organize partisan groups
and units, capture enemy arms and ammunition, destroy the enemy mercilessly, day and night, through ambushes and in open combat."

First the sabotage groups were formed, often consisting of extremely
young people from the big cities. One of these was Zoya Kosmodemyanskaya, whom I mentioned earlier. Others could not bring themselves to
kill innocent horses as Zoya had, and said, "I'm not a townie like Zoya,
who enjoys setting fire to stables."

Partisan units were set up by Moscow and were under Moscow's command. The Supreme Command was under Voroshilov, followed in 1942 by
the party leader in White Russia Panteleimon Ponomarenko. In fact, the
partisan units were therefore under the command of the NKVD or a party
organization.

For years there was general animosity between the White Russians and
the Ukrainian partisans who—not exactly innocent themselves—were still
able to prevent publication of Ponomarenko's memoirs in 1974.

A distinction should indeed be made between partisans in White Russia and those in Ukraine. White Russia had large-scale partisan activities
and the population supported them and joined up themselves, resulting
in bloody persecution by the occupiers, which again swelled the ranks
of the partisans. Tsidilkovski writes that, in Ukraine, on the other hand,

438.1

282.2.223

225.1.60

249.3.133–34

partisan units were set up on Moscow's orders and that "according to our observations, a large proportion of the population took practically no part in the resistance against the occupiers. Worse still, a considerable proportion of the young and middle-aged men served as politsay or *starosta* [village head], betraying and murdering Jews and Communists." 74.1.143

Partisan units consisted partly of soldiers who had escaped from encirclement or prisoner-of-war camps. 383.5.208

Minor campaigns near villages, like pinpricks against the enemy, led to reprisals in those villages. As a means of protection, the villages would then form self-defense groups, which was characteristic of all partisan areas. Open violence and robbery evoked the fury of the villagers: Ponomarenko pointed out this danger on 3 March 1943. 338.1.151 338.1.150

Kondratyev reports on a conversation he had with someone after the war, who with a smile, had told him that he had been part of a Bandera unit set up by the NKVD and had been given the assignment to terrorize the local population so as to encourage their sympathy for the partisan movement. 209.27.8

Supplying the partisans with food was a difficult problem. If you gave them food, you risked German revenge; but if you didn't, you would be shot just the same, but by the partisans. Later a kind of arrangement was made as to which unit could forage in which village. In the neighborhood of Bryansk "you paid a kind of tribute, at one time to the partisans, at another to the Germans, whoever turned up first." 338.1.152–53 473.2.5

In White Russia and Northwest Russia, whole villages retreated into the woods or the swamps in times of danger, under the partisans' protection. In the area around Minsk, 567,000 people were saved from destruction or deportation to Germany in this way. These came to be known as the "wood or civilian camps" where people hid during German punishment expeditions. 338.1.152

The partisans caused the occupiers a great deal of damage. They kept German units away from the front, and, by sabotaging railway lines, bridges, and roads, they caused German supplies to go astray.

"Many farmers feared the 'people's avengers' as much as they did the occupiers. . . . It was not uncommon for bandits to operate openly under the partisan flag. Furthermore, according to Sergei Kudryashov, in several places NKVD units operated as partisan soldiers, exercising repression against 'unreliable' villages." 243.1.92

"If the Bolshevik regime is supported by a cruel system of punitive measures, then it loses its former significance for the population of the occupied areas," wrote Nikolai Yonyayev. "Prompt measures were therefore taken to intensify to the extreme hostile relations between the population and the occupiers. Numerous partisan units carried out sabotage sometimes simply with the aim of provoking counter-repression and thus depriving the Russian population of possibly looking to the Germans as allies rather than enemies. If one discounts the remarkable inhumanity of this plan, it can be seen as one of Stalin's most ingenious inventions."

Some partisan contingents were highly praised; others enjoyed less sympathy. For example, when a commandant asked that the son of the house be relinquished to join the partisans and was refused, there was suddenly "an order from Stalin: the male population in that area over the age of sixteen must join the partisans. Get ready, boys."

During the war Ovidi Gorchakov, a future interpreter for Stalin and Khrushchev, was dropped behind enemy lines to carry out sabotage activities. Later he joined a partisan unit in White Russia. What he saw there—betrayal, cowardice, as well as courage—is described in his autobiographical account, *Vne zakona* (Outside the law). His task was ultimately to remove a local partisan commander who was as sadistic as he was dictatorial. This villain shot women who were not receptive toward him as well as anyone who disapproved of his conduct. History and the writers of memoirs do not mention this partisan unit. The affair took place in the summer and autumn of 1942 in the area of Mogilyov.

Vasil Bykov tells of a girl who had gone into hiding with the partisans in White Russia but then fled because the commandants wanted to sleep with her. Plenty of girls were there to carry out the most dangerous assignments. But if a girl screamed at night because she was being cornered, then she risked execution, since screaming betrayed the unit's position. "Live by the well, but don't drink the water?" the commandants argued. The story continues: the girl falls into German hands and is carried off to Austria, where she is well treated as a maid. Her employer maintains that communism and fascism are two ends of the same stick. When the Red Army arrives in Austria and she is raped by her fellow countrymen, she is afraid of being repatriated to White Russia.

Suspicions, insinuations, the secret settling of scores, it was all an integrel part of the times. Decent people were being killed—whether partisans or not—next to bastards who felt like fish in the water in the partisan units. There were also "wild" groups, semi- or entirely criminal, who passed

211.1.110

225.1.73

145.2
142.1

66.1

themselves off as partisans. These confusing circumstances are described
in accurate detail by Andrei Zhdanovich, who himself took part in all
kinds of action as a seventeen-year-old boy.   503.1

The population found itself between the devil and the deep blue sea.
They never knew whom they were dealing with. For example, what was
one to think of people who pretended to be partisans, who asked for and
were given food, and then came back the next day in German uniforms?
Neither party took prisoners—unless it was just long enough to extract
information.

Small partisan groups, often unorganized sabotage groups, have gone
unnoticed by historians and authors. No one writes about them; no one
knows about them. The survivors of these groups still have great difficulty
"justifying" their actions. These groups, ten to fifteen men strong, with-   326.1
out orders from any authority, operated on their own initiative. The many
citizens who helped those partisans have also remained largely unknown.   27.1.170

Vasil Bykov is a White Russian writer who, although he himself fought
in the regular army, has written fascinating accounts of the partisans in
his homeland. He spent many years researching the stories of survivors,
victims, and eyewitnesses. His primary interest is in the moral problems
that arose during the struggle and the influence the prewar past had on
the partisans. How was their behavior influenced by collectivization, by the
terror against the farming population, by the executions and provocation
campaigns? Why did so many join up as politsay, starosti, or mayors? "For
some the war has served only to dull the memories of earlier humiliations;
for others the war has enhanced those memories."   66.2.70

And what were you to do if a partisan commandant ordered you to
kill innocent people? How does a patriot feel who, unbroken by German
torture, is deliberately set free by the occupiers in the hope that his own
people will consider him a spy and a traitor? Should you sacrifice the   66.4
wounded in order to save yourself? Should you send people on a mission   66.3
where, unknowingly, they are risking their lives? Should you save yourself   66.6
by betraying another? What do you do with billeted German soldiers?   66.5; 66.7
What does a man feel who is led away into the mist to be shot by two partisans, and then helps them when they are wounded during an unexpected
skirmish, and the two turn out to be cowards? How does a partisan feel   66.8
who previously terrorized the population of a village and now asks for,
and receives, help and shelter from those very people? After all, a farmer's 66.2.11
wife whose flourmill he had smashed up during collectivization is now

helping him. "What kind of character is that? A good-hearted person or one indifferent to good and evil? What is it? A typical farmer's characteristic or that of a woman? Or is it a national trait? Azevich wanted to believe that after everything you had been through, before and during the war, life would change once the Fascists were driven out . . . that the people . . . must surely free themselves from class hatred, party prejudice, and all other enmity, to live in justice. How long can you keep fighting among yourselves?" Bykov asked himself: "People! How mercilessly they were toyed with. And then something was still expected of them. All the years of Soviet rule, they had simply been a means to an end, material for the realization of not too smart, sometimes stupid and idiotic, merciless plans implemented with hunger, injustice, and blood! All those years Azevich had tried to convince himself with a bleeding heart that this was right and proper, that it was necessary to achieve a higher goal and to secure the happiness of future generations."

66.2.72

66.2.69

Ales Adamovich, also a White Russian author, described an extraordinary, unlikely but true case of a German soldier from the feared Dirlewanger Division, infamous for its cruel reprisals, who saved a White Russian girl from destruction, defected to the partisans with her, and pretended for years to be deaf and dumb, forced even to keep up this facade after the war.

5.1

In this love story, worthy of a film, Adamovich goes on to write that, after the war, repressions were carried out against former partisans who, according to the government, had taken (or enjoyed) too many liberties in the war. The NKVD attempted to break any former contact between them by making sporadic arrests and false accusations. They were often seen as "hardened terrorists." Units from Beria's People's Commissariat combed the area, because "they have all been in occupied territory, in contact with the enemy. Some were left behind here; others stayed of their own accord. We have to find out why, what their objective was."

5.1.41

9

Repression

Counterespionage and Court Martials

The counterespionage agency SMERSH (Death to Spies) was in charge of investigating, in particular, political reliability, desertion, and "group flights"; verifying (the stories of) members of the military who had escaped encirclement or captivity; and, later, investigating the population of the liberated, formerly occupied areas. SMERSH agents relied on an extensive network of informers, the *sekretnie sotrudniki* (secret agents), who were otherwise known as *seksoty*. Members of this "Special Section" (Osoby Otdel) of the NKVD were feared and hated. These *osobisty* were entitled to execute suspects on the spot.

395.2.62

SMERSH agents were known for their superior equipment, their excellent weapons, and their healthy, well-fed constitution. They were generally recruited from among party members and former members of the militia. They were constantly busy gathering *kompromat*—that is, compromising material, particularly on officers. They also monitored and punished anyone spreading rumors or expressing dissenting opinions in conversation. Someone who praised a clutch of German tanks immediately fell prey to them. If, as an officer, you refused to carry out an obviously senseless order, again you became a victim of SMERSH. Boris Slutski, a SMERSH officer, later wrote:

481.1.21

For three incidents, three jokes,
We dragged the marksman out of his hole,
Judged and condemned,
So it was and so it will be.

407.1.92

For some time after his partial exemption from active service, the future regional novelist Fyodor Abramov was a member of the *osobisty*. He was not strict enough, however, and was forced to leave. Instead of capturing deserters, he says, they hunted down people who said they were suffering from hunger. Shortly afterward, during a postwar reunion, he wrote: "What a lot of butchers and thugs they were. Our own people. I could no longer stand the sight of the old bastards, dripping with ribbons and medals, weeping sentimentally, and I left." I described earlier how the *osobisty* treated escaped soldiers in verification camps and elsewhere. There, you could count on "beatings, insults, humiliation," writes Konstantin Vorobyov.

And Yelena Rzhevskaya: "Haven't you taken the oath?" "Where is your uniform jacket?" "And where is your rifle?" "According to the oath, you have to fight to the last drop of your blood." Even the wounded had to report to the first-aid posts with their weapons so as not to fall under suspicion.

One escaped Jewish soldier was asked, "How could you, a Jew, save yourself from the hands of the Germans? What assignment did the officer give you?" General Grigorenko was warned to look out for one Jakob Goldstein, "a Jew, who was taken prisoner by the Germans and survived. He was even nursed in a German hospital . . . a suspicious person." The truth was that Goldstein had never seen a German but had escaped encirclement.

Another Jewish soldier, a certain Freydin, was encircled in the autumn of 1941 while acting as examining magistrate at the court of the 251st Infantry Division at Vyazma and was only able to break out and reach the Russian lines with great difficulty. "He was subsequently arrested and sentenced to five years in a camp by the NKVD Special Consilium." He was later rehabilitated.

Once, when a group of soldiers suspected someone of being an informer, they urged him to feel just how well they had sharpened their knives. "Here, feel." He ran his finger along the blade. "No, with your tongue," they said threateningly. And he sloped off with a bleeding tongue. "Next time it will be your throat," they called after him.

There were three levels where "justice" was meted out: at the bottom, the NKVD Osoby Otdel, or SMERSH; then the military prosecutor; and finally the military court-martial. Of the 994,300 people tried by military court-martials, some four hundred thousand were sent to punitive battalions,

3.2.145

3.2.151

485.3.127

383.3.9

420.1.4

280.1.177

155.4.173

386.4.197

23.14.28, 30

often to a certain death. How many death sentences were pronounced
is not known. If one soldier reported another for spreading rumors or
for anything else, the commanding officer was obliged to report this to
SMERSH.

93.1.133

209.23.214

"Like most people, I did not believe in the justice of the court-martials
at the front. In such a court, for each justified punishment there were four
or five monstrous, fabricated judgments: ten years, to be commuted to
assignment to a punitive battalion," wrote Teodor Vulfovich.

488.2.255

"It is difficult," said artillerist Andrei Zharikov, "to comprehend the predominant general mistrust, the mutual spying, and the denunciations, not
only regarding concrete issues but also your comrades' thoughts. None of
this served to promote brotherly friendship in the officers' corps; it only
caused meanness. If you can prove that, although your friend may not be
a spy, he is capable of being a traitor to the Fatherland, you yourself will
never be under suspicion by SMERSH."

502.1.147

Human lives meant nothing. A drunken SMERSH man once said, "That
red Vanka shoots them down with a smile on his face."

230.1.160–61

Another said, "There are few arrests. You don't see what we're doing,"
and therefore "you had to report glowing successes to the demanding
bosses who gave you your verification assignments, in other words, your
planned tasks; you had to continually find and arrest enemies, spies, and
terrorists, unmask anti-Soviets and hand their cases over to the court-
martials."

93.1.138

And then there were the NKVD internal troops. Between 1942 and 1945
they arrested 3,715 spies and saboteurs, 88,859 traitors, 125,956 deserters,
and 251,408 conscientious objectors. It was not stated how those qualifications were defined.

34.1.12

Punitive Battalions and Companies

Vladimir Karpov, Hero of the Soviet Union and later chairman of the
Soviet Writers' Union, was placed in a punitive battalion for a while. He
writes of his experience, "I attacked many times. I was lucky; I wasn't even
wounded. The first company was wiped out almost in its entirety; of 198
men, six survived. Then the second company was killed, and, once again,
I was left unscathed. We were deployed in the most dangerous parts, sent
to an almost certain death, initially even without artillery support. Later
it was a bit better; the punitive companies attacked along with the others,
but they were still in the front."

446.1.107

No one knows how many *shtrafniki* (condemned persons) there were. Their units consisted of a permanent core of volunteers (one month's service in a punitive ballalion or company counted as six months elsewhere) and a varying proportion of convicts. If you were wounded, then your "debt had been paid in blood."

Sometimes punitive companies consisted entirely of criminals released from the Gulag.

37.3.4

The *shtrafniki* were gunned down by their officers at the slightest provocation. Commanding officers of punitive battalions were not required to justify killing their subordinates. You get used to it after a while, Captain Reyestrov told a visitor. "I shoot at them every day here and I never miss. I don't need them to love me." And to another visitor he said, "Let's go and have a drink, Captain, we're going to execute someone." And that was a daily occurrence.

380.1.36

380.1.35

After three-quarters of a battalion had been killed, the remaining soldiers were excused their punishment. With Karpov, however, this evidently did not apply. Punitive battalions were deployed on the grounds of Order No. 00227 of 28 July 1942.

380.1.34

Never had soldiers been treated so negligently and heartlessly: "Every front had between one and three punitive battalions and a few dozen punitive companies." The former were for convicted officers, the latter for lower-ranking soldiers.

238.1.10

Whole battalions of convicted officers were killed at Velikie Luki. Officers, badly needed at the front, were sacrificed senselessly here. I. Korzhik was punished for having been encircled. He escaped and, via the verification camp at Ryazan, ended up in a battalion that fought at Velikie Luki. Convicted soldiers were also deployed not even to gain ground but to find out where the enemy had set up their machine guns. According to Astafyev, this happened at the crossing of the Dnepr as well.

222.1

382.1.46

23.9.39

Across the entire front, from Murmansk to the Black Sea, these punitive battalions struck terror into the hearts of the enemy whenever they attacked, crying "guga, guga."

398.1.43

Blocking Units

In August 1941, and also, according to others, in the summer of 1942, the NKVD deployed barrier units. These *zagradotryady* operated either just behind the Russian lines or fifteen to twenty-five kilometers behind, with the task of finding deserters and stray soldiers and, in the event of

continued flight, shooting them. These units, too, were equipped with ex- 120.1.155
cellent weapons and had the most modern equipment: "Rosy faces, well
fed, as if they had spent a stretch at a health farm, well uniformed, with
new helmets. What distinguished them from the ordinary trench soldiers,
in particular, were their generously cut, rubberized trench coats, a luxury
not even afforded to every officer," says But.   64.1.43

A blocking detachment was two hundred men strong: "They don't like
fighting the Germans; they go for their own people." Admittedly they quite 64.1.51
rightly tried to stop soldiers fleeing in panic.

Yuri Nikolayev writes that, in his First Moscow Guard Infantry Division, the officers and sergeants were told before battle, "If one of your
soldiers is cowardly during battle and flees, then shoot him. If you fail to
restore order, then you will face a court-martial. . . . Furthermore, they
warned us all that there was a blocking detachment behind us, so we had
no way out."   314.1.219

"Because of the changed situation at the front, the blocking detachments
were disbanded on Stalin's order of 29 October 1944."   223.1.4

Executions

At the beginning of the war, in particular, "inexperienced officers made
overzealous use of executions." But officers, too, were gunned down by 380.1.34
their superiors in the panic of the first few weeks of the war, more often
than not for mistakes made by those very superiors. The commandant of 367.1.119
the western front, Zhukov, ordered "instructive executions" to be carried
out, for which each unit had to account for one or two victims. In peri- 120.1.135
ods of en masse retreat, in particular, there were plenty of executions.

Absence without leave for more than a couple of hours also carried the
death sentence, as Sergeant Zhukh found out after visiting his Spanish
lover, Maria Teresa, one night. The death sentence also applied if you 189.1
failed to bring back your shot-up tank to your own lines. And exactly 24.1.205
how were you supposed to do that? Desertion, of course, also carried the
death sentence. Civilians were afraid of wandering deserters hiding in the
woods and stealing food from the villages at night. Expressions of "defeat- 37.1.152
ism," for example, maintaining that the war would go on for a long time,
were also rewarded with the death sentence.

Soldiers were repeatedly shot for refusing to carry out senseless orders
or for willful mutilation. Men with wounds to the left hand were treated
with suspicion. In the event of real explosions, therefore, the men hid their

hands. "And cowards stuck a leg in the air, got wounded, and avoided
being unmasked immediately." All those executions did nothing to improve the morale. "The feeling of blind subjugation was intensified; in
those critical days, human life meant nothing; it seemed as if all officers,
at least all of ours . . . were vying with one another as to who could be
the cruelest, the most ruthless, the most so-called courageous," says Vasili
Berezhkov.

A drunken colonel once ordered that volunteer Leonid Likhodeyev, the
future author, be shot. The person who had to carry out the order whispered to Likhodeyev: "I'm going to shoot now, lad. Don't be scared; I'll
shoot in the air, and you run away."

For executions, the regiment was lined up in a horseshoe formation. A
pit had already been dug and the unfortunate condemned man was placed
in front of the pit, generally stripped to the waist. The sentence would
be read out, a soldier from the special section would shoot the man in the
neck, and that would be that. Yuri Levitanski, one of many witnesses, recounted that, afterward, he had heard, "Regiment! Forward, march! Sing!"
And in Vladimir Karpov's words: "During the war years, all the personnel
in our army lived under the permanent threat of execution. In the thousands of political accounts I have read, almost from the first day to the
last of the war, there are reports of executions. . . . The event was also
sometimes phrased as 'executed without trial.'"

Exiled Peoples

The banishment and deportation of sectors of the population considered
unreliable to inhospitable areas was nothing new. The best-known example is that of the kulaks, who, during the agricultural collectivization, were
allocated a plot of land elsewhere as "special colonists" (*spetsposelentsy*)
and were not allowed to leave there.

Ingermanlanders

At the beginning of the war, kulaks originally deported to Karelia were
driven out for the second time.

The Ingermanlanders, an originally Finnish-speaking sector of the population, who were living around Leningrad, suffered the same fate—as a
precautionary measure! The elderly among them were exiled to Kirghizistan; those eligible for national service, like E. Karkhu, were called up to
a reserve regiment consisting largely, as he himself says, of criminals. He

80.1.80

38.1.220

53.1

262.1

191.3.100

19.1.166

187.1.122

was called up only because he—the son of an exiled kulak—had kept quiet about his background.

In April 1942 Ingermanlanders were still being dismissed from the army and deployed in labor battalions, at Chelyabinsk, for example, where they built the metallurgical factory together with exiled Germans. Many of them perished from the exhausting forced labor and from hunger. "For us, any other version of the war that omits what we had to endure is false, untrue, willful suppression." Among those who died was an American Fin, who had come to the Soviet Union in the 1930s to help in the social construction of that country. In the camp at Chelyabinsk he broke stones, became confused, and repeatedly sang, "In America I had a house, number one; in America I had a car, number two; in America I had food, number three." 421.1.155 187.1.132 187.1.132

The technical and commanding section of the construction battalions lived more comfortably: in houses with their families, supplied with separate provisions.

Other Ingermanlanders were in camps in the province of Vologda, where they did not fare much better. Their only crime was that their passports stated "Finnish" as nationality.

Some Ingermanlanders in occupied territory were transported to Finland; some were placed in Estonia as farmhands. After the war, in 1947, they were forbidden to return to their former places of residence. Many then went to Karelia. In recent years several thousands of Ingermanlanders have moved to Finland, where they have been granted Finnish state citizenship. 421.1.157 421.1.159

Germans and Volga Germans

As early as 1936 the Gersch family, German farmers who had lived in Zhitomir since 1914, was deported to North Kazakhstan, because "as Germans, they are living near the Polish border and could defect to the enemy in the event of a conflict." 299.1.154

On 28 August 1941 an *ukaze* from the Supreme Soviet ordered the exile of the Volga Germans: "According to reliable information, there are thousands and tens of thousands of saboteurs and spies among the German population living in the Volga area, and they are planning to cause explosions on a signal from Germany. . . . No one informed the government of the presence of such a large number of saboteurs and spies; the German population is therefore harboring enemies of the Soviet people and of the Soviet government in its midst." 198.1.33

And on the grounds of this ridiculous, mendacious fallacy, they were driven out en masse: 1,084,828 people in 344 trains, followed shortly thereafter by another 120,000; they were sent to North Kazakhstan or were put into labor battalions, which constructed the metallurgical *kombinat* in Chelyabinsk (to the east of the Urals) in 1942. At Chelyabinsk there were fifteen camps for construction battalions, "and in each of them one hundred brigades of twenty-five to thirty men . . . a total of forty thousand to fifty thousand helped build that company." Perhaps as many as ten thousand died during the construction, and were left behind, unregistered, in mass graves. In fact, the survivors were unable to return after the war: they had no passports. Instead, they had to report to the police once a month. In addition to the Germans who worked at Chelyabinsk, there were also Ingermanlanders, Finns, Bulgarians, Romanians, and Hungarians.

It was said of the winter of 1943 that, "it was minus 42 degrees Celsius, but work was not interrupted for a moment. We hacked at the ground with picks, spades, and chisels and took the earth away in wheelbarrows. That's how we dug the construction pit for the foundations of the first rolling mill."

Russian Germans whose forefathers had lived in Russia often for more than a century were dismissed from the armed forces, along with Poles and Finns, and also taken to Chelyabinsk. Germans from Moscow city, from the provinces of Moscow and Rostov, altogether just under thirty thousand, were deported to Kazakhstan from 10 September 1941 on.

On 1 October 1949 a total of 1,099,758 Germans were still registered in the "Labor Army," either in "construction battalions" or as "special colonists." (Former) Volga Germans still emigrate to Germany to this day.

Chechens and Other Caucasian Peoples

Among the exiled peoples the Chechens are the best known. On 23 February 1944 the people in this Caucasian mountain republic were called together and surrounded. Suspecting nothing, they were given no more than half an hour to pack food for ten days and forty pounds of luggage per family, then they were loaded into Lend-Lease trucks that the United States supplied to the Soviet Union and taken to railway trucks. "Cattle trucks, bursting at the seams, without light or water, we traveled for almost a month to an unknown destination. . . . There was an outbreak of typhus and there was absolutely nothing done to combat it. . . . We buried the dead during short pauses at remote stops, next to the train in the soot-blackened snow." The dead were buried next to the train, because if anyone strayed more than five meters from the truck, they were shot without warning.

"Day and night," wrote Khadzhibar Bokov, "the truck was like a beehive, filled with the sound of religious singing. The people called on Allah to witness their suffering, to save them, the innocent children, the impotent old people, the sick. And they pleaded that those who had brought this monstrous evil upon them be punished." The party functionaries from Chechnya traveled to Kazakhstan in relative comfort, in a passenger train, with all conveniences and, once in Kazakhstan, went about their normal party business as usual.

"In Kazakhstan," Bokov continues, "we walked through the Kazakh steppes with a long line of carts. March was cold, and we were wearing light clothing. We were distributed among the villages where mostly Russians and Ukrainians lived. And they did not refuse us. . . . They let us warm ourselves, gave us tea to drink and milk for the children, to whom they also gave a piece of bread. They had no more to offer; everyone lived in destitution at that time."

A total of 106,000 families arrived in Kazakhstan in this way and twenty-three thousand in Kirghizistan. Chechens were also deported from Moscow and other towns. Chechen soldiers, too, were dismissed from the Red Army and deported to Kazakhstan, including some 700 officers, 1,696 sergeants and 6,488 privates. But because the Chechens were generally such good soldiers, officers often quickly changed the Chechens' nationality so that many remained in the Soviet army after all.

Their religion kept the exiles going. They were forbidden everything, including their national dance, the *lezginka,* as it was considered "bandit music." In the period from 1944 to 1948, according to the NKVD, 23.7 percent of all deportees of Caucasian origin died—44,704 people.

There was a prelude to this deportation. German parachutists had been dropped in this inhospitable area on 25 August 1942 and some Chechen functionaries had joined up with them. An uprising took place under the leadership of a certain Izrailov—and many Chechen civil servants died. "Bands of Chechens were wandering around in the mountains, killing the militia and security troops. Whether they were deserters or robbers, whatever they might have been, the entire people, young and old, was deported," Tatyana Shukova wrote. And in the words of Dmitri Zhukov: "Dogs were whining in the farmyards, and, in the barns, the unmilked little mountain cattle were screaming from pain."

497.2.100

48.1.163–64

48.1.164; 507.1.14

48.1.165

164.1

59.1.41

48.1.162

59.1.33

449.1.10

507.1.14

Claims have also been made that German soldiers, left behind by the
Edelweiss Bergjäger Division, had joined up with the Chechens. As early
as the spring and summer of 1943 Soviet divisions were deployed against
them.

In January 1943, during a meeting of the Politburo in which all others
kept quiet about this issue, a decision was made, on Stalin's initiative, to
deport the entire people, the majority of whom were innocent.

Z. Abdulayev, who, as a member of the NKVD, "fought against the
Chechens and Ingush who had established themselves in the mountains,"
quotes the following telegram in his book about this deportation: "Top
secret. To the People's Commissar for Interior Affairs for the USSR, Comrade L. P. Beria. For your eyes only. In view of the impossibility of transporting them and in order to allow operation 'Mountains' to progress
smoothly, I was obliged to liquidate more than seven hundred inhabitants of the village of Khaibakh. Colonel for State Security Gvesyano" The
colonel, as a result, was promoted and awarded a medal.

This massacre is confirmed in a letter to *Ogonyok* by Said-Emin Bit-
soyev, editor in chief of a newspaper in Grozny: "For more than forty
years you could only talk about this in whispers."

The freed areas were populated by Russians and people of other nationalities. Anatoli Pristavkin described in a novel how the residents and staff
of a Moscow children's home moved to Chechnya in 1944 and how
Chechens who had remained there continued to carry out attacks on the
intruders for a long time afterward.

At one point his train of evacuated Muscovite children comes to a
halt at a station. On the other rail is a goods train with barred windows
from which issue the sounds of children crying and incomprehensible
words. Later it turns out that those words meant "Water, water!" Yet every
adult pretended to hear nothing, "even the gray-haired driver of their
train strolled around at his ease, and people at the station went about their
business while stirring marching music blared from the radio."

After the war sixteen thousand demobilized Chechen soldiers went to
look for their deported relatives in Kazakhstan and Kirghizistan. They
searched for months.

In 1948 it was decided that the Chechens should remain exiled permanently. Only in 1957–58 were they able to go back. The return journey
was, again, a long one; the train stopped everywhere. "In those days,"

writes D. Zhukov, "the passengers made fires, cooked together, set up real markets. Here you could swap your things for bread rations, an ounce of tobacco, or canned food. Harmonica players, crippled by the war, expressed their sorrow in their music; blind singers earned a few coins and invalids without legs lined their pockets at the expense of good-natured passengers by performing all kinds of tricks, usually with marked cards. Everyone was trying to earn a crust of bread, as best he could, with his talents and skills. They lived like one big family; no one cheated anyone else."

507.1.14

In addition to the Chechens, others were deported: the Ingush, the Kabardino-Balkars (20,000), Karachi (40,000), Meskhets from Georgia in 1944 (115,000), Moslems from Georgia (80,000), as well as Kurds and a group of Armenian Moslems. Several tens of thousands of trucks were needed for these deportations and this in the middle of a war.

310.2.246–47

On the river Vasugan in Siberia where, from 1931 on, kulaks had been unloaded from boats, new exiles arrived. First, in 1941, came groups of people from Estonia, Latvia and Western Bukovina. Then, after the war, people of a dark complexion, from sunny Abkhazia in the Caucasus, arrived, exiled because they had supposedly planned an uprising with the aim of becoming part of Turkey. Of them it was said: "They will die like Jews in the winter."

273.1.134

273.1.134

Tatars and Kalmyks

The Tatars in the Crimea, accused of collaboration, were also deported. On 17 and 18 May 1944, 194,111 were taken away. Two partisan chiefs had reported to Marshal Budyonny, the commanding officer in this area, that "the vast majority of the Tatars from the mountains and from areas below the mountains had sided with the Fascists."

310.2.259

310.2.236

Crimean Tatars were dismissed from the army and transferred to construction battalions. The Tatar culture in the Crimea was virtually wiped out; the original place names disappeared.

Many did not even reach their destination, the Hunger Steppe in Kazakhstan. Others died there. Decades later Yelena Rzhevskaya described how a Tatar who had been deported as a child came in search of the area where he had been born, where everything had changed: the people, the names, the houses. He recalls "how Grandma could not walk, and two armed soldiers, who did not speak her language, took her under the arms and how her feet dragged over the stones. His little sister trotted along

383.7.362–63

with tiny steps, holding her mother's hand. Mother carried a heavy bale
of clothing on her head for the whole family."

Grandfather, who had never been afraid of anyone or anything, had
gone without protest, died on the way, and was buried on the Hunger
Steppe.

When new inhabitants notice that a Tatar has come to visit, he is chased
away, quickly taking water and earth with him for the family in Central
Asia.

On 27 December 1943 the Kalmyks, people from the steppe and nomads,
were deported north of the Urals and distributed over Siberia and Central Asia: their task, woodcutting. None of these people had ever seen
wood in the barren steppes by the lower reaches of the Volga and the
Caspian Sea.

Like their Chechen colleagues, their leaders traveled to their place of
exile in ordinary passenger trains. In Kalmykia the Germans, after first
executing all the Jews (in the capital of Elista), promised the Kalmyks a
free Kalmyk state. The kolkhozes were disbanded, and nomad customs
encouraged. Some of the Kalmyks sided with the Germans.

A Kalmyk cavalry corps, three thousand men strong, fought on the
German side but was disbanded by the Germans because of serious
crimes. Kalmyks in the army were then dismissed and sent to labor battalions, that is, all but General-Colonel Gorodovikov, general inspector
of the cavalry and Hero of the Soviet Union. Because Kalmyks were
excellent marksmen and officers did not want to lose them, the officers
quickly changed the Kalmyks' nationality whenever possible. The future
renowned litterateur David Kugultinov was dismissed "for being of Kalmyk
nationality."

Half of all the deported Kalmyks died, as did half the former soldiers
in a camp at Molotov (today Perm), where they worked on the Kamskaya
hydroelectric power plant in Kungur.

In 1944, 40,854 people were deported from Moldavia: "kulaks, former
landowners, collaborators from the German occupation, leaders and members of political parties, leaders and active members of illegal organizations and their families."

Secret Order No. 0078/42 of 22 June 1942 concerning the deportation of
all Ukrainians, signed by Marshal Zhukov and Beria, was not carried out.

Margin references: 383.7.362 / 245.1.24 / 310.2.253–54 / 310.3.257 / 310.3.260 / 245.2.11–12 / 245.1.24 / 331.1.57

The objective, Khrushchev recalled at the Twentieth Party Congress in February 1956, was to "exile all Ukrainians who have lived under occupation to remote areas of the USSR." The order was not implemented: there were too many Ukrainians, and there was nowhere to deport them to, but "otherwise they would have been deported."   188.4.129, 131

During the war a total of 1,514,000 people were deported as "special colonists." Their accommodations were abominable; a large number of evacuees had already been housed in the areas where they were sent, and these "special colonists" were one step down the ladder from the evacuees. At the end of the 1950s some of the restrictions imposed on them were lifted. Even later they were allowed, in principle, to return to their old homes, but other people had already occupied the homes for many years.

Occupation and Collaboration

Approximately sixty million people were living in the occupied areas. Just less than twenty-five million had managed to flee or were evacuated in time. It quickly became clear what kind of people the German occupiers were. The population, without question, would be given no consideration.

The fate of the Jewish inhabitants and the remaining Communists is described elsewhere. Wherever resistance was shown, retaliation campaigns were carried out mercilessly. Only rarely in my sources have I come across mention of a reasonable relationship between the occupiers and the local population.   144.1.74

In the beginning the people suffered little, as long as they weren't Jewish, a Communist, or a prisoner of war, but the inhuman herding together and internment of prisoners of war, in particular, quickly dispelled some people's initial relief, which had even evoked a celebratory mood in parts of Ukraine. The people were amazed at the height of the German soldiers, who were overconfident and cheerful.   383.1.68

In towns the occupiers appointed a "mayor," in villages, as I mentioned, a *starosta* (village head), both supported by police recruited from the local population (politsay). How many were in that police force is unknown; for a long time the subject remained taboo. At the beginning of 1942 there   274.1.165
were 60,421 members. The figure I came across for April 1944 was 191,166.   338.1.150

Some members of that police force executed their duties out of sympathy for the occupiers and hatred for the departed Communists. Others joined

up to avoid a worse fate, and they, especially, found themselves between
the devil and the deep blue sea. An equally forbidden subject was the
fact that Communists, too, were prepared to cooperate and collaborate.
Lev Razgon suggests that, in the Northern Caucasus, practically the entire
intelligentsia of Zelenchuk defected to the German side, "and even some
of our NKVD boys."

The occupiers were "amazingly loyal" to these defectors. A lot of former functionaries immediately changed sides. "The framework for cooperation with the Germans was prepared by the Soviet government," by the
experiences of many people in prisons, and by the terror aimed at farmers and others. Solzhenitsyn is inclined to see collaboration as a "tragic
phenomenon," caused by prewar events. Some "collaborators" joined up
on the orders of the Soviet authorities.

Wherever the German troops met with stubborn (military) resistance, as
at Rzhev, they hardened their attitude toward the local population. This
was also the case after the German defeat at Stalingrad and, even more
so, during the subsequent retreats.

The Germans acted even more savagely when hindered by partisan
activity, sending out retaliation expeditions, which spared nothing and no
one, and taking terrible reprisals.

All the inhabitants of the village of Leonovo were executed in February
1942 for helping the partisans. In Ola there were 1,758 victims, including
950 children. In White Russia, where partisan activity was well developed,
2,230,000, a quarter of the population, were killed. A total of 209 towns
were destroyed, and 628 villages "were wiped from the face of the earth."
Partisan activity evoked reprisals a hundredfold; some believe that those
campaigns cost "millions of people's lives."

As the Soviet troops liberated one occupied territory after another, they
acted with suspicion toward the local population, as they had been living
under occupation. That it was the mistakes of the political and military
leaders that had put the local residents in that position was conveniently
forgotten.

The units that arrived after the front troops, in particular, believed that
these people "are all tarred with the same brush; they are all deserters or
worse." According to Rzhevskaya: "The liberators did not return with a
feeling of guilt toward the population but as judges." In other words, "the
official bodies [of repression] had their work cut out for them!"

In captured Elista—the capital of the dissolved Kalmyk Republic—the *osobisty* even shot washerwomen and bakers, because their work had (also) benefited the Germans. Anyone who really had something on his conscience, however, had already beat it with the retreating Germans.

Girls and women who had consorted with the German soldiers changed their modern hairstyles straightaway. The punishment for genuine collaborators was the death sentence; punishment for the aforementioned girls and women was five years in the Gulag. Informers again took up their task; the NKVD and the *osobisty* had their hands full with tracking down and punishing offenders, for example, the engineer from the public works department in Odessa, who had managed to repair the water supply in order to stay alive and feed his children, or the woman with three children to feed who had taken a job as a secretary for the German authorities to save her family from starving to death.

Through her courage and reasonable relationship with the Kommandantur in Przemyl, Nikolai Lyubimov's mother had succeeded in saving the lives of a large number of Communists. This was exactly where the NKVD interrogator found her guilt lay. His argument, explains Lyubimov, was that "we should have let the Germans take as many people and cattle and everything else from the population as they wanted, and then the people would have hardened their attitudes, whereas my mother had contributed to their 'pacification.'"

To his credit Konstantin Simonov, in his novella *Sofia Leonidovna*, defends people like Lyubimov's mother. But this position did not help many. Years after the war people were still hesitant to talk about having lived under occupation. Questionnaires and job applications required such information.

Military Collaboration

Much has been written about General Andrei Vlasov's Russian Liberation Army (ROA). We have already seen that Vlasov was taken prisoner—or allowed himself to be taken prisoner—at Myasnoi Bor. In any event, over the following years he was able (or perhaps allowed) to form the ROA, which was comprised of Russians who fought in German uniform alongside the Germans. As late as 16 April 1945 tens of thousands of Russians were still ceremoniously pledging the oath to Vlasov and joining the ROA, which, by the end of the war, was reputed to have had as many as 320,000 men.

Some call Vlasov a traitor. Others, including Solzhenitsyn, see him as a true Russian patriot. His army, recruited from among desperate prisoners of war and people with a strong anticommunist conviction, fought in East Prussia and on the Oder (13 April 1945), and on 6 May 1945 liberated the center of Prague. The inhabitants of this city, in amazement, read the two slogans, written side by side on his tanks: "Down with Hitler" and "Down

259.1.154

with Stalin." On 2 August 1945 Vlasov was hanged in Moscow together with eleven other high-ranking officers from the ROA. They had previously been subjected to protracted torture, as they refused to admit to being traitors. As a result they received no public trial. "I'm not even going to describe how they were hanged," someone in the know told General

155.1.196–97

Grigorenko. Punishment for ROA soldiers was years in the Gulag. Vlasov's first wife, who had nothing to do with her husband's activities, was sentenced to five years in a camp.

Between 1945 and 1947, 148,079 members of Vlasov's army were sen-

371.2.179

tenced to long-term exile, and they were released in 1955. Opinion on Vlasov in current-day Russia remains divided.

With this I leave the issue of Vlasov and the ROA. Not only is the subject too complicated to discuss in a few pages, but it also lies outside the scope of this book.

In addition to Vlasov's Russian units, there were Lithuanian, Latvian, Estonian, Tatar, Crimean-Tatar, Azerbaijani, Georgian, Kalmyk, and other legions that fought on the German side, a total of some three hundred thousand men. Other estimations, however, arrive at lower figures, and

15.1.171

still others claim around a million.

Most of the Russians were deployed in the defense of the Atlantic Wall (where they were taken prisoner by the Allies). With the Russian armies

259.1.142

serving in the West, the German divisions could be deployed in the East. The Germans, incidentally, were extremely cautious with regard to foreign armed units. Hitler was against using them; the military leadership was in favor of them. The attitude toward the Ukrainian nationalists was even equivocal. In fact, particularly later in the war, the Ukrainian nationalists fought against both sides.

10

The Military

Mobilization

The mobilizations of June and August 1941 called up men who were born between 1890 and 1918 as well as younger men born in 1923. Those from the years in between were already in service. There was also a mobilization in 1942, described in a diary entry from May 1942: "The last people are going to the front. I saw a party being led away yesterday . . . grim, gaunt faces without a trace of life or courage, dull subjugation, hardly anyone smiled, heads bowed, few cheerful thoughts could be read on their faces." 455.1.94

"In the summer of 1943 not only many new lieutenants but terribly young soldiers, born in 1924, were drafted into the army. . . . They could do nothing but drill." 375.1.74

Gudzovski, a history student from Odessa, was standing in the courtyard of a barracks with several others. He heard the order: "Germans, five steps to the right; Estonians, Latvians, Lithuanians, to the left; people whose family or relatives have been arrested or convicted, to the front; the rest of you stay where you are." And so a person under suspicion was put into a "special construction battalion," which meant hard work and little food. 159.1.67

In 1943 almost everyone was called up; the medical examination was perfunctory. That had already been the case when the home reserve divisions were formed in 1941, and it was even more so for the later mobilization—if you can call it that—of men and boys who were in the liberated areas of Ukraine and other German-occupied areas. They were thrown into battle with neither proper preparation nor equipment. "In the morning a Red Army soldier went around to the farmhouses and made a list of old men and teenagers—all of whom had to go into the army,"

recounts Yelena Rzhevskaya. "The next day the same Red Army soldier
banged on the window: 'Come on out and line up!'"

Pyotr Grigorenko recalls, "Toward autumn 1944 it appeared that the
end of the war was approaching. The caliber of the 'human supplies'
pointed that way, too. Already no one was left in the country. The mobilization of boys born in 1927 was under way, in other words, seventeen-
year-old boys. . . . The Fourth Ukrainian Front was ordered to find human
reserves on the spot. There was a mobilization in Western Ukraine of
those born the same years as men already called up elsewhere; volunteers
in Trans-Carpathia were recruited, and the recuperating wounded and
sick returned to their units. The absence of people was so tangible that
the mobilization actually came down to a manhunt, the way slave traders
used to catch Negroes in Africa."

At the beginning of their training the regular recruits were placed in a
"reserve regiment" or "training regiment." All authors who have written
about their experiences there agree that those regiments had an extremely
daunting reputation: there was too little to eat, intense drilling, worn, ill-
fitting uniforms and footwear, and inhuman accommodations (filthy, stinking, and damp). Many fell sick from exhaustion. "The sick didn't even cry;
they simply moaned helplessly." Dysentery, bronchitis, anemia, and night
blindness were common, and, of course, perpetual hunger. The doors of
the barracks froze shut at night; people were either unable or unwilling
to open them and urinated on the stairs or on the porch. Anyone caught
doing so was arrested and beaten," wrote Viktor Astafyev. The only ones
who felt at home were the released criminals, who, in groups, terrorized
the young recruits and took their meager possessions. Barracks like these
were more like a camp in the Gulag than anything else.

Remaining in such a regiment was so intolerable that everyone longed
to get to the front: the sooner they got away, the better. The most horrifying account of such a regiment, in my view, is the novel by Astafyev,
who was "trained" at the end of 1942 near Novosibirsk. His tale is so realistic that it is doubtful it will ever be translated.

At the end of Astafyev's novel, which is entitled *Chertora Yama* (The
devil's pit), he writes that he guarantees the accuracy of every detail and
every personal and place name, even though he expects to be attacked by
the "professional veterans" who have claimed the truth about the war and
the victory for themselves.

383.5.215

155.4.168

23.7.246

Just a few details: A bed wetter is first tormented and then kicked to death by an officer. Kazakhs, understanding little or no Russian, are forced to eat pork; first they refuse and then they eat it, vomiting it up later. The Snegiryov twins are absent for four days and return with delicious farmhouse food for everyone. They are executed in front of the troops—on a Sunday, so as not to disturb the routine. "The Kazakhs cried; all the others mourned them in silence. Only the Orthodox believers mourned together. On a piece of paper, and using a pencil, they drew a cross and the image of the Mother of God—and they prayed before it . . . all night long they were on their knees, praying for the forgiveness of human trespasses." "What do you think, shall we go and pray at the front, too?" the commissar remarks sarcastically. "They'll certainly be praying there if they can manage it. There the wounded cry for their God or their mother but not for their political leader. Almost all the dead lie there with a cross around their neck. Before going into battle they sign up to join the party, but they put on their crosses before they attack."

To stop people from dropping off to sleep in political instruction sessions, the order is given unexpectedly to "stand" and then "sit." The counterespionage service attempts to recruit informers with promises and threats.

Starving boys steal food and rummage through the bins. The main character in Astafyev's *Chertora Yama* is the strong, Siberian Orthodox Kostya Ryndin, who keeps his faith despite all the baiting.

The "instructive execution" of K. D. Zelentsov, who had broken a captain's nose and glasses, is commuted to service in a punitive company. An officer recalls the retreat of 1941, when many soldiers shot their own men. "There proved to be far more people eager to fight against their own brothers than against the fascist enemy." They drilled, crawled through mud and snow, were not allowed to practice with their weapons, and were armed only with wooden sticks. Other authors, such as Vladimir Vinogradov, David Samoilov, Anatoli Genatulin, and Sergei Polyakov, describe comparable experiences with similar drilling equipment. A censor forced Vyacheslav Kondratyev to scrap a passage in which he had referred to wooden rifles and wooden machine guns.

Astafyev's novel is the first book to deal with the war from an Orthodox religious perspective. In the barracks the regime so destroyed and crushed the Russian character, spirit, and belief that people were conflicted in their loyalties between Soviet patriotism and Christian conscience.

474.1; 386.1; 127.9 348.1

209.12.297

111.1.227

23.13 These regiments, in particular, have had little mention. At Orenburg, in one such regiment, nine recruits slept in a pit dug from the earth and lined with turf. Two greatcoats were supplied for nine men, and a man 488.2.143 could turn to sleep on his other side only when ordered. Dmitri Sergeyev described comparable experiences in a reserve regiment. The scene is 395, nos. 2, 3 Siberia at the end of 1942: Nothing but drilling, the SMERSH officer recruiting informers; an "instructive execution" is carried out to keep discipline. Sergeyev: "In peacetime half the recruits would have failed the medical because of poor health or their age. Now, everyone was passed as 395.2.36 A1. Stalingrad left no room to breathe—it kept demanding replacements."

As soon as recruits had received some sort of uniform, "warm clothing was collected from each company—help for the front. That collection was considered voluntary. But if a soldier tried to hide any of his own 395.2.37 clothing, it was confiscated later during inspection anyway." You can't shoot? "Well, we'll see about that. Anyone who hasn't snuffed it in the first fight will soon learn to shoot, make no mistake. It's not as difficult as 368.3.117 all that."

According to Astafyev, poor training and the weakened condition to which the recruits were reduced was partly what caused the great loss of 23.13 human lives.

Once the "training" had been completed, the men were placed in a marching company, with good equipment and uniform (cap, gloves, woolen underwear, shirts, trousers, a uniform jacket and padded coat, felt boots, puttees, kit bag, mess tin, and spoon). You only got a rifle when you 295.1.166 reached the front.

Soldiers who spoke no Russian and barely understood it faced an even grimmer future. "Many of them died without ever having fired a shot at 282.2.339 the enemy."

The Road to the Front

The soldiers were generally transported to the front in freight trucks. The journey took many days: a stove in the truck and planks along the walls, and during brief stops in the fields everybody out to quickly do your business. Genatulin once described his fellow passengers: "Calm, patient Russians from different provinces, fast-talking Tatars from Kazan, quiet, ambitious Bashkirs who enjoy military service, mysterious forest people from Siberia with broad cheekbones and small eyes, unpretentious, cheerful, lively Kazakhs, adroit, friendly children from Central Asia—they were all traveling together to one war, slept next to one another, shared their body warmth with one another."

"The reserve regiment was finally behind them: the earth shelters with the fleas, the snowdrifts, the exercise alarms in the dead of the night." At the stations "crowded with people, here passenger trains, full of evacuees and the wounded and military transports shunting continually back and forth to the front, came to a stop. There is lively trade next to the train, soldiers attempting to supplement their scanty rations. There is brisk trade for hot water at the kiosk. Getting hold of a kettle of hot water to make tea is a major concern. When there is no kiosk, then it's down to a pump station or to the water pipe that feeds the locomotive." Getting hot water and swapping military clothing for food was apparently quite usual during stops at the stations.

127.4.18–19

348.1.112

After the train journey, the men generally continued on foot, sometimes hundreds of kilometers, traveling preferably by night to avoid airborne attacks.

Teodor Vulfovich writes that his regiment had their papers checked no fewer than four times on the way to the front by stocky NKVD boys. These NKVD boys should have been deployed against the SS Panzer Divisions, he writes, instead of against "these half-trained, half-uniformed young lads."

488.3.171–72

Sergei Polyakov went on foot to the front at Velikie Luki in February 1943: "There was a terrible snowstorm the first few days. We walked during the short daytime hours; we walked at dusk and in the night. During brief breaks, the soldiers dropped into the snow and immediately fell asleep. Officers ran along the column, waking the men, getting them to stand up. I had learned to sleep during a march: you walk with your eyes closed and you sleep. It's important that there are no bends in the road, because then you wander out of the rank and fall over." Polyakov covered 250 to 300 kilometers by foot in ten or twelve days. On the way he met a young woman, who said, "'Go on. They've all been left behind there. You don't know anything yet. No one will come back.' We soldiers walked on in silence."

348.1.113

During one such night march, wrote Aleksandr Shenkman, you bump into the man in front of you now and again, and you can cut your face on his weapon. Just before they reached the front line, they had their first hot meal in ten days. "The front is now close at hand. You can hear the shooting. We are walking over an ice road built in the thick woods. Horses, like animated skeletons—two soldiers supporting each horse,

441.1.98

one soldier on the left, one on the right, others pushing the sleigh from behind—are transporting our mortars."

In his story, "The Selizharovo Highway," Kondratyev wrote: "We arrived at the front line in the night and went straight into attack the following day. . . . What I saw was completely different from what we had done in practice attacks: a field full of neglected corpses, an unconsidered, unprepared attack. They chased us forward against the machine guns, over a minefield. After only two months nobody in our brigade was left—and we only had carried out three attacks." David Samoilov was on his way to the front at Tikhvin: "We could hear the rumble in the distance to our right, which reminded us of a stone-crushing machine, and we looked anxiously at the wagons full of wounded. Cart horses pulled slow, narrow wagons in which two or three wounded lay sheltered from the rain with tent cloth until, sometimes, all you could see was part of a bandaged head, arm, or

386.1.61 leg. The proximity of death was frightening."

At the front the marching companies were transferred to the front commandants. The escorts returned to the reserve regiment, unless an

216.3.58–59 extreme lack of officers at the front forced them to stay.

The Russian Infantryman

According to David Samoilov, in the presence of commandants the Russian infantryman "is submissive, agrees easily, promises rashly, is sensitive to praise, and is even enthusiastic about the strictness of the leadership." When there are no superiors about, however, the infantryman "grumbles and curses, threatens and boasts, and is extremely irritable." The third state he displays in battle. "Then he is a hero. He dies calmly, without any fuss. He will not leave his comrades in misery. . . . The Russian soldier is hardened, undemanding, carefree, and a confirmed fatalist. . . . Those

386.2.52 traits make him invincible."

Soldiers and sergeants had their heads shaved and were dressed somberly. No one had a watch. "And why should you?" asked Genatulin. To count how many more minutes you have to live? But most members of the military were crazy about such gadgets; after all, most of the soldiers were only eighteen or nineteen. Watches were the most coveted booty. They were taken from enemy bodies, too: "Why should the things go

127.12.141–42 to waste?" There were helmets, but no one wore them. The helmet made words ring and resonate; you couldn't understand each other properly, so you got rid of it. You only see soldiers wearing helmets in films and in paintings. They wore a *pilotka,* a cap with a red star on it; in the winter they wore a fur cap with earflaps. Helmets were used as a basin for washing or to light fires in. Wearing helmets was compulsory for German troops. A Russian wearing a helmet would be taken as a German and shot at by his own people.   313.1.139

Footwear was uncomfortable: shoes with puttees. Many authors mention the dead being robbed of good footwear, particularly boots, as they   209.2
were scarce initially. Viktor Berdinskikh writes that there was a problem   37.1.21
with footwear up until 1943: "You had to wear shoes, and worn out ones at that, tied round with string so the sole didn't fall off—and then into battle!"

A tent cloth that doubled as a raincoat was not available for everyone, and without it your uniform jacket and puttees got soaking wet. The men   230.1.162
washed in the evening: the superstition was that anyone washing in the morning would not make it to the evening. Sergei Polyakov describes how   488.2.124
a dead lieutenant, lying in no-man's-land, was gradually deprived of his weapons, clothing, underwear, and footwear: "The naked body yellowed and, for several days, served as a landmark for us."   348.1.117

For weapons, you had a rifle or a submachine gun, a couple of rounds of cartridges and some hand grenades, plus a small engineer's spade, a gas mask full of cartridges, a canteen, a knife, and a cloth for cleaning your weapons.

Some personal possessions were allowed: a medallion with your military and personal details, letters, paper, a stump of pencil, newspaper for rolling tobacco, a tinder box, a towel, shaving gear, your ration of bread, and sometimes booklets published especially for soldiers.

A Russian machine gun—the Maksim—weighed sixty kilos. Two men had to transport it; the gunner always has a second man with him, and four men carried the ammunition crate.   295.1.169

Golitsyn described how his Pioneers Company advanced in the summer of 1944 in the area of Chernigov: "On thirty carts with two mobile canteens, a smithy, with a sidecar for the captain, a still on a cart, cows, sometimes ten of them, our company was half a kilometer long and did not exactly present a military spectacle."   137.4.52

"Anyone who served in the army then [after May 1945]," wrote V. Yerashov, "knows about the strange, multicolored getups: some wore the gray Russian uniform, some the grass-green English or bluish Canadian jackets,

some were in padded jackets, in jackets covered with tent cloth, in red
American jackets with all kinds of headgear, whatever you had."

108.1.5

The Life of the Infantryman

Little has been written about the life of the ordinary infantry soldier.
Probably, Vasil Bykov assumes, because most of them were killed.

66.7.380

Concerning danger, an infantry company fared not much better than a
punitive company, and the most dangerous jobs in the infantry were those
of scout and sharpshooter. Nevertheless some preferred life as a scout
behind the German lines, because "no one is shooting at you or bossing
you around," wrote Vulfovich, evidently referring to his own people.

488.2.61

The infantry was generally deployed until no one was left. The men
were divided up roughly: big ones and little ones; tall ones for the infantry,
short ones for the mortars. Then a question was put to them: "Who wants
to have a jolly war?" Those who stepped forward became scouts.

"We, the infantry, the 'kings of the battlefield,' we are always suffering
from a cold, we are always coughing," wrote Yuri Belash. "What do you
hear when the infantry is marching in columns? Stamping feet and coughing. And what do you hear when you wake up in the morning? Coughing
that rolls through the trenches like artillery practice. Well, it's true, isn't
it? And why? We sleep on damp ground, we crawl over wet earth, we sit
in damp trenches, and almost all of us smoke. Not light tobacco, but the
heavy soldiers' stuff."

32.2.17

Genatulin writes: "What a soldier experiences during an attack you
can't call wild recklessness or fury; the feeling is more like ecstasy, like
bliss." But he also writes: "I had just recovered after heavy fighting in
which almost our entire battalion was wiped out in one day, and I had
not yet got rid of the sight of blood and the stinking breath of the dead
when we had to go back into hell. While I had thought and hoped that,
after everything we had been through, we would be sent to the hinterland for a long rest, now it suddenly dawned on me that if I also came out
of this fight unscathed they would send me back into the following battle
and then into another and another, until I was wounded or killed."

127.7.200

All the same, the front was often seen as a kind of liberation, because
"in the hinterland food was scarce, the discipline and treatment brutal."
When anyone was wounded and ended up in a hospital, he always wanted
to go back to his old unit, even though friendships at the front were

386.3.299

usually short-lived: a few weeks, a month at the most. Two months in battle is, after all, already too long. "You get so exhausted in that time that you only have one thought: get killed or wounded as quickly as possible to save you the agony; after all, there is a limit to what a man can bear." 209.5

Of course, everyone tried to stay out of danger as much as possible: "from the trench to the shelter, from the shelter to the battalion, regimental, or divisional command post; from ordinary private to writer, cook, aid to the political leader, and, if necessary, orderly." 375.1.76

The hard and fast rule was this: "Ask no questions, refuse no orders." 386.1.61 This was not fatalism but a cautious attitude with respect to life. Toward the end of the war people were more careful: nobody fancied dying at the last minute. Soldiers with a family were more wary than single young 216.2.240 men. During and after Stalingrad people started to gain a better understanding of the fighting and the losses were fewer, although, "for the infantry, being careful made no sense. But being carefree was accepting one's fate, one's familiarity with death." 349.1.169

War, according to Viktor Astafyev, is hard work: "We were working all the time, terribly hard . . . digging, digging, digging." 345.1.193

Yevgeny Nosov, then in the army and later well known as a litterateur, said that war is, "above all, patience, marching for hours on end, carrying heavy loads, pushing and pulling with all your might, digging with a substandard spade you have found in an empty farmyard, feeling cold, your teeth chattering, at your post, stamping your feet in your frozen felt boots, damp, rain, overcoming heat and thirst, sometimes waiting days for a stray field kitchen, gnawing on that miserable, stale, hard bread because you have nothing else, smoking dry grass and moss, lighting a fire with flint, sleeping with your boots on, often on damp ground and sometimes simply in a hollow in the snow, enduring being shot at with bullets and under heavy mortar fire, not to mention the fighting itself when you have to face the machine guns in the open or defend yourself from a tank with grenades." 316.1.5

Heroic deeds, according to Vyacheslav Kondratyev, only take a moment: "It's over in seconds, but daily life is days and nights, bloody, without prospect, because only death or wounding can free the soldier from the permanent, inhuman effort that was unbelievably difficult to keep up." 209.6

Vsevolod Osten, too, sees the most important characteristic of the soldier as the "limitless patience that no one else has." Pomerants writes of 326.2.89 the soldiers: "Patience that borders on and flows into the willingness to die, even if no one else comes to help you." 349.1.159

Polyakov wrote how nicely behaved the farm boys from Vologda were, quite different from their urban peers. They did not smoke, did not drink; they were honest, reliable, and accommodating. "One day the talk turned to girls. It turned out that they were all still virgins. One said, shyly, that he had had 'it' before the army, but 'very little of it.'" Vulfovich tells a similar story. Astafyev, on the other hand, had a different experience; he was used to unwashed, illiterate, uncivilized soldiers. "All their words were replaced with orders; they used the absolute minimum of words for communication among themselves and with officers; the air was blue with swearing, coarseness, and indecent expressions, military jargon, learned largely from criminals and all kinds of prison scum. . . . Far from human, almost animal . . . some of the front soldiers were like beasts." Viktor Nekrasov looked back fondly on the "perpetually . . . dissatisfied soldier, his cap pulled down over his ears, his puttees hanging loose, cursing the sergeant under his breath more than the Germans, who had plowed right through Europe and climbed the Reichstag."

In the Trenches and Shelters

Sleeping in the open air in the summer was not a great problem for Russian soldiers. In the winter they had to dig a kind of hollow in the snow, lay branches on the bottom, and sleep close together.

They often lacked the strength to dig a trench, or the soil was frozen, and in those cases they had no protection at all. Pomerants described the winter of 1941–42 in this way: "It wasn't war, it was simply murder." "The trench is the coldest, hardest place in the world—no fairy tales there," Vladimir Tendryakov once remarked.

Captain Anatoli Lebedev wrote: "In the spring the groundwater prevents you from digging a trench the way you're supposed to. And then the soldier's home is a small trench, sometimes waist-high. Soldiers spend all their time there. . . . Trenches are extremely unpleasant in the autumn mud and in the early spring when the snow melts. In the autumn the trench is full of sticky mud. You can't sit anywhere; there's nowhere to put your kit bag. In the April thaw the bottom of the trench is covered in slabs of thawed feces. In the winter the soldiers generally relieve themselves in the trenches, in the odd corner or dead end. That all freezes and is covered with snow. Then in the spring it all comes to the surface; you can't get through, you can't walk anywhere."

Yelizaveta Romanova, an army interpreter with one of the divisions,

348.1.113
488.2.153

23.14.25

309.2

136.1.163

349.1.160

460.1

257.1.49, 50

declared, while on the border with Romania: "In the trench it smelled like a trench: of damp, gun smoke, sour sweat, tobacco smoke, of a kind of disgusting eau de cologne, of rye porridge, iodine, machine oil, and burned iron."

374.1.11

Officers and Men

My information indicates that there was a wedge between soldiers and sergeants, on the one side, and between sergeants and officers, on the other. Officers, one often reads, treated their subordinates carelessly, pushing them forward into senseless attacks and ignoring any losses. The men were often of such an age that they could have been the young officers' fathers.

394.1.115

In critical situations officers had the right to shoot subordinates without any trial. Other officers were violent in other ways; corporal punishment, particularly at the front, was not unusual. Generals, too, would hit the lower-ranking officers.

446.1.110

Officers received a modest extra ration of cigarettes and food (chocolate). Those who shared this with the men lived longer at the front, Kondratyev writes, ominously. No wonder the standard tale in the field was of an officer who once hit or killed a soldier for a minor issue, after which the soldier's comrades fell on their superior and killed him in the next battle.

209.4.117

282.2.336

Soldiers who had their own opinion and expressed it openly were not terribly popular with the officers. The general idea was to keep your mouth shut and do what you were told; "no tittle-tattling" and "no philosophizing" were the favorite rules of thumb. Sometimes officers actually feared their own soldiers more than the enemy feared them, but officers who were careful with their men, who did not expose them to unnecessary danger, were adored.

32.2.22

303.2.132

Statistically, in periods of attack, a lieutenant's life expectancy was eight days; that of an ordinary infantryman was even shorter. Overexhaustion took its toll; there were rarely any replacements and leave was virtually unknown, except in very exceptional circumstances. This, of course, increased the tension among the men; they became careless, and fatalism dulled their wits. All the same, writes Boris Slutsky, without leave, without entertainment, without brothels, the Soviet army still vanquished the army that had all those advantages: "In the winter of 1941, in Moscow, with our

446.1.107

snow pits warmed by our own breath, we beat the Germans who were not
adapted to sleeping in snow pits."

407.3.47

Officers were not always suited to their task, which was not surpris-
ing after the purges in the higher ranks. They had little experience, were
usually overconfident, and were contemptuous of losses. Astafyev sees
those officers as out to avenge the insults and humiliation they themselves
had previously been subjected to, by taking their anger out on others
who were now in their power. Certainly there was a lack of good officers.
Indeed, some companies were led by sergeants.

23.12.29
326.2.141

Good officers did, however, emerge from the reserve, namely, teachers
and technicians. These officers had more respect for the men than did the
professional personnel, and they were also more competent with regard
to military strategy. Before you could become an officer, you were thoroughly checked for reliability. If any family member had been in the
Gulag, then you would not qualify for that rank.

209.4.123

David Samoilov writes that the soldiers expected care, justice, and skill
from the officers. If an officer did not fulfill those expectations, then the
soldiers had no confidence in that officer during battle "and, worse still,
they would leave him wounded on the battlefield or would put him out
of his misery."

386.1.66–67

At the end of the war many inexperienced, young officers remained. As
they knew neither fear nor caution, many of them died.

286.1.131

Whenever the officers suddenly became friendly, that was a sure sign that
the journey to the front was approaching, because at the front "there was
shooting and you couldn't have any mutual resentment."

187.1.133

Dmitri Sergeyev noted: "At the front, too, the relationship between
officers and men was far from humane, but the difference between their
relationship at the front and at the reserve regiment was immeasurable."
Golitsyn feels that, "in the second half of the war, the cliquishness and
arrogance among officers increased."

395.3.111

137.3.23

Even greater was the distance between soldiers and staff personnel. "Soldiers display no cheerfulness," noted the future litterateur Yuri Nagibin in
1942. "That is displayed only by rosy-cheeked men from the staff, men
who shave every other day and change the collars of their uniform shirts.
Those people write papers, eat in mess halls, are afraid of every plane,
and panic at every incident. The rest of the time they are full of cheerful
militant activity. The fighting is done by sick, exhausted, filthy half-wits
with frozen noses, a weary look, so weak you could knock them down with

a feather. Healthy, fat, cheerful people write papers, send other people into
battle, and get their uniforms at the military outfitters." 303.2.125

Samoilov complained of the suspicious atmosphere at the front. Keeping a diary or making notes was strictly forbidden. But the "relationship
between the front soldiers themselves was generally friendly. Sergeants
seldom insulted or humiliated the men. When the reserve regiments were
in the hinterland, then the soldiers liked to curse their superiors; there
they felt that all those bastards had ensconced themselves in the hinterland and, from sheer malice, bent over backward to make the men's lives
a misery with their draconian strictness and pointless activities. At the
front, though, most officers were easy-going, felt responsible for us, didn't
make us do anything for no reason, and lived pretty much as we did; they
shared the dangers with us, the ups and downs of life at the front." 386.1.66–67

New Terms of Address and Decorations

In the spring of 1943 new terms replaced the old: *commandant* became
officer, fighter became *soldier*. The officers were given new insignia: now
instead of circles and squares on the collar, there were stripes and stars
on the newly introduced epaulettes (*pogony*). There were some who asked
themselves whether the term *comrade* would now be replaced with *Your
Excellency,* as officers were addressed under the tsars. New decorations
were also introduced, named after Suvorov and Kutuzov, heroes of the
Napoleonic war, and another after Aleksandr Nevsky, who had vanquished
the Order of the Teutonic Knights in 1242. This latter decoration, incidentally, had been introduced earlier, on 30 July 1942. The wounded were
also decorated: those lightly wounded with a dark red stripe, a yellow
stripe for the seriously wounded. 323.4.99

"The honoring of ranks and positions reached its height after Stalingrad," according to Kardin. "The customs of the tsarist army were now
being copied. . . . Some saw positive signs for the future in this turn of
events." 188.2.139

This new order was to eradicate the "former fraternity." Officers were
now allowed to have an orderly, who carried out all kinds of chores for
them. Every morning Captain Rubinstein's orderly brought him a cup of 230.1.161
vodka and fried potatoes. During the day, when he had visitors, vodka
was brought again: "no one was drunk, but everyone was tipsy." After the 380.1.52
war Rubinstein disappeared from the scene for several years, the result of
alcoholism, a habit he acquired in the army.

As the war progressed, medals and decorations were handed out more freely; some had rows of them.

Even Prince Sergei Golitsyn received the Order of the Red Star in 1945 in Poland. David Ortenberg tells of a soldier who was to be declared a Hero of the Soviet Union, until it was discovered that his wife had been arrested. He was given a choice: either get a divorce or you don't become a Hero. He opted for the latter.

The Order of the Red Star was dubbed the ladies' medal, since officers rewarded their girlfriends with it. The medal soldiers most prized was the one "for proven courage."

After Stalingrad Viktor Nekrasov and other officers were as proud as Punch with their new uniforms: epaulettes were stiffened with tin or plexiglas and caps worn at an angle over the right ear; there was a sword belt, double uniform belts, a dagger and a knife, a German Walther pistol (superior to the Russian TT), and boots with the tops rolled down. This showy display of equipment and, of course, decorations and medals applied to all officers, Nekrasov said. "But in time the officers lost interest. Especially—and naturally at the request of those actually wearing the uniforms and medals—after the funds to pay for them were withdrawn and the right to free travel abolished."

For a few years after 1945 people still wore their medals, but thereafter no longer, except on 9 May, Victory Day.

Political Bodies

At the beginning of the war thousands of Communists—even those without any military knowledge—were called up "to take the lead." On 27 June 1941 twelve provincial party committees were given three days to supply one to ten groups of Communists, each consisting of five hundred men. The role the Communist Party played in the war was of tremendous significance, although perhaps it is more apt to refer to the role of the party members. The regime always claimed that the organizational role of the party and its members was decisive. That is certainly true, although the party also implemented a number of erroneous, ill-advised orders and many nonmembers fought no less bravely than party members. This is also true of soldiers whose families had been murdered by the Soviet regime or exiled or arrested as "kulaks" or "enemies of the people." The fact is that millions of soldiers were party members; it was customary for the men virtually to become members en masse automatically, just

137.4.65

309.1.68

309.1.67–68

7.1.34–35

209.6

before an attack. They would say: "If I fall in battle, then please consider me a Communist." 23.8.89–90
127.9.45

As many as 5.5 million members of the armed forces joined the party during the war. Astafyev sneers, "Yes, to bump up the number of Communists killed and bring honor and fame to the party. See how brightly the flame of the party burns in the winds of war." It is questionable whether the soldiers even cared about belonging to the party. Undoubtedly party members were often called on for a particularly risky assignment. 23.10.96

Kondratyev writes: "When you talk of the party's role in the war, you have to credit the political leaders, the party organizers of the various companies and battalions, and the Komsomol organizer. They sat alongside the soldiers in hideouts or in rapidly dug underground shelters and were the first to enter the battlefield when attacked, taking the lead, setting, as they said at the time, a personal example." They were people you could talk to, according to Zelenkov, who consider them the advance guard, the uniting force: no wonder the Germans killed them first when they took prisoners. 209.4.123

492.1.75

In the absence of a political leader or a commissar, ordinary soldiers could also consider themselves "political soldiers." Lieutenant Osten got on well with his political soldiers, but he knew, if he did anything wrong, that political soldier would shoot him dead without hesitation. 326.2.143–44

In July 1941 military commissars were appointed. Their task was to "promptly inform the Supreme Command and the government of any officers and political commissars who, through their conduct, besmirch the honor of the Red Workers and Farmers Army." These military commissars were also given the right to make decisions for the commandant. This meant the end of monocratic leadership; in 1988 Ortenberg, the editor in chief of the army newspaper, *Red Star*, referred to this change as "a sign of mistrust from the prewar years that cost our army dearly." On 10 October 1942, however, the "singular leadership" was reinstated and the position of military commissar abolished. 323.3.160

303.3.162

Officers had to deal with their political leader, whose official name, after October 1942, was "deputy commandant for political affairs." Officers were further monitored or hampered or both by "the representatives from headquarters," who visited them regularly and interfered in everything. The men would heave a sigh of relief when these people left. 400.6.124–25

For the soldiers, however, a political functionary (*politrabotnik*) was indeed an important visitor. He came to speak to them, gauge their mood, and give each of them a cigarette. "Soldiers who had enjoyed such luxuries only on feast days before the war politely stretched out their black, rough hands to the cigarette case, smoked and enjoyed the intelligent taste of fine tobacco," writes Anatoli Lebedev.

257.2.51

In turn, the NKVD officers from SMERSH, who were entirely independent of everyone, inspected the political organs.

282.2.300

At the beginning of the war, officers and political commissars were obliged to take the lead during an attack, to "guarantee, by personal example, the success of the infantry battalion's attack." German sharpshooters were equally aware of this procedure and, as a result, the commandants suffered severe losses. This foolish bravery was soon officially scrapped.

416.2.61

The enemy did not succeed in driving a wedge between those soldiers who were party members and those who were not, but the authority of the former remained great.

282.2.295

Kondratyev once had to take a bag of items to a "political section" thirty kilometers away and came across an animated party seated at a table groaning with provender. "A fat regiment commissar took the sack from me and shut the door without even thanking me." It was only the cleaner who gave him bread and vodka for his return journey.

209.4.117

"I recently read that the leader of the Riesman song and dance troupe procured girls for Colonel Brezhnev," Kondratyev wrote in 1992. "Didn't we know about such things occurring in other political sections? Of course, we knew! Sometimes we even saw these 'ideological inspirers' in the political sections of fronts, armies, and divisions growing fat, getting drunk, and indulging in debauchery."

209.9

Every military body had informers who had to report to SMERSH, the organization that had recruited them, about everything they heard. Everyone watched his tongue: "never talk about politics" was the unspoken rule. Word was, according to Rubinstein, that "if three officers had a conversation at the front, two of them told the KGB about it."

348.1.111

380.1.50

Informers had to be wary, too, because, as Vladimir But wrote, "at the front people do not forgive informers and the bullets are not marked." Rybakov added: "If you discover the bastard, he gets a bullet in his back during the fighting."

64.1.59

382.1.43

No one at the front cared for "questionnaires" or what these questionnaires said about you. "It was people doing the fighting, not questionnaires," Rybakov wrote. "Soldiers simply didn't fill them out. Who had a criminal record? Who had been exiled as a kulak or was the 'son of an enemy of the people'? Who simply came from the nobility or from the merchant class? Nobody knew, and nobody cared."

382.1.43

Supply Corps and Provisions

The difference between the provisions that were planned and those that were actually provided seems to have been phenomenal. In September 1941 each soldier was officially entitled to the following per day: bread, 900 grams; wheat flour, 20 grams; groats, 140 grams; macaroni, 30 grams; meat, 150 grams; fish, 100 grams; fat, 20 grams; vegetable fat, 20 grams; sugar, 35 grams; tea, 1 gram; salt, 30 grams; potatoes, 500 grams; cabbage, 170 grams; carrots, 45 grams; beets, 40 grams; onions, 30 grams; soap, 200 grams; tobacco, 30 grams; and three boxes of matches a month. At that time, in September 1941, 7.4 million men were entitled to those rations; in October 1941, "more than eight million men"; and in May 1942, "almost ten million men." From August 1941 on, soldiers at the front were also given 1 deciliter of vodka a day, to keep up "their health and activity under difficult war conditions."

82.1.95

82.1.93–94

471.1.95–96

Most important for the soldiers was the tobacco, followed by the bread, and in third place the vodka, which they normally received in little bottles (*shkaliki*).

322.1.140

There were mobile canteens, but generally the daily ration consisted of hard, dried bread (*sukhari*), which the sergeant weighed out and distributed by hand. The writer Yevgeny Nosov describes that bread as follows: "It is soulless bread without taste or form, spoiled because it's been kept for long periods, because of bad weather and transport, and because it is made from poor grain, like clay. It is impossible to bite off a piece of bread like that; it's almost like concrete. You can only break it up with the butt of your rifle or with a stone. Or you have to soak it and then you get a brown, sour porridge. And how are you supposed to do that in the winter?"

127.9.14

316.1.4

Others, who were more fortunate, had a different experience elsewhere. Lebedev writes: "There was generally enough to eat: 900 grams of good rye bread, buckwheat porridge for breakfast and lunch, usually with meat, something like goulash, and tea. The evening meal consisted of three courses. Big portions, calculated for a healthy man. In the first winter of the war, of course, there was plenty of confusion at the front. Soup, porridge, and tea arrived cold, sometimes with ice in it. The bread was so

frozen that you had to cut it up with an ax or even saw it. Chewing on
257.2.49 bread like that with ice cold soup gave little pleasure."

Later in the war, writes the same Lebedev, the food supplies were
well organized. Nonsmokers—of whom there were few, by the way—were
given sweets instead of tobacco. Here is how the smokers managed: "You
keep newspaper with the tobacco in your tobacco pouch (not in a tin).
You get a light from your tinderbox. Two or three strikes on the flint and
you have a spark on the end of your wick, in a cartridge. So you have a
light and not a flame, which is important, too. Matches are of little use;
257.2.50 they get wet and the box falls to pieces."

The menu generally consisted of bread, porridge with sugar, tobacco,
and vodka. Hot meals were a relief and a feast. Sergei Polyakov wrote that
348.1.123 he had never received a hot meal at the front, only bread.

Liquid food was served in one pan for two men, so, apart from your
32.1.76 rifle, the possession of a spoon was a matter of life or death. Experienced
soldiers knew never to eat before an attack, because, if you do, a stomach
wound is always fatal.

There are also numerous accounts of hunger being the predominant
feeling in the army, and sometimes, at the front, food not being delivered
for days. Soldiers would even go into the fields and dig for something edi-
313.1.138 ble there.

One continually reads that the soldiers ate horsemeat, even if the horse
had been dead for some time. Kondratyev talks of men at the Kalinin front
209.24.104 searching through the clothes of their dead comrades for food or tobacco.

Soldiers received parcels from the home front, which were made up "on
the directions of the party Central Committee." These parcels contained
food, tobacco, sometimes vodka, clothing, and a letter for the unknown
recipient. Often a correspondence was struck up between the recipient
386.1.69; 82.1.94 of the letter and the sender. Items were also stolen from those parcels.
Kondratyev writes about a political commissar who removed all the vodka
from the parcels so as "to increase the morale of the battalion comman-
209.9 dant and the commissar."

During the last years of the war American food was provided: in addition to the famous corned beef there were also daily rations, which con-
167.2.125 sisted of three portions packed in a box. The food was considered tasty
but not very nutritious. The amount of provisions reached their height in
Germany, where civilian homes were looted.

11

Ideas and Views

Patriotism or Something Else?

Unlike what Soviet propaganda would have had people believe, the soldiers were not fighting first and foremost for an ideal, such as communism or the Soviet government. Although that was true, of course, for some in the military, the majority was fighting because their fatherland, their own village, their own house was in danger and had to be defended. Soldiers had little incentive to defend "the system": the purges of officers were in the recent past, and the farmers' boys, who made up the majority of the Red Army, also had little reason to feel favorably toward the government. There was little Stalin had not done to ensure that his subjects hated his regime. He evidently realized this when he said, in a conversation with the American ambassador Averell Harriman in September 1941, "We cherish no illusions of our soldiers fighting for us. They are fighting for Mother Russia." 372A.49

Teodor Vulfovich wrote: "A generation of people went to the front who had been brutally insulted for years by events still fresh in their memories. It was a generation with a divided conscience. . . . We were ever patient with our own buggers. But we weren't taking any crap from foreigners. We weren't having that. That was our secret." In Vulfovich's view, 488.2.298 the soldiers believed that, after the war, they would all be liberated from "the cruelties of our Fatherland, from our own fears and endless humiliation." "Then, after the war, it will all turn out all right. Everything will be 488.2.136 renewed. But first, let's beat this terrifying, unbelievably strong enemy. We'll see after that. Then everything will be just and pure. We believed it would work out like that." Things turned out quite differently, however. 488.2.134–35

"We might have beaten the German Fascists, but we lost the war at home against our own people. It was our own fault. We foolishly spared them. Directly after the war they drove us into a corner and conquered us. . . . We are only the shadows of victors. We are the conquered, and we cannot admit that to ourselves."

488.2.252

According to Kondratyev, "There was much in the system we could not accept, but we were unable to imagine any other." In Astafyev's view: "We were both the victims and the oppressors. All of us, all our genes, our bones, our blood, even our shit, was saturated with the times and the stench Stalin made." Nevertheless, "when the war began, when the Fatherland was in danger, we tried to forget everything, so it would not hinder us in fighting a war," says Kondratyev. The young people "knew no other Fatherland. They were Komsomol members, volunteers, and they sacrificed themselves without hesitation. . . . The war was won by sick, worn-out boys in oversized greatcoats . . . those boys were the backbone of the victory."

209.4.115

23.17.184

209.4.115

209.4.116

That it was patriotism, Russian patriotism that drove the people can be seen from the attitude of many Gulag prisoners, who begged to be allowed to go to the front. It can be seen in the attitude of the children of deported kulaks, of murdered priests, and of others who were backed into a corner. "The people's age-old love for the Fatherland, passed down in our genes, was the source of our victory," says Kondratyev. "I don't think ideology played any major role in the war." On the contrary, according to the historian M. Zinich: It was "the instinct of self-protection, the protection of the family."

209.4.124

497.1.5

Thugs and victims fought shoulder to shoulder against the enemy. One example, as discussed earlier, is Kirill Meretskov, who went straight from the torture chamber to the head of an army.

According to Kondratyev, the motto "For the Fatherland, for Stalin," by which soldiers were supposed to go into battle, was devised by the political officers and was seldom if ever used. Senyavskaya, a historian who studied the psychology of the "front generation," quotes from the "political report" of an army unit: "The officially accepted war cries for the moment of attack were distributed among the Communists and the Komsomol members." The political bodies consciously spread and popularized the cry, "For Stalin." Not many were fanatically devoted to Stalin personally.

394.1.132–33

257.2.69–70

The classic Russian war cry "Hurrah," was still yelled in an attack, or "For the Fatherland," but the most common war cries were combinations of these slogans mixed in with filthy sexual references and profanity. Viktor Astafyev takes this even further: "We wanted no truck with Stalin, nor did we feel like shouting 'Hurrah' as we crawled away, dropping to the ground, falling asleep. . . . The only thought in your head was this: let death come as quickly as possible and bring an end to the suffering."   23.15

Yuliya Drunina recalls, "Personally I heard quite different things, not meant for a young girl's ears." And Grigori Pomerants adds: " Sexual force   100.1 is the most powerful, the most straightforward symbol of any might, and sexual curse words are one of the pillars of Russian social hierarchy—especially in a war."   349.1.163

A few realized that in defending the Fatherland they were also sustaining the regime. They had no choice, however. On the other side, the regime knew full well that, without the support of the people, it could not survive. Hence the rather humiliating wording of Stalin's radio speech to the people on 3 July 1941: "Comrades! Brothers and sisters! I am turning to you, my friends."

Whereas, in other countries, the war led to additional prohibitions, in the Soviet Union a number of things were now allowed, for example, city dwellers were allotted a plot of land and more tolerance was extended toward the church. According to Yuri Burtin, "This set an entirely different tone in the relationship between the people and the government." In   63.1.14 my opinion, however, Burtin's view of the issue is rather optimistic.

In any event, one cannot deny that, in the course of the war, a certain cohesion developed between the people and the regime, along with the notions of the "unity of Soviet states" and of a "Soviet people." The concept   102.1.76–77 of "Soviet patriotism" only gained genuine meaning during the war. After all, everyone had to pull together to survive. According to many, the concepts of "Russian" and "Soviet" were associated for the first time in the war.   20.2.205

When the Soviet regime collapsed in the 1990s the idea of mutual triumph also disappeared. When veterans of the war were later accused of having maintained Stalin's rule, Viktor Nekrasov refuted the accusation by saying that they had not been fighting *for* something but rather *against* something, namely, an intruding enemy.   309.2

Nationalism

No author writes about conflicts between members of different nationalities in the army, that is, about expressions of nationalism. On the contrary,

85.1   people were blind to one another's nationality. Friendships between peo-
         ple in the army were really genuine, write authors M. Gallai, V. Zelenkov,
122.1.9–10;   and Y. Rzhevskaya.
490.1.70; 3.8.11

         From 1943 on, however, nationalism was instigated from above; soldiers
         who hailed from "exiled peoples" were now dismissed from the army. And
         when Ukraine was recaptured and mobilization of Ukrainians began,
394.1.108   there was some animosity toward them, if not contempt.
              Kardin writes that the use of denigrating nicknames for Germans,
         such as "Fritz," "Hans," and "Kraut," were inevitably followed by further
         name-calling such as "Katsap" for Russians, "Khokhol" for Ukrainians,
         "Armyashka" for Armenians, "Chuchmek" for Caucasians, and "Yid" for
         Jews. "Then you get quarrels over 'bad' nations and 'good' nations, over
188.1.141   'national' sicknesses."
              When it came to political instruction of the troops, Uzbeks or Arme-
         nians were the preferred speakers in order to stress the common struggle,
         but the speeches were organized and prepared ahead of time and there-
394.1.106   fore were not real.
              There were legitimate problems with language. Caucasians and Central
         Asians understood little or no Russian, as mentioned earlier, and the Rus-
         sian officers were unfamiliar with the "native" languages. Boris Slutsky
         wrote in his memoirs that, in the winter of 1942, the officers were initially
         enthusiastic about the arrival of the Caucasian mountain peoples, as they
         were reputed to be excellent marksmen. When one of them was killed,
         however, "a dozen of his fellow countrymen surrounded the body. They
         prayed out loud and wept, and then they all took him away. Desertions
         and defections followed. The guilty parties prostrated themselves before
         the officers and, abhorrent to a Russian, they kissed the officers' hands. We
         had a lot of problems with them. It was not uncommon for the officers
407.4.151   to express their dislike of them in physical violence."
              Genuine "Great Russian" nationalism only emerged fully when, in his
         address in May 1945, Stalin spoke of "the Great Russian people" as the
155.4.190   "older brother," thus unleashing massive state chauvinism.

Hatred and "Fraternization"

         Although Ilya Ehrenburg and other propagandists preached hatred of
         the Germans, this had little effect initially. That changed, however, when
         the troops heard about, and then saw for themselves, the way the enemy

behaved toward the civilian population: they burned houses, hanged partisans, and murdered prisoners of war. That hatred turned to fury when the destruction camps in Poland and Germany were liberated, at Majdanek, for example, where they found the bodies, ashes, shoes, and collected hair of the victims.   295.1.171

Even without those horrifying images the ferocity of the troops had already increased. At first it was directed at standing their ground, and then there was the bitterness and pain of the defeats, and finally their anger screamed for revenge, tinged with the fear of being too late to save their fellow countrymen.   394.1.78–80

Marshal Zhukov was once asked how it was possible that the Russian reprisals in Germany, given the circumstances, remained within limits. He replied, "Were we entitled to revenge? Of course. But we controlled our fury. Our ideological convictions, our international feelings did not allow us to surrender to blind vengeance." That surely was interpreting affairs   345.1.191
through rose-colored spectacles.

Both sides took prisoners of war only reluctantly, and it is all the more remarkable that at times a kind of fraternization evolved. I do not wish to give the impression that this was a frequent occurrence, but it did happen sometimes.

—Neither side prevented the other from fetching food or water.   382.1.46
—No one shot at those fetching water on either bank of the river.   37.1.10
—When the Germans stopped fighting, the Russians took a break, too.   127.9.13
—Christmas 1942 at the Kalinin front was, in one case, celebrated
    jointly, the Germans supplying the food and the Russians the drink.
    Hearing sounds of a party, a political leader broke up the celebra-
    tion, took the Germans prisoner, and had the Russians transferred.   209.10.4
—One German left a chocolate bar for a young Russian soldier.   209.10.4
—A hungry Russian company came to get food from a German field
    kitchen, more than once, in fact, until another cook arrived.   216.2.45
—Germans did not shoot at a Russian who had been forced to stand up-
    right for several hours against the breast wall (parapet) as punishment.
—German and Russian spies suddenly found themselves face to face.
    "Nu, Gansy, davaitye rauchen," and, after a pause, "Nu a teperitsya,
    Fritzy, po domam, nach Hause. Aufviderzane." ("Well, Ruskies, let's   209.15.248–49
    go for a smoke" and "Well Krauts, let's go home. See you.")

Of this Kondratyev remarks, "Such incidents prevented people from becoming animals, something the war was inclined to do; it helped them to keep 'God's flame' alive." Soldiers who had experienced the German   209.14

313.1.140   occupation firsthand, however, were not inclined to be "charitable." "Noth-
188.4.137   ing is more intoxicating than blood."

Propaganda

Before the German invasion, propaganda had instilled the fact that, sooner
or later, there would be a war to free the populations of other countries
394.1.84   from capitalism. This was the mission of the land of victorious socialism.

Once the war was under way, however, this objective was abandoned,
the goal became victory over the enemy, and feelings of hatred were encouraged toward the intruders, their system, and their people. One example is Simonov's poem entitled "Kill Him." Almost every day the *Red Star*
published an article by Ehrenburg screaming for hate and revenge. Every
article, essay, and broadcast by and for the troops echoed the theme of
hate. At the end of the war the propaganda again changed its tune back
to that of the prewar years; once again the call was to "free Europe from
394.1.132   the chains of fascism," from "the yoke of capitalism."

Propaganda worked primarily by reducing heroic deeds to symbols and
then manipulating those symbols until they fit the desired mold. Those
who had been convicted of a crime were not deemed suitable examples,
unless, of course, the facts were carefully adjusted. Any deed that did not
conform to the official account was kept quiet. The story of the heroic
defense of the border fortress of Brest, for example, was permitted to
appear in book form only in 1964. The fall of Vlasov's Second Assault
Army, which was cut to ribbons at Novgorod, was also hushed up.

The background of a number of heroic symbols was often quite different
than was portrayed at the time.
  —Zoya Kosmodemyanskaya, who was hailed as a hero, had actually
    been reported to the Germans by angry neighbors because she had
    burned their stalls and killed their horses when implementing pol-
    icy ordering the destruction of anything that could be of use to the
    Germans.
  —Aleksandr Matrosov, who supposedly threw himself in front of a
    German machine-gun post where his body was peppered with bul-
    lets, had, in reality, been dragged in front of the post by the Germans
    when he tried to push down the barrel of the gun after having
394.1.142–43   crawled up above the hole. Although Matrosov's death occurred on
    27 February 1942, it was moved ahead to 22 February, the day the Red
    Army was founded.

—Of the twenty-eight soldiers in General Panfilov's battalion, who all fought to their death in the defense of Moscow at Dubosekovo, six, it later turned out, were still alive and one had been shot for desertion. Various authors, including Aleksandr Bek in his *Volokolamsk Highway,* based their theme on that supposed heroic tale.

—Oleg Koshevoy, the Komsomol hero of Aleksandr Fadeyev's *Young Guard,* a novel about a resistance group in occupied Krasnodon, turned out not to be a hero after all. Tretyakevich, who was named the "traitor" in the novel, later proved to have been the heroic leader.   25.1 By then, however, many innocent people had already been arrested and convicted of treason. Some of those arrested remained in prison until 1956 and were only rehabilitated in 1990.

In the 1990s much was written about Fadeyev's misleading book and about the "heroic" Panfilov soldiers.   343.1

All these symbols of heroism constituted war cries, legends, examples to be followed. The only facts quoted about the real figures were the ones that were useful for propaganda. "The political section needed 'extraordinary' deeds," wrote Kondratyev, "such as a duel between a soldier with a grenade or Molotov cocktail and a tank or the story of a plane shot down with a rifle."   209.27.7

Whether these symbols made much of an impression on the Russian soldiers is unclear. What is certain is that the only image they liked to be identified with was that of the prototype Russian soldier, "Vasili Tyorkin," of the poetic cycle of the same name by Aleksandr Tvardovski. "Vasili Tyorkin" was a simple soldier of flesh and blood, a farm boy, smart, natural, averse to extreme self-sacrifice; he didn't waste words.

> He is not the hero of a fairy tale
> A carefree giant
> But, with his soldier's knapsack,
> A person of simple nature
> He is not afraid of danger in the fight
> If he is not drunk
> And he is not drunk.   394.1.134

Censorship

The reports from the front by the Soviet Information Agency, the extraordinarily popular articles by Ilya Ehrenburg, and the poems of Konstantin

Simonov (and others) were widely read. Most admired was Tvardovski's aforementioned poetry about the Russian soldier Vasili Tyorkin. These poems were also read aloud and dramatized.

Contact with the home front was essential. Letters and parcels arrived from home; the home front received soldiers' letters folded into a triangle. Notification of death arrived in a blue envelope.

Lonely soldiers started correspondences with equally lonesome women in the hinterland by means of those parcels. Anyone who could write nice letters—for others, too—was popular among the troops. They were 394.1.63–65 referred to as *pismovniki* (letter writers).

It was customary for a soldier's entire village to send their greetings, and, in his reply, the soldier was also expected not to forget any of his fellow villagers. People quite rightly felt that they could boost the morale of both the troops and the home front by sending and reading aloud news of soldiers and civilians who had distinguished themselves by their actions.

Censorship ensured that men restricted themselves when reporting on the situation. The censor did not permit any mention of the medical per-11.5.55 sonnel or young boys taking part in the fighting to prevent the accusation 226.1.90 of violating international conventions.

Sergeant Bogdan Tarasov was delighted, but dismayed, to receive the following letter from his wife, which the censor had stamped but evidently not read:

Hello, there, my dear, beloved husband, Bogdan Tarasych. Greetings from your wife, Yefrosinya, and your children, Vanya and Nastasha. None of us had hoped or expected to receive a letter from you. When our troops came into the village and started distributing the post, there were more and more notifications of deaths. Our relatives and neighbors were either dead or missing. We, too, will die soon, here, I think.

We could live under the Germans, but now this is no longer any kind of life. Winter is almost upon us; there is nothing to eat or drink; no shoes to put on. The Germans left us alone and we only saw them for a week, in the summer of 1941, after which they moved on. They did leave Grandfather Maksim [the local village elder] in the village. He was a strong man, God rest his soul. He drove all the old and young people into the field to bring in the harvest—the rye harvest was better than ever that year. We harvested everything, down to the last stalk. He also gave stray horses to the people. And he distributed all the rye meal fairly; there was grain for every mouth. I had the whole storeroom filled with sacks of rye. And the cellar was filled with potatoes and other vegetables. And what's more, he gave us land from what was left of the kolkhoz. Everyone was given a plot. We had two are, and a horse, a cow, and a sheep. We even kept a pig for the winter.

And then our troops came. They were all hungry. Some food they took for themselves, the rest I gave to them; I was sorry for the poor boys. I thought: perhaps a good person will give my husband food, too. I have prayed to God and I pray for you. But now even God cannot protect you. They have hanged our local village elder. Because he served the Germans, they said. But it was his own village people he served; he helped the orphans. But they paid that no heed. They came with a half-tonner, grabbed him, and took him away. No matter how the people tried to stand up for him, it did no good. They were threatened with the same fate. They said that Grandfather Maksim was an enemy of the people and a traitor, while we saw him as our protector. The village women told how Grandfather was punished publicly. They are catching people in the woods, too, who they call deserters. These men try to kill them when they get caught. A gypsy in a long greatcoat went incredibly mad. So, you see, we are living in great fear now. You never know which will kill you first, our troops or the hunger. Thank God we saved the cow and there is hay for the winter. Our only hope is the cow, which feeds us all. Perhaps, by the grace of God, we will survive. I, too, wish the same for you. Greetings from the bottom of our hearts. Yefrosinya and your children.

290.3.86–87

It was not the censor's intention, incidentally, to intercept military secrets as much as to gauge, and conceal when necessary, the mood of the forces: that was the greatest problem. Still today the censorship archive for the armed forces, housed in the Central Archive of the Ministry of Defense, remains closed. Once it is opened we will have a more realistic picture of the mood of the troops. Historiography deals primarily with official documents and pays little attention to "verbal and written statements." However, there are a few exceptions.

394.1.5–6; 208.1

Letters from the front, which have now been published, all give a cheerful impression, in accordance with the propaganda. There are no letters about the "fatigue due to the continual risk" or about "conflicts with the leadership" or "natural reactions to defeat." Reports from the political sections of army units about soldiers' conversations have indeed been

394.1.47

394.1.61

retained, but even though they are essential to our knowledge of the soldiers' mood at the time, they are rarely studied.

Folklore

One extraordinary phenomenon of the war is the unofficial activities
that took place, that is, those the political bodies neither supported nor
initiated. One such activity took the form of ordinary soldiers amusing
their comrades and themselves with songs, fairy tales, stories, anecdotes,
sayings, and proverbs. What is striking in this is that the officially encouraged verses and the like made little impression on the men and came
362.1.94 across as fabricated.

Dmitri Pushkaryov's function in the administration enabled him,
throughout the war, to collect such folklore from one army section. He
cautioned against seeing this particular collection as universal. The artillery, the engineers, the air force, the navy, and the tank troops each had
its own specific folklore, as did the partisan units, the prisoners of war,
26.1.192 and those in the hinterland.

Favorite stories recounted the adventures and pranks of experienced
and smart peasant soldiers. David Samoilov—from another army section—described one storyteller who had a natural talent: "He told fairy
386.1.65–66 tales until his last listener had fallen asleep." The performers were divided
into singers (*pevuny*) and storytellers (*skazochniki*).

The content of the stories and songs were often based on existing folklore and simply were adapted to the current circumstances. Thus they
continually changed according to the shifting situation.

Homesickness, the anticipation of death, and suspicion of unfaithful
wives were familiar themes. These folklorists were "artists" who could
oblige the company with a story or anecdote made to order. Once again,
this folklore at the front had little, if anything, to do with the texts that
were officially permitted by, and distributed in, the political section's army
394.1.53 newspapers.

Trains to the front were the birthplace of folkloric expression, as was
kitchen duty, a stay in the hospital, or time spent in a reserve regiment.
Drivers often brought along new themes and songs.

The marching songs were official, but in the evening one heard quite
different, homemade lyrics. In trains, in particular, long stories were told.
Pushkaryov provides titles and sometimes the text of numerous poems
and stories. They are characterized by spicy details, laced with prison jargon, and peppered with risqué expressions.

Often, in the evening, sad, lyrical songs were sung, with "letters from home serving as a powerful stimulus. Some sang like nightingales after receiving news from home." The soldiers' repertoire was expanded considerably with the liberation of Russian girls in Poland and Germany; the girls had written their own songs about their lives and their fate. 362.1.99–100

362.1.86

At the end of the war the number of frivolous and erotic themes increased dramatically in expectation of the homecoming.

The Postwar Mood

Paradoxically many felt that wartime had been a kind of liberation, a taste of freedom. Yuri Burtin could already envision "the new social-political situation" before him, "characterized by changing relationships between the state and the people. At that time something like a union had already arisen between the two." "The war was a time of freedom of thought and deed, of the highest responsibility and initiative," wrote Yuri Sharapov in 1991. 394.1.89

63.1.14

440.1

During the war people felt that they were important, that a lot depended on them, and, even more strongly, that they were needed. Kondratyev wrote: "We felt like citizens in the full and real sense of the word. For our generation, the war was the most important event in our lives." Everyone felt the outcome of the war depended on him. "Nowhere did they feel as free, as unfettered and independent of the system, as at the front, in the trenches, in the tanks and the planes," says historian Yelena Senyavskaya. And Yelena Rzhevskaya said: "There was more freedom in the war, more room, less pressure from suspicion and the overall threat of danger. Those who behaved so selflessly in the war, one thought, could rely on the confidence of its leaders. After all, the children of 'enemies of the people' and even those 'enemies' themselves, had any of them been let out of prison, would have risen up with the criminals, the ex-kulaks, the priests, would have faced death in the eye for the sake of the Fatherland." 209.4.113

394.1.4

383.4.66

A greater trust in people, an end to the mass arrests of innocents, more freedom of expression, less restricted movement, abolition of the kolkhozes—all this is what the soldiers hoped, even expected at times, would happen after the war. After all, Stalin had seen that the people could be trusted, that they had remained true to him. People talked of this openly in the trenches, in Stalingrad, and elsewhere. 209.4.116

The general expectation was that things would improve, that life would be freer after the war. Pomerants heard young officers say that after the war they would hang the "popes" (political functionaries). There were open discussions of "our ulcers" at party meetings, and here he glimpsed the nascent germ of democracy. They had fought against fascism, and now they thought there would be an end to all tyranny. At the end of his novel, *Doctor Zhivago*, Boris Pasternak writes: "Although the relief and liberation that had been expected after the war did not come with the victory as they had expected, nevertheless there was a sense of freedom in the air during the postwar years."

However, Mark Gallai, a pilot who in 1957 was declared a Hero of the Soviet Union, wrote in 1995: "The naïve expectations of wartime that, after victory, the atmosphere of injustice, repression, and setting one section of society against another would never return were left unfulfilled." The government itself, however, never expressed such sentiments.

An incident that took place in Berlin the day after the Soviet victory, during a party for high-ranking officers, is very revealing. As recounted by eyewitness Yevgeny Dolmatovsky. Vsevolod Vishnevski (who, as mentioned earlier, had a loose tongue) said at this party:

"Everything has to be different from now on. We forgive Comrade Stalin his errors of previous years. The people demand an end to the persecution of innocent men! All prisoners, except Vlasov's scum, must be set free from the prisons, and the camps must be emptied."

"Shut up, Syeva," growled Marshal Chuikov threateningly, glancing across at Galadzhev, General Lieutenant and head of the political section at the front. But Vishnevski was not about to be stopped. He raised his glass: "To freedom! To the freedom of Lenin's country! No one can replace Lenin for us." Galadzhev went pale and clamped his thin lips tightly. I saw the lightning rage over Simonov's face. Looking for a way out of the situation, Simonov spoke up, "I propose a toast to the Eighth Guard Army and its soldiers." Ignoring everyone, Vishnevski continued: "It's no use hiding the fact that we are all being watched! It all has to change. I don't want anyone suspecting me of anything." General Galadzhev attempted to save the situation.

"Vsevolod Vitalyevich! We like you very much, and we don't suspect you of anything."

But Vishnevski retorted, "I want to be able to go to the Kremlin after the war without having to ask permission. I demand that they don't take my pistol from me when I come in."

Vishnevski had had his say and fell silent, but all those who were

present fell silent, too. . . . These heroes of the battlefield who had known
no fear were terrified on this first day of peace. . . . Present, too, of course,
was the head of the political section at the front, General Lieutenant
Galadzhev. What should he report to the "authorities"? After all, he was
obliged to report the incident. I looked at Galadzhev. He was pale, white
as a sheet.   98.1.63

"The spirit of the love of freedom and free thinking that the soldiers
had brought back from the front," Kondratyev wrote, "clearly did not
appeal to Stalin and his circle. In these 'young people in greatcoats without epaulettes' he saw 'the future Decembrists' [Russian officers who, in
December 1825, after defeating Napoleon and spending time in Western
Europe, demanded constitutional concessions from the tsar] and envi-
sioned the hardest measures to get rid of this political threat and once
again restore the prewar monotony and paralysis of the spirit. Soon after
victory the social atmosphere in the country became gloomy and oppres-
sive, with new waves of repression on the way."   209.25.411–12

Thus Stalin launched an attack on the generation of victors. The assault
began by referring to the people as "cogs," and this after victory had been
achieved by those who felt they were not at all little wheels within big
wheels but were indeed "citizens" and distinct "personalities."   209.6

Church and Religion

Many thought that the slightly improved attitude of the government toward
the church and religion was a sign of the anticipated postwar humaniza-
tion of the regime. The newspaper *Bezbozhnik* (The godless) had already
been shut down at the beginning of the war, and antireligious propaganda
had been halted. In 1942 citizens were given leave to move around the   279.1.74
streets freely at night to attend the Easter service.   207.1.138

In occupied Ukraine the Germans reopened many churches, reinstated
religious services, and again allowed people to have christenings.

Presumably these German measures forced Stalin to make a gesture,
and therefore, on 4 September 1943, he entered into discussions with three
metropolitan bishops who were requesting the release of seventeen imprisoned bishops (in the end ten were released). The building that had
housed the German Embassy before the war was now the domain of Sergi,
the metropolitan of Moscow. Other concessions were promised, for example, the reinstatement of seminaries and the publication of the magazine

The Moscow Patriarch Bulletin. The election of a patriarch and the calling
of a synod of bishops were also agreed on.

77.1.45

Of the 5,770 requests submitted in 1944 and 1945 for the reopening of
churches, only 414 were granted. Stalin asked the amazed church leaders,
"Why do you have a shortage of priests?" Sergi smartly replied: "One
reason is that we trained a priest and he became a marshal of the Soviet
Union." When they took their leave at 3:00 in the morning, Stalin touched
the elderly Sergi's arm and said, "Your Holiness, this is all I can do for you
for the time being."

468.1

77.1.45

207.1.139

On 12 September 1943 Metropolitan Sergi was elected patriarch. In
March 1943 the chief surgeon of a military hospital was given leave to take
up his former post—after sixteen years of imprisonment and exile—as
Bishop Luka.

217.1.206

The worst persecution of soldiers displaying signs of religious views
came to an end.

217.1.207

Leonid Panteleyev writes that, in 1943, someone asked the political
leader why the government had adopted a different attitude regarding the
church and religion. The reply: "There have been absolutely no changes
in this area. . . . We comrades are neither little children nor fools. We
understand the way things work. It cannot harm the politics of the Soviet
government if a few old men and women get married in church. This will
earn us tanks, planes, grain, and meat from America." In the same vein
he noted that "priests, mullahs, rabbis, and Catholic and Protestant ministers had returned from the prisons and from exile in the thousands."
V. Kozhanov characterized the propagandist book destined for abroad,
The Truth about Religion in the USSR, as "the most deceitful book in the
world." In 1944, in Leningrad, Kozhanov saw dozens of uniformed soldiers
attending a mass. On the other hand, an orthodox priest who had set up
a primitive church in a barracks in occupied territory, where he proceeded
to lead a church service, was shot, along with his wife, when the Red Army
liberated the area, because he "had desecrated a Soviet institution."

329.1.165

232.1.48

380.1.42

23.13

Several authors have written that soldiers were either religious or became
religious during the war. *Das Kapital* is not much help to you at the end
of your life, but "the Lord, who created our soul" might be.

380.1.42

In *The Devil's Pit* Astafyev portrays the Orthodox soldier Kostya Ryndin
as one who has not forgotten the lessons of his wise old grandmother,
Sekletinya: "All those who rise up and sow war and fratricide upon the
earth will be cursed and struck down by God." He was one of the few

recruits able to withstand the inhuman treatment they were given, the only one who came through it unharmed.

Astafyev also wrote: "Perhaps the Communists' most heinous crime is that they have made the people atheists, have robbed them of their belief in a heavenly hereafter, the belief that in that hereafter there is light and that there dwell God and the Holy Virgin."   23.13

12

Generals and Victims

Methods of Warfare

The Russian loss of human lives was extremely high. The losses were caused initially by incompetent leaders, by Stalin's strategic errors, by interference from political commissars in military affairs, and by the absurd habit of attempting to capture cities on the anniversary of important Soviet memorial days in honor of such days, as was the case at Kiev, Königsberg, and Berlin. Losses were also caused by the Soviet Union's lack of preparation for the war and by throwing inexperienced soldiers into battle, as happened with General Levashov's parachutists. The general was killed along with his men.

383.9.57

Other officers forced their subordinates to attack continually to enable them to report "activity" to their superiors. Others reported that areas had been taken when they were still in the hands of the enemy. "The generals pinned one more medal on their chests, the price—a few thousand Ivans and Chuchmeks [Caucasians]—was not important," according to

127.11

Anatoli Genatulin. A human life was worth nothing; no heed was paid to such losses. However, if a piece of equipment was lost, a tank, a cannon, a rifle, you had to explain yourself, but never for the loss of people's lives. In this the past played a role: had they been careful with human lives in the civil war, during agricultural collectivization, or during the purges? Not at all; one human life more or less was insignificant. "It is unbearably hard to see that your death is in vain, that they send you there just to tick

209.15.75

off another attack," declared Kondratyev.

Victories were often gained "at any price." Zhukov himself called the "frontal attacks" "the four-stage strategy": three waves of attacks level the ground, and the fourth goes over it.

Wrong decisions were without consequence for the guilty party. The official view on this issue is well illustrated in such common sayings as "The war writes everything off" and "Victors are not judged." Yuri Belash wrote a poem on the subject. These are the final lines:

Here and there on the sodden field
Lay still the gray mounds of corpses in bullet-riddled coats . . .
Someone, somewhere, had made a mistake.
Something had been neglected.
But it is the infantry that pays the price for all those mistakes
In full, with its blood.
We march on, mum.   209.27.71

There were needless attacks: General Aleksandr Gorbatov pointed this out, Kondratyev experienced them himself, and Astafyev described how the soldiers were herded into the Dnepr. People were often unaware of the horrific facts, stated a marshal who later boasted that "our heroes came over the river Istra up to their necks in ice-cold water, fell through the thin ice, and still took the city of Istra."   23.15

And so Russia, starting with the countryside, was gradually depopulated. Hence Astafyev's nickname for Zhukov: "the poacher of the Russian people"—which is why, in 1995, Astafyev refused to accept a memorial medal   23.15
(on the fiftieth anniversary of victory) that displayed Zhukov's portrait. "He fought with figures not with skill. Zhukov has covered half of Europe with the bodies of Russian farmers," Astafyev said in an interview with *Ogonyok*. In 1988 he wrote, "We simply didn't understand how to wage   23.16.32
war. . . . We drowned the enemy in our blood, we covered the enemy with our corpses."   23.3

The future film director Dovzhenko noted on 14 August 1942: "The world will be amazed at our power, might, and heroism. And we, ourselves, will forget all about the terrible, shameless, sickening chaos and bungling, our needless, thankless losses as a result of pig-headedness, obliviousness, despotism, and devious boot-licking."   100.2.12

The Generals

Ruthlessness and contempt for human suffering characterize virtually all Russian army leaders, with at least one exception: Konstantin Rokossovski. Many authors place this hero of Stalingrad strategically higher than

Zhukov. In any event, his men worshipped him. Was this because he had "been inside" or because many of his men had "done time"?

Rokossovski systematically refused to sign death sentences. As both a former Gulag prisoner who had had his teeth knocked out and an "enemy of the people," he knew what it was all about. He did, however, have great admiration for Zhukov, but he regarded Zhukov's behavior toward his subordinates as unacceptable. In 1949, on Stalin's orders, Rokossovski was made the minister of defense and vice premier in Poland, although his Polish was poor. During the de-Stalinization campaign, Khrushchev ordered Rokossovski to write an article criticizing Stalin. He refused. The next day Kirill Moskalenko replaced Rokossovski as the minister of defense.

86.1.173–74

Other army leaders had no objection either to behaving in an extremely coarse manner toward their subordinates or using their fists. Andrei Yeryomenko beat his men and always had his Mauser at the ready to shoot them. Vasili Chuikov, the commandant of the Sixty-second Army in Stalingrad, shot down officers with his own hand. "People were afraid of him, a rough, even cruel officer, the hard hero of Stalingrad, with the coarse lines of his lion's face, foul-mouthed, he walked around with a stick that he sometimes brought down on the shoulders of his subordinates. Staff personnel tried to keep out of his way." Ivan Konev was more careful with his soldiers and showed more concern for regular provisions and rest.

147.1.105–6

382.1.47

23.13

Nikita Vatutin paid no attention to losses. He urged his people on, so that, according to Igor Nikolayev, "even eighteen-year-old boys went in search of a quick death in order to free themselves of such inhuman ordeals." Khrushchev wrote, "In other words, at that time it was considered heroic to smash someone in the mouth. Later, I noticed that Yeryomenko had even hit a member of the military council. . . . Budyonny hit you in the face, too, and Zakharov."

313.1.148, 154

71.2.28

Incompetent, paranoid, and extremely cruel are words that describe Stalin's "eyes and ears," the schemer Lazar Mekhlis. As the highest military political leader, he paid a visit of inspection to virtually every front, usually with devastating consequences.

It was he who caused the Crimean disaster, allowing the Germans to take 120,000 Russians prisoners. After the defeat in the Crimea, he reported to Stalin, squirming, literally crawling on his knees to him and referring to himself as "that filthy Jew." Mekhlis was more interested in "ideology"

332.4.89

and whether people were really crying "for the Fatherland, for Stalin" than in strategic issues. He was always ready to shoot officers, such as when he executed the commandant of the artillery of the Thirty-fourth Army, General V. S. Goncharov, whom he shot "in front of the lined-up staff officers."

379.1.85

Mekhlis forbade troops to dig trenches in the Crimea, because that was defensive—and therefore defeatist—behavior. He was deployed on many a front. He ordered charges everywhere. He got in the way of military commandants, and accused them of cowardice and everything under the sun. This "Patriarch of the Great Fear" was probably by far the most hated man in the Soviet armed forces.

64.1.58–63

"Yes, our army leaders were primarily brutes who had no sympathy for people or soldiers. They couldn't give a damn, just like now," said Yuri Levitanski.

262.1

Marshal Zhukov

Georgi Zhukov and Stalin were together during the war dozens of times but never at the front. Only once was Stalin at the front lines, for three hours on 5 August 1943 at the little village of Khoroshevo on the Kalinin front. Here he discussed, with General Yeryomenko, the forthcoming operation for liberating Smolensk. That day Stalin decided that celebratory shots would be fired when big cities were captured, and that was the case with Orel and Belgorod.

109.2.11

Whether Zhukov and Stalin liked each other is debatable. According to the army leader, after Stalingrad Stalin learned more about the military profession, but at the beginning of the war he had, in Zhukov's opinion, committed grave errors, even leaving aside the unjust Order No. 00270, which called for prisoners of war to be treated as traitors. Zhukov felt that Stalin had given this order to exonerate himself for the initial defeats. According to Vladimir Karpov, this order was partly to blame for soldiers who had been captured being afraid to escape to their own troops.

191.3.100

Yelena Rzhevskaya writes that Zhukov once described Stalin as follows: "He was terrifying. He had, you know, these eyes. The way he looked at you, such eyes. Sometimes he was in a good mood, but that was rare. If there had been successes at an international or military level, then he would even sing sometimes. He was not devoid of humor, but it was rare. . . . Men went to him as to an object of dread. Yes, if he summoned

383.2.171   you, you went as if to some terrible fate." Zhukov was one of the few who
dared to contradict Stalin. Stalin once said to a gathering, "What should
I actually talk to you about? Whatever anyone says to you, you all say,
'Yes, Comrade Stalin,' 'Of course, Comrade Stalin,' 'Absolutely correct,
Comrade Stalin,' 'You have made a wise decision, Comrade Stalin.' Only
323.4.96   Zhukov here argues with me."

In 1988 Zhukov's "unpublished memoirs" showed, however, that he had
been afraid to contradict Stalin when the latter had contemptuously dis-
508.2.99   missed warnings of the approaching war.

Zhukov has been endlessly honored and venerated as the savior of the
Fatherland. Brodsky wrote a wonderful poem commemorating Zhukov's
death in 1974.

Nevertheless, almost everyone stresses his cruelty, the merciless orders
that needlessly cost hundreds of thousands of lives. His cursing was one
thing, but he also humiliated people. He once said to a general, "Who are
86.2.145–46 you? A sack of shit, but not a general."

Viktor Astafyev is particularly critical of him for his cruelty and contempt for the loss of human lives. "Oh, what a monstrosity of a 'father
and teacher' he was. What a scourge of the Russian people! He and his
Comrade Stalin burned the Russian people in the flames of war. Any
discussion of the war should begin with this serious accusation, and then
maybe you will get to the truth, but that is something we will never live
23.15   to see."

In 1996 A. N. Mertsalov published his *Inoi Zhukov* (The other Zhukov),
282.3   in which the marshal is belittled both as a person and a strategist. The
extent of Zhukov's ruthlessness was also illustrated later in his role in
Russian nuclear testing on 18 March 1954. Of the forty thousand soldiers
who were exposed to an actual nuclear explosion during the exercises, no
188.7.228   more than a thousand were still alive at the beginning of the 1990s.

Aleksandr Vasilevski, Georgi Zhukov, and Konstantin Rokossovski were
the great names behind the planning of the counterattack at Stalingrad.
During Khrushchev's regime, however, Marshal Yeryomenko claimed the
honor in his memoirs, as did Khrushchev. "Why did you write that?"
383.2.174   Zhukov later asked him. "Khrushchev asked me to," was the reply.

And when Khrushchev approached Zhukov through another marshal
requesting that he write an article criticizing Stalin, the reply was, "Marshal Zhukov, four times Hero of the Soviet Union, says to tell you he
86.2.138–39 doesn't know that marshal."

The Victims

In 1944 the Soviet army had lost virtually its entire prewar cadre: of the five to six million men in June 1941, four million had been taken prisoner or killed by the end of that year. It is impossible even to estimate the number of fatalities the war claimed among the armed forces and civilians in Russia—first, because the forces largely carried no "medallion" (the little case containing the soldier's name, civil status, rank, and address) and by no means did everyone have a Red Army service record book when the medallions were scrapped. That book, with a photograph of the holder, was introduced on Stalin's orders because he felt that "defeatists and traitors" were going to the hinterland under the guise of wounded soldiers. "The divisions of the Red Army have become a halfway house." The men, incidentally, who were superstitious, were not enthusiastic about wearing the medallions, which meant that the men in a unit only knew one another personally, by sight. On 12 April 1942 it turned out that "no more than a third of the actual number of personnel killed had been registered," also making it impossible to inform the relatives.

A second reason for not being able to account for the number of fatalities is that "burial books" were not maintained properly, which is quite understandable with encircled units or rapidly retreating troops.

A third reason is that after 1943, in Ukraine in particular, millions of men were "mobilized," sometimes with no uniform, army boots, or training, and thrown into battle. Hundreds of thousands of them were killed. Moreover, no record was kept of who had been killed among the partisans, illegal resistance fighters, or hastily formed home reserve detachments. Prisoners in German concentration camps had the greatest difficulty being recognized as war victims and participants in the war.

Fourth, there is the problem of how many defected and then died on the German side? Do they count among the Soviet losses? And what about those who died in German prisoner-of-war camps? Were they not military losses as well?

Fifth, how many thousands lie unknown and unidentified in mass graves or trenches?

And finally, sixth, the number of servicemen who died of their wounds in one of the 1,105 hospitals is not known. Some were still registered as "missing."

The estimations of the number of victims therefore vary absurdly from seven million to twenty-seven million. Demographically, the number one arrives at is 21.78 million victims, that is 11.5 percent of the population. The percentage for Great Britain is 0.9, for the Unites States 0.3, for Yugoslavia 10.9, and for Germany 12.7.

105.1.32–33

According to General-Major Gurkin, who was the first to give "precise" figures for each individual military operation, the direct losses amounted to 8,406,704 and the "sanitary losses" to 12,932,113. How many of the latter died afterward he does not say. Lazar Lazarev writes in his memoirs that, at a conference in 1995 on "human losses in the Great Patriotic War," the figure of "around nineteen million official records of those killed, missing, made prisoner of war, and servicemen who died of their wounds" was mentioned, and no one disputed it.

160.1

256.2.183–84

We know of roughly forty thousand places where members of the military are buried—"Around 6.9 million dead lie buried there"—but another 1.5 million or even more lie in the bogs and the woods.

206.4.11

At Stalingrad, so it is said, all those who died are recorded: approximately seventy-two hundred on plaques, the rest in card trays. When someone asked about his unit, no one in the unit was known. After a great deal of pressure, the employee in the Central Army Archive replied, "as an exception," that the man's unit had indeed perished at Stalingrad but that the archive could only produce twenty-eight names.

290.1.174–175

After the war Stalin asked Vice Premier Nikita Voznesensky how great the losses were. When the vice premier replied, "fifteen million," Stalin said, "That's rather a lot. Cut it in half." That is how Stalin arrived at the "approximately seven million" in his speech on 9 February 1946. At the Paris Peace Conference in 1947 Molotov talked of seven million dead servicemen and women.

249.1

Later Khrushchev mentioned to President John F. Kennedy the nice round figure of twenty million military and civilian victims. Others talk of twenty-seven million victims, including 8,668,400 members of the armed forces.

288.1

Still other figures emerge: the right-wing publicist Vadim Kozhinov claims there were 6.5 million military deaths and 13.4 million civilians killed; the historian B. Sokolov arrives at eleven million and "around fifteen million," respectively; the historian Viktor Kozlov claims 15.3 million military casualties, Yuri Geller as many as twenty-two million. The strong tendency was to estimate as slight a number of losses as possible. Also unknown is exactly how many people were in the armed forces during the war. Some say "more than twenty million," others "around twenty-nine million."

191.3.164

282.2.364

Politically this is a highly charged issue and therefore is fiercely contested. This is even more the case when one attempts to compare the Russian losses with those of the Germans. One person gives a ratio of 1.7 to 1, another says 5 to 1, and yet another claims a ratio as high as 14 to 1. It all depends on the political standpoint of the person doing the calculations, on whether or not one wants to believe the Russians did well.

Exactly how many victims there were, dead or missing, no one knows, and everyone complains about that. What is known—or so everyone says repeatedly—is that of those called up who were born in the years 1922 to 1925, 3 percent returned from the war alive.

The "official" losses, that is, 8.7 million, can be divided up in percentages among the various peoples as follows: Russians, 66.3; Ukrainians, 15.9; White Russians, 2.9; and "others," 14.9. Dividing the losses by section, 230.1.171 we arrive at 86.6 percent of the infantry, 6 percent of the tank troops, and 2.2 percent of the artillery. 237.1.16

Dead and Buried, or Not?

In 1962 Vyacheslav Kondratyev visited the places near Rzhev where he had fought in 1942. "What was that? One, two, and then another. I stiffened— I hadn't expected this. I felt a lump in my throat . . . on the pale green grass lay three bleached skulls. 'Oh, guys, I whispered, how can this be? We're twenty years on and you still haven't been buried? How can that be?'" 209.24.433

Dead soldiers were committed to the earth not only in mass graves but also in trenches and pits. I read an account of a potato storage pit that first had to be cleared of rotten potatoes and then the dead were piled in. Their faces barely covered, they lay side by side, all mixed up together, men and women. 316.2

Many of those reported "missing" either rest in mass graves or still lie unburied. People continue to come across unburied bodies, like at Myasnoi Bor near Novgorod, where remains of the Second Assault Army lie in the swamps.

At Volokolamsk, in the 1990s, "forty forgotten and neglected military cemeteries were discovered." One of those cemeteries contained 730 guards 425.1.134 who had been listed as missing in 1941. On top of it all was a dung heap. Even known military cemeteries have been plowed over. Elsewhere, 152.4 houses, stadiums or other buildings have been built on top of the mass graves, forgotten or not. Conscientious young people are doing all they can to identify and lay to rest unidentified corpses. Russian Field Marshall

Suvorov, who died in May 1800, once said, "You can never consider a war finished until the last soldier has been committed to the earth." Suvorov's words resemble the title of a book from 1997, by Victor Konasov, on the same subject: *Until the Last Soldier Is Buried.*

193.1

Toward the end of the war Lazar Mekhlis confirmed the fact that ordinary soldiers were allowed to be buried in mass graves, wherever they lay; officers had to be buried in inhabited places, and more senior officers in towns. Anyone dying in a siege was usually reported as "missing," which was considered a "disgrace" for the surviving relatives.

400.3.726
457.1.229–30

Astafyev described how the Russians collected the remains of their dead at the Dnepr and buried them any old way, without any respect.

23.13

The proud war cry, "No one is forgotten, nothing is forgotten" displayed at the Piskarev War Cemetery in Saint Petersburg is rather ironic in this light and is far from the truth.

When retreating, there was often no way to bury the dead, and, when attacking, frequently so many people died that an entirely different unit saw the dead in the field as "strangers," and left them where they lay. So when people inquired about their relatives years after the war, they were only told, "X does not appear in the list of those who were killed, died from their wounds, or are missing."

316.2

425.1.128

It should be mentioned, incidentally, that the Germans gave each of their dead his own individual grave, with a birch wood cross bearing the name. Straight lines of crosses. Afterwards, they virtually all disappeared. German war graves in town squares and the like were, in any event, cleared away when the Russians recaptured their country. Only in the last two years of the war, when the Germans were retreating rapidly, were they unable to bury their dead. Then the local inhabitants, on the Russians' orders, had to bury them. A brass memorial plaque was placed in Leningrad at the site where a German war cemetery had been, much to the annoyance of some Russians, who considered it scandalous that the Germans took care of their war graves and the Russians did not.

302.1.72

152.4

Sometimes the Russian mass graves were unmarked; in other places a 122-mm grenade shell marked the site; and, very seldom, a pyramid was left with the names of the fallen.

Grave robbers have also been at work. At first they operated individually, and then later, professionally, in groups. First in line were the Germans, as German medallions could be sold for a lot of money in Germany. Later the robbers also started looking for gold jewelry and gold teeth.

Graves were desecrated by the hundreds. Taisya Belousova wrote in 1995, "The 'elite' of the grave robbers, looking for gold, says, 'I don't dig up Slavs.' He gave no answer to my question as to whether they dug up Jews . . . which persuaded some Jewish communities to place concrete covers over the sites of mass executions."

35.1

On the Sunday before Easter the Russians visit the graves. Astafyev noted: "Every spring, when the snow lies blue in the woods and thawed patches appear, when the willow starts to burst into leaf, then all the cemeteries are filled with the sound of weeping. And every time I hear it, that weeping, my heart skips a beat and I think that if all the women on earth should come together at the graves of soldiers, then the world would tremble and kneel before such immense grief."

23.20

War Invalids

The fate of the war invalids was lamentable. Those who were seriously disabled refused to go home: "What use is a blind man to her?" Others ended it all, refusing food or jumping from the Red Cross boat transporting them from Stalingrad to the Volga.

13.2.89

After the war you could see invalids at and around the stations and kiosks, playing the harmonica, singing melancholy songs, selling tobacco, getting drunk, arguing and cursing the government that did too little for them. "Zhora from the refreshment bar," handicapped himself, knows exactly how to deal with disabled soldiers and those with shell shock— precisely how much he should serve them and which topics of conversation he should broach.

409.1.115

Anatoli Zhigulin writes that, in the winter of 1943–44, the militia in the city of Voronezh dared not approach the invalids in the market. "They stand side by side, ready to kill you. There was something like a market invalid caste. After the war they gradually disappeared."

504.2.75

Surgical aids such as crutches, prostheses, or wheelchairs were practically nonexistent. In the absence of Soviet prostheses—a few of the disabled were given American models—people had to manufacture their own crutches themselves. Horrific sights were common: torsos on a board with four little wheels, moving themselves along with spindles in their hands. . . . Most passers-by, women in particular, gave a little something to the unfortunate creatures. The pensions were a pittance, and finding suitable work was difficult.

461.1.5

303.1.44

209.5

In 1946 and 1947 the most noticeably and seriously disabled were
removed from the cities and housed in little villages. The worst cases were
placed out of sight, on the island of Valaam in Lake Ladoga. This applied
especially to the people on those little boards and others whose "appearance spoils the image of the big cities aesthetically," as someone cynically
wrote. *Literaturnaya gazeta* of 25 May 1988 published a photograph of
Aleksandr Podogenov on Valaam, sitting, without arms or legs, immobile
on a cushion.

Disabled prisoners of war had to prove that they had not been disabled
by a Soviet bullet. When proof from a Soviet front hospital could not be
obtained, the disabled prisoners were typically asked, "Did a guard shoot
at you while you were trying to flee Kolyma?"

Every year invalids had to report to the medical examination board,
even those who were missing an arm or a leg, "as if their arms and legs
could have grown back in the meantime."

Medical Care and Hospitals

Concerning personal hygiene, a soldier's greatest concern was the struggle against lice and scabies. There was (sometimes) a *banya* (a house or
hut with a steam bath) and the clothes could be boiled in a "louse killer"
(*vosheboyka*). In the first years of the war, in particular, the delousing was
"colossal." Cutting off your hair and rubbing in a kind of ointment (Sol-
idal) or petrol helped somewhat against this plague, which caused such
itching that the afflicted could not sleep. Every soldier's ideal was to have
a red-hot steam bath in the bathhouse and be really clean for a change.

Right at the front the *sanitarka*, women especially charged with the task,
were busy fetching the wounded from the battlefield and carrying them
to a medical post, where they administered first aid. The wounded man
was then sent to the first-aid post (*medsanbat*), where he could have sur-
gery and be bandaged. Then, if necessary, he was taken either to a surgical or evacuation hospital in the hinterland.

On arriving at the hospital, the wounded were first washed, in the *banya*
if possible. The sisters there were "cheerful girls, who would laugh and say,
'You are no longer men to us but wounded soldiers so don't be shy.'"

You can surely imagine the scenes in the hospital: a steady influx of
wounded men, surgeries being performed on rows of operating tables,
amputations without anaesthetic. "Oh, that anaesthetic at the front! They

303.1

324.1

45.1

98.1.71

209.4.113

257.2.50

209.24.263

put a cloth over your face and pour a couple of drops of something on it; it's as if you're suffocating. You scream, you can't breathe. Your arms and legs are strapped down, you can't move," wrote Grigori Vasilchenko. Conditions were primitive, and doctors and nurses fatally weary. 465.1.128

There are also many stories of parasites getting under the plaster of Paris casts, causing unbearable itching and driving the victims mad.

The greatest fear among the recuperating men was that they would not be sent back to their old unit. Toward the end of the war men came to be treated for gonorrhea or syphilis. 229.1.81

Were there separate officers' hospitals, with special "generals' rooms"? Indeed, Viktor Berdinskikh refers to "party hospitals." A last note: there were no dentists in the Russian army. 254.1.80 37.2.164 400.2.101

Kondratyev is one of many who have described in detail how those with relatively light wounds trudged to the *medsanbat* on foot, stumbling, sometimes for days on end, seeking food and shelter on the way, knocking on the door of a farm or digging up something to eat from a field. 209.24.258 Sashka, the main character in one of Kondratyev's novels, realized that, now, no one welcomed them as heroes on the way to a hospital, "that was only when we were traveling through Siberia [on our way to the front]." Yuri Nikolayev later told his daughter "how they transported us, 209.24.245 a train full of wounded from Bryansk to Orel in cattle trucks, with two nurses, how they reassured us that 'the maggots will clean the wound' and how in Orel no one was waiting for us and how the wounded walked and crawled in a long line to the other end of town where the hospital was located." 314.1.221

Anyone who was wounded was obliged to take his weapon with him, or else he would not be treated; worse still, you could then expect an unpleasant interrogation by the "Special Section."

Men were pleased to be wounded, because, at least then, you did not have to fight for a while. But in 1943, during the tank battles at Kursk, those who were exempt from fighting because of wounds were called back into service. There are several reports of this. 348.1.126

A seventy-year-old surgeon recalled in 1993, "You know, there were no sheets or blankets. There was not always enough to eat. The nurses brought their own things from home . . . potatoes and sheets, socks and spoons. We were all in it together. Brothers and sisters. And if someone was dying, then we sat up all night with him, so he could depart with a pure soul . . . not left all alone . . . so he could die as if he was at home." 43.3

Astafyev describes how, toward the end of the war, patients did as they pleased. He tells of a soldier with a bullet wound in his lung who could blow cigarette smoke out of his back. Others could pass wind in accompaniment to the song, *Boys, Unharness the Horses*. The largest audiences were attracted by a soldier "who could support a small kettle of water with his massive, erect member—that magician drew a crowd. He was a Greek by nationality and said that, for a Greek, this was the most normal thing
23.14.27   in the world."

13

After the War

Victory Day

The German capitulation was signed on 9 May at forty-three minutes after midnight. Stalin declared 9 May the Day of Victory, so that Prague could still be "liberated" by Soviet troops and not by Vlasov's army, which had, in fact, driven the Germans out of Prague.   381.1

"Toward evening on 9 May, the order from the Supreme Commander concerning the end of the war and the salute in honor of the victory was made known. When I went to Berzarin, the army commandant [the first garrison commandant of Berlin], he was shouting, laughing, into the telephone, 'Order from Comrade Stalin! Nine hundred cannons and three hundred salvos. Aim the barrels at the center of Berlin and shoot high.'

"It was 9:00 in the evening. In Berlin the salute in honor of the end of the Great Patriotic War began. The cannons were fired from a distance, from almost the same sites where they had stood in the days of the attack on Berlin . . . the roar of the cannons became increasingly louder. Independent salvos from automatic weapons joined the cannonade; the heavens were filled with differently colored machine-gun salvos. Continual explosions rang out over the ruins of the city. In the background the grim silhouettes of the Reichstag and Brandenburg Gate. More and more shrapnel whistled over our heads, falling like hail on the broken asphalt. . . . The rain of shrapnel finally became so dangerous that we were forced to change our position.

"The cannonade stopped as suddenly as it had started, and silence, a majestic, overpowering silence, reigned all around. It was Victory. It was

Peace. The Great Patriotic War was at an end," wrote the film producer
L. Saakov in 1986.

On the morning of 9 May, Polish soldiers who had come to Berlin
with the Soviet troops held a mass, led by the head chaplain, Kupsz. "Afterward, we drove in several cars to the center of Berlin, to the Reichstag,"
recalls Svetlana Davydyuk. "An unbelievably enormous crowd was gathered there. The Reichstag was smoldering and teeming with people trying to write their names on the walls and the pillars. On the steps up to
the entrance, the famous Lidiya Ruslanova was singing her no less famous
number, 'Felt Boots, Felt Boots,' to the accompaniment of a military
ensemble."

Decades later the predominant feeling on 9 May was that of sadness.
"On 9 May I go to the Bolshoi Theater. There are fewer and fewer veterans from the front. I search the crowd for an ordinary soldier, an infantryman, someone from the trenches, with only one medal. . . . I seldom
find one. But there are plenty of people looking like officers; you recognize them instinctively by certain characteristics. And they are not wearing ordinary medals either; only officers were rewarded with Suvorov
and Kutuzov medals," writes Anatoli Genatulin. In the image of the poet
Viktor Korolyov: "Once a year, on 9 May, he stands there with a good-
natured look in his old man's eyes, sometimes holding up a notice saying '1st company, 134th regiment, 225th division.' He comes here as before
and looks around him, true to his hope: perhaps someone will turn up
suddenly."

"The pomp and circumstance," wrote P. Borkunenko in 1990 in a letter
to *Ogonyok*, "are far removed from our memories of the dead. Here, on
the first level, stand the generals, dripping from shoulder to navel with
decorations. Look what heroes we are. But did you know, comrade generals, that many soldiers, including myself, do not wear their medals? We
are ashamed of such a victory, of the millions of dead, of the destruction
of the country."

Equally honest is the writer Anatoli Ananyev: "I think of those villages,
the tumbledown cottages of the widows for whom the kolkhoz chairman
had no concern, nor anyone else either. So that's how they lived, no pension, no privileges. And only on the Day of Victory do they set up a little
table in front of their *izba* (hut) on which they arranged the photographs
of their dead family members alongside a bottle of vodka and some glasses,
so that anyone passing might remember the dead. They couldn't even
afford to put out any kind of snack."

The Victory Parade

On 24 June 1945 the victory parade took place on Moscow's Red Square. "We stayed in some institution or other, and for fifteen days we rehearsed for the parade. On the first day we went to learn the parade step at 8:00 in the morning. The inhabitants of Moscow saw us and wept, 'Such brave boys, they survived, but mine was killed . . . our boys didn't live to see this,' they cried out loud. Little boys ran back and forth, getting in our way. So then we had to practice from 4:00 to 8:00 in the morning," writes Viktor Berdinskikh.   37.1.22

The generals and marshals were to be given new, sea-green worsted uniforms as in tsarist times, but nobody had the skill to make the uniforms. Finally, they found tailors in the Polish town of Lodz, who sewed one thousand uniforms from thirty-eight hundred yards of cloth. The uniforms were embroidered with an oak leaf for the marshals and laurel leaves for the generals. All the others were simply given a new uniform.   442.1 The dress rehearsal for the parade was on 23 June.

A military orchestra of fourteen hundred musicians played Mikhail Glinka's "Slavsha!" Then, to a thundering drumroll, a battalion of two hundred men cast down an equal number of German banners and standards in front of the Soviet leaders at the mausoleum—the same way French banners had been thrown at the feet of Tsar Alexander after the war against Napoleon.

Stalin did not wish to lead the parade, feeling that he was too old to ride a horse, so the honor went to Marshal Zhukov. At precisely 10:00, he rode out of Spasski Gate of the Kremlin on the white horse, Tsepki, onto Red Square. Marshal Rokossovski ordered the parade "Tenshun!" and reported, "Comrade Marshal of the Soviet Union! The troops of the field army and units of the Moscow garrison stand ready for the victory parade."

Zhukov rode alongside the regiments, which, with their leaders, all represented one of the fronts: Karelian front, Meretskov; Leningrad front, Govorov; First Baltic front, Bagramyan; First White Russian front, Sokolovski; Second White Russian front, Trubnikov; Third White Russian front, Vasilevski; First Ukrainian front, Konev; Second Ukrainian front, Malinovski; Third Ukrainian front, Tolbukhin; Fourth Ukrainian Front, Yeryomenko.

A slight rain was falling and clouds obscured the heavens. Stalin did not flinch at the rain, so Zhukov, too, bore the drizzle unruffled. The film director Dovzhenko was in the crowd. When Zhukov spoke of the fallen,

Dovzhenko was the only one to doff his hat. No minute of silence, no pause, no funeral march, as if those millions of victims "had never even 100.3 existed." Yevgeni Khaldei took a wonderful photograph of Zhukov gliding over the pavement, as it were, on his white mount.

In 1957, on the express wishes of Zhukov, the horse's life was spared and it was allowed to spend its twilight years on a stud farm in Strelkovo in 165.1 the area of Stavropol where it had come from.

In his address Stalin spoke of the people, those whom he referred to as "cogs" in the machine of war. Earlier, in May, he had lavished praise on the people. But this "correction confirmed a sharp turn in state politics," 52.1 as would become apparent all too quickly.

Demobilization

Millions of servicemen and women were demobilized in the space of two years. This was naturally a cause for great happiness for those whose families were waiting for them, alive and well, but those whose house had been destroyed or their family killed "went home with little enthusiasm." "Many had neither home nor family to return to, and home meant just such a barracks as this one. Here, in this barracks, you were fed, and, however you wanted to put it, it was Europe. At home there were shortages, hated bosses, the NKVD, the kolkhoz, working days (a 'working day' is not a 'day' but a calculation unit for paying wages in a kolkhoz; the 'working day' is worth more or less depending on the activity one is being paid to do). You are not allowed to go here, you are not allowed to go there; this is not allowed, that is not allowed; everyone was aware of the kind of 382.1.57 life they were returning to."

Back in the devastated areas, houses were ruined, families broken up, dramas at home.

Few returned; there was an enormous shortage of men. So the men had plenty of choices. One woman complained, "Now they can do whatever 205.1.45 they like; now they can."

Once they were home many demobilized servicemen resented "civilians" who, in the meantime, had grabbed all the best jobs. Disappointed, "after all we had done, it all seemed a lot of nonsense to me—the institute, the teaching, after that work. . . . I had the feeling I had already done the most important things in my life and from now on, from now on nothing interesting was going to happen," was Vyacheslav Kondratyev's 209.25.33 sentiment.

In a demobilization center, a Latvian said to L. Rubinstein, "There's nothing good awaiting Latvians or Jews. You and I, Major, now we are up to our necks in shit with our wounds and our decorations. . . . I've nothing to lose—my entire family has been arrested in the Fatherland."   380.1.50

The train journey home was difficult. Viktor Astafyev was crammed into the toilet with his young wife and two others, and afterward on top of the coal truck. His wife said of the train journey, "At the stations there was weeping and swearing, screaming. People were fighting, heartrending cries for help, soldiers shooting in the air for silence, to bring people to their senses, to create a kind of order among people who were beside themselves."   213.1

On the side of the packed carriages were the words "We won!" "We've come from Berlin!"   383.4.66

Astafyev recalls, "People laden with bundles, bales, buckets, sacks, and cases ran screaming and howling to the train. People were falling over, tripping, dropping things, retrieving them, banging on the carriages, yelling, cursing everything and everybody in creation. Men swore at women and together they all swore at the railway people, pleading with one, pointing out the children, their bandages and their medals. In some places crutches were used to emphasize the message."   21.12.62

The Spoils of War

A distinction can be made between recuperation (recovering what has been stolen), the spoils of war (the government confiscating enemy possessions), plundering, and soldiers' booty.

S. Aleksandrov described an example of recuperation when he had to transport 350 horses from Berlin to White Russia in May 1945. They went in four separate groups, each taking a different route for fear of stray troops and nationalistic "gangs" still wandering about. The disassembly of   10.1.139
factories and the confiscation of works of art are examples of the spoils of war.

Marshal Ivan Konev saw the Sistine Madonna in Dresden, and said, "Into the plane with her and off to Moscow." When officers suggested that the painting should be properly packed and sent by train, Konev said, "So I can go in a plane and she can't?" Konstantin Akinsha and Grigori   309.4.51
Kozlov wrote *Beautiful Loot: The Soviet Plunder of Europe's Art Treasures* (New York, 1995) about the thievery, or plundering, of art after the war by the Red Army.

And then there was the more or less regulated soldiers' booty. As discussed earlier, men were allowed to send one or more packages home, depending on their rank. What did they take? One took nails; another took an ax; a third, needles for the sewing machine and clothing. Soldiers liked to take harmonicas for themselves and one or more watches. Some took a whole armful. The short German army boots were also treasured possessions.

Stalin's motto, "Steal what has been stolen," was a great motivator at the front. Was the motto intended to placate the soldiers, to encourage them to fight ever more fiercely, or, in the case of officers, was it to acquire "compromising material" to be used against them later?

188.3.8

Some had more opportunity to steal than others. The infantry and artillery had to carry everything themselves; officers and members of the military from the hinterland, in particular, could send off chests and crates virtually without restriction. Anyone who came home without any booty was ridiculed.

23.12.86

V. Kardin writes that, in the first few months after the war, officers of standing could "organize" anything, "from black caviar to nice young girls." And when things got too hot for someone like that, he was quickly transferred. Baklanov wrote in his memoirs that, in the autumn of 1945, some soldiers set fire to a trailer full of their commandant's booty because either they "didn't like him or out of a sense of justice."

188.4.139

28.2.20

A. Zubov wrote: "Stalin demoralized the victorious army (consciously or unconsciously) when he permitted free looting of the conquered countries. Rows of Studebakers full of looted goods, sometimes whole trains full, along with the wives of generals from the front who had plundered the abandoned houses in Budapest and Danzig. There were soldiers who raped women, completely ignoring the 'terrible warnings,' and stuffed their pockets with loot. We paid a great price for all that Asian barbarism. The price for that plundering was our freedom. The plunderers were not only the individual soldiers and officers; the Soviet state behaved in exactly the same way."

500.1.75

"The division commandant, Major-General Shatskov, dispatched five or six trucks with photographic equipment and the like, and several trucks full of furniture," noted Grigori Pomerants. Viktor Kozlov remarked, "Searching for such 'booty,' which became a considerable part of army life, has not, for some reason, received any attention from the military authors."

349.1.171

230.1.167

Zhukov Falls from Grace

Intrigues and accusations aimed at Marshal Zhukov began virtually immediately after the war.

On 24 May 1945 Stalin asked a number of generals what they thought about Zhukov becoming Generalissimo. They all thought it was a wonderful idea, except Zhukov, who said he would then be in the company of such characters as Franco and Chiang Kai-Shek. Stalin, of course, got the title. 17.1

Just after the victory parade, several dozen generals and admirals who had been in close contact with Zhukov were arrested. In Berlin Zhukov had already chased off the infamous chief of police, Vsevolod Merkulov, who had come to arrest officers. Later, in June 1946, Zhukov used his pistol to drive away people who came to search his dacha. At an important meeting of the Politburo with his generals in May 1946, Stalin accused Zhukov of disloyal conduct, a tendency toward "Bonapartism," and of plotting a coup d'état, but the military supported Zhukov. 134.1.39 / 332.1.30–31 / 75.1

The editor of Zhukov's memoirs, A. D. Mirkina, quotes Zhukov: "In 1947 I expected to be arrested at any moment. I prepared a suitcase of linen. All my closest colleagues had already been arrested. How did things work then? People's fates were decided during lunch or dinner. Then they discussed business, naming people's names. Stalin would suddenly say, 'Lavrenti, take measures.' Beria would stand up and go to the phone in the next room. He dials a number: 'Ivanov, Semyonov, Stepanov.' And they were arrested that evening." 397.1.15

Zhukov was dismissed as commander of the land forces and was more or less exiled to the military district of Odessa. Shortly afterward he was transferred to Sverdlovsk. By New Year of 1947 it was already clear that Zhukov had fallen from grace. Only General Telegin and his wife dared celebrate New Year's Eve with him. The marshal burst into tears and demanded, "Why are they doing this to me? Never in my life have I feigned loyalty; I have served the Fatherland and the party in good conscience." 177.16

Some friends said to Telegin, "What on earth possessed you to visit Zhukov now that he's out of favor? Now you can expect big problems." In 1948 a number of Zhukov's colleagues were arrested, including General N. V. Kryukov and his wife, the singer Lidya Ruslanova, and Telegin. Some were severely tortured and sentenced to heavy punishments. Telegin, arrested on 24 January, was beaten, finally confessed to everything

that was required of him, and was sentenced to twenty-five years of forced
labor. Kryukov and Ruslanova were accused of excessive appropriation of
war booty. Although this, in itself, was correct, their arrest was actually
related to Zhukov.

Although "mass robbery of the German population and of destroyed,
empty houses in 1945–46 was unchallenged and generally acknowledged,"
wrote Arkady Vaksberg in 1990, it was used against you "if you fell out
of favor. Otherwise people kept quiet about it." Nevertheless, with regard
to Zhukov, Stalin did not take it that far. When Abakumov suggested that
the marshal be arrested as the head of a military conspiracy against the
"leader," Stalin said, "No, I won't have Zhukov arrested. I know him well.
In four years I have got to know him better than I know myself."

Even long after the war the Soviet leaders were not terribly keen on
Zhukov. Nikita Khrushchev dismissed him from the army in 1957, where-
upon Zhukov, embittered and abandoned by many, retired to his dacha
and started to write his memoirs. Party leader Leonid Brezhnev, together with Mikhail Suslov, the ideological super arbitrator, attempted
to stop publication of the memoirs but only succeeded in getting them
amended.

Despite Zhukov's express request to Brezhnev that he not be cremated
but buried, after Zhukov's death Brezhnev quickly had him cremated.

Zhukov will always remain famous as the commander who won the war
for Russia. Many praise him excessively; others take offence at his stern,
cruel conduct, at his contempt for human lives. "But have those critics
ever thought about what would have happened had I not taken such harsh
measures to retain almost every front line? I am convinced that, had that
been the case, we would not have been able to hold Moscow and would
have been forced to roll back to behind the Volga, where hastily formed
reserve armies were being trained."

Repression of Veterans

No sooner had the war ended than the regime set to work to stifle the
fledgling spirit of freedom the soldiers had brought home with them.
These men had seen a lot: they had witnessed Stalin's mistakes during the
first years of the war as well as the standard of living in the areas they had
occupied in Europe. Remarkably, in a report from the political leaders of
the Second White Russian front of 6 February 1945, a parallel was drawn

between these soldiers and the tsarist officers who had tasted the freedom and way of life in Europe during the Napoleonic War.

394.1.91–92

Kardin asked a fellow officer in 1945,"What will happen tomorrow?" "Tomorrow begins the start of a new 1937," was the reply. The year 1937, for Russians, is synonymous with the time of the Great Terror. "Stalin will not forgive us for the defeats of 1941 and 1942, which were his own miscalculations; he will want to suppress the spirit of independence and the love of freedom."

188.4.140

188.1.242

Any expressions of gratitude toward the returning servicemen and women were soon no longer heard.

Stalin was afraid of freedom-loving, independent-thinking people, people who had seen more than was good for them. After all, "a time of unlimited expectations . . . hopes of 'softening,' of earned confidence, of long-awaited humanity" was dawning.

104.1

194.1.32

The attack began with a judgment in August 1946 by the Leningrad magazines, *Zvezda* (The star) and *Leningrad*. Formally the judgment concerned literature and music, but the party campaign was actually aimed at the intelligentsia. The tone was set by Leningrad Party Chief Andrei Zhdanov. The "Leningrad Affair" was subsequently embarked on, and its victims were not only the defenders of Leningrad during the war (Aleksei Kuznetsov and his comrades) but also the city itself, which was far more open and liberal than Moscow.

The message of the attack was clear: an overabundance of independence had to be stamped out. Campaigns against "toadying idolization of the West" and "cosmopolitanism" followed shortly thereafter, translated as repression aimed at everyone who has seen too much in the West, plus the Jews. A third set of victims were former prisoners of war; although they had already paid their "penalty," they were arrested again. After all, who had seen more of the West than the armed forces and the prisoners of war?

"It was in Russia, not Germany, where masterworks of poetry and philosophy were burned at the stake," wrote Nikolai Panchenko, referring to the works of the famous poetess Anna Akhmatova. Amazed, the people became aware that a new war had begun, the "cold" war, bringing renewed terror to their own country. Less and less was being written about the war; the view was that the war should already have been relegated to history. For twenty years, until 1965, there was no parade on Victory Day.

328.1

209.25.335

383.4.47

The war had been won, but the peace had been lost.

122.1.9

Traumatized Veterans

There was virtually no help for the demobilized servicemen and women. These veterans did, however, enjoy certain privileges: one trip a year free of charge, no income tax, and a small financial allowance for medals and decorations received. They did not have to line up at the railway ticket office, at the pharmacies, or in the shops. When food was scarce they could buy extra in special shops, and they could even take a rest in a sanatorium. In some villages they were given firewood, their houses were fixed up, and their vegetable garden was plowed. Generally they made no demands; they felt they had simply been doing their duty.

Most veterans had to look for work and lodgings themselves. Their independent behavior and self-supporting attitude, and their unwillingness to overlook injustice were not popular with their superiors. After all, the system demanded obedience. Instead, many veterans felt that they could do as they pleased, and many families broke up because the husband and wife had become estranged, and, moreover, there was an abundance of willing women.

"I came home," writes one woman who was born in 1928, "in December 1945. There was nothing to eat; it was cold. We were hungry and there were no cattle, not a single cow, nothing. That whole winter I went with the sleigh to the place where the abattoir buried its animals. If a dead horse was brought in, then we took off the meat, as much as we could. . . . When spring came, we changed to grass, made soup from it, baked grass cakes."

Astafyev wrote: "After the war it was worse in some ways than during the war. At the front, at least you belonged somewhere; you more or less got fed." Kondratyev recounts how he and his comrades walked around in patched uniforms even into the 1950s. Even General Pyotr Grigorenko, a lecturer at a military academy, was happy to be able to earn a little extra to feed his large family.

Forty, fifty years after the war, some veterans were still waiting for a house or a telephone. Their situation became increasingly worse, ever poorer. Women, in particular, had a hard time, no matter how often they might say, "Well, I survived the siege" or "I saved the wounded." Young people would add, "I'm sick of hearing about that siege of yours."

The joy of the victory and returning home safely soon intermingled with bitterness and disappointment as the lack of attention and recognition became apparent.

The veterans buried their worst recollections of the war deep inside. They did not talk about these memories, preferring to keep silent about the horrors. "It was not forbidden, but it was still too fresh in our minds. It was only later that the nightmares came." 127.10.10–11

But on 9 May, when the victory was celebrated, everything would again surface. As the years passed, professional help became less available and the veterans looked back more and more to the time they spent in the war.

By the 1990s the veterans had more or less been written off; they were no longer given any priority. "In the pharmacies they are entirely 209.15.80 persona non grata with their crutches; there they are seen as something like pariahs of the local health system. As soon as a veteran hands over his prescription with the word *free* underlined, the pharmacist's face turns grim." 316.1.3–4

Kardin wrote to the Soviet Veterans' Committee a few years ago about the need to organize a system for all kinds of aid for the veterans. "Such help is not necessary—the help of the young pioneers is sufficient," was the reply. Indeed, young pioneers sometimes did shop or do chores for the 188.1.255 veterans.

Their victory had benefited others and had been misused by the "plunderers," as Baklanov refers to them: "All that the front generation achieved has been made use of by people without honor or conscience—plunderers, in other words." The *hinterland rats*—a term used in the military— 28.3 reaped the harvest, grabbed the best jobs. "When we came back from the war," says Boris Slutsky, "I became aware that no one needed us."

War traumas were hidden deep inside. Over the years they returned as 188.6 nightmares, as "sorrow, hate, anger, pain, terrible fatigue and anxiety," wrote Genatulin. 127.2.71

Vladimir Krupin was once asked to write an article about four Heroes of the Soviet Union who lived in his district. On investigation, it turned out that "one of them was in prison because he had hung his decorations and medals on a dog and had shot at the portrait of the Father of the People with a hunting rifle; a second, an invalid, was driving around in a creaking, three-wheeled carriage and had been shunted off somewhere." 241.1.40

After the war many people experienced a backlash, confronted with disappointments that were hard to swallow. Worse, in the 1990s, even public opinion turned against the veterans. People accused them of lying about the war in lessons to schoolchildren. People told them they had fought for nothing, because the country had been poor and remained poor. People said they were conservative, that they longed for the order and regularity of the old regime, and that, in fact, they were Stalinists.

Veterans were treated rudely and were sworn at in shops and in the street: "When are you all going to finally kick the bucket?" "What kind of victor are you? You brought the country to rack and ruin. That's what you did." "You reinforced the Stalin regime." Sometimes they were even punched, ridiculed for their rows of medals that one could buy now for a song in Berlin, or their decorations were torn off. "If you hadn't won, then we'd be drinking Bavarian beer here now."

The veterans, too, to their dismay, saw that the victory had not brought the country what everyone had expected. They, too, saw that the losing side was living far better than they were and that all kinds of shit had floated to the surface.

"If you want to know how the victory over fascism turned out for us, then look how Hitler's vanquishers rummage around in the dustbins and die in poverty. . . . If we no longer know what we were fighting for, then that is a real defeat, a defeat after the victory," wrote Mikhail Savitsky in 1995.

Many veterans, therefore, look back to the war with a kind of nostalgia, to a time when they were honored, when they were needed, when they (finally) felt like fully-fledged citizens, when they experienced camaraderie and genuine friendship, "when we were the People with a capital letter, when we held the fate of the Fatherland in our boyish hands," as Kondratyev writes. "The truth is that, in October 1941, boys and girls, young men and women, brought up with the idea of a Utopia, delayed and subsequently halted the advance of the Fascists with their unselfish, mindful courage."

"We were as one, like the fingers of a hand. It is not true that socialism never existed. It was there once . . . in the war . . . I am a witness to it . . . a witness nobody needs . . . an old scarecrow . . . life is casting off our generation . . . we are all superfluous," one veteran told Svetlana Alekseyevich.

For many, the war turned out to have been the best time of their lives. When they gather together now, every year on 9 May, there are fewer and fewer, "and then we don't talk about all the horrors we saw, but we do talk about the camaraderie." And the veterans are not Stalinists, "They don't

need Stalin or the Soviet regime . . . but they simply want recognition and a minimum amount of respect." At best they cherish "nostalgia for 209.15.80
the cast-iron national values and the former greatness of the unified state that, for them, will always be their Fatherland." 394.1.167

How many veterans committed suicide or succumbed to drink? 209.4.116–17;
209.2

The War Generation

Did a "war generation" really exist? Or was it a generation with universal traits? The binding element of that generation is the misery they all endured and the constant proximity of death. But there was also the feeling of freedom, a proud awareness that it was they who had done the job. The characteristics of that generation are said to be independence, lack of fear, the ability to make their own decisions but also to carry out orders without question, and the tendency to suppress their stress with vodka. The 446.1.112
members of that generation are afraid of losing one another: they recognize one another, without question, as comrades in adversity. 13.6.308

Someone once said that a generation is not formed by the blood in its veins but by the blood that flows from those veins. All those of that generation have nightmares. "I'm not in the war," says Yuri Levitanski, "the war is in me." 262.1

Opposing the view that a war generation indeed exists is the fact that soldiers' perception of what occurred in the war differs considerably from that of officers, as it also varies among the various forces—the infantry, the artillery, the tank troops, the anti-aircraft units, the partisans, the air force, and the navy. Nevertheless, they are all united by their common 188.6
need to forget.

To speak of a "lost generation" after the war was not permitted. Still, many felt lost; they were unable to readapt to family life or to hold down a job; there was a great deal of drunkenness, and there were suicides. 209.6
Rubinstein refers to this as well. Both Kondratyev and the poetess and 380.1.52
front soldier Yuliya Drunina committed suicide. Both gave voice to the views of the front generation.

Only after several years did the survivors feel the need to return and visit the former battlefield. The majority of veterans who attended these sad gatherings were not those who had been at the front; those attending were staff officers, personnel from the hinterland, including those often referred to as "professional veterans." And, indeed, they were often

209.9 conservative, even Stalinist in their views. The real front soldiers had seen enough of what Stalinism had brought about in the war.

It was not the victory that had been taken from the Russians but their hope for improvement, and that caused deep resentment. No Russians were invited to the fiftieth anniversary of D-Day. "They swallowed that pill with a bitter and, for all of us, hurtful aftertaste, in silence and with-
11.3.79 out complaint." In 1995 Mikhail Ananyev declared, "Russia lies in ruins,
14.1.15 like Germany in 1945, if not worse."

The fiftieth commemoration of 9 May 1945 led to the melancholy thought that nothing had been right, that it had all been to no avail. These thoughts were seen as part of the cause of the decline and subsequent col-
85.1 lapse of the Soviet Union.

Although the victory in the war was one of the few things people could be proud of, even that feeling was lost—a loss encouraged, egged on, by people who never tired of writing that nothing had ever been right. Who cared that this made the young generation uninterested and cynical?

And then, to top it all, people saw a new breed of fascism rearing its head in the1990s, replete with uniforms, boots, couplers, and anti-Semitic ranting and raving. Who would ever have thought that the Russian trans-lation of *Mein Kampf* would be openly on sale in the Moscow metro and that fascist Blackshirts would be marching through Moscow and other
188.3.4 cities, celebrating the anniversary of Hitler's birth?

"We didn't go off to war only to see idiots strutting around in black SS uniforms in our recaptured home, waving banners bearing the swastika, which we had ripped down from the buildings in each city we conquered,"
209.7 wrote Kardin.

And thus the veterans were branded as "occupiers," as "Stalin zombies," forced to live in poverty, lumped together with Hitler's hangers-on, read-
102.2.190 ing that, in Yalta, the Western Allies had let themselves be taken in. And what's more, all the while knowing that, in Germany, the veterans get their
57.1 pensions on time.

Kondratyev wrote prophetically about the fiftieth commemoration of the victory: "It will be unforgivable if, on that day, the veterans have to turn up half-starved, in old shoes, in patched suits, robbed of their sav-ings by the democratic government of Russia. Who will then defend such
209.15.80–81 a Russia and her government?"

The Hinterland

Vasily Belov writes:

The hunger among the people began imperceptibly, nothing serious at first; I think no one in the kolkhoz was terribly surprised when an old woman died of exhaustion. Nor was anyone surprised by the fact that the door stood continually open almost all the time because of the constant stream of beggars. Old people of all shapes and sizes trailed constantly along the roads, from far and wide, with sticks and knapsacks. Impoverished old people and invalids wandered around with baskets, and young people, too, with linen bags, made for school, traipsing from village to village, from house to house. There were all manner of children, from tiny tots who had barely learned to walk, to older children. And women would ask them, "Are you a boy or a girl?" It was difficult to tell from their clothes.

The beggars sought shelter as long as there was still daylight and were seldom refused. The farmer's wife would seat them at the table, dish up that evening's soup, ask them their names, where they came from, if they had a family and a home, what news there was from those far-off places. The beggars warmed themselves on the old couches, and those who were good at telling stories gathered a company of listeners around them. 36.1.76

The Afonin family was hungry, too. In December 1943, in Western Siberia, this is what happened to that family: "My little sister and I slept on the stove and mother in the bed. In the evening I told Yuliya stories until deep into the night, and then she slept with her back toward me. I put my arms around her, and we went to sleep like that. In the morning I awoke, and my sister was already cold. I was scared and I screamed out, but mother had already left the house long before." 7.1.28

For adults, the beginning of the war meant that you had to work longer days; no one had a day off anymore, and absence from work or arriving late met with extreme punishments. 497.1.68

Workers (mostly women) in the war industry were considered to have been mobilized from 26 December 1941, and therefore absence from work was considered desertion. This earned a prison sentence for 121,090 people in 1942; 367,047 in 1943; and 265,966 in 1944. In 1941 there were 1,458,185 people prosecuted for being absent without leave or arriving more than twenty minutes late for work; in 1942, 1,274,644; in 1943, 961,545; and in 1944, 893,242. 497.1.68

Children from fourteen onwards could be sent to technical schools, often far from home. Many could not stand the hard existence in the factory— because that is what actually came down—the hunger, the loneliness, and they took to their heels.

Farmer A. P. Muratovskikh recalls what happened to her as a girl: "At the age of fourteen they took us from the kolkhoz to be trained at a technical school. We didn't want to learn to be locksmiths or bench workers. Everything was done by force. They took us to Nizhni Tagil, put us in front of a workbench, showed us how it worked, and then forced us to work. I was terribly homesick; after all, they had taken me away from my family by force. We couldn't stand it; we planned to run away together from the 'factory training.' It was December and 40 degrees below freezing. We left on a coal train. The militia took me off the train three times, held me for a while, and saw how thin I was: I was 1 meter, 70 centimeters, tall, and I weighed 35 kilos [5 feet 7 inches and 70 pounds]; only my eyes were normal. Then they let me go, and I got on another train. Eight days I was traveling. I arrived at Kotelnich and managed to get to my village without anyone seeing me. I spent the whole winter on the couch and hiding in the cellar. Luckily there were good people at the kolkhoz machine and tractor station, and they let me learn to drive a combine 37.2.152   harvester."

Similar scenes occurred in Ukraine after it was recaptured: "They took young lads for the 'labor front' under the guise of teaching them in the 'factory school' . . . took them to the ends of the earth, to the Kuzbass, and put them to work in the mines of Prokopyevsk," noted Vasili 232.1.41   Kozhanov.

Children got into trouble for "stealing" stalks of corn after the harvest or taking something else for their hungry brothers and sisters. They had 127.13   children felling trees, too. After the war, children fifteen or sixteen had to clear minefields at Staraya Russa. "We worked all day as long as there was still light. And that went on until November 1946. . . . Of the 103 people so employed, 38 survived, and many of them had wounds and bruises," 242.1.21   reported N. Krylova in 1985.

The extreme scarcity of food and other goods meant money became greatly devalued. Bartering boomed, at least as long as people had something to barter with. But then you had to make sure that you did not end up in prison for "speculation," because, whatever else disappeared in the 497.1.46;   war, repression continued unabated.
497.2.114

Without their own little plot of ground, millions would not have made it—neither in the countryside nor in the towns. The farming population received no bread coupons, except for the teachers, nurses, and agronomists working in the villages. Mere words cannot possibly describe how serious the hunger was and the lengths to which people went to fill their bellies: chaff, grasses, bark. Infectious and noninfectious diseases made the rounds: sore throats, tuberculosis, diarrhea, dysentery, scabies, and typhus, while at the same time the number of doctors had fallen by more than half. The historian Zinich puts the number of doctors at 64,000, whereas there had been 141,700 before the war.   497.2.96

Mothers worked away from home all day, in the factories or farming the land. They were often away for part of the night as well. So many men had been killed that people started to refer to the children by their grandmother's or grandfather's patronymic. The children then used the   422.1.185 "matronymic," their mother's name, such as Pashin, Verin, or Alfeyevnin.

Quite out of the ordinary, Major Rubinstein had been given a few days of leave to spend with his family in Kuybyshev. On the way, women at stations asked him for bread, something to eat, and especially for soap. Once home, with a suitcase full of food, he was confronted with his hollow-eyed family. His wife "was afraid to approach him, she was so ashamed of her appearance. . . . Before me stood an old, consumptive woman, as dry as a bone, in a musty dressing gown, with no voice, a scarf around her neck and a headscarf, in whom I had difficulty recognizing my twenty-six-year-old, adored and healthy, always neat and tidy Irochka."   380.1.31

Another soldier, Anatoli Genatulin, saw his children when he came home: "He had been a rather weak, sickly little fellow for three years already. No pants on, skinny bowlegs, his tummy sticking out, his neck like the floppy stem of a flower growing on poor ground." Sergei Golitsyn   127.1.96 described children in White Russian villages by the river Berezina at the beginning of 1944: "The children, especially, looked completely dead beat, five or six to a family, grim, silent, with waxy old people's faces, little arms and legs as thin as matchsticks, covered in weeping sores, they hardly spoke, they whispered, they didn't run, they didn't play, they hardly smiled."   137.2.213

In the countryside, work in the kolkhoz provided almost nothing, because the grain all went to the state. But you had to pay taxes, register for war loans, and so forth. And you also had to pay in kind from what you grew on your own piece of land. Women described after the war how

37.2.151   they were shut up in the kolkhoz office until they paid or registered for
the state loans.

And mowing grass for your own cow, longer than the permitted three
days? That was forbidden. And if you did it anyway, then that grass was
127.1.101 confiscated.

Some war orphans, who were found in the captured villages, left with
the soldiers, as "sons of the regiment." For thousands of other children,
extra children's homes were set up, which was a solution, as long as the
497.2.46–47 management "behaved respectably." After the war, the innumerable war
orphans presented an acute problem. In 1948 it was calculated that 2.5 million children had lost their parents from acts of war or starvation. There
were also many children who had ended up wandering far from home,
having run away from orphanages or forced labor. And then there were
the children who were left alone because their widowed mother had been
arrested for "stealing" food. Boarding schools were set up for them. Unfortunately, however, the personnel sometimes (how often?) stole from the
494.1.133–34 young children or sexually assaulted them.

The Famine

After the war famine broke out, and this lasted from 1946 to 1948 and
for part of 1949. It was caused by an unprecedented drought in Russia to
the west of the Urals, by lack of manpower—the farmers had all been
killed—by a shortage of machines, and by the fact that the government
had no money left for agriculture—although there was money for arms,
for the race to create the atomic bomb—and the government refused to
break into the state grain reserves. Even the grain the farmers had with-
held for planting in the following year was confiscated; after all, the government had to realize its five-year-plan. Moreover, for political reasons,
grain was still being exported to Eastern Europe and France, which received .5 million tons.

The grain harvest in 1940 was still 95.6 million tons, but in 1945 it
was down to 47.3 million tons, and in 1946 it was as low as 39.6 million
483.1.6   tons. In 1947, 4.8 million tons from the grain harvest was added to the
496.2.29   state reserves, and 1.1 million tons were exported. In 1946–47 a total of
2.5 million tons were exported, and even in 1948 another 3.2 million were
496.2.149 exported. In other words, there was no need for anyone to have gone hun-
496.2.178 gry. "From 1 October 1946, the number of villagers provided with bread
dropped from twenty-seven million to four million," calculated Zima, the

specialist in this aspect of the famine. This meant that "in the winter of 1946 and 1947, part of the urban population and almost the entire rural population had to find alternative sources for bread until the new harvest, either buying it at the market or at 'commercial' prices." 496.2.12

Child mortality in 1947 was high, up to 319 deaths per thousand. The famine and the consequent sickness not only claimed some two million victims but "crime" also increased sharply. People stole grain from the field or robbed shops. Thousands of show trials were held in order to scare the people off. Harsh punishments were meted out to 21,285 kolkhoz chairmen who kept back grain, nevertheless, so that they could provide their starving fellow villagers with something to eat. 496.2.11 496.1.48

Mainly women and young children were arrested; women disappeared into the Gulag with their children for up to seven years. "The Gulag was an enormous 'mother and child center.'" Desperate parents left their children behind or sent them out to beg. "Hundreds of thousands of widows, invalids, and orphans populated the Gulag, which, for most of them, meant an escape from starvation, because at least there they were given something to eat. But if the hunger did not break you physically, then the camp crippled you morally." 496.1.53 496.1.58

The party machinery and the government, from the highest to the lowest levels, "experienced no shortages and were provided with all the necessities." 496.2.57

Thanks to the UNRRA, the United Nations help organization, which was also active elsewhere in Europe, and the American Red Cross, many managed to survive. Long after the war the famine was still not a subject for discussion. At the very most one spoke of *nyedorod* (crop failure). 496.2.146–47

PART 4

A Provincial Town during and after the War

14

Shadrinsk

Shadrinsk is a reasonably unknown small Russian provincial town on the east side of the Urals, with a prewar population of some thirty-five hundred, situated on the railway line from Sverdlovsk to Kurgan-Omsk, on the river Iset. The region is fertile, thanks to the black earth, so that, before the war, Shadrinsk was a kind of center of the "granary of the Urals." The industry was aimed at serving the agricultural sector and processing agricultural products: grain mills, a slaughterhouse, silos, a sack factory, felt boot manufacturing, a repair shop for agricultural machines, a vodka distillery, and some small-scale craftsmen. Shadrinsk also had a training college, a financial training institute, and a nursing college.

Historically Shadrinsk was a fortified town, founded in 1663 to prevent attack by "non-Russians." Before the war it still consisted of low wooden houses, sometimes with a stone foundation. Governmental buildings were built of brick. The streets were wide, mostly unmetaled, with grass verges. Electricity was provided by the town's own 760-kilowatt power plant, but there was no running water or main sewerage. Open plots between the buildings bore witness to the several churches that had been demolished.

The Start of the War

In the first few days of the war several hundred people, including women, went to enlist, more symbolically, I believe, than realistically, as volunteers for the front.

On 25 June 1941, in the center of the town, you could hear the many agricultural tractors driving through the main streets, destined for the front. 434.210

On 2 July a thousand Communists were transported to the front as "political soldiers."

434.87 Also in 1941 as many as 135 Komsomol girls joined the army. At the beginning of July of that year eleven "girls eligible for national service" 433.160;
433.146–47 went to war. Only two of them survived.

In May 1942 another fifty-two girls voluntarily joined the forces: as a telephone operator, nurse, or anti-aircraft artillery operator. A total of some 433.160 five hundred girls and women were working in the army or in hospitals.

On 18 September 1941 all men between the ages of sixteen and fifty 433.89 had to undergo military training after work. Railway workers were called up, and women had to replace them. On 10 October 1941 the government set itself the task of training fifty-two thousand women and girls through- 433.200 out the country as train drivers, boilermen, and wagon masters. In Shadrinsk those women were all accommodated in an overfull community center, along with the men. "All sorts of things were going on there; for 433.201 a seventeen-year-old girl, such a life was extremely difficult."

In the winter of 1942 a man who had initially been declared unfit for work because of an atrophied arm was nevertheless called up as a writer 434.3 for an army unit. In August 1943, when a serious shortage of soldiers re- sulted "after the bitter massacre at the Kursk front," that same man was 434.179 recruited into the active army, without a medical examination. Even those 434.15 under eighteen were called up at that time.

The 367th Infantry Division was formed from recruits from in and around Shadrinsk. Their training "progressed at accelerated speed" and consisted of marching and "drilling" with wooden sticks instead of rifles. The local population prepared "carts with field kitchens, and brought 433.121 horses, fodder and equipment" for them.

The training was already completed on 1 September 1941 and seventeen trains took the division to the front in Karelia, the Finnish front, where they arrived on 18 December 1941. Not only the lower ranks but also the officers had practically no experience.

They were met with harsh conditions in Karelia: "There was water under the snow . . . we had to lay a wooden causeway, otherwise the horses sank into the mud. It was swampy; there was nowhere to get warm. We made the trenches from timbers and snow, the huts from conifer branches. There was no chance to build a *banya*. We swelled up from the cold. Some- times we failed to recognize one another. We spoke in whispers, as our 433.128 sore throats had left us no voice."

Within two months, the division lost 7,610 of its 10,910 men; 2,967 of them were "missing." Their bodies still lay unburied in the swamps up until the end of the 1990s. In 1991 two hundred bodies that were recovered there were successfully identified.   433.131

The war took a high toll among the inhabitants of Shadrinsk and the surrounding area. More than twenty thousand people, some two-thirds of the prewar population, left for the front and more than eleven thousand failed to return.   432.125

Refugees

The war may have taken many of the inhabitants of Shadrinsk but it also brought others to the town: refugees, evacuees, factory workers, soldiers, and the wounded, a total of some sixteen thousand newcomers. Most of them came from the "western areas." Some refugees—it is difficult to   434.88
distinguish between refugees and evacuees—"looked at us as if we were foreigners. They touched us and felt our clothes."   434.146

Another diarist noted on 17 January 1942: "I heard a lot of complaints about Jewish refugees who had settled in the town and the villages. In the villages the new inhabitants behave as free as you please. They take (steal) potatoes and newly baked bread and, if the host is out, then they milk his cows and so forth." "The most noticeable were the Jews, with their gut-   434.219
tural speech. The children picked it up straightaway, and the little ones teased them over it. . . . At first the Jewish women were covered in gold and wore a lot of lipstick . . . not all of them were able to move into work-ers' canteens and other warm places." A. N. Martinova's mother arrived   322.38–39
from Karelia after a train journey of fifty days—she had been told that it would take fourteen. Her train was continually shunted to a siding to let military transports or trains carrying the wounded through. After ten days her food supplies were finished.   435.38

She traveled in "a freight train with wooden beds to the left and right of the entrance, from wall to wall, over the entire length of the carriage. On these beds families sat or lay. In the middle of the carriage was a small iron stove, the *burzhuyka*—there was no toilet." Two of her younger   435.58
brothers died during this train journey.   435.60

She was accommodated in a village in the area along with her mother, with a family with tuberculosis at the infectious stage. Her mother noted, "There were a lot of evacuees in Mekhonka, and some of them were quite well off. They sent the prices soaring, buying everything, milk, meat, bacon. These were generally people of a non-Russian appearance. It was unheard of to come across a local inhabitant between the ages of eighteen and fifty in Mekhonka; they were all at the front. But there were a lot of healthy, blooming young men among the evacuees. How I hated them, how I despised them." They were given two hundred grams of bread a day. "I can't remember getting anything else on our ration cards, very little, evidently. We never saw any butter, meat, or sugar."

One time, some refugees got off the train in Shadrinsk, people from Mogilev and Vitebsk, although they should have been further along the line. An "evacuation post" was then set up at the station.

Some evacuated women behaved antisocially and made sure they did not have to work in the local kolkhoz. "It is amazing how all these evacuees appear to be sick and don't want to work in the kolkhoz. . . . In the queues for food they say some evacuees have brought a whole lot of money with them." From a diary dated 15 July 1941: "They stop and stare in the street, those Muscovite ladies, and laugh out loud at the Shadrinskers, particularly the women from Shadrinsk, who are dressed poorly and tastelessly. They might well laugh at us, those ladies; they have brought two cooks and wagons full of food with them."

Forty-eight Norwegians, who had fled to the Soviet Union by boat in 1940, found shelter in Shadrinsk. During the war the men returned to Norway to fight with the resistance.

Children from Leningrad and Moscow were evacuated to Shadrinsk, where ninety-six of them, primarily orphans, were housed in municipal orphanages. A total of 182 children came from Leningrad, and they were housed in four boarding schools. "Even the children were sleeping two to a blanket." Children from Leningrad were also put up in the surrounding villages.

Nine hundred children of evacuated technical specialists came from Moscow, another 120 from Vitebsk.

The most interesting group of children—360 of them—came from Moscow, and they were under the charge of A. I. Fotiyeva, a civil servant from the party's Central Committee. These children of members of the Central Committee and the government went to the village of Yermakovo, since Shadrinsk was already full. Here, a children's *kombinat* (school) was set up for them; the "Kremlin children" went to school like all the others, but "each child had a fictitious surname." The children of Molotov and those of Vice Premier Andrei Andreyev are reputed to have been among them.

In July 1942, in Shadrinsk, there were two hundred families of the high-ranking military, each with two or three children. Owing to the dearth of fathers who had been killed or were away, those families lived in wretched conditions. Thus, for those children, too, a boarding school was opened. The evacuated children were "housed in the best buildings in Shadrinsk." A total of 217 orphans were adopted during the war.

433.79
434.39
321.95

Factory Workers

Various factories were transferred to Shadrinsk, along with their personnel, during the mass evacuation in the summer and autumn of 1941. The following arrived in Shadrinsk:
- —A branch of the Moscow car factory, ZIS (Stalin factory): 1,689 workers and 3,500 family members. "People and factories arrived at the same time. There was no storage space; the machines were unloaded in the open air. Everything was lugged around by hand, cleaned, and assembled in cold halls." 433.178
- —From Prilutsk (in Ukraine), a factory producing fire-fighting equipment, combined with a Moscow instrument factory. This became Factory No. 815, and from then on it produced mortars and mortar shells.
- —From Osipenko on the Azov Sea, a mechanical engineering college.
- —From Yuryuzan (near Chelyabinsk), a metal factory producing such items as nails and horseshoes.
- —A textile factory from Klintsy (in Ukraine), manufacturing uniform jackets, parachutes, gloves, and the like, together with a factory from Zaporozhe.
- —A tobacco factory.
- —A factory producing field telephones: 2,529 in 1942 and a total of 247,000 up until 1945.
- —A graphic institute from Moscow from the Association of State Publishers (OGIZ).

Everything, everybody, was already working for the war industry at the beginning of 1942; "a total of 4,250 boys and girls learned new specialties on the job at the workbench." 434.88

This influx of new people meant that the local population either had people billeted with them or they were put out of their houses to make room for those considered to be more important. 433.66

433.67 Each person was supposed to have three square meters of space. Here is one description: "We were living in a cellar with windows at street level. In the evenings enormous toads came and looked at us, standing on their hind legs, their white throats swelling as they breathed . . . water streamed down the walls; it was cold and damp. The gray stones sucked the life out 433.30 of me and I contracted tuberculosis in the middle of the war."

And if you had to go to the toilet in the night, "then you had to jump out into the frost in your bare feet and stand dancing from one foot to the other for two or three minutes in the snow. It was not easy, using the overfull municipal toilets. That was the narrative of life in wartime that 434.91 you don't talk about so readily." "In the last few months of 1941 the streets 433.15 were teeming with people, like a provincial capital." Shadrinsk became 434.147 more and more "a Babylon of the hinterland."

Three churches were demolished for the bricks. Just at the last moment 433.117 Moscow stopped the demolition of the cathedral. Warehouses were converted into accommodations. Wooden barracks were erected, each big 433.111–12 enough to house three hundred people.

Two hospitals and a theater came to Shadrinsk from Chelyabinsk, 434.72 which itself had to make room for Moscow's Gorki Theater. Shadrinsk's own theater company was sent to perform in the countryside. Then the artists, the professors, and the writers arrived. From Moscow came a scientific institute for the study of artificial fertilizer, which was to organize 428.1.96 the cultivation of sugar beets in Shadrinsk. In the course of the war some evacuees went on to Tashkent, and later some people returned to the lib- 433.80, 89 erated cities or to devastated areas to help in the reconstruction.

Part of the Central State Archive of Literature was stored in Shadrinsk in a former grain depot, where it was the prey of rodents, naturally. The Central State Archive, along with its personnel, was housed in the Voskre- 434.78 senskaya Church.

The Wounded

Two hospitals were set up for wounded soldiers: No. 1726 with 1,000 beds and No. 3108 with 425 beds. At the beginning of July 1941 the first train-load of wounded arrived from Ukraine. One time a train full of wounded servicemen arrived from Tikhvin; they were frozen Estonian soldiers, who spoke little or no Russian and only could say, "Give me bread." They were so emaciated and weak that at the beginning they were allowed to eat only 433.143 very little. Another train brought four hundred to five hundred wounded, and they were accommodated in a building that had room for eight hundred men. The number of wounded there soon rose to fifteen hundred. "We just put two beds side by side and, in the middle, we placed someone with, for example, a plaster cast around their torso and to the sides we placed people with a wounded arm or leg. There were also wounded lying on stretchers in the corridors."

Many young girls went to work in the hospitals. It was demanding work, lifting, carrying, dragging, assisting in operations, removing plaster casts, and cleaning wounds. "In the evenings you often saw a cart with wooden boards unloading the dead from the morgue. They were taken to the churchyard and buried in one big pit. Many people died here." Anyone on the road to recovery helped on the hospital's small land holdings, growing vegetables and looking after the pigs. _{433.155} _{433.153}

In 1943 Hospital No. 3108 was moved nearer to the front and its personnel with it, to Makeyevka in Ukraine. Later still, the hospital was moved to Poland. _{433.156}

The authorities received reports every day about who received treatment, how many patients were recuperating, how many had recovered, and how many had died, all transmitted in code, under the strict supervision of the counterespionage service, "which was always there when the wounded were admitted; the agents generally stood unnoticed on the sidelines." _{433.145}

The nurses wore military uniforms. There was much work to be done; there was a shortage of medical personnel and of stretchers. Sometimes two nurses carried a wounded patient together, hands crossed, to the second floor. "We were eighteen or nineteen at the time, thin girls, dead skinny, and a patient sometimes weighed one hundred kilos. We stood beside the operating table without complaint, ready to help the wounded who were coming in." _{433.147}

"Sometimes you had just got home and gone to sleep when a patrol came to pick you up. Then there was a new party of wounded. You helped however you could; one you carried on a stretcher, another you took under the arms. And when they were sent back to the front, they kissed you, hugged you, and thanked you. Then came the letters; they asked you to send a volume of Yesenin or Pushkin." _{433.149}

"Most of the wounded were nervous. You felt that nervousness especially when we were retreating; soldiers from those areas took it very badly. To be honest, not all the wounded believed in the victory. Then you tried to encourage everyone and improve their morale, and then they said,

433.147–48

'Nina, you're the only one among us who believes it.'"

"There were also wounded soldiers who had their quirks, particularly among the commandants. They usually didn't like porridge; you had to

433.158

give them fried potatoes."

Schoolchildren and civilians visited the hospitals regularly and brought little gifts for the patients, read to them, or played music.

The Military

A cavalry unit in training was billeted in Shadrinsk as was a training

433.40

school for aircraft engineers. To make way for them, an orphanage from Vitebsk was moved to another village. From Moscow came a military political school whose students were sent to join the troops at the front

433.58; 433.57

after six months. An NKVD infantry division was billeted near Shadrinsk.

There was also a camp with some one thousand prisoners in Shadrinsk. "You could tell the difference between them and the Red Army soldiers and other columns who marched through the town, because they didn't sing. They walked under guard to and from their work—what work that

433.41

was I am not sure—and they walked in silence, a silent gray mass." Sometime in 1943 a camp for ten thousand prisoners of war was set up in the area of Shadrinsk.

In the summer of 1942 one inhabitant of Shadrinsk came home from work and was surprised to find a wounded soldier in his bed: "He stayed in our bed at our house for a week and a half before he was able to get to

433.28

his own village [under his own steam]." In mid-1942 several dozen men came from Leningrad to work in the telephone factory. They were "so weak they could not get to the second floor; they crawled up on their

433.175

hands and knees."

On 24 March 1944 I. A. Shavkunov, a soldier who had been declared unfit to fight, returned, dressed in summer uniform, "the soles of his shoes tied on with string." His household effects had been sold by an officer, who had also taken his wife to Tashkent. The Military Affairs Department gave him five liters of vodka and 555 cigarettes. These he could sell on

434.110

the market, so he could at least get a little money. This soldier had infec-

434.108–9

tious tuberculosis "and limited mobility; he walked on crutches." He had nothing left and was totally devastated. For several years he tended the garden of the aviators' school and, when that was relocated, he was out of work.

Mortality in the war years was high because of starvation, lack of medication, and continual, exhausting work. Life in Shadrinsk was still reasonable, since it was in a fertile agricultural region and many of the townspeople had a cow, sometimes one of their own, sometimes shared. Many inhabitants grew vegetables on the small plot of land they were allocated. In 1943 some 14,728 people had their "own kitchen garden." In 1944 another twenty thousand people requested such a piece of land. Many of the inhabitants also worked in the war industry, where the rations were somewhat more generous.

432.118
432.122

433.119

Work and Working Hours

People worked seven days a week, twelve to fourteen hours in a factory, where it was cold in the winter and the metal stuck to your fingers. It was quite normal for people to remain in the factory for days on end and sleep there in the production hall.

433.49

434.182

At home the children were waiting by an empty cupboard, because the shops were empty, too. The factory did provide a meal, though usually a rather meager one: "At lunchtime there was soup with two or three pieces of frozen potato floating in it and a bit of cabbage or nettle soup in the summer and, as a second course, fried sugar beets with a thin, watery wheat porridge."

433.50

Some women took their children with them to work; others found a place for their children in a crèche, for which two orphanages had to move to the next village.

433.71

In May 1943 A. P. Pustynnykh went to work at the SAAZ, the factory that produced detonators. She recalls:

The work was terribly hard; we worked twelve hours a day and eighteen hours on Sunday (shift change). Mostly young people and older people worked there. The little children were at the workbenches, which were too high for them, so they piled two or three crates on top of one another in front of the workbench, climbed up, and set to work just like the adults. Being late for work was a serious offence there; they could fine you, but usually they sent you to cut wood. The working conditions were really bad. We had poor food, usually nettle soup for lunch containing nothing more than finely chopped nettles (generally not even any potato).

The people were tired; they often fell asleep in the production hall or on the toilet. That led to a lot of accidents. Fatigue breaks you, you doze off, and your hair gets caught in the workbench. But worse things happened. Zina Shurulchik, for example, was scalped; the hair was pulled off her head along with her scalp; she was in the hospital for a long time, but she recovered.

There were also accidents with the die punch presses. That is dangerous work; you should only work with tweezers and sometimes you were too late, so you grabbed it with your hands and then your fingers got torn off. Working on the manufacture of mine detonators demands great precision. The people were terribly weary, didn't get enough to eat, and therefore their production was sometimes rejected.

One time a military representative rejected a whole batch of detonators and sent us away to dismantle them. That was extremely dangerous work and required a great deal of attention, so we worked in pairs, relieving each other after a certain amount of time. There were three girls working there that day. Suddenly we heard an explosion and, when we ran outside, we saw that parts of the walls had been destroyed and the windows were hanging out. The girls who were working there were in a bad way. One died on the spot, another had serious burns and died in the hospital, and the other lost her legs.

491.49

The following report dates from 1943: "It was as bad as this: we had been working during the night, and during the day we had to cut wood for the factory. Or you had worked for twelve hours in the factory and then you were sent to the electric power plant, to unload coal from a train. We also went to dig ditches in the peat bog in the village of Glubokoe. Everything was done by hand. It was hard, but we didn't show we were tired. There was nothing in the shops, but we couldn't buy anything anyway, because we had no money. We didn't ask for wages, we just asked for bread."

433.190

Another woman recalls, "It was very hard, we still had to help at the kolkhoz, too. After the night shift we cut corn, lifted potatoes. What else could you do? We had children who had to be fed. I wouldn't wish it on anybody to have to go through what we went through." And if you turned up five minutes late you were given a dressing-down, twenty minutes late a court-martial, and anyone taking anything from the field could count on a district court case.

434.189

434.152

And, as mentioned earlier, there were no days off. The first day off after four years of war was 9 May 1945. "That day brought us a surge of joy, bitterness over the losses, and hope."

435.30

Agriculture

Working on the land was not much better. "At night we separated the chaff from the corn and, if you didn't turn up, then you were given a reprimand or they did not give you a horse to plow your own piece of land or you did not receive any grain. It was compulsory to sign up for a state loan; if you had no money, it was 'find it or borrow it,' as long as you signed up. You paid tax (butter, meat, wool, eggs), but we were exempt, because Osip was at the front. Your wages were not paid out in money; we worked for a mark in the workbook, but each month we were given ten to twelve kilos of flour." 435.87

The harvest was an ordeal, stretching out far into the autumn because of the lack of manpower and machines, by which time the first frost had often already set in.

Grain was reaped with sickles and gathered with pitchforks. 428.1.94

"We harvested the potatoes in the autumn. It rains, your feet stick in the mud. As soon as you have one foot out, the other is sucked in. You dig in that sticky ooze, your arms up to the elbows in mud. You crawl across the whole field, a bucketful at a time. You get wet, shivering from the cold, but think of the delicious potato cakes waiting for us! It was even more difficult in the winter; you had to clear the snow from a piece of ground first, then find the potato plant, and then, all together, hack the frozen soil open: you were glad of every potato." And another noted: "In the winter 434.194 we harvested frozen potatoes with a crowbar." 434.187

After the grain "harvest" you could glean the fields and then, the following spring, dig up the potatoes left in the frozen ground: what a delicacy! 435.80

"Black potato cakes were a favorite . . . and were sold on the market at five rubles a piece. And then came all the nettles and the wild garlic and then the cow started to give milk again. And so you eked out an existence until the new potato harvest." 434.12–13

The greatest famine was always in the spring, and the worst ones, in particular, were in the spring of 1943 and that of 1944. "There was nothing more in the house that you could sell or exchange for oat chaff or anything else edible." In 1943 a more intelligent approach to harvesting was 435.32 employed. That autumn everyone was allowed to help with the potato harvest, and you could keep 10 percent of what you dug. Thousands of workers came voluntarily after the night shift. 434.19

Nevertheless—regardless of all the trials and tribulations—the government continued to make life unnecessarily difficult for the people. Anyone with a cow naturally had to have hay for the animal. If you had mown
a secret little haycock in the hours of darkness and were caught, that
resulted in a penalty. They would rather have the hay rot away than let
the people have it. "If you took one straw in the war, they said: stolen
property. They would rather burn it than give it to the kolkhoz farmer.
They were constantly making everyone afraid of being persecuted. No one
had permission to mow his own grass. If your son had not gone to work
that day, they said to the parents: your son is not working. Then those parents were not allowed to let their cow graze with the herd. If you didn't
go to work yourself, then your cow could stay home, too. They knew how
to get to you: leave your cow without fodder and you without milk. Well,
then, you were soon running off to work . . . we worked day and night."

Once someone had to pay meat tax but the calf he brought was two
kilos underweight: "The policeman made up a bill of indictment for the
court, and I was tried. Then I had to hand over the cow." Another farmer
said: "We were hungry. You worked from dawn till dusk and there was still
nothing to eat, only potatoes, no bread. It's a good thing we still had our
own cow." Having their own cow, not only in the country but also in the
"town," as well as having the kitchen garden, is what kept many people alive.

Schoolchildren regularly helped at the kolkhoz. "In the first couple of
years the littlest ones collected corn stalks; the norm was a half a sack.
After that they got us to lift potatoes. Apart from that, all the kolkhoz gardens were ours. We schoolchildren and old grannies weeded the gherkins,
carrots, beets, and rutabagas. The boys cut the cabbages, and the girls
collected them in woven baskets. Our mothers were in the fields day and
night, harvesting grain, mowing; everyone had a cow and the kolkhoz cattle had to be fed, too. And at night we were called out to grind the corn."

The factories in Shadrinsk had a joint "agrarian subsidiary business," thir-
teen kilometers outside the town, which supplied the factory canteens
with extra food. The farm was seventy hectares, with fifty cows and thirty-
five pigs. Factories and other institutions could have 202 hectares, the local
population 581 hectares.

Factory workers were supplied with food by the Department for Workers Provisions (ORS), in other words, a shop exclusively for the personnel
of a particular company. These were abolished after the war, and normal
trade resumed.

Plowing was occasionally done with a horse, but generally with oxen, which were also used as beasts of burden.   434.140

In June 1943 the factories in Shadrinsk, taken together, had 691 horses, 1,666 cows and bulls, 1,000 pigs, and 254 sheep; the local population had 2,552 cows and 325 sheep and goats (on 1 January 1945, the factories had 119 cows and the local population 2,496, as many cows had already been transported to the devastated areas in the west).   433.98, 101

Bread was baked in a bread factory, eleven thousand kilos a day. You   433.60
were given 125 grams for a child, 400 grams, and later 600 grams, for older people, and for heavy work you were given 800 grams. "As a child, you   434.217
were given 125 grams of bread made from oat straw. Our mother had three children . . . toward the end of the war they started selling oat straw. Mother soaked it in the evening, salted it in the morning, sieved it and made pancakes from it; there was nothing in the shops." In addition to   435.80
potatoes, other vegetables were eaten, as long as they had any others, and all kinds of edible wild grasses.

The woods and marshes were a rich source of free berries and mush-rooms, which you could also sell at the market. One person noted that, in   435.81
1943, "bull's black pudding with pureed frozen potatoes" was eaten as a main dish.   434.8

A loaf of bread cost four hundred rubles at the market, as much as a bucket of potatoes cost.   435.80

Quite soon after the war began one item after another was withdrawn from regular sale: matches (people started using tinderboxes), electricity (reserved for the factories), soap (water and ash instead), and boots (re-placed by clogs).

For washing soldiers' clothing, a kind of local soap was put into opera-tion, which used animal waste as raw materials. The shops did sell picture postcards featuring Hitler with a potbelly or with one eye or pictures of tanks and artillery. The local craftsmen often supplied the shops with infe-   435.80
rior goods. There were no new clothes to be had. Toward the end of the war,   433.171; 433.190
people could get shoes with wooden soles. There were also shoes on sale for four hundred rubles with a sole made from treated cardboard, which fell off after one or two days. Therefore children walked barefoot whenever   434.26
possible: "We didn't feel the cold or thorns; we were used to anything."   433.32

In 1944 "we were given American gifts, the only time during the war: I got a brown, rather strange dress made of crêpe-satin and a white fur jacket with short sleeves. It was just my size."   433.65

Nevertheless, they say they did not feel poor, "because almost everyone lived like that."

433.31

Off to School

As early as 1940 a military instructor was appointed to the schools to prepare the boys for military service; the girls were taught nursing. During the war part of the education corps consisted of evacuees; they took the place of the lesser skilled teachers from Shadrinsk, who were sent to the villages. The schools started a month later than usual, on 1 October, to give the personnel the opportunity to help on the land.

434.158

Teachers helped in the kolkhoz by organizing activities for wounded patients in the hospitals and by collecting money and goods for the front. "In the summer holidays, they collected firewood, repaired the school buildings, gathered medicinal herbs, and helped with the harvest until far into the autumn." When the pupils arrived at school with a frozen nose or frozen cheeks in the winter, they would rub goose fat onto their faces.

433.161
434.162

Many schools were cleared out to make room for hospital beds. There were forty to fifty children in each class, and there were three shifts. The classrooms were rarely heated. Pupils sat there in fur coats and gloves. There were only a few textbooks for each class. Because ink was unavailable, the children wrote with a liquid made from the juice of beet roots or with soot. And because there were no exercise books, they wrote on newspapers or in the margins of old books. "We teachers didn't have any free time on any of the school holidays during the war: we were sent into the fields with the children to weed, glean, and dig potatoes. If there were no workers available, then the teachers were deployed for grinding corn at night, and then we went straight on to school, unwashed, with straw still in our hair."

433.44

One woman recalls, "From the second class on, we went to the fields after school to gather corn. The stubble was prickly, so by the time we went home our hands were covered in blood. But it was back to the fields the next day."

434.142

Every school had its own kitchen garden where the pupils grew all sorts of things. In the summer of 1942 schoolchildren collected moss in the marshes around Shadrinsk and dried it for the hospitals. They said that moss was better than cotton wool, because "it absorbed moisture easily and dispelled unpleasant odors."

434.43

It was exceptionally cold that first winter of the war—down to fifty-three degrees below freezing—and there was a lot of trouble with wolves, "Oh, there were loads of them and they attacked people." Wolves were seen "even with manes. Great big ones. They bit through the throats of the cattle." The plague of wolves lasted until long after the war.

434.11

434.130; 435.81

One day a girl's felt boots froze solid to her feet. Only when hot water was poured inside and onto the boots did "they thaw a bit and she could take her frozen feet out of them."

433.45

The houses were heated with wood, but you had to go thirty-five to forty kilometers (twenty to twenty-five miles) outside town in order to get the wood. Peat was also burned as was *kizhak*, a mixture of manure and straw. "You were given five cubic meters of wood a year. And you had to cut it yourself. The snow was so high," one woman recounts, "that it came up to the waist of a sturdy man. Everything was covered. First, Mother stamped out a pathway. I was small and the ax was big. I came out of school at two o'clock, took the ax and the sleigh, and went to help Mother cut wood. I said to my mother, 'I always hear little children crying on the way.' Mother asked, 'How do they cry?' I said, 'Like this, Ah-ooo-ooo-ooo. I went after them, but they kept going farther away from me.' To which my mother replied, 'Oh, Daughter, don't stray from the path, those are wolves with their cubs.'"

433.95

435.81

Starting in the autumn of 1944 fourteen to sixteen year olds were mobilized for training colleges. If you had had at least four classes of primary school, you could be called up for an FZU (technical college), usually far from home. Fifty-five girls and thirty-five boys from Shadrinsk were called up. Those who ran away were arrested and imprisoned. A. Yurina ran away twice and was imprisoned, shut up in a pigsty. Because she had been talking to some other girls during work, her boss once made her go out into the mud and work all day, soaking wet, in the freezing cold.

434.44–45

434.140

435.84

People were plagued by the so-called state loans. You were held in the town hall until you signed up. Often you had to sell scarce food in order to get the money to pay the taxes. Tax collectors were as feared as they was hated. Tales spread of one tax collector who had been shut up in a cellar and of another whom someone poured milk over. People with livestock paid tax in kind: 40 kilos of meat, 100 eggs, and 270 liters of milk a year.

434.132

434.141

435.88

Transportation

People moved around on foot. One or two of the town's inhabitants had
a bicycle. Technical specialists traveled by horse or by horse and cart.
Trains did not accept any passengers, but it was possible to jump onto a
moving freight train. The Ministry of Railways was sent a report every six
hours regarding the progress of military transports; for important transports, reports were sent every hour. The NKVD and militarized railway
personnel guarded the line. During the night, too, people could be called
on to carry out work that would tolerate no delay. American locomotives
arrived at the end of the war, namely, the EA, "a powerful machine with
an automatic coal supply."

Entertainment and Contact

People sold their rations to get hold of a cinema ticket—that was the
only way to get money. In the last years of the war, American and English
films were shown, such as *Charley's Aunt*—"the whole auditorium was
rolling in the aisles"—and *The Thief of Baghdad*. In 1942 and 1943 as many
as 520,723 children and 974,839 adults visited the cinema, which showed
a new program every week.

In the Iovleva family, the children were read to in the evenings from
Mark Twain's works and from Tvardovsky's *Book of the Soldier*.

People had a great need for mutual contact: they went in and out of one
another's houses, just for a chat. What brought them close together was
the communal sorrow, the hunger that affected everyone, and the poverty.
People who knew each other well checked each other's hair for nits. "What
could you do about it? There was a war on." The center of social inter-
course was the market, the bazaar. You could buy things there—mostly
fish from the Iset but also milk, a piece of bread, potatoes, and potato
cakes made from frozen potatoes. And you met up with other people.
There were always invalids at the bazaar, "on little carts. They traded in
tobacco, played the harmonica, and sang and swore." Beggars and men-
tally disturbed people also frequented the market regularly. Everyone gave
them something, because "it was not done to refuse them; they were beg-
ging 'in the name of Christ.'"

The Front

People not only collected warm items for the army; parcels—thousands of them—of food, clothes, and tobacco, and particularly letters, were sent to the front. And letters were sent back from the front, from totally unknown soldiers. Whole truckloads of gifts were also sent to the front; once, on the side of such a truck, there was written "Siberian *pelmeni*" (a kind of dumpling). "We bought meat, too, and made *pelmeni*, but we didn't eat them ourselves; we had them frozen and then sewed them into little bags to go to the front. We bought woolen socks and tobacco, sewed the tobacco into little pouches, and sent it all to the front." 435.63

From 1943 on, the inhabitants of Shadrinsk were sent in small groups to liberated areas for a few months at a time, to Stalingrad, for example, and later to Moldavia, to help with the reconstruction. Cows, sheep, pigs, horses, and agricultural machinery were also sent to these areas. Three 435.99 hundred cows were transported by train to the area around the Ukrainian Sumy, and then went on by foot for another week. 435.90–91

At the end of 1943 and the beginning of 1944 a total of 12,700 evacuees returned to their liberated homes. The last 17,265 evacuees left in 1948, 432.118 bringing the population back down to 35,675 on 1 January 1949. 432.132

Women

Like elsewhere, the majority of the work and care was left to the women and girls: the work in cold factory halls, during the day and often at night or both, the responsibility for food and warmth, and the care of the children. "And the women carried out unparalleled work in the hinterland. They manufactured grenades, sewed soldiers' uniforms, made fur coats and felt boots, were woodcutters and carpenters." Seventy percent of personnel in the companies were female. 433.160 433.161

"Now those women can't believe it: how did we manage to keep it up, how did we stand it? It was probably because they believed in and hoped for better times, and because they all had kitchen gardens, too, where they grew all sorts of things. Without exception, they also worked in the company farms and helped with the harvesting in the kolkhoz. In the spring they tried to get frozen potatoes out of the ground, from which they made potato cakes. God forbid you got caught doing so, of course.

"That's how the women were all over Russia, in the towns and in the villages. . . . Could it be that that is how the country kept its head above water in this great struggle?"

433.164

Genatulin's description of the women in the hinterland does not only apply to the women of Shadrinsk: "These female soldiers who experienced no less of the misery of the war than their men folk and came through it, those historic women of Russia, they have not been decorated or rewarded with money, honor, or privileges. In the years when the war is commemorated, they are not offered any gifts; no statues are erected in their honor. Probably having already experienced the real highpoints of their lives, they spend their final years living modestly or even in poverty, content with their scanty kolkhoz pension and the free firewood.

After the War

The first day off, after four years of war, was 9 May 1945. After that, nothing changed for some time. In fact, the reins were tightened even more. "Destitution and lack of the absolute essentials accompanied us constantly in our postwar life." The heavy punishments for arriving to work late and for absence without leave remained in force for another six years. Forty to fifty people were punished every month, more than the number punished in 1940.

"The annual loans for the economic recovery were handled in exactly the same way as during the war. You were summoned to the village soviet where you were told the amount for which you had to buy obligations , and all you had to do was sign." Perunova had to sell two packages of booty from Germany to get the money: "All that was left of those two packages was a German knife, and I'm still using it to this day."

The horse entrusted to Tolmachova's keeping died. She was fined twelve thousand rubles. One of the milkmaid Antonina's cows also died: again another twelve-thousand-ruble fine. By morning Antonina was paralyzed. "That's how we lived during and after the war."

"In the war horses and bulls were removed from the village, as were harnesses, saddles, and carts. We did all the plowing with cows in the war. Well, then the war was over and where was the kolkhoz farmer supposed to get things from? You got nothing for the 'work days' [a calculation unit for agricultural work] you had earned. All the grain went to the state; your own kitchen garden was your only hope, and it went on like that. When

rationing was abolished in 1947, town dwellers could buy bread, but where
were farmers supposed to get the money?"   435.33

After the war the Muscovite technical specialists gradually departed,
sometimes leaving their second "war family" behind. Others stayed on
and did not return to their prewar family. In 1946 A. N. Martinova went   435.30–31
back to Karelia. Her second husband had been arrested, because he had
been a prisoner of war. Her mother was arrested in 1949, and her son
had been placed in a children's home. In 1949 the mother was released in
an amnesty, and in 1957 she was rehabilitated.   435.66–67

In November 1947 A. Beznogova's father was arrested. They had to leave
their home—the four of them lived in a kitchen—"within twenty-four
hours; there is no room for enemies of the people here," they were told.
The father returned in 1953.   435.83

In the spring of 1945, 240 internees arrived in Shadrinsk; they were mostly
young Germans and included 196 women, all "shabbily dressed, with
wooden clogs." They remained there until August 1948. Among them were
44 Catholics, 195 Lutherans, and one atheist; 33 were members of a fascist
party, 13 were members of other nationalist parties, 133 had been members
of the Hitlerjugend or Bund deutscher Mädel, and 81 did not belong to
any party. Socially the group was composed of 96 workers, 132 farmers,
6 manufacturers and craftsmen, and 6 shopkeepers.   435.117

In Shadrinsk they had to work in the factories or the fields; other tasks
included loading and unloading heavy goods. They produced buttons,
pots, and aluminum spoons; others helped to build a steel mill. They were,
or very soon became, just as poor as the Russians and begged from house
to house for food (*klingeln*), sold their best clothes to buy something to
eat, and stole potatoes from the fields; driven by hunger, they bartered
with whatever they could lay their hands on.

These internees were free to walk around and were housed in barracks.
They were "nicely dressed, at first," according to Russian standards, "smart
dresses, as colorful as butterflies."   433.36

"I can see them now: big people, big noses, white, they all smoked. Later,
on feast days, they played the harmonica in the street."   435.81

One of them, Hilde Rauschenbach, after having returned to Germany,
wrote about her experiences and impressions in her book, *Von Pillkallen
nach Schadrinsk* (From Pillkallen to Shadrinsk). Her account shows that   366.1
the Russian people displayed not a trace of enmity toward them, but
rather sympathy. The Russian guards at their barracks were strict but not

exaggeratedly so, and they were not sadistic. In 1989 Rauschenbach went back to visit Shadrinsk and maintains a friendly relationship with many of the people there. But how did those Germans end up there?

In February 1945 Stalin had ordered that Germans who were fit for work be deported to the Soviet Union to help rebuild the devastated economy. "But several days later, when it was announced that Goebbels was using this [or the fear of such an eventuality] to increase the resistance of the Wehrmacht, the order was rescinded as not conforming to international law."

393.2.94

Shortly afterward "westerners" (*zapadniki*) arrived in Shadrinsk, people who had been deported from the western areas during and after the war. They, too, were always starving. One of them said: "Why do they always laugh at me? My name is not Zakhar, but Seicher. Before the war I was a surgeon," and he looked down at his mutilated hands. The *zapadniki* lived behind a high fence in one wooden barrack. "We children were afraid of them. We were strictly forbidden to stand by the fence; we thought they did not look much like ordinary people, and that made us even more afraid." V. Schmidt, a young man deported from Moldavia to Shadrinsk as a child, had the greatest difficulty pursuing a higher education after the war because of his origins. The provincial Komsomol committee intervened on his behalf, after which he was admitted to the school of his choice "along with other such unfortunates."

435.75

435.75

428.1.90

Immediately after May 1945 Shadrinsk saw transports going to the east: preparations for the attack on Japan that had been agreed on. They had come from Germany with their booty. "An open truck, the walls hung with carpets. There was a white grand piano inside, with someone playing, another was milking a black and white cow, and they were laughing and shouting."

435.4

In January 1947, in anticipation of their release, forty-nine Poles were taken from Shadrinsk to Odessa, and in July 1947 a total of seventy-two sick, dystrophic Germans were transferred to Frankfurt on Oder for repatriation.

435.118

In May 1949, in the province of Kurgan—to which Shadrinsk had belonged since 1943—it was decided to "clean up all the prisoner-of-war cemeteries," because they had all been neglected, were not separated, or had been destroyed or razed to the ground. "Not one single grave had any identification. It was impossible, therefore, to establish the exact number of graves, as there was neither a cemetery book nor a plan of the graves."

435.119

There were two cemeteries in Shadrinsk: one for the Ministry of Internal
Affairs' Camp No. 514 and the other for Labor Battalion No. 1085, a battalion for internees and prisoners of war. It was rumored in Shadrinsk,
in 1946, that a letter had been thrown from a train full of ex-prisoners;
so many fostered (vain) hopes that people who had been registered as
missing would return. And indeed, in 1963, a few of those missing soldiers
came home. 435.119 435.33 435.74

Health Issues

A special hospital was set up for victims of radiation sickness. "For many
years, the people living on both sides of the Urals knew nothing of the
activities of the Mayak experimental atomic energy complex in Chelyabinsk." Despite the prohibition to do so, people stuck to their old customs
of drinking water from the Iset, drinking milk from cows that had grazed
on the riverbanks, washing their linen in the river, watering their kitchen
gardens with that same polluted water, swimming in it, and eating fish
from the Iset. "And then people were getting sick and were dying from an
unknown 'radiation sickness.'" 435.9

The hospital was guarded by the militia: "The surgical department was
upstairs and downstairs was the secret, guarded department." Personnel
from other departments "were surprised at the frail frames of some of the
'bald old people' lying in the beds; these were actually dying children with
swollen lymph glands, whose hair had fallen out. It was terrible." 435.9–10

The Start of a Better Life

Bread rationing was abolished in 1947. It was a joyful day: "You got three
days' worth of bread." But it did mean long queues in front of the bakers.
Farmers walked twenty kilometers (twelve miles) into town for bread,
but "no one considered that such a long distance." "People started queuing the evening before; they wrote the number of your place in the queue
on your hand with an aniline pencil." There was no sugar available until
1953. From 1948 on, workers were given holidays—twelve days a year—and
pensions. The taxes in kind and the state loans continued to weigh heavily, however. 435.96 435.33 435.5 435.82

The almost annual price reductions "gave hope of a better life. All sorts
of foods appeared in the shops: various kinds of cheap honey, salmon, red
and black caviar in barrels, and pyramids of tinned 'crab.'" 436.6

In 1953, after an amnesty for primarily common criminals, danger on the streets and in trains increased sharply. Criminals tossed a coin to see which of them should kill some passenger or other or throw them out of the train. "But starting in 1961 life began to get better. We bought a television that year, a Volkhov; before that we used to watch TV at the neighbors. And then we bought a washing machine, a vacuum cleaner, and a refrigerator."

435.77

435.10

The farms attached to factories and institutions continued to constitute an important source of food, even after the war. In 1946 Shadrinsk produced 236 centners (1 centner = 100 kilos) of grain, 134 centners of oats, 91 centners of peas, 885 centners of potatoes, 85 centners of cabbage, 1.8 centners of gherkins, 72 centners of carrots, and 57 centners of beets. Housewives preserved mushrooms, blueberries, cranberries, gherkins, cabbage, and beech buds. And anyone with a cow, a pig, or chickens had little to complain about.

435.211

435.78–79

No maintenance was carried out in the town during the war. Pavements (made of wood), bridges, and fences had been neglected or used for firewood. In 1950 an effort was begun to provide sewerage and water mains, and fifteen hundred trees were planted (the original trees had presumably been used as firewood).

435.14

The factories helped to supply the schools with firewood for heating. In 1948–49 the schools were given 25,000 new textbooks, 130,000 exercise books, pens, pencils, and chalk. Nevertheless, in some schools three children still shared a desk, and teaching was still done in three shifts; some classes had fifty to fifty-five children.

435.45

435.43

Ninety-six orphans were adopted in 1945 and an additional sixty-six in 1946. Living accommodations remained abominable. In 1947 one family, including the parents and three children, were housed in a kitchen. "Father slept on the couch, Mother on the blanket chest, and we three on the stove."

435.44

435.83

Another house was somewhat roomier, with "a living room and a kitchen, windows with curtains, a rubber plant, a rose, and tulips by the window. In the right-hand corner was a commode and, above the commode, a mirror and a big frame full of photographs. Against the right-hand wall a bed, to the left a blanket chest. On the floor we had rugs we had made ourselves. There was a bed in the kitchen, a big Russian stove, a kitchen table, and stools. There was a basin in the corner by the door. The floorboards were unpainted."

435.73

Houses were built for technical specialists working in the industry built by German prisoners of war. Hilde Rauschenbach saw how the people

435.31

sometimes lived in earthen shelters: "I first went down a couple of steps, and then bent to get through the low door. To the right a partition had been made, and behind it stood the cow. It was almost dark in the room; there were no windows, and the only light came from a petrol lamp. In a corner, on the ground, was a wooden bed. To the side was an iron stove and next to it a wooden table with two chairs. The walls were covered with clay. The roof was made of straw and manure, covered with earth and then green grass." 434.204

Train tickets were only for the military, until long after the war. "If you could, you grabbed hold of a truck—some people managed to climb onto the roof—even on the buffers or the open platforms, in order to hitch a ride." In 1940 several religious-minded people had asked that the Voskres- 435.35 enskaya Church be reopened. This was not permitted, however, until 25 June 1946. 434.93–95

The schoolchildren practiced for the celebrations of 1 May and 7 No- vember, the latter commemorating the October Revolution. "We started marching twenty days beforehand—six abreast. The order was to keep your distance between the rows and in the row as well. We learned new songs: 'The Volga and the Don Are Wide,' 'Rolling Rivers,' 'Russians and Chinese Brothers Forever,' and 'We Shake Off the Old World' and the 'Marseillaise.'" 435.71

Not until 1956 were girls "given their first pretty dresses made from artificial silk, dark blue with little white flowers and puffed sleeves—I couldn't have been more delighted." These artificial silk dresses were for special occasions. 435.73

"At the market you could buy milk, cream, hot junket, potatoes by the piece, mushrooms, berries, fried fish, and hot potato cakes." You could 435.34 also have your picture taken; there was a barber and a small cafe. There were postcards for sale, often from invalids, who were sometimes united in ambiguous collectives of craftsmen.

War invalids were always visible at the market, but there were also those who had been disabled from childhood and old people without any means of support. Many of them sold little cups of tobacco: one person might be 435.27–28 missing an arm, another missing a leg or both legs. They moved around on little boards with wheels on all four corners. A harmonica player was often around "and they sang of the war and their fate, where they had been wounded, and how they lived now. And there were a lot of new songs— the more plaintive the songs, the more people came to listen. Women stood wiping away tears." They sang, for example, "I lie in the hospital, seriously 435.34–35 ill / Of heart pain. One wound heals / another weeps, and the third I will die of"; and they sang, "In a white coat, spattered with blood / the nurse came and stood close by / recognized her own brother in him / and began to wail."

435.35

The children of Shadrinsk did not see ice cream until 1949: "It was expensive and not everybody could afford it." As treats they were given pieces of dried carrot, rutabaga, and pumpkin, and later pieces of dried beet. Other treats were little balls of white clay and the first milk from a cow that had just calved.

435.79

435.71

In 1947 seventeen children were still not attending school because they had no shoes. Those who were the worst off received aid: in 1946 these children were given 1,890 pairs of felt boots by means of a school fund, 360 pairs of shoes, 6 short fur coats, 75 suits, 95 jackets, 170 pairs of trousers, 85 dresses, and 1,905 pairs of slippers. And all children were given 50 grams of bread and a piece of sugar at school. In 1950, as a student, V. N. Iovleva was given a cheap winter coat, "Nobody had anything . . . apart from food, your purchasing power was nil."

435.43

435.44

435.7

Shadrinsk had many small firms, some of them hardly worth mentioning, but still they employed large numbers of personnel. They produced, for example, felt boots, furniture—which drew plenty of complaints because of rickety construction or fraud—hats, fur coats, methylated spirits, shoes, bread, and construction materials. There were also tailors and seamstresses, basket making and textile manufacturing. One small firm made nails, and another manufactured hardware. There were saddlers, too. Other firms made glue, jugs, buttons, brushes, children's toys, and musical instruments. The goods were generally of an inferior quality; indeed, many of the items customers brought in for repair "disappeared." One very good product was a kerosene stove manufactured by the firm of Truzhenik (The worker), which was exceptionally effective and economical to run.

435.23

Any complaints or comments met with the response, "It doesn't matter; it's for the village, and they put up with anything there. And that was true." Others said, "Go ahead and complain, but who to? We're not subordinate to anybody in Shadrinsk."

435.21

Individual craftsmen worked quickly, skillfully, and cheaply. They produced anything and everything: hand-painted wooden spoons, paintings on glass, portraits, fine stockings, and blankets. Some made and repaired shoes, others were wagoners or hawkers of fruits and vegetables, and still others knitted scarves from goats' wool, sewed fur coats, repaired sewing machines, or made artificial flowers from scrap metal and soap. There was even a doctor who received patients at his home. 435.18

Shadrinsk is a little Russian provincial town that fought to rise above the horrors of the war and all the shortages. The people who lived there do not appear in the history books but, nevertheless, together they succeeded in keeping the hinterland alive, and, in so doing, they made a considerable contribution to victory in a cruel and bloody war and, thereafter, to building a more organized life.

Abbreviations

Sources

Index

Abbreviations

AV	Avrora		NM	Novy mir
DN	Druzhba narodov		NS	Nash sovremennik
DV	Dalny Vostok		NV	Novoe vremya
IS	Istoriya SSSR		OG	Ogonyok
IZ	Izvestya		OI	Otechestvennaya istoriya
IZC	Izvestya TsK KPSS		OK	Oktiabr
IU	Iun'ost		EE	Eastern Europe
KE	Kentavr		PR	Pravda
KO	Knizhnoe obozrenie		RG	Roman gazeta
KOA	Koltso A		RO	Rodina
KOD	Kommersant Daily		ROG	Rossiiskaya gazeta
KOM	Kommunist		RV	Rossiiskie vesti
KON	Kontinent		SE	Sever
KP	Komsomolskaya pravda		SI	Sibir
KZ	Krasnaya zvezda		SM	Svobodnaya mysl
LG	Literaturnaya gazeta		SO	Sibirskie ogni
LO	Literaturnoe obozrenie		TE	Teatr
LR	Literaturnaya Rossiya		UR	Ural
MG	Molodaya gvardiya		VE	Veteran
MO	Moskva		VI	Voprosy istorii
MZ	Mezhdunarodnaya zhizn		VIZH	Voyenno-istoricheskii zhurnal
NE	Neva		VL	Voprosy literatury
NG	Nezavisimaya gazeta		VO	Volga
NINI	Novaya i noveyshaya istoriya		ZN	Znamya
NIZH	Nauka i zhizn		ZV	Zvezda

Sources

1 Abdulaev, Z.
    1. Vspolokhi. Groznyi 1991, 176 pp.
2 Abdulin, M.
    1. Pereprava, pereprava. DN 1985.4.201–10.
3 Abramov, F.
    1. Belaia loshad'. ZN 1995.120–31.
    2. Kto on? ZN 1993.3.140–60.
4 A'chil'diev, S.
    1. Deti voiny. ZN 1991.1.168–81.
5 Adamovich, A.
    1. Nemoi, ich werde dich schützen. ZN 1992.12.3–50.
    2. Blokadnaia kniga. Glavy kotorych v knige ne bylo. ZV 1992.5/6.8–19.
6 Afanas'ev, A.
    1. O voine kak o voine. OG 1995.18.36–40.
7 Afonin, V.
    1. Proshchanie Slavianki. SO 1989.3.25–36.
8 Akinkhov, G.
    1. Evakuatsiia. Khronika. SE 1991.6.105–19.
9 Aleksandrov, G. A.
    1. Tovarishch Erenburg uproshchaet. PR 1945.18.4.
10 Aleksandrov, S.
    1. "Osoboe zadanie." SO 1987.5.137–52.
11 Alekseev, M.
    1. Stalingradskaia tetrad'. LG 19851.1.
    2. Moi Stalingrad. MG 1993.3.30–65.
    3. Polveka i kazhdyi den'. MO 1995.5.79–86.
    4. Moi Stalingrad. Kniga vtoraia. NS 1998.5.6–93.
    5. Moi Stalingrad. MG 1993.2.35–70.
12 Alekseev, V.
    1. Kommentarii k detstvu. IU 1985.5.25–65.

13 Aleksievich, S.
1. Soldatskoe zhenskoe serdtse. OK 1985.2.9–26.
2. U voiny ne zhenskoe litso. RG 1985.10/11.57–92.
3. Nravy. OG 1993.11.31.
4. My s vami—odnogo bezumiia liudi. LG 1995.22.2.
5. Moia edinstvennaia zhizn'. VL 1996.1/2.205–23.
6. U voiny ne zhenskoe litso. Minsk 1985.
14 Anan'ev, A.
1. Ostanemsia slabymi—pokoia ne budet. DN 1995.3.14–16.
15 Andreeva, E.
1. General Vlasov i Russkoe Osvoboditel'noe Dvizhenie. DN
1991.5.170–205.
16 Andrianova, A.
1. Deti Leningrada. NE 1996.1.214–16.
17 Anfilov, V.A.
1. Samye tiazhkie gody. LG 1989.22.3.
2. Desiat' neizvestnykh besed s marshalom G. K. Zhukovym v mae-iiune
1965 g. VIZh 1995.3.39–46.
18 Anisimov, N. V.
1. Eshelon dlinoi v chetvert' veka. VIZh 1989.6.72–82.
19 Annenkov, Iu.
1. Kulatskie deti. MO 1990.10.159–69.
20 Anninskii, L.
1. "Spasti Rossiiu tsenoi Rossii." NM 1994.10.214–21.
2. Ruki tvortsa. DN 1996.6.203–7.
21 Antonov-Ovseenko, A.
1. Beriia. IU 1988.12.66–84.
22 Asadov, E.
1. Frontovaia vesna. MG 1988.3.161–209.
23 Astaf'ev, V.
1. Tam, v okopakh. PR 1985.25.11.
2. Da prebudet vechno. LG 1987.7.10.
3. Tsena. LG 1988.18.5.
4. Britovka. MO 1991.8.3–37.
5. Prokliaty i ubity. NM 1992.10–106.
6. do. NM 1992.11.188–226.
7. do. NM 1992.12.268–46.
8. do. NM 1994.10.62–110.
9. do. NM 1994.11.37–101.
10. do. NM 1994.12.57–134.
11. A ia vse pomniu to shosse. DN 1995.4.4–6.
12. Tak khochetsia zhit'. ZN 1995.4.3–113.
13. Tak khochetsia zhit'. LG 1995.8.2.
14. Veselyi soldat. NM 1998.5.3–58.
15. Letter dated 7 June 1982. LG 1994.16.10.
16. Nepodspudnyi Astaf'ev. OG 1995.18.30–32.

17. Letter dated 28 December 1987. VL 1995.1.184.

18. Oberton. NM 1996.8.3–51.

19. Ia—poslednii kto razocharuetsia v cheloveke. IZ 1997.6.12.

20. DN 1985.5.235.

21. LG 1995.9.5.

22. Snachala snariady, potom liudi. RO 1991/6/7.52–56.

24 Astapov, V.

1. Podvig evakuatora. NE 1995.5.205–9.

25 Azhgikhina, N. A.

1. Zalozhniki legendy. OG 1990.44.25–27.

26 Bakhtin, V.

1. Narod i voina. NE 1995.5.186–93.

27 Bakhvalov, A.

1. Nikto ne zabyt. NE 1989.9.170–73.

28 Baklanov, G.

1. Vysota dukha. ZN 1990.5.3–10.

2. Vkhodite uzkimi vratami: nevydumannye rasskazy. ZN 1992.9.7–54.

3. I togda prikhodiat marodery. LG 1995.26.4.

29 Baltermants, D.

1. Predvestnik Pobedy. OG 1986.45.10–12.

30 Baruzdin, S.

1. Review of "Samo soboi." Moskva 1985. ZN 1986.7.232.

31 Belaia, M.

1. Letter. LG 1999.28.4.

32 Belash, Iu.

1. Lozhka. In Rasskazy. ZN 1985.4.72–86.

2. Frontoviki. TE 1985.8.3–37.

3. Okopnye stikhi. Moskva 1990, 400 pp.

33 Beliaev, A.

1. Kapitan Vasilii Tokarev. SI 1990.5.36–70.

34 Beloborodov, G. S.

1. "Brali vraga ezhovymi rukavitsami." VIZh 1993.9.9–12.

35 Belousova, T.

1. Chernyi poisk. LG 1995.5.4.

36 Belov, V. I.

1. Takaia voina. IU 1985.11.75.80.

2. Medovyi mesiats. NS 1995.3.62–85.

37 Berdinskikh, V.

1. Riadovye fronta i tyla. Rasskazy ochevidtsev. VO 1989.5.3–22.

2. Kolkhoz nekuda devat'sia. Ustnye rasskazy Viatskikh krest'ian. ZN 1993.10.140–52.

3. Vosstanie Dmitriia Panina. NM 1997.3.168–74.

4. Riadovye fronta i tyla. Rasskazy ochevidtsev. VO 1989.6.146–65.

38 Berezhkov, V.

1. Zhestokost'; Ne streliat'. NE 1993.8.218–24.

2. Peklo. NE 1994.3.203–6.

39 Berezhnoi, I.
    1. Ogon' na sebia! VO 1985.1.58–128.
40 Berggol'ts, O.
    1. Ob etoi knige. AV 1994.1.4–13.
    2. Dnevnye zvezdy (glavy iz vtoroi knigi). MG 1995.5.115–18.
41 Bezborodova, I. V.
    1. Inostrannye voennoplennye i internirovannye v SSSR: iz istorii deiatel'nosti
       Upravleniia po delam voennoplennykh i internirovannykh NKVD–MVD
       SSSR v poslevoennyi period (1985–1953 gg). OI 1997.5.165–73.
42 Bezymenskii, L. A.
    1. Die Rede Stalins am 5 Mai 1941. Dokumentation und Interpretation. OE
       1992.3.242–64.
    2. Informatsiia po-sovetski. ZN 1998.5.191–99.
43 Bianki, V.
    1. Gorod, kotoryi pokinuli ptitsy. ZV 1994.1.105–13.
44 Bitsoev, S. E.
    1. Letter. OG 1990.42.3.
45 Blazhnov, I.
    1. Letter. OG 1991.41.7.
46 Bobylev, P. N.
    1. Repetitsiia katastrofy. VIZh 1992.6.10–16.
    2. do. 1992.7.14–21.
    3. K kakoi voine gotovilsia General'nyi shtab v 1941 godu? OI 1995.5.3–20.
47 Bogorov, E.
    1. Blokada v kadre i za kadrom. NE 1981.1. 202–6.
48 Bokov, Kh.
    1. Ekho nevozvratnogo proshlogo. MO 1989.1.160–67.
49 Bol' Bab'ego Iara. OG 1990.42.6.
50 Bonner, E.
    1. Poezd v 43-i god. LG 1995.9.5.
51 Bonwetsch, B.
    1. Nastupatel'naia strategiia—nastuplenie—napadenie. OI 1998.3.20–25.
52 Bordiugov, G.
    1. Ukradennaia Pobeda. KP 1990.5.5.
53 Borin, A.
    1. Ia vystreliu v vozdukh, a Vy begite. LG 1997.30.4.
54 Borkunenko, P. F.
    1. Letter. OG 1990.43.3.
55 Borodulina, K.
    1. No i nad gorodom. Iz zapisok blokadnitsy. NE 1990.1.195–97.
56 Borshchagovskii, A.
    1. Kak pisateli antisemitami rabotali . . . LG 1993.27.10.
57 Brogaevich, I.
    1. Letter. OG 1991.26.4.
58 Bukhanov, N.
    1. Review of N. Dorizo, "Iakov Dzhugashvili. Byl' i legenda." MO 1988.2, 3.

59 Bugai, N.
    1. Pravda o deportatsii chechenskogo i ingushskogo narodov. VI 1990.7.32–44.
60 Bukov, K. I.
    1. Trevozhnyi oktiabr' 41-go. KE 1991.70–79.
61 Bulovatskii, M.
    1. Letter. OG 1992.1.29.
62 Burka, Iu.
    1. Voina, pora svobody. "Vasilii Terkin' i dukhovnaia atmosfera voennykh let."
       OK 1993.6/7–16.
63 Burtin, Iu.
    1. Voina, pora svobody. OK 1993.6.7–16.
64 But, V.
    1. Orel—reshka. DN 1995.4.23–95.
65 Butov, M.
    1. Response to questionnaire. XN 1995.5.185–86.
66 Bykov, V.
    1. Poliubi menia, soldatik. DN 1996.6.6–37.
    2. Stuzha. ZN 1993.11.7–76.
    3. Zhuravlinyi krik. In Sobranie sochinenii I. 25–119.
    4. Zapadnia. In Sobranie sochinenii II. 453–99.
    5. Poiti i ne vernut'sia. In Sobranie sochinenii II. 207–362.
    6. Kruglianskii most. In Sobranie sochinenii III. 121–206.
    7. Znak bedy. Sobranie sochinenii IV. 5–248.
    8. V tumane. DN 1987.7.3–61.
    9. Politruk Kolomiets. ZV 1999.5.7–10.
67 Kholendro, D.
    1. Sto stranits voiny (Dokumental'naia povest'). IU 1995.5.10–28.
68 Kholmogorov, M.
    1. Voiny i marodery. VL 1997.1.3–25.
69 Kholopov, G.
    1. Po tu storonu blokadnogo kol'tsa. ZV 1986.5.42–124.
70 Khorkov, A. G.
    1. Ukreplennye raiony u zapadnykh granits SSSR. VIZh 1987.12.47–54.
71 Khrushchev, N. S.
    1. Deleted.
    2. Vospominaniia OG 1989 33.29.
    3. Vospominaniia OG 1989.35.16.
    4. Vospominaniia OG 1989.34.10.
72 Chudiakova, N. D.
    1. Sud'ba odnogo muzeia. NE 1994.9.289–94.
73 Khvostov, V., and A. Grylev
    1. Nakanune Velikoi Otechestvennoi Voiny. KOM 1968.12.56–71.
74 Tsidilkovskii, I. M.
    1. Polveka s poluprovodnikami. UR 1996.10.125–63.
75 Tsitriniak, G.
    1. Ugolovnoe delo marshala Zhukova. OG 1993.11.12/13.

76 Tsvetaev, V.
    1. Poslednii podvig G. K. Zhukova. MO 1986.11.146–54.
77 Tsypin, V.
    1. Patrioticheskoe sluzhenie Russkoi Pravoslavnoi Tserkvi v VOV. NINI
       1995.2.41–47.
78 Chashchina, L.
    1. Vzyskanie pogibshikh. NE 1990.10.108–81.
79 Chebotaev, M.
    1. Stradaia za liudei. SO 1991.7.280–97.
80 Cheremnykh, I.
    1. Okopnaia pravda. SI 1988.3.74–86.
81 Cherepanov, V. V.
    1. Shli na front dobrovol'no VIZh 1996.1.9–16.
    2. Pitanie bylo kaloriinym. VIZh 1999.1.93–96.
83 Chernov, A.
    1. Smertnyi paek OG 1989.40.12–15.
84 Chernov, I. E.
    1. Sapery. OK 1986.6.166–81.
    2. do. 1986.7.141–81.
85 Chukhrai, G.
    1. My pobedili v toi voine. LG 1995.23.3.
86 Chuev, F.
    1. Marshal Rokossovskii. MG 1995.9.157–80.
    2. Marshal Zhukov. MG 1995.8.134–56.
87 Chukovskaia, L.
    1. Zapiski ob Anne Akhmatovoi. NE 1989.7.99–143.
88 Chukovskii, K.
    1. Iz dnevnika 1932–1969 ZN 1992.11.135–94.
89 Daev, S.
    1. Mirnye liudi s ruzh'iami. NE 1996.6.212–19.
    2. Vozdushnye 'izvozchiki' na boevom kurse. NE 1997.3.210–13.
90 Danilov, V.D.
    1. Gotovil li General'nyi Shtab Krasnoi Armii uprezhdaiushchii udar po
       Germanii? In Gotovil li. 82–91.
    2. Sovetskoe glavnoe komandovanie v preddverii Velikoi otechestvennoi voiny.
       NINI 1988.6.3–20.
    3. Stalinskaia strategiia nachala voiny. OI 1995.3.33–44.
91 Davydiuk, S.
    1. Tsvety v porokhovom dymu. DN 1995.4.122–44.
92 Davydov, A.
    1. Zdes' moia ostanovka. AV 1987.6.37–45.
    2. Tak bylo. NE 1997.5.234–35.
93 Delagrammatik, M.
    1. Voennye tribunaly za rabotoi. NM 1997.6.130–39.
94 Direktivy I. V.
    1. Stalina V. M. Molotovu pered poezdkoi v Berlin v noiabre 1940 g. NINI
       1995.4.76–80.

95 Diuzhev, Iu.
    1. Ubity i prokliaty. SE 1994.5/6.150–57.
96 Dmitriev, L.
    1. Blokadnyi dnevnik. ZV 1997.2.172–99.
97 Dolinina, A.
    1. Razmyshleniia ob "Osadnoi zapisi" A. N. Boldyreva. NE
       1999.1.184–89.
98 Dolmatovskii, E.
    1. Ochevidets. Pisateli na voine. OK 1995.5.3–78.
99 Dongarov, A.
    1. Mezhdu Reinom i Volgoi. RO 1991.5.39–40.
100 Dovzhenko, A.
    1. Iz dnevnikov. LG 1989.15.2.
    2. Pishu, razluchennyi s narodom moim. OG 1989.19.10–13.
    3. 'Ia prinadlezhu chelovechestvu kak khudozhnik'. PR 1989.11.9.
101 Drabkin, Ia. S.
    1. Pamiati L'va Kopeleva (1912–1997). nini 1997.6.113–21.
102 Dragunskii, D.
    1. Natsiia i voina. DN 1992.10.176–81.
    2. "Voiny u nikh ne v pamiati, voina u nikh tol'ko v krovi." Zn
       1995.5.183–200.
103 Drugaia voina. 1939–1945 Pod ed. Iu. N. Afanas'eva. Moskva 1996 490 pp.
104 Drunina, Iu.
    1. Tucha nad temnoi Rossiei. PR 1999.15.9.
105 Eliseev, V. T., and S. N. Mikhalev
    1. Tak skol'ko zhe liudei my poteriali v voine? VIZh 1992.6/7.31–34.
106 Eliseeva, N. E.
    1. Tyly deistvuiushchei armii okhraniali voiska NKVD. VIZh
       1998.6.16–25.
107 Eliashevich, A.
    1. Chetyre oktavy bytiia. OK 1990.4.193–202.
108 Erashov, V.
    1. Koridory smerti. Moskva 1990 336 pp.
109 Eremenko, V.
    1. A vse ona, voina. DN 1980.5.141.149.
    2. Tri chasa s I. V. Stalinym. VIZh 1993.12.6.–12.
110 Erin, M. E.
    1. Nemtsy v sovetskom plenu (po arkhivnym materialam Iaroslavskoi
       oblasti). OI 1995.6.133–42.
111 Esaulov, I.
    1. Satanicheskie zvezdy i sviashchennaia voina. NM 1994.4.224–39.
112 Farsobin, V. V.
    1. Na frontakh voiny za rulem avtomobilia. In V gody voiny. Stat'i i ocherki.
       p. 219–32.
    2. Zametki byvshego serzhanta gvardii o voine. VI 1995.5/6.121–30.
    3. Review. V. B. Konasov's Sud'by nemetskikh voennoplennykh v SSSR.
       Vologda. VI 1996.11/12.147–49.

   4. Review of Gotovil li Stalin nastupatel'nu-iu voinu protiv Gitlera?
      Nezaplanirovannaia diskussiia. Sbornik materialov. Pod ed. G. A.
      Bordiugova. Sostavitel' V. A. Nevezhin. Moskva 1995 186 pp. VI
      1995.10.167–69.
   5. Nado sobrat' svidetel'stva o sud'be plennykh i zakliuchennykh v SSSR. VI
      1996.10.172–73.
113 Filatova, I.
   1. Letter. OG 1989.48.4.
114 Filin, N.
   1. O gibeli, o slave, o liubvi. MG 1996.5.25–46.
115 Filippov, N.
   1. Kak soldaty na peredovoi. AV 1986.5.131–34.
116 Firsov, F.I.
   1. Arkhivy Kominterna i vneshniaia politika SSSR v 1939–1941 gg. NINI
      1992.6.12–36.
117 Frank-Kamenetskii, M.
   1. Lish' tot. . . LG 1988.24.8.
118 Deleted.
119 Frezinskii, B.
   1. Poety-frontoviki Il'e Erenburgu. VL 1993.1.270–82.
120 Gagarin, S.
   1. Pravda i legendy o voine. VL 1989.7.133–59.
121 Galkin, O.
   1. Rasskazy frontovikov. NE 1995.5.42–59.
122 Gallai, M.
   1. Vyigrav voinu, my, k neschast'iu, ne vyigrali mira. DN 1995.5/6.9/10.
123 Ganichev, V.
   1. Oni vyigrali voinu . . . a vy? NS 1995.5.113–28.
124 Deleted.
125 Gavrilov, L. M.
   1. Dalekoe i blizkoe p. 189–204. In V gody voiny. Stat'i i ocherki. Moskva
      1985. 238 pp.
126 Geller, Iu.
   1. Nevernoe ekho bylogo. Dn 1989.9.229–44.
127 Genatulin, A.
   1. U rodnogo poroga. NS 1979.2.90–102.
   2. Romashkovaia poliana. In Nas ostaetsia malo. 53–72.
   3. Tri protsenta. In Nas ostaetsia malo. 9–12.
   4. Son soldata. DN 1980.5.15–28.
   5. Dobroe solntse Kimmerii. ZN 1983.5.113–25.
   6. Vozvrashchenie k pobede. NM 1985.5.116–18.
   7. Otets. In: Nas ostaetsia malo. 191–202.
   8. Strakh. VO 1987.7.17–50.
   9. Vot konchitsia voina. Moskva 1988, 368 pp.
   10. Nas ostaetsia malo. Moskva 1988, 335 pp.
   11. Piatyi fort. LG 1993.16.6.

   12. Ur. ZN 1996.5.141–44.
   13. Krasivaia. VO 1996.8/9.53–57.
   14. Maiskaia noch' za Oderom. To, chego ne spisali gody. LG 1999.23.6.
128 Gerasimov, G. I.
   1. "'Mobilizatsiia est' voina . . .'" VIZh 1999.3.2–11.
129 Gerasimova, S. A.
   1. Ne pora li pereosmyslit' rol' i znachenie boev pod Rzhevom? VI
      1998.5.173–175.
130 Gerulia, H.
   1. Interview. OG 1995.18.41.
131 Ginzburg, L.
   1. Zapiski blokadnogo cheloveka. NE 1984.84–108.
132 Gishko, N. S.
   1. GKO postanovliaet. VIZh 1992.3.17–20.
133 Deleted.
134 Glebov, I. S.
   1. Intrigi v General'nom shtabe. VIZh 1993.11.37–43.
135 Glinka, M.
   1. Chelovek na koleniakh. Zapiski piatidesiatiletnego. NE 1989.3.146–62.
136 Goikhberg, M.
   1. Do, vo vremia i posle voiny. OK 1998.12.158–67.
137 Golitsyn, S.
   1. Most. DN 1985.5.191–96.
   2. Iablonovaia vetka Belorussii. DN 1987.4.212–20.
   3. Zapiski bespogonnika. NS 1995.7.7–25.
   4. do. NS 1995.8.51–80.
138 Golovanov, Ia.
   1. Palachi i zhertvy "Dela No. 555." OG 1992.5.16–19.
139 Goncharov, V.
   1. Rukopashnia s germantsem. LG 1999.23.6.
140 Gorbachev, M. S.
   1. Uroki Voiny i Pobedy. PR 1990.9.5.
141 Gorbatov, A. V.
   1. Otkrytaia dver'. OG 1988.20.24.
142 Gorchakov, O.
   1. Vne zakona. KO 1987.18.12.
   2. Vne zakona. Moskva 1990 528 pp.
143 Gordeev, I. A.
   1. Kaliningradskaia oblast' VI 1945–1946 godakh. 1995.4.172–73.
144 Gorina, G. N.
   1. In: Pomnit' vechno. p. 74.
145 Gorinov, M. M.
   1. Budni osazhdennoi stolitsy: zhizn' i nastroenie Moskvy. OI 1996.3.3–28.
146 Gorianin,A.
   1. Pochemu Stalin schital ugrozu germanskogo udara blefom? Russkaia
      mysl' 1979.19–25 June pp. 1, 2.

147 Gor'kov, Iu.
    1. Kreml'. Stavka. Genshtab. Tver' 1995. 384 pp.
    2. O kharaktere voenno-operativnykh planov SSSR nakanune VOV. Novye arkhivnye dokumenty. NINI 1997.5.108–29.

148 Gorodetsky, G.
    1. Grand delusion. Stalin and the invasion of Russia. Yale University 1999 384 pp.

149 Goryshina, T.
    1. Radi zhizni. NE 1999.1.190–94.

150 Gotovil li Stalin nastupatel'nuiu voinu protiv Gitlera? Nezaplanirovannaia diskussiia. Sbornik materialov. Pod ed. G. A. Bordiugova. Sostavitel' V. A. Nevezhin. Moskva 1995 186 pp.

151 Grafchikov, V.
    1. V boiakh za Mamaev kurgan. Zapiski voiskovogo razvedchika. SO 1985.5.100–113.

152 Granin, D.
    1. Obiazanny raspriamit'sia. LG 1991.19.6.
    2. Daty, kotorye vsegda s nami. LG 1993.23.6.
    3. Drug moi Ales'. VL 1995.1.315–22.
    4. Krest nad gorodom. LG 1996.20.3.
    5. Strakh. NE 1997.3.141–43.

153 Grechina, O.
    1. Spasaius' spasaia. 1. Pogibel'naia zima (1941–1942 gg). NE 1994.1.211–82.

154 Gribachev, N.
    1. Kogda stanovishsia soldatom. MO 1986.7.3–121.

155 Grigorenko, P.
    1. Vospominaniia. ZV 1990.4.180–204.
    2. do. ZV 1990.5.192–205.
    3. do. ZV 1990.6.190–200.
    4. do. ZV 1990.7.166–207.
    5. Pis'mo v redaktsiiu zhurnala 'Voprosy istorii KPSS'. UR 1991.6.4–25.

156 Deleted.

157 Grossman, V.
    1. Iz zapisnykh knizhek. VL 1987.6.157–77.
    2. Zhizn' i sud'ba. OK 1988.1.3–127.
    3. do. OK 1988.2.27–103.
    4. do. OK 1988.3.25–150.
    5. do. OK 1988.4.3–142.
    6. Ubiistvo evreev v Berdicheve. ZN 1990.6.144–57.

158 Guderian, H.
    1. Panzer Leader. London 1974.

159 Gudzovskii, I.
    1. My—obuza, my vragi . . . RO 1991.6/7.66–68.

160 Gurkin, V. V.
    1. Liudskie poteri Sovetskikh Vooruzhennykh Sil v 1941–1945 gg. Novye aspekty. VIZh 1999.2.2–13.

161 Gusev, B.
   1. Dom na Rashetovoi. AV 1996.5.54–75.
162 Gusev, G.
   1. Bessmertie nashei Pobedy. NS 1995.4.3–20.
163 Hoffmann, I.
   1. Podgotovka Sovetskogo Soiuza k nastupatel'noi voine 1941 goda. OI
   1993.4.19–31.
164 Ibragimbeili, M.
   1. Plody proizvola. LG 1989.17.5.
165 Icka, I., and M. Babak
   1. Marshal Zhukov. OG 1986.51.27.
166 Il'ina, L.
   1. Blokadnyi dnevnik 1941 goda. AV 1991.11.8–20.
167 Ipatov, V.
   1. S odnosel'chanami—na zapad. SE 1997.5.93–106.
   2. Ladvinskii dnevnik. SE 1995.11/12.116–30.
168 Istoriia diplomatii tom 4. Moskva 1975 ed. S. A. Gonionskii e. a.
169 Istoriia SSSR 1991.1.8.
170 Ivanitskii, G. M.
   1. Sovetsko-germanskie torgovo ekonomicheskie otnosheniia v 1939–1941 gg.
   NINI 1989.5.28–39.
171 Ivanov, S. P., ed.
   1. Nachal'nyi period voiny. Voenizdat 1974.
172 Ivanov, V.
   1. Tashkentskii dnevnik 1942. OK 1997.12.89–113.
173 Ivanova-Romanova, N.
   1. Kniga zhizni. NE 1989.4.68–102.
174 Ivanovskii, I.
   1. Letter. OG 1989.7.4.
175 Ivashova, L., and A. Emelin
   1. Gulag v gody Velikoi otechestvennoi voiny. VIZh 1991.1.14–24.
176 Ivin, M.
   1. I veritsia s trudom . . . NE 1993.11.248–66.
177 Iz zhizni i deianii velikogo polkovodtsa. NS 1992.5.3–19. Ed. Vadim
   Kozhinov.
178 Izvestiia TsK KPSS 1990.1.216–20.
179 Iakovlev, N.
   1. Zhukov. Stranitsy zhizni legendarnogo marshala. OK 1985.5.3–124.
180 Iakushevskii, A. S.
   1. Faktor vnezapnosti v napadenii Germanii na SSSR. IS 1991.3.3–16.
181 Iampol'skii, V. P.
   1. Vmesto bavarskogo piva pulia i golod. VIZh 1997.1.12–17.
182 Kaganovich, Iu.
   1. Blokadnye vospominaniia. ZV 1996.3.181–89.
183 Kamianov, V.
   1. Preodolenie. NM 1987.5.235–58.

184 Kaplin, L. A.
     1. Letter. OG 1988.33.4.
185 Kapushchinskii, R.
     1. Imperiia. ZN 1994.2.116–23.
186 Karakov, L.
     1. Slavnye stranitsy. VIZh 1972.10.83–87.
187 Karkhu, Eino.
     1. U kazhdogo byla svoia voina. SE 1995.7.119–35.
188 Kardin, V.
     1. Ne zastriat' by na obochine. DN 1989.2.240–55.
     2. Viktor Nekrasov i Iurii Kerzhentsev. VL 1989.4.113–48.
     3. K voprosu o belykh perchatkakh. Moskva 1991 47 pp.
     4. Neob"iavlennaia voina. Iz zapisok riadovogo uchastnika OK
        1995.1.107–60.
     5. Chut' bol'she sutok. OG 1995.5/10.48/49.
     6. Navazhdenie. LG 1996.19.6.
     7. Review of A. Mercalov's, "Inoi Zhukov." ZN 1997.7.227–28.
189 Karim, M.
     1. Pomilovanie. DN 1986.8.3–84.
     2. Derevenskie advokaty. DN 1988.8.3–99.
190 Karmazin, V.
     1. Kto sochtet . . . NS 1986.8.158–71.
191 Karpov, V.
     1. Marshal Zhukov, ego soratniki i protivniki v gody voiny i mira. ZN
        1989.10.8–71.
     2. do. ZN 1989.11.78–172.
     3. do. ZN 1989.12.81–166.
192 Kasack, W.
     1. Sluzhenie kul'ture ne byvaet bessmyslennym. DN 1997.7.177–83.
193 Kashurko, S.
     1. Letter. OG 1989.19.29.
194 Kaverin, V.
     1. Epilogue. NE 1989.8.4–99.
195 Kazakov, M.
     1. Nad kartoi bylykh srazhenii. Moskva 1971, 232 pp.
196 Kazarin, V.
     1. Ognennyi farvater. VO 1987.7.137–56.
197 Kersnovskaia, E. A.
     1. Naskal'nye zhivopisi. ZN 1990 nos. 3–5.
198 Kichikhin, A. N.
     1. Sovetskie nemtsy: otkuda, kuda i pochemu?. VIZh 1990.9.28–38.
199 Kirshin, Iu., and N. M. Ramanichev
     1. Nakanune 22 iiunia 1941 g. Po materialam voennykh arkhivov. NINI
        1991.3.3–19.
200 Kiselev, A.
     1. Iosif Stalin i voina v Zapoliar'e. SE 1995.4/5.114–26.

201 Klemin, A. S.
    1. Voennye soobshcheniia v gody. VOV. VIZh 1985.3.66–71.
202 Klipel', V.
    1. Soldaty otechestva. DV 1984.8.8–94.
    2. do. DV 1984.9.73–100.
203 Kolesnik, A. N.
    1. Voennoplennyi starshii leitenant Iakov Dzhugashvili. VIZh 1988.12.70–79.
204 Kolesnikov, A.
    1. Riadovoi. NS 1995.10.77–82.
205 Kolesnikov, M.
    1. Riadovoi. MO 1995.5.43–47.
206 Konasov, V. B.
    1. K istorii sovetskikh i nemetskikh voennoplennykh (1941–1943 gg). NINI 1996.5.54–72.
    2. Sud'by nemetskikh voennoplennykh v SSSR: diplomaticheskie, pravovye i politicheskie aspekty problemy. Ocherki i dokumenty. Vologda 1996, 320 pp.
    3. Review of S. Karner, 'Im Arkhipel GUPVI'. Wien 1995. NINI 1997.6.208–10.
    4. . . . Poka ne pokhoronen poslednii soldat. Ocherki i dokumenty. Vologda 1997, 107 pp.
    5. K voprosu o chislennosti nemetskikh voennoplennykh v SSSR. VI 1994.11.187–89.
    6. Novyi podkhod k uchetu bezvozvratnykh poter' v gody VOV. VI 1990.6.185–88.
207 Kondakov, S.
    1. Bitva za Rossiiu prodolzhaetsia (Tserkov' i VOV). MG 1994.9.136–42.
208 Kondrat'ev, V. A.
    1. O publikatsii pisem sovetskikh liudei perioda VOV. IS 1986.6.96–105.
209 Kondrat'ev, V. L.
    1. Ty proshel stoverstnyi put'. LG 1984.23.1.
    2. Ve noe rzhevskoe pole. LG 1986.18.6.
    3. Chto bylo . . . ZN 1988.10.6–55.
    4. Ne tol'ko o svoem pokolenii. KOM 1990.7.113–124.
    5. Paradoksy frontovoi nostal'gii. LG 1990.9.5.
    6. Kakaia zhe ona, pravda o voine?. PR 1990.20.6.
    7. Men'she vsego v okopakh my dumali o Staline. ROG 1991.24.6.
    8. U sorok pervogo. OK 1991.3.202–4.
    9. Sashka segodnia u Belogo Doma? LG 1992.26.2.
    10. Razum protiv bezumiia. DN 1993.4.3–6.
    11. Letter to A. Adamovich. VL 1995.1.273.
    12. Iz perepiski. VL 1995.1.270–314.
    13. Letter. LO 1995.2.20.
    14. Letter. DN 1995.4–81.
    15. Pomnit' o smerti, dumat' o zhizni. KOA 1.1993/1994.74–83.
    16. Den' Pobedy v Chernove. In Na pole Ovsiannikovskom. 402–46.
    17. Bor'kiny puti–dorogi. In Na pole Ovsiannikovskom. 482–551.

18. Ovsiannikovskii ovrag. In Na pole Ovsiannikovskom. 101–39.
19. Zhit'e–byt'e. In Selizharovskii trakt. 185–227.
20. Vstrechi na Sretenke. In Krasnye vorota. 3–144.
21. Ne samyi tiazhkii den'. In Sorokovye. 199–220.
22. Sorokovye. Rasskazy i povesti. Moskva. 1988, 464 pp.
23. Selizharovskii trakt. Moskva 1985, 368pp.
24. Na pole Ovsiannikovskom. Moskva 1985, 575 pp.
25. Krasnye vorota. Moskva 1988, 413 pp.
26. De schande van Rziev. Amsterdam 1991, 192 pp.
27. Oplacheno krov'iu. RO 1991.5/7.8.

210 Konisskaia, M.
1. Zlye gody. NM 1992.6.65–102.
211 Koniaev, N.
1. Vlasov do Vlasova. AV 1995.7.69–113.
212 Kopelev, L.
1. Razrushenie stereotipa. OG 1989.36.23.
213 Koriakina-Astaf 'eva, M.
1. Znaki zhizni LG 1995.25.10.
214 Koriakov, M.
1. Frontovoi dnevnik. ZN 1992.5.170–92.
215 Kornilov, V.
1. Devochki i damochki. DN 1990.5.5–76.
216 Korobeinikov, M.
1. Pered kontsom voiny. ZN 1985.5.108–17.
2. Podrobnosti voiny. Moskva 1988, 253 pp.
3. Sud'bu my vybirali sami. MO 1995.5.56–61.
217 Korolev, St.
1. Pravoslavie i Velikaia otechestvennaia voina v 1941–1945 godakh. MG
1990.5.204–8.
218 Korolev, V.
1. Vernost' frontovomu bratstvu. AV 1989.5.49.
219 Korotkevich, L.
1. Nam zhizn' dana . . . NE 1986.2.112–31.
220 Korsunkov, V.
1. Review. VO 1991.5.175.
221 Korzhavin, N.
1. V soblaznakh krovavoi epokhi. NM 1992.8.130–93.
2. do. NM 1996.1.152–80.
3. do. NM 1996.2.123–62.
222 Korzhik, I.
1. Tragediia ofitserskikh shtrafnykh batal'onov. VE 1988.40.3.
223 Kosenko, I. N.
1. Kogda Rodina zvala v boi. VIZh 1992.11.2–7.
2. Pochemu Berlin ne byl vziat v fevrale 1945 g.? MG 1995.5.44–54.
224 Kostev, G.
1. Neizvestnyi podvig admirala Kuznetsova. LG 1988.24.6.

225 Kostrov, M.
    1. Zhikhari Polistov'ia. NE 1989.11.58–82.
226 Kostyrchenko, G. V.
    1. Sovetskaia tsenzura v 1941–1952 godakh. VI 1996.11/12.87–94.
227 Koval', M. V.
    1. Tragediia Bab'ego Iara: istoriia i sovremennost'. NINI 1998.4.14–28.
228 Kovalev, I. V.
    1. Rel'sy Pobedy. NS 1985.5.40–50.
229 Kovalevskii, A.
    1. Nynche u nas peredyshka. Frontovoi dnevnik. NE 1995.5.63–108.
230 Deleted.
231 Kozlova, N.
    1. Stseny iz zhizni 'molchalivogo men'shinstva'. NM 1998.7.251.
232 Kozhanov, V.
    1. Voina vezde naidet. Prifrontovye byli. DN 1994.11/12.9–51.
233 Kozhedub, A.
    1. Dolgi nashi. DN 1992.7.150–64.
234 KozhInov, V.
    1. Zagadochnye stranitsy istorii xx veka. NS 1988.11/12.186–212.
235 Krasavin, Iu.
    1. Svidetel'stvo o zhizni. ZN 1992.12.54–109.
236 Krichevskii, I.
    1. Skhodstvo kazhdogo portreta bylo zavereno u komandira chasti. LG
       1997.30.4.
    2. Zhukova podvel Vasilii Ivanovich. LG 1999.28.4.
237 Krivosheev, G.
    1. V pervykh srazheniiakh. VIZh 1991.2.10–16.
238 Kriuchkov, F.
    1. Iskupit' krov'iu. VE 1989.31.9–10.
239 Kruglov, A.
    1. Sosunok. DN 1989.11.135–63.
240 Kruglov, V.
    1. Tsena bestsennoi pobedy. MG 1990.5.195–203.
241 Krupin, V.
    1. Ianki gou khoum. MO 1995.5.39–42.
242 Krylova, N.
    1. Stranitsy podviga. OG 1985.22.21.
243 Kudriashov, S.
    1. Predateli, "osvoboditeli" ili zhertvy voiny? Sovetskii kollaboratsionizm
       (1941–1942). SM 1993.14.84–98.
244 Kudriavtsev, M.
    1. Topograficheskoe obespechenie voisk v Velikoi otechestvennoi voine. VIZh
       1970.12.21–29.
245 Kugul'tinov, D.
    1. "Ot pravdy ne otrekalsia." OG 1988.35.24.
    2. Chuvstvo khoziaina zhizni. VL 1988.8.3–25.

246 Kuklin, L.
    1. Nam v sorok tret'em vydali medali. AV 1985.5.4–66.
247 Kukuev, L.
    1. Polevaia sumka. SI 1985.3.18–51.
248 Kulish, V. M., and V. Oskotskii.
    1. Epos voiny narodnoi. VL 1988.10.27–87.
249 Kumanev, G. A.
    1. V ogne tiazhelykh ispytanii (iiun' 1941–noiabr' 1942 gg.). IS 1991.2.3–31.
    2. Eta nasha pobeda. LR 1992.51.3.
    3. O chem vspominal P.K. Ponomarenko. OI 1988.5.132–39.
250 Kurochkin, V.
    1. Na voine kak na voine. MG 1965.8.74–128.
251 Kuznetsov, N. G.
    1. Nakanune. Moskva 1996, 344 p.
    2. Nakanune (glavy iz knigi). MO 1988.5.165–178.
252 Kvachadze, V.
    1. Dva goda v roli Stalina. DN 1998.2.89–111.
253 Labas, Iu.
    1. Chernyi sneg na Kuznetskom. RO 1991.6/7.36–37.
254 Lavrin, A.
    1. Otets i syn. IU 1993.5.76–81.
255 Lavrov, V. S.
    1. V kovarstve Gitler ne ustupal Bismarku. VIZh 1996.2.16–23.
    2. Diplomaticheskie zigzagi Germanii nakanune napadeniia na SSSR
       (O poezdke V. M. Molotova v Berlin i polete R. Gessa v. Angliiu). MZ
       1994.1.82–88.
256 Lazarev, L.
    1. Bez strakha i upreka. ZN 1995.6.187–93.
    2. Fakty—upriamaia veshch'. ZN 1999.5.181–90.
    3. Dukh svobody. ZN 1988.9.218–29.
257 Lebedev, A.
    1. Bol' i nenavist'. SE 1988.11.69–95.
    1. do. SE 1988.12.32–85.
258 Lebedeva, N. S.
    1. Chetvertyi razdel Pol'shi i katynskaia tragediia. In Drugaia voina.
       237–95.
259 Levin, I.
    1. General Vlasov po tu i etu storonu linii fronta (vospominaniia, vstrechi i
       dokumenty). ZV 1995.6.109–56.
260 Levin, Iu.
    1. Doroga vela v Reichstag. UR 1985.5.114–23.
261 Levinskii, D.
    2. Na iuzhnom fronte. ZV 1995.5.53–64.
262 Levitanskii, Iu.
    1. Rasskazyvaet. ZN 1997.5.170–82.
    2. Ia ne uchastvuiu v voine, ona uchastvuet vo mne. LG 1995.12.4.

263 Likhotkin, G. A.
    1. Kratkaia zapis'. NE 1994.1.304–14.
264 Lipkin, S.
    1. Sobstvennaia zhizn'—eto klad. ZN 1998.1.180–89.
265 Lisiutkina, L.
    1. Georgiia Iur'evna—ditia voiny. LG 1995.9.5.
266 Litvinova, F.
    1. Vospominaia Shostakovicha. ZN 1996.12.156–77.
267 Liubimov, N.
    1. Sukhaia groza. Glavy iz knigi "Neuviadaemyi svet." DN 1994.8.96–118.
268 Losev, A. I., and V. I. Kazakov
    1. Korpus voennykh topografov. VIZh 1992.10.79–82.
269 Lotarev, M.
    1. Parad obrechennykh. NE 1996.5.142–51.
270 Lysenko, A. E.
    1. Religiia i tserkov' na Ukraine nakanune i v gody Vtoroi mirovoi voiny.
      VI 1998.4.42–57.
271 Madaichik, C.
    1. Katyn'. In Drugaia voina. 225–36.
272 Maiorov, G.
    1. Dvenadtsat' dnei i vsia zhizn'. MG 1986.5.203–13.
273 Maksheev, V.
    1. Khazan, Sashni i drugie. Iz khroniki spetsposelentsev. SO 1991.11.133–70.
274 Malinovskii, V. V.
    1. Kto on, russkii kollaboratsionist: patriot ili predatel'. VI 1996.11/12.164–66.
275 Mar, N.
    1. 'Est' upoenie v boiu . . .'. IU 1986.8.67–75.
276 Marchenko, V.
    1. Bezhentsy. NS 1995.5.50–57.
277 Markova-Kadnevskaia, E.
    1. Idut po voine devchata. Zapiski snaipera. VO 1986.5.3–50.
278 Maser, W.
    1. Der Wortbruch. Hitler, Stalin und der zweite Weltkrieg. München 1984[4],
      463 p.
279 Medvedev, R.
    1. Oni okruzhali Stalina. IU 1989.3.66–81.
280 Meletinskii, E.
    1. Moia voina. ZN 1992.10.148–79.
281 Mel'tiukhov, M. I.
    1. 22 iiunia 1941 g. Tsifry svidetel'stvuiut. IS 1991.3.16–28.
    2. Ideologicheskie dokumenty maia-iiunia 1941 goda o sobytiiakh Vtoroi
      mirovoi voiny. OI 1995.2.70–85.
    3. Repressii v Krasnoi Armii: itogi noveishikh issledovanii. OI 1997.5.109–121.
282 Mertsalov, A.
    1. Stalinizm i voina. Iz neprochitannykh stranits istorii (1930–1990 gg).
      Moskva 1994, 399 p.

2. Inoi Zhukov. Neiubileinye stranitsy biografii stalinskogo marshala. Moskva 1996, 92 pp.

3. Review of "Inoi Zhukov." ZN 1997.7.

4. Review of "Grif sekretnosti sniat—voprosy ostaiutsia." SM 1993.3.114–16.

283 Mezhenko, A. V.

1. Voennoplennye vozvrashchalis' v stroi. VIZh 1997.5.29–34.

284 Mikoian, A. I.

1. V pervye mesiatsy Velikoi otechestvennoi voiny. NINI 1985.6.93–104.

285 Milstein, M.

1. Vom Nachrichtendienst liegt vor . . . Neue Zeit 1990.26.31–33.

286 Mindlin, V.

1. Poslednii boi—on trudnyi samyi . . . ZN 1985.5.124–71.

287 Mindlina, M. G.

1. Letter. OG 1991.13.4.

288 Moiseev, M. A.

1. Tsena Pobedy. VIZh 1990.3.14–16.

289 Molodiakov, V. E.

1. Review of V. A. Nevezhin, "Sindrom nastupatel'noi voiny." OI 1998.3.183–85.

290 Morozov, V.

1. Golos pogibsh'ikh. VO 1993.12.174–75.

2. Pokhoronka. SE 1995.7.74–85.

3. Prosmotreno voennoi tsenzuroi. SE 1995.7.85–88.

291 Moskva voennaia.

Sost. K. I. Bykov. Moskva 1995, 744 pp.

292 Moskva voennaia. IS 1991.6.101–22.

293 Murashev, G.

1. Frontovichka SE 1995.3.53–82.

294 Muratov, E.

1. Shest' chasov s I. V. Stalinym na prieme v Kremle. NE 1993.7.280–88.

295 Murzin, N.

1. Stseny iz zhizni. UR 1988.10.155–76.

296 Musaelian, A.

1. Letter. ZN 1988.5.236.

297 Deleted.

298 Nabatov, Iu.

1. Nakazanie bez prestupleniia. UR 1990.3.142–49.

299 Nakhtigal', A.

1. Na kostiakh trudarmeitsev. UR 1991.8.153–56.

300 Nachal'nyi period voiny. Moskva. 1974. Ed. S. P. Ivanov.

301 Nadzhafov, D. G.

1. Sovetsko-germanskii pakt 1939 goda: pereosmyslenie podkhodov k ego otsenke. VI 1999.1.154–67.

302 Nagaeva, I. M.

1. Bez vesti propavshaia . . . pamiat'? VIZh 1998.1.70–75.

303 Nagibin, Iu.

1. Terpenie. NM 1982.2.25–53.

    2. Voina s chernogo khoda. Volkhovskaia tetrad'. DN 1992.5/6.119–43.

    3. Buntashnyi ostrov. IU 1994.4.66–86.

304 Narinskii, M. M.

    1. Kak eto bylo. In: Drugaia voina. 32–59.

305 Nazarov, A.

    1. Pesochnyi dom. OG 1991.26.14–17.

306 Nekhoroshev, M.

    1. Generala igraet svita. ZN 1995.9.211–19.

307 Nechaev, E.

    1. Poslednie zalpy. NM 1985.5.55–114.

308 Nedelin, M.

    1. Millerovskaia iama. MO 1995.5.84–98.

309 Nekrasov, V.

    1. Kak ia stal sheval'e. ZV 1989.11.67–69.

    2. Tragediia moego pokoleniia. LG 1990.12.9.

    3. O svoei partiinosti. LG 1991.12.6.

    4. Iz neopublikovannogo DN 1995.3.25–58.

310 Nekrich, A. M.

    1. Doroga k voine. OG 1991.27.6–8.

    2. Nakazannye narody. NE 1993.10.246–84.

    3. do. NE 1993.9.223–61.

311 Neustroev, S.

    1. O Reichstage—na sklone let. OK 1990.5.130–44.

312 Nevezhin, V. A.

    1. Sovetskaia politika i kul'turnye sviazi s Germaniei (1939–1941 gg). OI 193.1.18–34.

    2. Metamorfozy sovetskoi propagandy V 1939–1941 godakh. VI 1994.8.164–71.

    3. Rech' Stalina 5 maia 1941 goda: oborona ili lozung nastupatel'noi voiny? OI 1995.2.54–69.

    4. Stalinskii vybor. OI 1996.3.55–73.

    5. Vystuplenie Stalina 5 maia 1941 g. i povorot v propagande. Analiz direktivnykh materialov. In: Gotovil li. 147–67.

    6. Sindrom nastupatel'noi voiny: sovetskaia propaganda v preddverii "sviashchennykh boev," 1939–1941 gg. Moskva 1997, 288 pp.

313 Nikolaev, I.

    1. Osen'iu sorok tret'ego. OK 1995.3.136–56.

314 Nikolaev, Iu. T.

    1. ". . . u Vas est' chitatel'! . . ." NM 1994.4.219–21.

315 Nikolaev, V.

    1. Moskovskii romans. Moskva 1988, 63 pp.

316 Nosov, E.

    1. Memuary i memorialy. IU 1998.5.2.7.

    2. Fanfary i kolokola. LG 1990.9.5.

    3. Sinee pero Vatolina. MO 1995.5.13–28.

317 O pereselenii nemtsev, prozhivaiushchikh v raionakh Povolzh 'ia. VIZh 1990.9.37–38.

318 O pereselenii nemtsev iz g. Moskvy i Moskovskoi oblasti i Rostovskoi oblasti.
      VIZh 1992.4/5.22–23.

319 O podbore i vydvizhenii kadrov v iskusstve. RO 1991.6/7.74.

320 Obrosov, A.
        1. V poiskakh broda. MO 1991.6.6–46.

321 Ocherki istorii Shadrinska. K 50–letiiu Kurganskoi 322 oblasti. Otv. Ed. P. V.
      Surovtsev. Shadrinsk 1993, 207 pp.

322 Ogloblin, A.
        1. Na Nevskom platsdarme. NE 1987.6.137–48.

323 Ortenberg, D.
        1. Iiun'–dekabr' sorok pervogo. Moskva 1984, 351 pp.
        2. God 1942. Rasskaz-khronika. Moskva 1988, 464 pp.
        3. God 1942. MO 1988.3.158–73.
        4. Stalin, Shcherbakov, Mekhlis i drugie. Moskva 1995, 208 pp.

324 Oskotskii, V.
        1. Voina "uchastvuet vo mne." RV 1998.27.5.

325 Osokina, E. A.
        1. Liudi i vlast' v usloviiakh krizisa snabzheniia 1939–1941 gody. OI
           1995.3.16–32.
        2. Krizis snabzheniia 1939–1941 gg. v pis'makh sovetskikh liudei. VI
           1996.1.3–23.

326 Osten, V.
        1. Letter. ZN 1989.11.234.
        2. Vstan' nad bol'iu svoei. Kaliningrad 1995, 479 pp.

327 Palkin, I.
        1. Neizvestnye soldaty. ZV 1988.5.167–79.

328 Panchenko, N.
        1. Response to questionnaire. LG 1995.9.5.

329 Panteleev, L.
        1. Ia veruiu. NM 1991.8.132–80.

330 Parsadanova, V. S.
        1. Deportatsiia naseleniia iz Zapadnoi Ukrainy i Zapadnoi Belorussii v
           1939–1941 gg. NINI 1989.2.26–44.

331 Pasat, V.
        1. Deportatsiia iz Moldavii. SM 1993.3.52–61.
        2. Evakuatsiia nemetskikh kolonistov s territorii Bessarabii i Severnoi
           Bukoviny v 1940 godu. OI 1997.2.87–106.

332 Pavlenko, N. G.
        1. Razmyshleniia o sud'be polkovodtsa. VIZh 1988.12–29–37.
        2. Istoriia voiny eshche ne napisana. OG1989.25.5.
        3. Byla voina . . . Razmyshleniia voennogo istorika. Moskva 1994, 416 pp.
        4. Interview. RO 1991.6/7.87–90.

333 Pavlov, A.
        1. Babii front. VO 1988.6.121–53.

334 Pavlov, A. G.
        1. Sovetskaia voennaia razvedka nakanune VOV. NINI 1995.1.49–60.

335 Pechenkin, A. A.
     1. Byla li vozmozhnost' nastupat'? OI 1995.3.44–59.
336 Penkov, M.
     1. Vizit na sosedniuiu planetu. NS 1995.5.8–14.
337 Perechnev, Iu. G.
     1. O nekotorykh problemakh podgotovki strany i Vooruzhennykh Sil k
        otrazheniiu fashistskoi agressii. VIZh 1988.4.42–50.
338 Perezhogin, V. A.
     1. Partizany i naselenie (1941–1945 gg). OI 1997.6.150–54.
339 Pervye gody voiny.
340 Pestova, Z.
     1. Vospominaniia o syne. NM 1992.9.182–206.
341 Petrov, A.
     1. Ver sind si? Ver? NE 1995.5.220–23.
342 Petrov, B. N.
     1. O strategicheskom razvertyvanii Krasnoi Armii nakanune voiny. In:
        Gotovil li. 66–76.
343 Petrov, N., and O. Edel'man
     1. Novoe o sovetskikh geroiakh. NM 1997.6.140–51.
344 Petrov, V. P.
     1. 1941: Taina porazheniia. NM 1988.8.172–87.
345 Petrovskii, Iu.
     1. Liki voiny. Gumanizm sovetskoi voennoi prozy. ZV 1985.5.190–97.
346 Plimak, E.
     1. V Sovetskoi okkupatsionnoi Germanii 1945–1946. KON 84-138.
347 Poliakov, G.
     1. Vrag ne proshel. AV 1997.3/4.22–30.
348 Poliakov, S.
     1. Zapiski malen'kogo soldata o bol'shoi voine. SE 1995.9.108–26.
349 Pomerants, G.
     1. Zapiski gadkogo utenka. ZN 1993.7.134–73.
350 Pomnit' vechno. Was im gedächtnis bleibt. Herausgeber P. Fraenkel. Moskva
     1995, 320 pp.
351 Popov, I. I.
     1. "Poidite i ostanovite ikh sami!" OI 1997.6.154–57.
352 Postanovlenie Politbiuro TsK VKPb 27.6.1941. RO 1991.6/7.47.
353 Pozhenian, G. M.
     1. My eshche pozhivem na opolzniakh svoikh beregov. LG
        1995.9.5.
354 PR 1941.1.1.
355 PR 1990.9.5.
356 Prikaz oo 227. VIZh 1988.8.73–75.
357 Prikaz 270. VIZh 1988.9.26–28.
358 Pristavkin, A.
     1. Review of 'Nochevala tuchka zolotaia'. OK 1987.6.204–6.
     2. Nochevala tuchka zolotaia. ZN 1987.3, 4.

359 Prishvin, M.
    1. Dnevnik 1939 Iiul'–dekabr'. OK 1998.11.126–46.

360 Pron'ko, V. A.
    1. Review of I. T. Mukovskii, "Zvitiaega i zhertovnist." Kiiv. 1997, 568 pp. In
       VIZh 1998.2.184–86.

361 Pron'ko, V. A., and V. A. Zemskov
    1. Taina doklada Berii. NG 1993.23.12.
    2. Vklad zakliuchennykh Gulaga v pobedu Velikoi Otechestvennoi voiny. NI
       1996.5.131–50.

362 Pushkarev, D. N.
    1. Po dorogam voiny. Vospominaniia fol'klorista–frontovika. Moskva 1995,
       310 pp.

363 Putko, A.
    1. Epitalama po–frontovomu. Rasskazy. DN 1993.6.91–99.

364 Razgon, L.
    1. Boris i Gleb. IU 1990.4.76–81.
    2. Nachal'nik politsii. OG 1996.50.43–45.
    3. Nepridumannoe. IU 1989.2.34–61.

365 Raspopov, A.
    1. My—sapery. SE 1985.2.63–91.

366 Rauschenbach, H.
    1. Von Pillkallen nach Schadrinsk. Meine Zeit im Lager 6437 und das
       Wiedersehen nach 43 Jahren. Leer 1993, 178 pp.

367 Razin, V.
    1. Rasstrel kommunista. NS 1992.10.104–19.

368 Razumovskii, L.
    1. Deti blokady. NE 1999.1.4–68.

369 Deleted.

370 Reginia, L.
    1. Obozhzhennyi fashizmom. O sud'be i tvorchestve Vitaliia Semina v
       Tret'em reikhe i v sobstvennoi strane. NE 1995.5.164–85.

371 Reshin, L.
    1. 'Tovarishch Erenburg uproshchaet'. NV 1994.8.50–51.
    2. Kollaboratsionisty i zhertvy rezhima. ZN 1994.8.158–79.

372 Rishina, I.
    1. Lish' tot dostoin zhizni i svobody. LG 1988.24.8.

372 ARO 1991.6/7.

373 Rokossovskii, K.
    1. Soldatskii dolg. VIZh 1984.4.52–55.

374 Romanova, E.
    1. Sutki v pekhote. NS 1999.3.3–22.

375 Rossiianov, O.
    1. Donets ostalsia pozadi. UR 1996.5/6.38–81.

376 Rozanov, G. L.
    1. Stalin—Gitler. Dokumentarnyi ocherk sovetsko–germanskikh
       diplomaticheskikh otnoshenii 1939–1941 gg. Moskva 1991, 224 ff.

377 Rozenberg, A.
   1. Dva dos'e "Krasnoi Kapelly." VIZh 1995.6.18–30.
378 Rozhkov, A.
   1. Zhivu i pomniu. NE 1988.1.185–91.
379 Rubtsov, Iu. V.
   1. Lev Zakharovich Mekhlis. VI 19998.10.69–93.
   2. G. Zhukov. KOD 1998.1.9.
380 Rubinshtein, L. M.
   1. Ispoved' schastlivogo al'pinista. ZV 1995.5.5–52.
381 Runin, B.
   1. Literaturnyi vecher 1945 goda. LG 1991.27.11.
   2. Moe okruzhenie. Zapiski sluchaino utselevshego. Moskva 1995,
      224 pp.
382 Rybakov, A.
   1. Roman-vospominanie. DN 1997.3.3–94.
383 Rzhevskaia, E. M.
   1. Voroshennyi zhar. NM 1984.5.6–75.
   2. V tot den', poslednei osen'iu. ZN 1986.12.157–77.
   3. Zhiv, bratok?. NM 1987.5.3–11.
   4. Dalekii gul. DN 1988.7.3–69.
   5. Znaki prepinaniia. Moskva 1989, 413 pp.
   6. Podo Rzhevom. In Znaki prepinaniia 160–96.
   7. Segodnia kupat'sia zapreshcheno. In Znaki prepinaniia. 359–75.
   8. Pobeda obnazhaet rany voiny.DN 1995.5/6.10–13.
   9. Dorogi i dni. DN 1996.6.42–74.
   10. U voiny—litso voiny. VL 1996.11.182–221.
   11. Posleslovie. DN 1996.12.8–32.
384 Saakov, L.
   1. Berlin 1945 . . . ZV 1986.5.3–15.
385 Safronov, V.
   1. Otpusti menia, pamiat'. VO 1988.10.115–19.
386 Samoilov, D.
   1. Liudi odnogo varianta. Iz voennykh zapisok. AV1990.1.42–83.
   2. do. AV 1990.2.50–96.
   3. Pamiatnye zapiski. NE 1994.4.299–312.
   4. Itak, pis'mo napisano. NE 1998.9.176–197.
387 Sandalov, L. M.
   1. Perezhitoe. Moskva 1966.191 p.
   2. Oboronitel'naia operatsiia 4-i armii v nachal'nyi period voiny. VIZh
      1971.7.18–28.
388 Savchenko, L.
   1. Moia sud'ba. NE 1995.1.151–58.
389 Savitskii, M.
   1. Esli pobedy i net, to pobediteli ostalis'. DN 1995.5/6.15–16.
390 Schwendemann, H.
   1. Die wirtschaftliche Zusammenarbeit zwischen dem Deutschen Reich und

der Sowjetunion von 1939 bis 1941: Alternative zu Hitlers Ostprogramm?
Berlin 1993 398 pp. Reviewed in OI 1995.3.210–13.

391 Sekretnye dokumenty iz osobykh papok. VI 1993.1.3.22.

392 Semidetko, V. A.
    1. Zapadnyi voennyi okrug k 22 iiunia 1941 g. VIZh 1989.4.22–31.

393 Semiriaga, M. I.
    1. Sud'by sovetskikh voennoplennykh. VI 1995.4.19–33.
    2. Russkie v Berline 1945 g. MZ 1994.5.89–95.
    3. Predatel'? Osvoboditel'? Zhertva? RO 1991.6/7.93–94.

394 Seniavskaia, E. S.
    1. 1941–1945. Frontovoe pokolenie. Istoriko-psikhologicheskoe issledovanie.
    Moskva 1995.220 pp.

395 Sergeev, D.
    1. Dvesti zlotykh. SO 1989.1.108–12.
    2. Zapasnoi polk ZV 1992.3.36–105.
    3. do. ZV 1993.4.81–124.

396 Sevost'ianov, G. N.
    1. Pravda o zimnei voine 1939–1940 g. NINI 1999.1.141–47.

397 Sidorovskii, L.
    1. Marshal Pobedy. AV 1990.5.6–16.

398 Simashko, M.
    1. Gu-gu. DN 1987.8.5–80.

399 Simkin, G.
    1. Rasskazy. VO 1985.5.8–42.

400 Simonov, K.
    1. Sofiia Leonidovna. DN 1985.2.3–67.
    2. Raznye dni voiny. tom 1. 1941 god. Moskva 1977, 576 pp.
    3. Raznye dni voiny. tom 2 1942–1945 gody. Moskva 1977, 779 pp.
    4. Uroki istorii i dolg pisatelia. VIZh 1987.6.42–51.
    5. Zametki k biografii G. K. Zhukova. VIZh 1987.7.45–50.
    6. Besedy s A. P. Pokrovskim. OK 1990.5.116–29.
    7. Zametki k biografii G. K. Zhukova. VIZh 1987.10.56–64.
    8. Georgi Schukow ueber die sowjetische Fuehnung 1940/41. Marscistische
    Blaetter 1988.2.73.

401 Sindalovskii, N.
    1. Geroicheskii faktor voiny i blokady. NE 1999.1.174–83.

402 Sipols, V. Ia.
    1. Eshche raz o diplomaticheskoi dueli v Berline v noiabre 1940 g. NINI
    1996.3.145–61.
    2. Torgovo-ekonomicheskie otnosheniia mezhdu SSSR i Germaniei v
    1939–1941 gg. V svete novykh arkhivnykh dokumentov. NINI
    1997.2.29–41.

403 Skriabin, S., and N. Medvedev
    1. O tyle fronta v nachale Velikoi Otechestvennoi voiny. VIZh1984.4.32–38.

404 Sladkov, N.
    1. Lermontovskaia tragediia. ZV 1990.5.3–31.

405 Slepukhin, Iu.
    1. Chas muzhestva. NE 1991.6.113–41.
406 Slipchenko, L.
    1. Pravda o nepravdopodobnym. Iz vospominanii uznitsy getto vblizi Odessy. UR 1990.5.156–69.
407 Slutskii, B.
    1. Chetvertyi anekdot. DN 1988.11.92.
    2. Iz "Zapisok o voine." OG 1995.17.48–51.
    3. Zarubki pamiati (Iz knigi "Zapiski o voine"). VL 1995.3.38–82.
    4. Iz "zapisok o voine." NE 1997.1.143.158.
408 Smirnov, S.
    1. Iz frontovykh zapisnykh knizhek. LG 1991.25.9.
409 Sofronov, V.
    1. Otpusti menia, pamiat'. VO 1988.115–19.
410 Solianov, F.
    1. Kak my s diadei pisali povest' o Varshavskom vosstanii. NM 1995.6.233–43.
411 Sollertinskaia, L.
    1. Shostakovich, voennye gody. ZV 1986.9.169–78.
412 Soloukhin, V.
    1. Katyn', Katyn'. LR 1993.2.14.
413 Soobrazheniia po planu strategicheskogo razvertyvaniia Sil Sovetskogo Soiuza na sluchai voiny s Germaniei i ee soiuznikami. NINI 1993.3.40–45.
414 Sopelniuk, B.
    1. Valenki. OG 1998.38.25–29.
415 Spasov, O.
    1. Polykhan'e. Dokumental'naia povest'. ZV 1988.1.158–72.
416 Stadniuk, I.
    1. Ispoved' stalinista. MG 1992.11/12.71–155.
    2. Ispoved' bez pokaianiia. MG 1991.3.27–74.
    3. od. MG 1991.4.32–65 and 97–135.
    4. od. MG 1991.5.116–128 and 161–96.
417 Deleted.
418 Stalin, I. V.
    1. Sochineniia tom 6. Moskva 1947.
    2. Sochineniia tom 7. Moskva 1947.
    3. Sochineniia tom 10. Moskva 1949.
    4. Sochineniia tom 11. Moskva 1949.
    5. Istoriia SSSR 1991.1.8.
    6. Rech' 5 maia 1941 g. in: Iskusstvo kino. 1990.5.10–16.
419 Stalin, Beriia i sud'ba armii Andersa v 1941–1942 gg. (Iz razsekrechennykh arkhivov). NINI 1993.2.59–90.
420 Starshinov, N.
    1. Na podvigi obrecheny. NM 1990.5.3–4.
421 Stepanov, A.
    1. Ingermanlandskaia tragediia. DN 1994.3.151–59.

422 Stupnikov, A.
    1. V Viatskoi tylovoi derevne. ZV 1989.2.183–96.
423 Sukhov, F.
    1. Ivnitsa. VO 1986.12.21–70.
424 Sud'ba voennoplennykh. i deportirovannykh grazhdan SSSR. Materialy Komissii
    po reabilitatsii zhertv politicheskikh repressii. NINI 1996.2.91–112.
425 Suleimanov, G.
    1. Chertopolokh zabveniia. UR 1989.5.128–136.
426 Suprunenko, D.
    1. Voina ubivaet pravdu. IU 1991.6.16–17.
427 Suris, B.
    1. Sosed po frontu. NE 1990.10.198–202.
428 Surovtsev, V. P.
    1. Zhivaia byl'—zhivaia bol'. Shadrinsk 1995. 144 pp.
429 Suvorov, V.
    1. Ledokol. Den' M. Moskva 1996. 575 pp.
430 Svintsov, V.
    1. Prokliaty i ubity. ZN 1997.8.228–30.
431 Szonyi, D.
    1. Letter. OG 1990.49.2.
432 Shadrinskaia letopis'. Shadrinsk 1998, 2d ed. 140 pp.
433 Shadrinsk voennoi pory. Tom 1. Ed. S. B. Borisov. Shadrinsk 1995. 218 pp.
434 Shadrinsk voennoi pory. Tom 2. Ed. S. B. Borisov. Shadrinsk 1995. 248 pp.
435 Shadrinsk poslevoennyi. Ed. S. B. Borisov. Shadrinsk 1995. 128 pp.
436 Shafranovskii, I.
    1. Blokadnaia zima. AV 1992.I.97.
437 Shalamov, V.
    1. Poslednii boi maiora Pugacheva.NM 1988.6.115–23.
438 Shaposhnikov, V.
    1. Tsena pobedy. LG 1988.22.6.
439 Shapovalov, A.
    1. Letter. OG 1989.29.19.
440 Sharapov, Iu.
    1. Kak pred gospodom Bogom chisty . . . KZ 1991.22.6.
441 Shenkman, A.
    1. Iz frontovogo bloknota. ZN.1985.2.93–115.
442 Sherstennikov, L.
    1. Sputniki slavy. OG.1987.50.25.
443 Shestinskii, O.
    1. Angel'skoe voinstvo. NE 1990.1.69–87.
444 Sheviakov, A. A.
    1. Sovetsko-germanskie ekonomicheskie otnosheniia v 1939–1941 godakh. Vi
       1991.4/5.164–70.
445 Shishenkov, Iu.
    1. Molnii chelovecheskikh sudeb. DN 1987.5.207–19.
446 Snajder, B.
    1. Neizvestnaia voina. VI 1995.1.104–13.

447 Shpak, A.
 1. Blokadnaia neft'. NE 1988.1.140–47.
448 Shubkin, V.
 1. Odin den' voiny (23.8.1942). LG 1987.23.9.
449 Shukova, T.
 1. Gde zhe pereprava?. LR 1993.28/29.10.
450 Shul'kin, S.
 1. Vospominaniia balovnia sud'by. NE 1999.1.148–61.
451 Shur, G.
 1. De joden van Wilno. Een kroniek 1941–1944 Amsterdam 1997. 224 pp.
452 Deleted.
453 Taluntis, E.
 1. Tot zharkii ianvar'. ZV 1987.5.100–113.
454 Tarnov, V. V.
 1. Parad, izumivshii mir. VIZh 1989.1.61–72.
455 Tkhorzhevskaia, L.
 1. Da sviatitsia imia tvoe. (Iz dnevnikov 1941–1944 gg.). UR 1996.5/6.82–106.
456 Tendriakov, V.
 1. Den' sed'moi. DN 1986.1.146–60.
 2. Donna Anna. Nm 1988.3.42–61.
457 Tiagunov, B.
 1. Nikto ne zabyt? ZN 1988.10.226–30.
458 Trukhanovskii, V. G.
 1. Speech in: Velikaia otechestvennaia voina: fakt i dokument v istorchieskikh issledovaniiakh i khudozhestvennoi literature. IS 1988.4.38–41.
459 Tumanov, Iu.
 1. Buivol, bednyi buivol. OK 1992.4.3–20.
460 Turkov, A.
 1. I eto vshe v menia zapalo . . . LG 1995.9.5.
 2. Raduius' i negoduiu. DN 1995.5/6.12–13.
461 Ukhanov, I.
 1. Pobeda byla i budet za nami. MG 1995.5.5–12.
462 Uspenskii, L.
 1. Voennye dnevniki. NE 1987.1.165–171.
 2. do. NE 1987.2.186–192.
463 V gody voiny. Stat'i i ocherki. Ed. A. M. Samsonov. Moskva 1985 238 pp.
464 Vaksberg, A.
 1. Taina oktiabria 41 g. LG 1988.20.4.
 2. "Delo" marshala Zhukova: nerazorvavshaiasia bomba. LG 1992.5.8.
465 Vasil'chenko, G.
 1. Dolia russkogo soldata. MG 1995.5.119–29.
466 Vasil'ev, A. F.
 1. Review of 'Drugaia voina'. VI 1997.9.155–158.
467 Vasil'ev, V.
 1. Chtoby zhili Leningradtsy. ZV 1989.1.124–30.

468 Vasil'eva, O.
       1. Tainaia vecher'ia. LR 19991.39.20–21.
469 Velikaia otechestvennaia voina: fakt i dokument v istoricheskikh issledovaniiakh
       i khudozhestvennoi literature. Beseda istorikov i pisatelei za 'Kruglym stolom'.
       IS 1988.4.3–44.
470 Veltmeijer, R.
       1. Vriend en vijand. Assen 1996.283 p.
471 Veniaminovna, V. V.
       1. 'Narkomovskie' grammy. Vizh 1995.5.95–96.
472 Vetrogonskii, V.
       1. Vozvrashchaius' zhivym . . . AV 1995.5.76–80.
473 Vinogradov, I.
       1. Riadovye dvadtsatogo veka. Iz knigi o sebe. AV 1995.5.11–69.
       2. I nastupilo molchanie . . . NE 1995.5.4–29.
474 Vinogradov, V.
       1. Rasskazy. NS 1995.6.18–28.
475 Vishlev, O.
       1. Pochemu medlil Stalin v 1941 godu? (iz germanskikh arkhivov). NINI
           1992.2.70–96.
       2. Nakanune 22 iiunia 1941 goda (po materialam germanskikh arkhivov).
           MG 1997.6.103–62.
       3. Zapadnye versii vyskazyvanii I.V. Stalina 5 maia 1941 g. (po materialam
           germanskikh arkhivov). NINI 1999.1.86–100.
476 Vishnevskii, V.
       1. "Sami pereidem v napadenie." Iz dnevnikov 1939–1941 godov. MO
           1995.5.103–10.
477 VIZh 1992.3.20.
478 VIZh 1992.8 inside cover.
479 VIZh 1992.11.10.
480 Vladimov, G.
       1. Iasnaia Poliana. LG 1990.27.6.
       2. Za zemliu, za voliu . . . ZN 1996.2.8–27.
481 Vnukov, N.
       1. Kompaneevka i dal'she. AV 1990.10.12–27.
482 Volfson, B.
       1. Letter OG 1991.39.13.
483 Volkov, I. M.
       1. Zasukha, golod 1946–1947 godov. IS 1991.4.3–19.
484 Vorob'ev, E.
       1. Moskva. Blizko k serdtsu. Moskva 1986.480 pp.
485 Vorob'ev, K.
       1. Ubity pod Moskvoi. Moskva 1987.159 pp.
       2. Eto my, Gospodi! In Povesti. Moskva 1988.12–109.
       3. Pochem v Rakitnom radosti. In Drug moi Momich. Moskva 1988. 105–77.
       4. Drug moi Momich. Moskva 1988. 636 pp.
       5. Ubity pod Moskvoi. Moskva 1987. 159 pp.

486 Voznesenskii, A.
   1. Rov.IU 1986.7.6–15.
487 Voznesenskii, N. A.
   1. Voennaia ekonomika SSSR v period Otechestvennoi voiny. Moskva
      1948.191 pp.
488 Vul'fovich T.
   1. Tam, na voine NM 1986.6.134–73.
   2. Tam, na voine. Moskva 1991.303 pp.
489 Witness to history. The photographs of Yevgeny Khaldei. New York 1997.
   96 pp.
490 Zatonskii, D.
   1. Byla-li VOV oshibkoi? DN 1995.4.2–16.
491 Zaural'e 1910–1940-kh godov v vospominaniiakh. Shadrinskii al'manakh.
   Vypusk 2. Sost. S. B. Borisov. Shadrinsk 1998. 49 pp.
492 Zelenkov, V.
   1. Komu voina, a komu mat' rodnaia. NS 1997.9.69–82.
493 Zemskov, V. N.
   1. K voprosu o repatriatsii sovetskikh grazhdan 1944–1951 gody. IS
      1990.4.26–41.
494 Zezina, M. R.
   1. Sotsial'naia zashchita detei-sirot v poslevoennye gody (1945–1955).VI
      1999.1.127–36.
495 Zilin, P.
   1. Podvig naroda i uroki istorii. OK 1985.5.158–68.
496 Zima, V. F.
   1. Poslevoennoe obshchestvo: golod i prestupnost' (1946–1947gg). OI
      1995.5.45–59.
   2. Golod v SSSR 1946–1947 godov. Proiskhozhdenie i posledstviia. Moskva
      1994. 264 pp.
497 Zinich, M. S.
   1. Budni voennogo likholet'ia 1941–1945 vyp.I. Moskva 1994. 125 pp.
   2. do. vyp 2.1994. 143 pp.
498 Zolotusskii, I.
   1. Voina i svoboda. LG 1988.8.6.
499 Zubchaninov, V.
   1. Povest' o prozhitom. OK 1997.8.64–134.
500 Zubov, A.
   1. Pobeda, kotoruiu my poteriali. KON 84.71–76.
501 ZV 1986.5.55.
502 Zharikov, A.
   1. ". . . v polk pribyli Sibiriaki." So 1989.5.145–51.
503 Zhdanovich, A.
   1. Kholodnoe utro. Leningrad 1990. 352 pp.
504 Zhigulin, A.
   1. Zhertvy i palachi. LG 1990.20.6.
   2. Oblomki "chernykh kamnei." DN 1998.7.74–75.

505 Zhilinskii, I. I.
      1. Blokadnyi dnevnik. VI 1996.6/7.3–13.
      2. do.VI 1996.5/6.5–27.
506 Zhuk, A.
      1. Nachalo. NE 1995.4.162–78.
507 Zhukov, D.
      1. Eto bylo. LR 1989.14.14.
508 Zhukov, G. K.
      1. Vospominaniia i razmyshleniia. Moskva 1970. 701 pp.
      2. Iz neopublikovannykh vospominanii. KOM 1988.14.87–101.
      3. Vospominaniia i razmyshleniia. Moskva 1990, 10th ed.
      4. Address PR 1990.9.5.

Index